MEN
IN
ARMS

FOURTH EDITION

ARMS

A History of Warfare
and Its Interrelationships
with Western Society

MEN
IN
ARMS

FOURTH EDITION

ARMS

A History of Warfare
and Its Interrelationships
with Western Society

RICHARD A. PRESTON
SYDNEY F. WISE

HOLT, RINEHART AND WINSTON
New York   Chicago   San Francisco   Atlanta   Dallas
Montreal   Toronto   London   Sydney

Library of Congress Cataloging in Publication Data

Preston, Richard Arthur.
  Men in arms.

  Bibliography: p.
  Includes index.
  1. Military history. I. Wise, Sydney F.,
joint author. II. Title
D25.P7 1979   909   78-21298
ISBN 0-03-045681-9

Prefaces

PREFACE TO THE FIRST EDITION

The authors wish to thank the following people who have helped in the preparation of this book by their encouragement and by reading all or part of it—without, of course, acquiring any obligation for its accuracy or opinions: Colonel C. P. Stacey, Director of the Historical Section of the General Staff of the Canadian Army; Dr. D. M. Shepherd, Department of Classics, McMaster University; and the following members of the Faculty of the Royal Military College of Canada: Wing Commander E. C. Snider, RCAF, formerly Head of the Department of Military Studies; Lieutenant Commander J. B. Fotheringham, RCN, his successor; Dr. David Dooley, of the Department of English; and Dr. J. W. Hodgins, of the Department of Chemistry. We are also indebted to President Walter C. Langsam, of Gettysburg College, for kindly editorial supervision and to C. K. Smallman, of the Royal Military College, for reading the proofs.

Our gratitude is also due to Miss Joyce Houston, who patiently typed several drafts of the whole manuscript, and to several other typists who helped with parts of it.

We also wish to record our indebtedness to the resources of the libraries at the Royal Military College of Canada and at the United States Naval Academy. The librarian at the former, John Spurr, has made an invaluable contribution to this book by building up the largest collection in Canada of books on military history.

The theme of this book, the interrelationship of warfare and society in the West, is capable of virtually unlimited extension in scope. It is also complicated by fundamental differences of opinion. As a result its compression into the pages of a small book has been very difficult. The task of the authors has been primarily one of generalization and selection. Many interesting and important topics have had to be left out in order to provide a short continuous narrative of the part that warfare has played in the history of our society. The authors believe that this process of simplification, or perhaps even of oversimplification, was justified by the need for a brief outline of a subject which urgently demands the attention of all thinking men and women. A comprehensive bibliography is appended for the guidance of those who desire to read more widely and more deeply.

Richard A. Preston
Sydney F. Wise
August, 1955   Herman O. Werner

PREFACE TO THE REVISED EDITION

The major alteration in this new edition of *Men in Arms* has been in Chapter 20, which has been rewritten and greatly enlarged. Not only have there been significant developments in international politics and in strategic thought since 1955, and a very rapid rate of change in military technology, but the nature of the forces shaping the postwar world has now become more apparent and, it is hoped, has been treated here with more clarity and perspective than was possible at an earlier date. There have also been numerous alterations in other parts of the book, and many new works in the field of military affairs have been added to the bibliography.

The authors wish to thank the Commandant of the Air Force College, Toronto, and the editors of the *Air Force College Journal* for permission to use material from R. A. Preston's article "The Great Debate on Strategy."

April, 1962   R. A. P.
                                                   S. F. W.

PREFACE TO THE SECOND REVISED EDITION

The need for a new printing has provided an opportunity for a thorough revision of *Men in Arms,* not merely to bring it up to date with events since publication of the first revision in 1962 but also to revise it in line with new scholarship since the first edition was issued in 1956.

To ensure that the body of the text conforms with modern scholarship, we asked many good friends to comment on those portions of the text in which they have specialized. Many sections of the book were then amended, and some were rewritten. For their generous help, we are deeply indebted to John R. Alden, John Curtiss, Arthur Ferguson, Richard G. Glover, D. J. Goodspeed, the late Sir Basil Liddell Hart, Robin Higham, Trevor Hodge, S. Shepard Jones, J. A. Leith, Jay Luvaas, A. J. Marshall, Harold Parker, T. R. Robinson, Theodore Ropp, D. M. Schurman, W. Willis, Monte Wright, and Norman Zacour. All these submitted criticisms, and their advice has greatly improved the book. Any errors that remain are, of course, to be attributed not to our distinguished critics but to the obstinacy of the authors.

Despite the appearance of new scourges and the revitalization of ancient ones, war is still the greatest danger to the continued existence of the human race. This second revised edition of this book therefore appears to be justified.

R. A. P.

April, 1970 S. F. W.

Preface to the Fourth Edition

We are indebted to the following colleagues for advice about, material to be used for, and corrections in the additional chapter for this fourth edition: I. B. Holley, T. Ropp, and Major Lorenzo Crowell of Duke University, and Brereton Greenhous and Captain Vincent Bezeau of the Directorate of History, Canadian National Defence Headquarters. The responsibility remains ours.

R. A. P.

November, 1978 S. F. W.

Contents

List of Illustrations

List of Maps

Introduction

The history of human society has been punctuated by war; but the study of military history has all too often been undertaken as if war always existed in a vacuum. Probably because by far the greatest number of those who have concerned themselves with the study of war have had a professional interest, there has been a tendency to concentrate on campaign narratives, battle outlines, and studies of the qualities of leadership shown by great commanders. All too often the necessity for an adequate background of political, economic, social, and cultural history for the full understanding of military events has not been realized. Attention has been concentrated on a few aspects of military history to the exclusion of others. The history of operations has not always been written and studied with enough awareness of the history of military administration and of supply; weapon development has been sometimes treated as if it were a watertight compartment in the general structure; and it is only recently that, as a result of a renewed interest in amphibious warfare induced by the lessons of recent wars and by the complications produced by the rise of a third arm, there has grown up a tendency to treat war as a whole rather than as separate military (in the narrow sense of the word) and naval narratives.

The study of military history has almost always been undertaken as a means of learning lessons for the future conduct of operations. It has long been realized that while the opportunities for training commanders in war or mimic war are limited, a vast amount of experience lies buried in the story of past warfare. But the study of narratives of campaigns requires a background knowledge not merely of the history of weapon development and of army organization but also of political, economic, and social history. Similarly the study of warfare must include enquiry into the social and technical changes which have affected it. Without these wider investigations military history by itself is of little value.

The increasing extent to which modern war involves civilians makes it imperative that they should study military history and the history of warfare in relation to society. In the period between the two world wars, as a result of a distaste for things military which grew out of the bitter experiences of the first war, the study of military history was relegated to a minor place in the whole historical picture. This was unfortunate. The degree to which civilian life is affected by war, and to which civilian energies are absorbed by it, makes it essential that civilian leaders of society, whether businessmen, engineers, manufacturers, administrators, clergymen, or politicians, must study and understand warfare. In war time, many civilians have to make decisions which are vital to the war effort. Indeed, in modern times the higher direction of war in all countries has been in the hands of civilians and not of soldiers. The history of warfare should, therefore, be widely studied.

There has been some disagreement about whether it is better, for the purpose of learning the lessons of military history, to concentrate on a few campaigns and battles studied in great detail or to cover many wars, campaigns, and battles in a wide survey. By presenting the full picture, intensive study comes closer to recreating the fog of war; but it provides only a relatively few illustrations of the principles involved. Surveys oversimplify the story of fighting but give a more varied experience by the repetition of numerous examples. The ideal solution of this dilemma is that the reader should use both methods. The most important thing is that his reading should be carried on over many years and that it should not be limited to the duration of a course or to the preparation for a professional examination. Battlefield experience, war games, maneuvers, and tactical exercises without troops are all important ways of learning about war; but they are too few to provide the necessary experience. Only by much reading can the mind of the future commander be trained.

Although this book does not concern itself primarily with the history of tactics, or even of strategy, the reader should be familiar with the basic principles of war. Within the last half century, soldiers and military historians have discovered and enumerated certain basic precepts of conduct which operate in warfare and which have regularly affected the decision in past conflicts. These precepts appear to be permanent despite changing conditions. Although originally worked out in relation to land strategy, they are equally applicable to sea and air warfare. At the tactical level they also have some validity, although here their application is more affected by circumstances of time, place, terrain, comparative strength, and relation to the overall plan of the higher command. Study of military history in terms of these principles helps to draw the attention of the student to those aspects of a very complicated picture that can help him to absorb the many lessons history can teach.

However, the principles of war must be used with some circumspection in the reading of military history. They are not rules like those in a game, nor scientific laws. They are not infallible guides to conduct which will ensure success. Lists of them prepared by different authorities in different periods or countries vary somewhat in wording and in the number of principles enumerated. Soviet military authorities, ignoring western principles, list a smaller number of "permanently operating factors" which do not exactly coincide with those of the West. Certain of the principles of war as explained in official texts in the West are so full of qualifications that their application requires the exercise of considerable judgment. In some cases this may be little more than the application of plain common sense. Some principles are qualified by others in the same list; and not all the principles are applicable to every given situation. The principles of war are warnings of what will probably be the result of a certain kind of conduct rather than positive guides to action. They should be regarded as excellent pedagogical devices for aiding the student of history, rather than as rules of thumb for the direction of operations. They are no substitute for wide reading. Military history, even when studied in the light of the principles of war, must be regarded chiefly as a means of training the judgment of the future commander by the multiplication of experiences. Perhaps the chief value of emphasis upon the principles of war in the study of military history is that it enables the modern student to understand more fully that he can learn much from past warfare, even though weapons, modes of organization, and means of communication were very different.

As the lists of principles of war propounded by different arms of the service and in different countries vary somewhat, the student of military history may become confused unless he understands that they must not be regarded as all-inclusive rules covering every aspect of every military operation. New principles have been enunciated and added from time to time; and the nature of some principles differs very considerably from that of others. While some are aids to successful planning and action in strategy or tactics, others may more properly be described as general conditions which, if present in an army, aid it to victory. The principles, in the form in which they are usually outlined in military manuals, should be familiar to all those who read about warfare as well as to all soldiers and potential commanders.

This book, however, does not limit itself strictly to the operational field in which the principles apply. It has a dual aim: to provide the professional military student with a background for his reading of military history, and to provide the civilian with an understanding of the significance of military developments in the evolution of society. It is an attempt to relate the history of warfare to the history of society in the West and to trace their effects on one another. Put in its proper setting the history of conflict looms large in the story of man.

1
Warfare and Society

Warfare may be defined as any conflict between rival groups, by force of arms or other means, which has claims to be recognized as a legal conflict. Under this definition there may be a state of war without actual violence or clash of arms. It excludes riot and acts of individual violence but includes insurrection and armed rebellion, especially that which is of sufficient extent to be regarded as civil war.

The conflicts of primitive man may be classed as warfare if they were the result of organized group activity with some continuity of purpose and action; but if they consisted only of incidental and casual acts of violence they cannot be considered as warfare. Primitive societies include many stages of development, from the simple social organization of the Eskimo to the more complex and differentiated societies of the Zulu or of the Indians of the Pacific Northwest. Their basic feature is that, having no written form of language, they rely upon oral tradition for the transmission of knowledge. Primitive life is ruled by custom; social relationships within the group, and the techniques for providing the necessities of life, have been sanctioned by the unvaried experience of generations. Primitive warfare is conditioned by the same rule of custom that governs the other activities of the primitive group. Since society is static, the techniques and weapons of war are static also and in this way differ from those of civilized societies in which methods of making war are subject to constant change.

Primitive warfare is distinct from that waged by civilized peoples in every major respect. Specialization of function in primitive societies is almost nonexistent; each member of the group participates in all its activities. Thus there is no professional, or "regular," military class whose only function is that of waging war. Just as in most primitive groups there is no ruling class, so in war there is no command structure, no means of enforcing orders or discipline. The war chiefs of the North American Indians were those warriors who had distinguished themselves by their individual exploits; their prowess attracted others to follow them on the war-path; but they did not act as commanders in our sense of the term. The lack of any principle of authority, other than custom, means that the tactical organization of civilized armies is never achieved. The simplest form of attack is to ambush an enemy, preferably by employing missile weapons from a distance. Many primitive groups never get beyond this technique, and very few of them are prepared to engage in a stand-up pitched battle or to attack fortified places. Usually primitive war parties break up after the initial engagement and the individual fights for himself.

Rational planning for war, undertaken by military staffs or political bodies in civilized nations, does not exist in the primitive approach to conflict; the war plan may be no more than the auspicious dream of a war chief, as among the Crow people of the Plains. Because its food resources are too scanty, because its warriors are also the hunters and food suppliers to the whole community, and because the members of its war parties are free to go home if the spirit so moves them, no primitive society is capable of extended campaigning. Because a primitive society can ill afford to lose one of its vital food producers, although casualties in primitive war are usually light, the loss of a few men usually causes the abandonment of fighting. The Seneca, joining with the British against the Americans in the battle of Oriskany (1777), quite understandably regarded the death of thirty-three braves as a tribal disaster.

Finally, the motives for primitive war only vaguely resemble those of organized, civilized states. The economic motive is not very important; most primitive groups have little to tempt an attacker. Wars for the acquisition of territory or the domination of another people are equally unusual. War generally is undertaken by a group of individuals, or by the whole tribe, as a matter of prestige; that is, war is fought for the glory which attaches to the outstanding warrior, or for revenge.

The nature of primitive warfare is closely related to the state of the social, political, and economic organization of primitive society. Change in the methods of making war occurs if there are changes in the organization of the group, either as the result of internal innovations, or as the result of influences from other cultures. Such change might come about through the mastering of a technique, such as metallurgy, which makes specialization possible. It may occur through the evolution of political institutions, such as kingship. When the royal principle was established among the Zulu, it resulted in the emergence of an individual who had the power to command. The Zulu, organized into regiments (*impis*), and led by powerful kings, such as Chaka, broke through the barrier of custom which impedes change and evolved a system of warfare intermediate between that of more primitive groups and that practiced by civilized societies. Similarly, most primitive peoples, upon encountering the European, have imitated Western techniques of war, with varying degrees of success. The Plains Indians obtained horses from the Spaniards and became cavalry warriors; firearms added to their effectiveness; but although the Sioux succeeded in vanquishing Custer's troops at the battle of the Little Big Horn (1876), Indian progress in armament was not matched by an advance in social organization, and Indian command and tactics remained rudimentary.

In civilized societies warfare is a condition which is distinguishable from many other forms of violence by the fact that it is an accepted form of behavior on the part of certain groups within the community. The endemic disorder of the Middle Ages, although frequently regarded by authorities in church and state as illegal because it threatened the integrity of the Christian polity in Europe, was in fact warfare. The political unity of medieval Christendom was largely theoretical; conflict between groups was a recognized method of settling differences; and military operations were planned and carried through in an organized fashion. In modern times the type of conflict which predominates is warfare between nation-states. Such conflict must be classed as warfare even though it is often alleged to be unjust or illegal. Philosophers have wrestled, although not very successfully, with the problem of distinguishing between just and unjust wars on the basis of the morality of causes. Today, under the charter of the United Nations, it is claimed by some authorities that warfare of the old type between nation-states is illegal and that the only legal military action is an international police action to prevent or punish aggression. But powers that have opposed the United Nations forces have claimed that they fought for legitimate ends and that their cause was both just and legal. It is still impossible to find any significant difference between wars which are legal or just and those which are illegal or unjust.

Therefore, any organized armed conflict between national or ideological groups must be regarded as warfare.

The requirement that to be classed as warfare a conflict must be in some degree an organized activity might suggest that war is a condition which develops with the development of civilization. Indeed, some philosophers, like Rousseau, and some anthropologists, like W. J. Perry and the school of "diffusionists," have implied that war and civilization had a common origin. Some anthropologists have pointed to certain stone-age tribes, like the Eskimos, to suggest that primitive man was "peaceful"; and it is abundantly clear that war has been intensified as man has become more "civilized." From these sources, it is possible to draw the inference that war is "unnatural." If it is "unnatural," then there is powerful support for the belief that war can be eliminated from society; for if man is not by nature a combative animal, then it is conceivable that a cure can be found for the disease that has always plagued civilization.

On the other hand, the majority of anthropologists disagree with the belief that the most primitive man did not know war. They regard his food-gathering and wife-seeking raids as a primitive form of warfare. Clearly the march of civilization, while it has intensified war at certain levels—for instance, in the resounding clash of nations—has actually abolished its manifestations at other levels, such as within the area of the nation-state itself. Few will deny that, within that sphere, the nation-state has become one of the most important man-made instruments for the advancement of civilization. War is not the product of the nation-state and extreme nationalism, as is sometimes said. It occurred before the nation-state existed. Hence, in the light of these circumstances, modern war between nations may be looked upon as a reversion to barbarism which has not yet been controlled by the growing civilizing forces that have trained men within the state.

Whether one accepts the thesis that war is the child of civilization or the contrary one that war stems from human nature, it is clear that development in warfare has been closely related to the process of historical change. Man's social, political, economic, and cultural progress has been affected both for good and for ill by the incidence and impact of armed conflict. The verdict of war has been, time and again, the deciding factor in the process of historical change. The Persian Wars saved Europe from Asiatic tyranny. The Roman Empire was established by warfare, and warfare contributed to its destruction. William the Conqueror, as his name indicates, exercised his influence upon the history of England because of a successful war. And so it has gone through the centuries. War has always been the arbiter when other methods of reaching a decision have failed. The judgment it has given is based on might rather than on right; it is never a moral judgment. At times right has prevailed, but whether this was accidental or due to inherent moral strength is a question upon which agreement is impossible.

But war has also been much more than a crude trial by combat deciding the course of history. It is intimately involved with the whole historical process. The nature of war itself has been fashioned by social factors and by technical development; war in its turn has affected social and technical progress or retrogression.

That war has been affected by social and technical change needs little elucidation. Weapons are the products of contemporary technology. Armies reflect the society from which they spring. When social or industrial revolutions take place, when power is passed from one economic class to another, when new techniques of administration or of distribution are discovered, warfare is automatically affected. The ever-accelerating rate of scientific discovery in our own time has made this clear as never before; so much so, that one British writer on military affairs, General J. F. C. Fuller, has gone so far as to say that weapons account for 99 per cent of victory. While few would agree with so extreme a statement, it is a fact that superior weapons favor the user. Because of the present acceleration in invention, success in war depends more than ever before on the facility with which soldiers adapt their organization, tactics, and doctrine to the use of improved weapons. It may equally depend upon the extent to which military leaders bring their forces into line with the society from which they come and which they are designed to defend. Armies that are anachronisms will be swept away like the *condottieri* of Renaissance Italy. In the past, partly through a conservatism inherent in their craft, soldiers have been peculiarly slow to adopt weapons and methods that were ready to hand. Resistence to improvements in military efficiency has sometimes resulted from militarism, which includes among other things a distortion of military values by an overemphasis upon the superficialities of military traditions and the insulation of the military craft from society at large. Only in very recent times has scientific research been accepted by the soldier as an important part of defense; and only slowly is it becoming understood that an army cannot stand aloof from the rest of the community.

The complementary thesis, that war has a continuous effect in the shaping of society, raises more contentious issues. Some thinkers have concluded that war has been a constructive force in social and technological progress. The German economist Werner Sombart argued that war fostered the modern economic system and therefore modern society: the medieval knight was the earliest example of the specialization of labor; the growth of professional armies developed the spirit of discipline and the organizing spirit essential to modern capitalism; the cost of war led to the expansion and development of credit; and the demands of modern armies for standardized products on a huge scale compelled the introduction of the techniques of mass production in the basic metal-working and textile industries. The American social philosopher Lewis Mumford contends that the machine was propagated by war; that the invention of gunpowder stimulated the production of the basic element of modern civilization, iron; that since the gun was itself a primitive single-chambered combustion engine, it inspired also the invention of power-engines; that war produced the military engineer who was the prototype of the industrial director and something very different from the simple craftsman of the Middle Ages; and that in the professional army was elaborated the ideal form of organization for a purely mechanical system of industrial production. A host of writers have dwelt upon the military virtues as they are revealed by individuals, especially in time of crisis; and some, like Nietzsche, have argued that war must therefore be an ennobling experience for society as a whole.

A contrary view has been advanced in Toynbee's *Study of History,* in which, along with due recognition of the importance of the military virtues, it is shown that war has been the "proximate cause" of the breakdown of every civilization in the past. Toynbee's description of the death-symptoms in the "time of troubles" of previous civilizations is uncomfortably similar to the nationalist wars of our own day. A great many other writers have shown that war is a great destroyer, both of materials and of moral standards. Some have attempted to distinguish between militarism and other military characteristics and have come to the conclusion that there is a strong tendency, perhaps an inevitable one, for the efforts expended in necessary defensive organization and operations to lead to excesses of the military spirit which, in the end, tend to destroy the society that it was the original intention to defend. Many books and articles, inspired by the revelations made by scientists about the atom and hydrogen bombs, and by the impact of total warfare, have resurrected the theme of Armageddon and of the destruction of civilization, perhaps even of man himself.

The most detailed investigation of the impact of war upon society is Professor J. U. Nef's *War and Human Progress,* in which many of the claims of the "constructive" school about the contributions made by war to society are shown to be either false or exaggerated, and in which it is contended that it is the "limitations" on war, rather than war itself, that have led to social and technical advance.

War may be limited in several different ways. It may be limited in duration, in space or location, in intensity or mode of fighting, in its impact upon the contending peoples, or in objective. All of these forms of limitation may not be present at the same time. The origin of such limitation is diverse. Shortness of the duration of wars is more likely to be brought about by a preponderance of strength on one side than by lack of zeal of the contestants; limitation in location may be caused by the localized nature of the issues in dispute; restraints in the mode of fighting, lack of impact upon the civilian populations, and limitation of objective can be caused by physical limitations as well as by a climate of opinion which places restrictions on the nature of warfare. Limitations of this latter kind existed in theory in the Middle Ages and were a powerful restraint in the eighteenth-century Age of Enlightenment.

It is obvious that the concept of limitation is opposite to the concept of totality in war. Furthermore, just as limitation can never be absolute, so also totality in war is a relative concept rather than an absolute one. Total warfare in the most complete sense would mean fighting with all resources and all kinds of weapons without any restrictions imposed by humanity or by expediency, killing all prisoners and civilians without respect for age or sex, disregarding completely the rights of neutrals, and using psychological techniques to wipe out individual personality and to obliterate all standards. No warfare has yet reached this stage. The conqueror does not wish to find at his feet a pestilence-ridden lazarhouse. Absolute totality in warfare can only mean chaos and a return to barbarism. Hence, when we speak of total warfare, we really mean approximation to totality, and when we speak of limitations upon warfare we mean that the growth of civilizing influences, or the lack of ability to overcome physical barriers, has exercised restraint upon warfare and so has lessened its impact upon society.

Man's increasing power of construction has been closely parallelled by the growth of his power of destruction. Similarly, his greater capacity for destruction has been matched by, and to some extent has produced, a desire to place limitations on warfare in the name of humanity. Through the centuries, the forces moving toward totality, on the one hand, and toward limitation, on the other, have been roughly in balance with a tendency first to one side and then to the other. Just as the Middle Ages and the eighteenth century were periods of limitation, so the ages of the Reformation and of the French Revolution saw increasing approximation to totality. The nineteenth century was a period when it seemed as if man had a choice between two alternative paths. The twentieth century shows a swing toward total warfare but is also marked by more conscious efforts than ever before to control the scourge of war.

The invention of the atomic bomb seemed to threaten civilization and perhaps even the very existence of man. Although it suggested that war had stimulated the rate of scientific development beyond what was possible in peace time, war has now become a destructive force of boundless potentiality. Failure to divert atomic power from warlike to peaceful uses accentuated the danger which was suspended, like the sword of Damocles, above man's head. Movements to abolish war, which had already been stimulated by the horrors of modern strife, were greatly strengthened. Pacifism, limitation of armaments, collective security, and even the creation of a super-state by general consent have been advocated as means by which war might be ended. The annihilating power of the new hydrogen bomb is so vast that some responsible statesmen, scientists, and military men have begun to say that the frightfulness of the weapon will, in itself, be a deterrent against the onset of another major conflict.

It is just possible that the human instinct for self-preservation will eventually save mankind from extermination; however, it is equally possible that it will not. Observers have been surprised to find that the development of a Soviet nuclear capability, which was at one time feared as a possible precipitant of a third world war, has so far had a quite different effect. The nuclear equilibrium, or stalemate, of the two great powers, achieved about 1959, established a state of mutual deterrence—a balance of terror. It unfolded a nuclear umbrella under which lesser powers continued to wage war while the super-powers, although sometimes giving clandestine support, held back. Even when they became more involved, the two super-powers accepted restraints on their operations and shunned the temptation to resort to nuclear weapons. Moreover, both revealed a reluctance to share atomic secrets even with their closest friends and preached against the dangers of proliferation.

Nevertheless, the nuclear arms race continued with little abatement, despite efforts to restrain it by diplomatic agreement. New developments in defensive weapons or first-strike capability may upset this delicate situation and lead to worldwide disaster. But it had become obvious that the solution of the problem of war at this level could be achieved only by the conquest of one super-power by the other and the establishment of a world state, or, alternatively, by self-denying agreement.

Because the super-powers are beyond control by general international agreement, and because statecraft has been incapable of abolishing or containing war except fortuitously, by the fragile nuclear balance, scholars have turned to a more intensive study of war and its causes in order to learn more about its prevention. The earlier debate about whether war was a result of human nature or of developing civilization now seems too simplistic. Attempts to maintain peace by arbitration, disarmament, international organization, and collective security have proved equally frustrating. In 1958-59, the year when the possibilities of the balance of terror were first realized, new research institutes sprang up at Duke, Harvard, Northwestern, Princeton, Michigan, Stanford, and elsewhere to explore what came to be called the science of peace. One of the most promising lines of approach in these programs was the study of conflict resolution and crisis management, in the belief that, if, under the nuclear umbrella, antagonisms between states could be prevented from passing the point of no return, war could be contained.

The balance of terror has, thus, fostered a more scientific approach to the study of the origins of warfare by social scientists and other scholars from a variety of disciplines. No one expects easy solutions. Even if an overall theory of the causes of war can eventually be produced from work done in several widely scattered fields of endeavor, there will still remain the serious problem of persuading statesmen to apply theory to practical situations. Nevertheless, these studies constitute the most promising steps toward peace being taken at present, except for the negotiations between the superpowers about nuclear arms limitation, which were inaugurated in November, 1969.

The study of the history of warfare, its relation to society, and the impact of social and technical developments, which is the purpose of this book, can help us to speculate more fruitfully upon this search for a means to control or limit conflict and, so, to eliminate a present danger to man and his civilization.

2

Classical Warfare:
The Age of the Phalanx

"Civilization begins, because the beginning of civilization is a military advantage," wrote Walter Bagehot in his *Physics and Politics*; "progress is promoted by the competitive examination of constant war." Most modern historians believe that the explanation of the origin of civilization is much more complex than this purely military interpretation. Civilization is associated with the growth of urban life, of a complicated social structure, and of extensive control over the physical environment. To achieve civilization, the oral transmission of knowledge must be superseded by a written language so that successive generations may build upon the accumulated knowledge of their predecessors. These conditions only arise out of a combination of circumstances: favorable topography, soil, and climate; the existence of mineral resources; knowledge obtained from other peoples; the perfecting of new techniques, institutions, or ideas in response to certain stimuli. In this process, warfare must play a part.

All these influences seem to have contributed to the emergence of the Greek civilization. Very early in the second millennium B.C., an Indo-European people appeared almost simultaneously in Greece and in the Troad (northwest Turkey). That they were almost certainly Greeks is known from decipherment of the script (Linear B) they later learned; history calls them Mycenaeans. The warlike nature of the Mycenaeans is recorded in the Homeric epics, in their grave furniture, and in their great citadels of Mycenae and Tiryns. They fought in war chariots and were armed and armored with bronze. By about 1400 B.C., they had become sufficiently powerful to overcome the Minoan sea empire and occupy its capital of

Knossos, on the island of Crete. The siege of Troy, sometime during the thirteenth century, appears to have been the military climax of Mycenaean civilization, for, shortly thereafter, Mycenaean power fell into decline. The Mycenaean strongholds, Athens excepted, proved vulnerable to the onslaught of a new wave of more primitive Greeks, the Dorians, from the north. Their weapons of iron gave the Dorians military superiority. By about 750 B.C., these Greeks, in their turn, had become literate, learning their alphabet from the Phoenicians. Gradually they evolved the city-state, the characteristic Greek form of political organization, and with it a complex social structure in which, in many states, simple tribal kingships gave way first to wealthy oligarchies and then, by the sixth and fifth centuries B.C., to democracies. Political uniformity, however, was hardly a Greek characteristic; Sparta, for example, remained a monarchy to the end. During the same period the Greeks produced a "civilized" fighting body, the phalanx, the germ of all future European military development. The story of Western civilization, and of organized warfare in the West, must thus begin with Ancient Greece.

While it is possible to speak of the civilization or culture of Greece and, despite its many dialects, of a Greek language, politically Greece was marked by extreme diversity. The political unit was the city-state. Even in times of great peril, consciousness of a common identity as "Hellenes" never transcended strong local loyalties and a jealous regard for local political independence. This molecular political structure of Greece was inherited from the original tribal fragmentation of the Hellenic peoples at the time of their migration and was preserved by the geography of the Greek peninsula. Settlement concentrated on the infrequent coastal plains and in the river valleys which were geographically isolated from neighboring areas by high mountain barriers. The early Greek city-state was the limit of its inhabitants' horizon. Particularism bred of isolation was, in the course of time, strengthened by distinctive historical and religious traditions which made for a powerful group-sense. This sense of community and locale was the most important barrier against the establishment of a single state embracing the whole Greek mainland.

Greek unification was therefore not accomplished by a gradual historical process, since that process was working against it. It was eventually imposed by force of arms, but until the fourth century B.C. no single state was powerful enough to achieve it.

Moreover, Greek armies and military techniques were peculiarly unsuited to the act of conquest. Despite their great political differentiation, it is a most interesting fact that all the Greek states, with the exception of Thessaly and Aetolia, fought in the same way and with the same formation. This formation was the phalanx, a solid rectangle of heavily armored infantrymen carrying shield and spear and drawn up eight deep. The relatively advanced state of Greek metal-working crafts made possible the provision of arms and armor for a large proportion of Greek armies. The phalanx was more than a mere huddle of men drawn together in self-preservation, for discipline and endurance were required to maintain cohesion and to prevent the opening of a dangerous gap in the front rank. Discipline was based on morale, the morale of free men. Although the institution of slavery was a part of Greek city society, the dominant feature of that society was a large, and free, middle class.

A battle between phalangite armies was a test of weight and stamina, with the two formations, locked closely together, contending until one side or the other broke ranks and fled. There was no place in warfare of this nature for generalship; once battle was joined, the individual was submerged in a mass of sweating bodies and, since reserves were unknown, there was no chance of outside assistance. Outflanking as a conscious maneuver was never used, except by the Spartans. In battles between the citizen-soldiers of other states, outflanking occurred by accident or through the tendency of each man in the phalanx to sidle to the right in an effort to avoid exposing his unshielded right side. The highly trained Spartans took advantage of this tendency by wheeling, outflanking their enemy's left, and then rolling up his line from that flank. Victory in phalangial warfare was limited in extent, for the phalanx, by itself, was incapable of achieving a crushing success. It was too unwieldy and immobile to be adapted to pursuit. Casualties in early Greek warfare were light, and most hoplites (heavily armored infantrymen) lived to fight another day.

Greek warfare remained stationary for several centuries. The phalanx was the standard military technique from the Homeric Age until after the Peloponnesian War (431-404 B.C.). Only part of the explanation for this extraordinary conservatism lies with the unwillingness to alter what was known and proven. Greece was not exposed to attack from an outside power employing different techniques until the invasion from Persia in the early fifth century.

Neither example nor incentive was present to compel innovation. Moreover, the social prestige of the infantry soldier has perhaps never been so high as in the ancient Greek world. The heavily armored hoplite, with crested helmet and massive shield, was for the Greeks the highest embodiment of military attainment, sanctioned by the triumphs of the past and the hero-image of an Achilles. It was an honor to serve in the phalanx; the most desirable position was in the front rank; and military service was the privilege as well as the duty of every free citizen. Only the aristocrats and the middle class fought as hoplites, however, because only they could afford the cost of the armor. The bulk of the free population served as lightly armed troops or rowed in the fleet. Moreover, there was no competing tradition of a cavalry elite, because most of Greece, owing to poor pasturage, was unsuitable for horse-breeding. Only Thessaly, in the north, and Boeotia developed significant cavalry forces. Neither state was able to use cavalry effectively away from its homeland plains.

The predominance of infantry can be accounted for on grounds of social prestige, military tradition, and political structure, and also because no strong competing traditions existed. But the paradox remains that in a country four fifths of which was mountainous, the Greeks were employing a formation which could be effective only on level ground. Only on the infrequent plains of Greece could the phalanx retain that solidarity which was its essential attribute. Enhancing the paradox is the fact that although most of the towns in Greece were fortified in one way or another (the Athenian Acropolis is an outstanding example), there were few sieges and no developed siege procedure.

Greek military development was highly specialized, both in the methods employed and in the terrain chosen for battles. This was so because warfare in Greece was profoundly affected by the fundamental economic problem of Greek history. The cultivable area of Greece was very small; through terracing and other artificial methods of coping with an unfavorable environment, Greece probably supported a somewhat larger population in the fifth century than in modern times. But food shortage was chronic, with the attendant evil of overpopulation. In part, these difficulties were overcome by the great colonizing activity of the seventh and sixth centuries B.C., which eased the population pressure by emigration. The thin line between subsistence and deprivation, however, meant that the primary objective of the Greek army in the field was the crops of its antagonist, because destruction of the harvest would bring the enemy to his knees. This tended to limit war in several ways: fighting was generally restricted to the autumn harvest period, and battles almost always took place in the open fields, because the threat of crop removal by an invader would always bring the townsmen out to fight in the open.

At the beginning of the fifth century B. C., Greek warfare was running in channels already ancient, its frequency conforming to the rhythm of the seasons, its techniques adapted to the conditions of economic life, and its continuance guaranteed by military conservatism, social custom, and democratic politics. In democratic Athens, for instance, commanders could be called to account by the Assembly when they lost a battle. They, therefore, tended to be orthodox in their manner of fighting, as the least blameworthy course. For this reason, it is hardly surprising that no one state had been able to dominate Greece politically. Leaving aside the obstacles of limited resources, rugged terrain, and complicated diplomacy, the conventionalized, severely restricted military methods pursued by the Greeks set sharp bounds to the ambitions of any city-state. In the fifth century, however, Greece was required to face the greatest power of the Mediterranean world, and, although this challenge was met, it brought changes that were to alter the nature of Greek civilization.

The army of imperial Persia reflected the social and political organization of the empire; it was composed of men from many nationalities and language groups. Its core, however, was the Persians themselves, and those closely affiliated to them in race and religion. The best infantry, whether the Immortals of the Persian royal guard or the Medes and Elamites, consisted of regular professional troops. Although they carried daggers or short spears for close fighting, their basic weapon was the bow, and their standard tactic was to launch their arrows at an enemy from a distance, behind the protection of wicker shields planted in the ground. Other than their shields, they wore little or no protective equipment, a fact that astonished the Greeks. The cavalry of the Persian homeland probably came from the landowning aristocracy and their adherents; the Medes, Elamites, Bactrians, and Sakai also produced excellent horsemen. The basic weapon of cavalry, as well as infantry, was the bow; although some body armor was worn and the

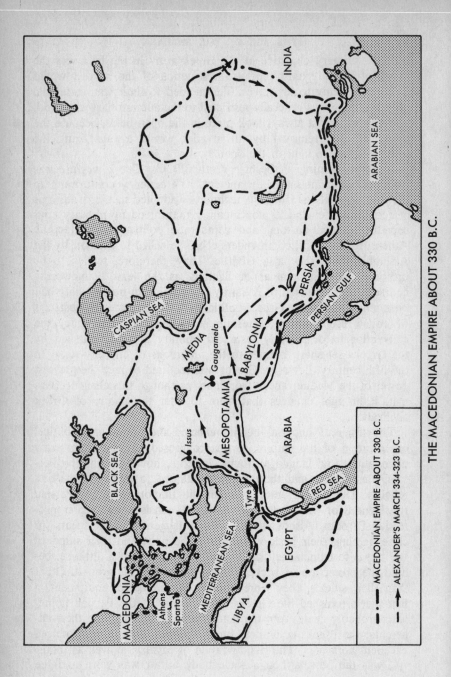

THE MACEDONIAN EMPIRE ABOUT 330 B.C.

- - - MACEDONIAN EMPIRE ABOUT 330 B.C.
→ - ALEXANDER'S MARCH 334-323 B.C.

Sakai had axes, the function of the cavalry was not shock but the fixing of an enemy by a combination of speed and missile fire, so that he could be destroyed by the infantry. These tactics had won Persia an Asian empire, but they proved unsuitable in Greek terrain against heavy infantry fighting on ground of its own choosing.

The Persian offensive against Greece was an attempt to prevent the Greek states from further helping their sister communities of the islands and eastern coastline of the Aegean Sea. In the decisive engagement of the first Persian expedition, the battle of Marathon (490 B.C.), the Athenian phalanx proved superior to Persian numbers. The hoplites closed swiftly with the Persian infantry, and, although the Sakai broke the deliberately weakened Greek center, the great superiority of the heavy infantry in close combat was decisive on the wings and brought victory. There appears to have been little Persian cavalry at Marathon. In the subsequent battles of the second Persian expedition, Greek infantry successfully withstood the Persian combination of cavalry and infantry missile fire that had proved so lethal in Asia. In the stand of Leonidas and his Spartans at the pass of Thermopylae (480 B.C.), where the terrain was unsuitable for cavalry, the Persian infantry understandably refused to close with the hoplites, and the Spartans were eventually worn down by a hail of arrows from both front and rear. At Plataea (479 B.C.), in a preliminary engagement, the allied Greek phalanx was able to protect its flanks from cavalry assault by resting them against a mountain spur and a wall and indomitably kept ranks under steady missile fire. In the main battle, some days later, the Persian general, Mardonius, caught the Greeks dispersed during a retreat, and his cavalry halted the Spartan contingent. Spartan discipline held up under prolonged missile fire; then, when the Persian infantry was fully committed, the Spartan commander, Pausania, launched his hoplites in an attack that smashed through the wicker-shield wall and put the Persians to flight. The Greek victories against the Persians were defensive in character, won by fighting on ground of their own choosing. It is noteworthy that the Greeks never took the offensive or offered battle in areas like the plains of Boeotia, where their shortcomings would have been revealed.

The truly decisive battle of the war, however, was fought not on land but at sea. The Athenian statesman Themistocles was aware that the Persian menace would persist as long as the Persian fleet was able to act as flank guard and support to a land army invading

Greece. He succeeded in persuading his fellow citizens to devote the profits from a newly discovered vein in the state-owned silver mines at Laureion to the building of a fleet of 200 triremes, and, in the decade after Marathon, Athens by this supreme effort emerged as a naval power. The outstanding naval victory of Salamis (480 B.C.), won chiefly through a combination of ramming and boarding, resulted in Xerxes's withdrawal, with part of his army, from Greek soil. Mardonius, left with the bulk of the army and acutely sensitive to the threat to his communications now posed by the dominant Greek fleet, was driven to seek a swift victory. The result was the decisive Greek triumph at Plataea.

It has become commonplace to say that the thwarting of Persian imperialism allowed Greek civilization to reach its fullest flower and thus permitted a great cultural legacy to be bequeathed to western society. As far as the Greeks could ascertain, however, the threat from the East had not ended, and the continued existence of this supposed threat had the widest political and military consequences. The Persian intrusion into the homeland had exposed a serious Greek weakness: the inability of the various states to cooperate when threatened by an outside power, owing either to long-standing jealousies or to the unwillingness of some states to sacrifice their own territories to Panhellenic requirements.

The necessity for coordination of effort in time of war drove certain of the Greek states into an alliance, the Delian League, so called because the treasury of the League was established on the sacred island of Delos. Members of the League were required either to contribute ships to the fleet or to render an equivalent in cash to the League treasury. Because Athens was the premier naval power, it was perhaps natural that she should be given headship of the League and be made responsible for its administration, although, had Sparta been more enterprising, the leadership would clearly have gone to her.

Under her great leader Pericles, Athens proceeded to transform the League from a defensive alliance of freely associated states into an empire based upon the coercive force of the Athenian navy. States wishing to secede from the League were brought to heel by military action and their contributions were increased; democratic governments on the Athenian model (and dependent upon Athenian support for their existence) were set up in all member-states; in 454 B.C. the treasury was moved from Delos to Athens upon the feeblest of pretexts; in 449 the final transformation took place. In that year when the war with Persia ended, the members of the League expected that their contributions would end also. Instead, on the legitimate ground that her navy was performing a Panhellenic function by patrolling the Aegean, Athens insisted that their contributions should continue. Thus she irrevocably committed herself to a policy of naval imperialism. At the same time, Sparta was following much the same course in the Peloponnesian League she headed, except that she tended to support oligarchies, not democracies.

The middle years of the fifth century saw the splendor of Athens at its height; the building of the Parthenon and of other magnificent structures, the sculpture of Phidias, the poetry and drama of Aeschylus and Sophocles, the flowering of a great intellectual center. In this period Athens had a liberal democratic form of government, in which, in the words of Pericles, "power rests with the majority and not with a few; in private disputes all are equal before the law; and we ourselves personally either decide policy or at least form a sound judgment on it." At the the same time Athens was enjoying an age of great commercial prosperity. A changeover from subsistence agriculture to the cultivation for export of the vine and the olive, and the creation of large-scale pottery and metal-work manufactures, had made Greece the premier trading nation of the Mediterranean, and Athens the wealthiest and most important commercial center in Greece.

To all these achievements, however, the Athenian navy made an important, if not decisive, contribution. Its dominance of the eastern Mediterranean and Aegean safeguarded the channels of Athenian trade and guaranteed Athenian control of the vital wheat-producing areas around the Black Sea. Commercial wealth made possible the flourishing of Athenian culture and a leisure class to support it. It is scarcely necessary to point out the significance of the construction of the Long Walls linking Athens with its port of the Piraeus (456 B.C.). The fortunes of Athens were tied so intimately with sea power that she was attempting to make herself into an island.

The operation of the Athenian navy required thousands of men. Because the poorer citizens rowed in the fleet, the navy was always the stronghold of Athenian democracy; the army was a more likely source of potential oligarchs. Naval-induced prosperity brought certain problems. Manufacturers resorted to slave labor on a large scale, with the result that individual artisans were unable to compete and many free citizens were unable to find employment. The navy thus became a means of easing economic distress.

Although Pericles might have justified Athenian imperialism on the grounds that "our city as a whole is an education to Greece and our individual citizens excel all men," it might equally be shown that Athens was forced to convert the Delian League into an empire based on money contributions because of social and economic dislocation stemming originally from her very success as a naval-commercial power. Whether or not this is so, Athenian statesmen realized that, for Athens, there could be no return to the orbit of a parochial city-state, set predictably within the constellation of its fellows. Her sea-borne commerce demanded an expensive fleet, which only commerce-derived wealth and the Delian contributions could maintain; inexorably, therefore, she was driven along the road to empire.

The threat posed by Athens to the autonomy of other Greek states caused them to cluster about the only state in Greece which had the military power to check her. Sparta was unquestionably the most formidable land power in Greece; but she owed this pre-eminence to a peculiar set of political and social arrangements comparable to nothing in history except perhaps the "national socialism" of modern totalitarian states. In the eighth century B.C., when other Greek states solved the problem of a steadily increasing population and a relatively diminishing food supply by colonization, Sparta turned instead to the conquest of neighboring Messenia. The food shortage was relieved by dividing arable Messenian land into equal allotments for each Spartan family. Since the land was cultivated by the Messenians, Spartan males were left free to engage their energies in the one great object of their state, the maintenance of an iron rule over the Messenians and other subject populations, collectively known as the Helots. Every Spartan, female as well as male, was trained, in the appropriate age-group, to physical perfection through a competitive program of athletics; perpetuation of the best stock was achieved by placing eugenic control in the hands of the state, which rejected unfit infants, encouraged the marriage of fine physical specimens, and expelled the cowardly and the idle. From the age of seven (when he was taken from his mother) to the age of sixty, no Spartan male was free from military discipline and service. From this system emerged the best heavy infantry of the age, greatly superior even to other Hellenic hoplites. To this end was sacrificed the many-sided diversity of Greek culture: the narrow preoccupation with the forging of a remarkable military instrument meant the stifling of all other activities as mere distractions. For this reason, after the Messenian Wars there is no tradition of Spartan development in the plastic arts, poetry, drama, or philosophy; Spartans were forbidden to compete in the Olympic games since these were diversions from truly military procedures; and the political structure congealed into a dictatorship of the minority as early as the seventh century B.C. It is the great irony of Spartan history that, having labored at enormous cost to construct an irresistible army, the Spartan people were unable to use their creation in large-scale ventures outside their own territory. They were living atop a volcano. As Aristotle put it, "the Helots may be described as perpetually lying in wait to take advantage of their masters' misfortunes," and thus, even in the Persian Wars, Spartan participation was limited and unwilling.

A prime cause of the Peloponnesian War (431-404 B.C.) was the anxiety of the commercial state of Corinth over Athenian trade expansion. Corinth succeeded in dragging a reluctant Sparta into war when Athens chose to apply an economic boycott to the city of Megara, a clear demonstration to all Greek states that Athens was prepared to use her naval dominance to control the distribution of food imports.

It is remarkable that in a war which was literally a death struggle between the two most powerful states of the Greek world, almost no military innovations took place, with the exception of the occasional use of light-armed troops (*peltasts*) which were employed with some success against the slow-moving phalanx. The great length of the war must therefore be ascribed to the binding force of tradition acting as a brake upon military techniques, and also to the inability of the Spartan land power to achieve a swift and crushing decision against the Periclean strategy of avoidance of land battle. In order to defeat Athens, Sparta found it necessary to fight her on her own element, the sea. Sparta's victory was made possible by an Athenian naval and military disaster at Syracuse in 413 B.C. In Sparta's acceptance of Persian money to build a fleet lies the explanation of her final victory; in return, Persia was permitted to

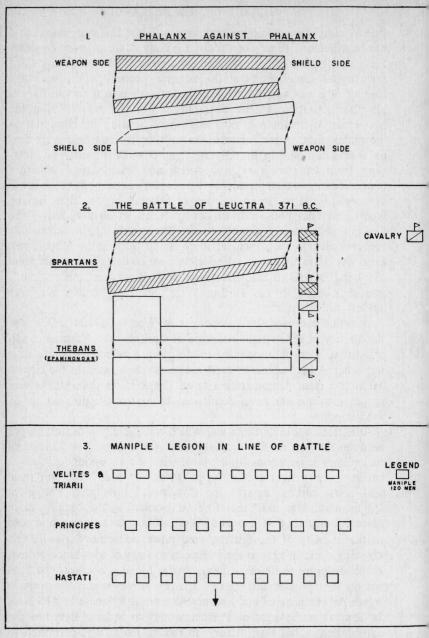

1. PHALANX AGAINST PHALANX

WEAPON SIDE   SHIELD SIDE

SHIELD SIDE   WEAPON SIDE

2. THE BATTLE OF LEUCTRA 371 B.C.

SPARTANS

THEBANS
(EPAMINONDAS)

CAVALRY

3. MANIPLE LEGION IN LINE OF BATTLE

VELITES &
TRIARII

LEGEND

MANIPLE
120 MEN

PRINCIPES

HASTATI

MILITARY FORMATIONS OF THE ANCIENT WORLD

repossess the Ionian states lost by the Empire in 479 B.C. The war left in its wake a trail of devastation, especially in Athenian territory. In addition, Greek society proved too frail to withstand the stresses of fratricidal war. Everywhere, but particularly at Athens, there occurred a struggle for power between contending classes, resulting in violent political upheavals, dictatorships, and the rapid alternating of power from class to class.

The period between the end of the Peloponnesian War and the establishment of Macedonian hegemony in Greece was one of political chaos, social disintegration, and economic distress and, at the same time, of the most rapid military development. Victory in the war proved lethal for Sparta: it forced her to become, as the only state capable of giving order to Greece, an imperial power; but Spartan governors and garrisons, men trained exclusively in military matters, were unable to achieve the political flexibility that their new position demanded, and the harshness and rapacity of Spartan rule soon led to resistance. In addition, the underlying contradiction of Spartan might reasserted itself: the maintenance abroad of garrisons weakened the Spartan grip on the Helots and rendered their imperial policy half-hearted. Even more important, the necessity of providing garrisons drastically weakened the core of Spartan strength, the army. Thus, when the brief period of Spartan domination was ended by Thebes at the battle of Leuctra (371 B.C.), the proportion of Spartans to Helots in the battle order had dropped from the normal four in ten to one in ten.

It is doubtful, however, whether even a fully mobilized Sparta would have been able to cope with the new army of Thebes. The place of honor in Greek armies had traditionally been on the right, perhaps because of the tendency of the phalanx to edge in that direction. The Theban leader Epaminondas cunningly weighted his left flank to a depth of forty-eight ranks and refused his center and right. No orthodox phalanx could stand up to this overwhelming concentration of weight upon one point. When the Theban left enveloped the enemy, Epaminondas then used the Boeotian cavalry to mop up the broken remnants. The first Greek army able to take decisive offensive action had been created by a coordination of different arms.

Thebes was no more successful than Athens or Sparta in holding Greece together as one political unit. In part, Theban power was curbed by the same shortage of manpower that had restricted Sparta and by the same failure to create a form of government transcending the concept of the city-state. The expansion of the slavery system, and the concentration of wealth in fewer hands, coupled with devastation and unemployment resulting from the Peloponnesian War and subsequent conflicts, heightened the class struggle in every Greek state, including Thebes, and rendered military success fleeting and meaningless. It was left for a state which the Greeks considered barbaric, or at least not quite "Greek," to impose upon the peninsula the centralized rule of a conquering power.

In constructing an empire, Macedonia did not have to break through the city-state habit of mind, for it had clung to the institution of monarchy, a form of government long abandoned in Greece itself. Therefore, extensions of Macedonian rule were merely extensions of the personal power of the Macedonian king. The basis of Macedonian strength was an army which was perhaps the most powerful military force constructed before the coming of gunpowder. Although its creator, Philip II, had borrowed inspiration during an enforced stay in Thebes, the army was founded ultimately upon the social resources of Macedonia itself. The country was predominantly rural; from its free peasantry came the phalangite, differing from his Greek counterpart in that he wielded a somewhat longer spear, since the Macedonian phalanx was deeper and heavier than the Greek model. From its land-holding aristocracy came the prime striking force of the army, the cavalry of the King's "Companions," some two thousand strong. To these basic elements Philip added mercenary cavalry components drawn from the neighboring state of Thessaly, and also infantry units of different kinds, including slingers and javelin-throwers, whom he had probably seen in action in Greece.

The result was the first balanced army of historic times, an army equipped to fight over any kind of terrain and against any enemy. It could operate defensively and offensively with equal efficiency. Philip must also be regarded as the founder (at least for the Greek world) of scientific siege warfare; his army contained a full siege apparatus, including towers, rams, and torsion-catapults, the latter invented shortly before Philip's reign began. The army was kept in the field by selective conscription for set periods; in this way the Macedonians obtained the first standing army for year-round campaigning. With the long campaigns of Philip's son, Alexander, the Macedonian army transformed itself from a national conscript army into a professional army with a history and esprit of its own.

Militarily, the dissension-torn Greek states could not resist the new army of Macedonia. In the battle of Chaeronaea (338 B.C.) the irresistible Macedonian horse supplied the margin of victory and made Philip master of Greece. It was Philip's ambition to lead a united Greece against the traditional Persian enemy, and to this end he had himself appointed Captain-General of the Hellenes. His assassination left the project to his son Alexander, who assumed the title and the ambition after quelling Greek insurrections. There were factors besides royal ambition, however, which encouraged the idea of an expedition against Persia. Such an attack against the "barbarians" had been preached for many years by political publicists like Isocrates, whose propaganda, truly imperialist in nature, was based on the superiority of the Greeks as a people and hence their undoubted right to govern others. Although Panhellenism as a unifying force had never been strong, Isocrates's arguments fell on fertile soil, for, in the fourth century, the Greek export economy was being slowly strangled by the rise of competitors like Carthage and by the growth of home manufacturing in Italy, the Black Sea areas, and the Persian Empire itself. As a result, population once more began to press upon food supply; and as before, many Greeks began to think in terms of overseas expansion as the solution of their difficulties. This situation explains one of the most marked phenomena of the military history of the fourth century: the presence on foreign soil of large numbers of Greek mercenary troops. As Isocrates put it, "many, through lack of daily sustenance, are compelled to serve as mercenaries, and to die fighting for the enemy against their own friends." In 401 B.C. 10,000 Greeks took service with Cyrus the Younger in his abortive attempt to seize the Persian crown from his brother Artaxerxes II; their exploits, described by Xenophon in his *Anabasis,* are the best known of many such adventures during the century.

At the moment in Greek history when social and economic exigencies were forcing Greeks to look abroad, a channel for the release of pent-up energies was provided by the perfected Macedonian war machine, with a military genius at its head and a rich and unwieldy empire as its target. It does not seem that at the outset Alexander contemplated the overthrow of the Persian Empire and the construction of another in its place, but an unbroken string of victories led him on beyond the limits of the world previously known to the Greeks. Syria, Egypt, Babylonia, the Persian heartland itself, the fringes of the great Russian steppes, the western ranges of the Himalayas saw his army pass, until, in northwest India, weary and homesick after eight years of campaigning (334-326 B.C.), the Macedonian veterans refused to go farther and Alexander was forced to turn back. In this unprecedented march (which the Romans failed to equal) each component of the army was tested in turn, as different terrain was entered and as different enemies were encountered. The light-armed peltasts proved their worth in arduous mountain fighting, while the siege train met the difficult challenge of the island fortress of Tyre successfully in a long and hazardous siege. The conquest of Tyre was the most spectacular of Alexander's successes in siege warfare; it was emulated many times in the capture of other strongholds.

The greatest element in the Macedonian technique of conquest, however, and that which constituted the most significant advance on traditional Greek warfare, was the combination of the rock-like phalanx with light and heavy cavalry. The union of an always dependable infantry base with the mobile shock supplied by cavalry was too much for the valorous but heterogeneous Persian masses, whose chief advantage, numbers, was vastly outweighed by steadiness, missile fire, cavalry shock, and generalship.

More than any previous commander, Alexander possessed the attributes which, in modern times, are associated with generalship; and it is this imponderable of generalship, the uniformly skillful wielding of an almost perfect military instrument, which is the most difficult factor to measure in accounting for the conquest of Persia. The qualities of Alexander as a general emerge most clearly in the most critical battle of the whole campaign at Gaugamela on the river Tigris (331 B.C.). Alexander, adhering to the old custom, always entered the battle personally at the head of his cavalry, but never until he had concluded that the decisive moment was at hand. Thus at Gaugamela he withheld his Companion cavalry until the Persians had been totally engaged, and then launched an assault which crumpled the Persian flank, drove it in upon the center, and turned an apparent Persian victory into a rout. Alexander showed the qualities of greatness in other ways. He invariably followed up his victories on the field with a relentless pursuit; and he fought in all weather and in every season. As a strategist, he was the master of his age. When the Persian campaign began, the Persian fleet dominated the eastern Mediterranean and menaced Alexander's communications. Rather than risk a defeat at sea, Alexander systematically worked his way down the Mediterranean coastline, capturing and garrisoning every seaport until Persian naval superiority had been nullified.

The great empire constructed by force of arms survived Alexander's death by only a few years. Its enormous extent and the consequent communications problem made centralized administration almost impossible; the empire tended to break down into well-defined regions or national blocs. The Greeks, especially the Macedonians, were too conscious of their own virtues to mix freely with the Persians and with other groups, and so there could be no supranational basis for the empire. It required more than an invincible military machine to win and hold this great territory; the failure of the Graeco-Macedonian conquerors to institutionalize their military triumphs into a positive political system meant that once the arresting personality of Alexander was removed, the empire rapidly disintegrated.

The career of Alexander was much more than a transitory *tour de force*. His conquests were made possible by an army which itself was the product of centuries of Greek development. This army broke down barriers that could never be restored, vastly widened the area of international commerce open to the Greeks, and, in place of the old particularism, substituted the concept of the Mediterranean world. The Macedonian army served as the transmitter of Greek civilization. The "islands" of Greek culture left in its wake Hellenized the Mediterranean world and provided the foundation, not only for the Roman Empire, but for the coming of Christianity.

3

Classical Warfare: The Age of the Legion

"We find that the Romans owed the conquest of the world to no other cause than continual military training, exact observance of discipline in their camps, and unwearied cultivation of the other arts of war. Without these, what chance would the Roman armies, with their inconsiderable numbers, have had against the multitudes of the Gauls . . . or the Germans? The Spaniards surpassed us not only in numbers but in physical strength. We were always inferior to the Africans in wealth and unequal to them in deception and stratagem. The Greeks, indisputably, were far superior to us in skill in arts and all kinds of knowledge." These words, set down by the military writer Vegetius when night was falling on the Roman Empire of the West, indicate how closely the meticulous Roman approach to war was bound up with the construction of the most durable and extensive empire of ancient times. And, notwithstanding the deference of Vegetius to superior attributes of other peoples, the Romans alone possessed the political and administrative capacity to consolidate the gains of their generals and thereby bridge the gap from city-state to empire.

When Greece, having repulsed the Persians, was just entering upon its greatest days, Rome was a barely civilized city-state fighting for existence on a peninsula dominated by Etruscan warlords and the Greek cities of southern Italy and Sicily. By 265 B.C. Rome had become the master of Italy and was preparing to embark upon the conquest of the Mediterranean world. Favored by geography, Rome was sure of a place of some importance in Italy. The city straddled both the River Tiber and the main north-south trade route; and the rich plain of Latium supported a dense population which provided an ample reservoir for Roman armies. Early Rome was a farming community; its people were conservative, unostentatious, and practical in outlook; the society was marked by a singular toughness and cohesion despite its rigid division into patricians and plebeians. All the virtues held by the Romans tended to involve obedience to some established authority: to the family, to the state and the laws, and to the gods. On this solid base the Roman republic was founded, its chief organ of government being the conservative, patrician Senate. The two chief magistrates, the consuls, were elected annually; in addition to their civil duties they also shared the command of the army. This peculiar dual command, designed to lessen the possibility of military tyranny, was often a military drawback. The annual changeover made continuity of policy difficult and the election of inexperienced commanders possible; the day-to-day rotation of command resulted in deadlock when the consuls disagreed, a deadlock that could be broken only by the election of a dictator for an emergency period.

The Roman army mirrored the society of which it was a part. It was a levy of the citizen-body, or rather of those citizens who could meet the property qualification which conveyed the right (and obligation) to serve. Each citizen-soldier was responsible for providing his own equipment; grading within the army was determined by wealth; and the mass of the common soldiery was composed of small farmers. The early Roman army was not much different from the armies of its neighbors in that it was an infantry force using a phalanx close to the Greek model. Its great strength lay in the simple patriotism and rigid discipline characteristic of Rome and in the attention the Romans seem always to have paid to matters of training and drill. From very early times, and certainly by 400 B.C., soldiers were paid by the state.

The first stride in Rome's climb to the headship of Italy was the development of the legion, the standard infantry formation of all later Roman armies. Roman tradition assigns this innovation to the Second Samnite War (326-304 B.C.), and there is no cause to question it. The Samnites were people of the mountainous region bordering on Latium, and in meeting them on their own ground the Romans found that the phalanx could neither maintain ranks nor achieve the mobility required to come to grips with the enemy. It was therefore broken down into self-contained units called maniples ("handfuls") of 120 men. The legion was an open formation of thirty maniples, plus five in reserve, arranged in a checker-board pattern. The mature legion had a high degree of flexibility and range of tactical employment; the first line of maniples, for example, could retire through the openings in the second line without throwing it into confusion, and the second line could similarly advance. For the single shock of the heavy phalanx the Romans substituted a series of smaller shocks by units infinitely more maneuverable and versatile, a tactical system that made much greater demands upon the individual soldier and that was attained only by the strictest training and discipline.

Rome was primarily an infantry power, and this was never more so than in the period of expansion on the Italian peninsula. One legion (i.e., one field army) numbered roughly 6,000 men, half of them heavy yeoman infantry and the remainder lightly armed skirmishers (*velites*) and a small body of cavalry to cover the flanks. In battle order, the first two lines of maniples were composed of the heavy infantry (*hastati* and *principes*), equipped with shields, helmets, body armor, short, broad-blade thrusting swords (*gladii*), and throwing spears (*pila*). Although the commander had many methods of attack at his disposal, fundamental tactics were simple: the front line let fly its *pila* and charged at the run, to fight at close quarters with the sword. If this initial wave was repulsed, the second line took over, using the same procedure. The third line, a mixture of heavy and light infantry, was held in reserve. Later Roman generals were to exploit the potentialities of this reserve to the fullest extent.

The perfecting of the legion as an instrument of war was a gradual process which took place over many years; but even in its semi-developed state it was so vastly superior to the crude tactics of her neighbors that by the middle of the third century B.C. Rome controlled almost the whole of peninsular Italy. Military success, moreover, had been turned to political advantage by an imperial policy which was at once enlightened and practical. Each Italian state was treated, not as a subject of Rome, but as an ally; there was no interference with local autonomy. Rome merely reserved the control of foreign policy to the Roman Senate and, in time of war, required contingents of troops from each dependent state. This liberal policy, coupled with the eventual extension of Roman citizenship and Roman culture throughout Italy, secured for Rome the attachment of other Italian states, an attachment cemented by the building of admirable roads of military as well as commercial importance. The roads were tied in with Roman colonies to form a military network throughout the peninsula. Unlike Greek colonies, the Roman colonies remained units of citizens under Roman direction and were to form an important part of the resistance to Hannibal.

It would have seemed that in 265 B.C., with the reaching of her "natural" frontiers, Rome had also reached the limit of her legitimate aspirations; but at this point she was pulled into the wider theater of Mediterranean affairs. Rome, it is fair to say, had conquered Italy almost in self-defense and against the inclinations of the Senate. (At times, to evade its own regulation against the waging of aggressive war, the Senate trumped up fictitious aggressions by others.) Rome now collided with the mercantile state of Carthage, in North Africa, whose navy controlled the western Mediterranean and therefore menaced Roman interests in southern Italy. At this point the political effect of the long wars of expansion came into play: the continual demands upon Roman manpower had forced the Senate to make concessions of a democratic nature; in 265 B.C. the democratic assembly was able to override the misgivings of the Senate and force a war against Carthage.

The Romans found that, to deal effectively with Carthage, to strike at the African heart of her empire with land forces, they must first beat her on her own element, the sea. Although the Romans at no time felt at home on the sea or ever gave much consideration to sea power, they met the Carthaginian challenge by constructing a fleet, using as model a Carthaginian trireme that had been driven ashore. At first, due to lack of experience in naval tactics and the mishandling of ships in bad weather, Roman losses were enormous. Losses, however, were made up by drawing upon the plentiful resources of Italy in men and materials; and naval shortcomings were surmounted by turning battles at sea into boarding encounters through the use of grappling hooks and swinging gangplanks. Thus Rome overcame her difficulties and henceforward was a naval power.

The First Punic War (265-241 B.C.) had brought Rome her first offshore possession, Sicily. Although Rome did not at this time maintain a permanent fleet, she had, in effect, deprived Carthage of the naval leadership of the western Mediterranean. Under the leadership of Hamilcar Barca, and later of his son Hannibal, in the interval between the First and Second Punic Wars, Carthage attempted to restore her position by absorbing Spain. When Carthage and Rome clashed in this area in 218 B.C., the possession of sea power should have given the advantage of the offensive to Rome. Hannibal, however, forced his enemies to conform to his own strategical conceptions. He saw that the Roman navy was no more than the outwork of a state whose true vigor was on land and that his only chance to crush Rome lay in entering Italy and endeavoring to detach the Italian confederates. He crossed the Pyrenees, the Rhone River, and the Alps, thereby outflanking the Roman navy. Then, by a series of smashing victories, he brought Rome almost to her knees.

Hannibal's victories were won by a conglomerate army made up from the many subject peoples of Carthage. Through the force of his personality, and as a result of long training, he had welded this army into a sensitive, disciplined weapon which would respond to his guidance even in the heat of battle. Cavalry formed a high proportion of its total strength and was its most potent arm. When directed by the consummate tactical sense of Hannibal, the mobility and shock-power of the Carthaginians were too much for the mechanically efficient but poorly led Roman legions. At the River Trebia hidden cavalry forces fell upon the rear of the Roman legionaries who had hitherto been more than holding their own; at Lake Trasimene the Roman army in marching order blundered into an ambush and was slaughtered before it could deploy; at the crowning disaster of Cannae (216 B.C) the largest army Rome had ever put in the field was destroyed through the outstanding generalship of Hannibal and the stupidity of the Roman commander. The consul at Cannae, C. Tarentius Varro, a Roman businessman whose day it was to be general, discarded the open order of the legion and crowded his 80,000 men in a phalangial formation on a plain ideally suited for cavalry action. When engaged by the Carthaginian infantry the huge Roman block lost its coherence; when Hannibal's cavalry swept in to envelop it on both sides, the Roman army became a tightly packed huddle of struggling men, powerless to use their arms.

In three calamitous battles Rome had lost well over 100,000 men and an immeasurable amount of prestige. That it did not collapse is a tribute not only to her own toughness and resiliency, but also to her imperial and military policy. Many slaves were freed and, along with under-age youths, were enlisted to restore the shattered legions; 173 senators were appointed to take the place of those who had fallen at Cannae; and a policy of disengagement was substituted for the aggressive policy which had brought such unfortunate results. Under the leadership of Fabius Maximus, called *Cunctator* (the Delayer), Roman units hung about the Carthaginian camps practising the familiar techniques of guerrilla warfare, nibbling at Hannibal's limited manpower, but refusing at all times to come to grips. Much depended, however, upon the conduct of the Italian states and their response to the proclamation of Hannibal: "I have come not to fight against you but to attack Rome in your behalf...I have come to restore freedom to the Italians and to assist you to recover the cities and lands that you have one and all lost to Rome." Rome's past imperial policy was vindicated when Hannibal failed to receive any significant help from the Italians. Without their assistance he could menace Rome but not besiege it; and he had to content himself with methodically devastating the Italian countryside. Meanwhile, because of Roman sea power, reinforcements from Carthage had to march one third of the way around the Mediterranean to reach him. For thirteen years this war of mutual frustration continued, although Hannibal's chances of success had really vanished by 207 B.C., when a Carthaginian army of reinforcement was totally defeated at the River Metaurus in northern Italy.

In Scipio Africanus, Rome finally produced a general of stature comparable to Hannibal. He was not a general of the old type, reaching military command through the ascension of the prescribed political ladder. Appointed to command in Spain, in a series of hard campaigns he had trained his army to a high standard of excellence. Under Scipio the maniple became more than ever before the true combat unit. Each maniple had objectives and methods of its own; through the perfection of its parts the legion became one of the few infantry forces of the pre-gunpowder period to hold its own with cavalry. Scipio borrowed Hannibal's tactics of envelopment and applied them to his infantry by masking his third-line reserves behind skirmishers and shooting them out from either wing upon the flanks of his enemy. He also repaired somewhat the Roman deficiency in cavalry by increasing its numbers and by recruiting horsemen among peoples more accustomed to that form of war than were the Romans. In 205 B.C. he was given the direction of an army, not for a year, but until Carthage was defeated. Taking full advantage of control of the sea, he carried the war to North Africa, forced Hannibal to return to protect his own homeland, and defeated him in the decisive battle of Zama (202 B.C.), where his balanced and flexible army outmatched Hannibal's medley of mercenaries and conscripts.

This surprisingly swift end to a long war had been brought about by a fundamental recasting of the old Roman citizen army. Roman military organization had been shifted from its base to begin a new line of development which was to culminate in the professional army of Julius Caesar. Scipio's army did not change its composition yearly as one annual levy replaced another. Although the qualifications for service remained the same, in practice Roman citizens were henceforward enrolled for long service that, by the second century B.C., seems to have averaged six years. The only limitation on length of service was the sixteen-year maximum civic obligation. Rome owed her victory over Carthage to the qualities of discipline upon which the legion was based, to her facility in appropriating the techniques of other societies, including that of sea power, and to the imperial policy that had brought her the nearly unanimous support of the Italian confederacy.

Carthage was the most formidable opponent the Romans were ever called upon to face. When, in the second century B.C., Rome turned her face to the eastern Mediterranean, there was no comparable power to block the way. The Macedonian successors of Alexander, who did most of their fighting in Greece, had successively discarded the complexities of his magnificent army, until nothing was left but the original phalangial nucleus, now even more unmanageable than its predecessor, and with its flanks guarded only by a few inferior horsemen. This array was adequate to the conditions of Greek warfare but was anachronistic when confronted with the legion. The superior Roman cavalry drove in its flanks, or the speedy maniples took it in the rear. At the decisive battle of Pydna (168 B.C.), where the wings of the phalanx happened to be well guarded, the Greek infantry drove irresistibly forward but, whether through poor marching or uneven ground, a small gap opened in the front rank, the maniples poured in, and the phalanx was split as a brittle stone is split by ice. With Macedonia disposed of, it was not many years before every state bordering the eastern Mediterranean had acknowledged the Roman republic as suzerain.

Rome's rapid expansion from city-state to empire in all but name set in motion broad social and economic processes which altered completely the nature of the Roman state and society and profoundly affected Roman military organization. Although many of the territorial gains of the late republican period were justified in the rhetoric of the traditional defensive policy, more than a century of responsibility for foreign and military affairs was working to transform the Senate into an arbitrary body drawing its members from one exclusive class, the war-wealthy *nobiles,* and was changing its goals from a quest for defensible frontiers into an undisguised adventure for riches and territorial aggrandizement. This rapacious policy was symbolized by the ruthless sacking of Carthage in 146 B.C. The Senate had no imperial program similar to the sensible federal policy followed on the Italian peninsula. As new territories were added, governors (proconsuls) were sent out from Rome, nominally under the centralized authority of the Senate but actually having a largely free hand. Because the proconsul was commander of the army in his province, he presented a potential danger to the security of the state.

Domestic problems went much deeper. Several factors stemming from the long wars had conspired to weaken gravely the old base of the Roman state, the class of small farmers. Hannibal's widespread devastation of the rural areas had caused Italian agriculture to stagnate. The Italian population dropped by 17 per cent during the Punic Wars. Much of this decrease was due to the casualties suffered by the farmers who had formed the mass of the Roman armies. For many veterans, the task of re-establishing their holdings was too great, especially for those near Rome, who had now to compete with the quantities of cheap grain pouring in from new provinces like Sicily and from Egypt. The *nobiles,* prevented by law and social taboo from engaging in commerce, found an outlet for their war profits by converting the small peasant holdings into vast ranches, or *latifundia,* and changing from grain cultivation to vines and olives, crops much more suitable for the lands south of the Apennines. Such products involved a long-term capital outlay that the small peasant could not undertake, nor could he compete as labor with the abundant masses of slave labor available to rural entrepreneurs as a by-product of Roman conquests.

The result of these social and economic movements was to drive many Roman farmers into the cities to swell the rootless urban proletariat and be manipulated by politicians prepared to exploit their bitterness. In social terms, a great wedge had sundered the connection between the governing class and the citizen body; in military terms, the property qualification for military service could no longer be depended upon to fill the legions. The old military framework was further weakened by the tendency of many members of the upper classes, who had hitherto officered the legions, to buy their way out of service in order to enjoy a life of ostentatious leisure which would never have been tolerated in earlier Rome. For the solid virtues of the antique Roman state were being corroded as well; in the train of Roman armies came not only slaves and tribute but also exotic cults from the east, much more exciting than the formal state religion, and strongly individualistic codes of conduct such as Stoicism and Epicureanism, which broke down the sense of duty to the state. Yet the typical legionary remained a countryman, believed in the old Roman religion, and responded to traditional civic and patriotic appeals.

During the second century B.C., the demands made upon Roman manpower were immense. The wars with Macedonia; the expansion into Asia Minor, Egypt, and Gaul; the Third Punic War; and, above all, the terrible wars of pacification in Spain, which continued virtually throughout the century, meant continual levies upon the small landholders, who formed the backbone of the army. The new provinces required permanent garrisons, beginning with the stationing of two legions in Spain from 197 B.C. By the end of the century, the garrison army numbered eight legions, or about 42,000 men. Because garrison service tended to be even longer than the service performed by those called up "for the duration" to meet a war crisis, and even an absence of two or three years could ruin the small farmer, military service became increasingly unpopular among the very class that formed the bulk of the armies. The attempts by Tiberius and Gaius Gracchus, during their respective tribunates (133 B.C., 123 B.C.), to meet the distress of the small holders and discharged veterans through land reforms met with failure but were a precedent for the land-allotment policies of the political generals in the last century of the Roman Republic.

The time was ripe for the emergence of men who knew how to use social unrest to promote their own careers. Those who could summon the help of armed force were naturally in the best position, and the first century B.C. witnessed the marriage of politics and the army in the persons of four outstanding generals. The first of these, Gaius Marius, was repeatedly elected to the consulship (contrary to law) on the basis of vigorous demagogic appeals. Because in 107 B.C. he threw the legions open to volunteers from the whole citizen body, Marius has usually been considered the creator of the wholly professional and proletarian Roman army. But this measure was simply a reflection of the desperate manpower crisis that had caused similar measures in the past, and of the social and economic distress that had brought Marius the political support of those upon whom the draft bore hard. A century before, Scipio Africanus had been required to raise his expeditionary force exclusively from volunteers; throughout the second century, volunteers had repeatedly been called for from among those eligible for the levy; and in 152 B.C. the draft had been by lot rather than by selection, because the magistrates tended to pick those who already had some military experience. The inflation caused by trade expansion and vast imports of specie as the result of Roman conquest had had the effect of greatly lowering the property qualification in real terms; during the century, that qualification was further lowered by legislation from 11,000 *asses* to 4,000. Marius, then, was scraping the bottom of the barrel. Moreover, although, because of the Marian reform, the proportion of volunteers in the army greatly increased, particularly from propertyless citizens attracted by the promise of a land grant upon discharge, the compulsory levy based upon property continued to operate. While the professional character and quality of the army rose after Marius, the citizen-draftee was still to be found alongside the long-service volunteer.

Marius also was once regarded as the inventor of the cohort, but it is now thought that this tactical innovation evolved gradually during the second century to meet the onrush in battle of such peoples as the Spanish and Gallic tribes, who did not use the phalanx. Whatever the explanation, the result was that the maniple was replaced as the tactical unit by the cohort of 360 heavy infantrymen.

This innovation did not greatly reduce the efficiency of the legion; if anything, discipline was stricter than before and foot and arms drill was kept at a high level by the use of professional gladiators as instructors. To compensate for the loss in mobility sustained by the creation of the cohort-legion, Marius placed the bands of mercenaries who had long been associated with Roman armies on a regular footing. Henceforth Balearic slingers, Numidian and Gaulish horsemen, and other auxiliaries gathered from the provinces figured as permanent and indispensable parts of the Roman field force. The professional approach to war may be seen in the careful attention paid to such procedures as a vigilant order of march, the equipping and provisioning of the individual soldier, and the exemplary use of camp and field entrenchments.

Because only from the general could come tangible rewards of loot or the grant of a parcel of land upon discharge, the immediate result of the reform of Marius was to divorce the army from its allegiance to the state and make it almost the personal property of its general. The army's attachment to the Roman state was further weakened when, as an outcome of the Social War (91-88 B.C.), the inhabitants of the Italian provinces were admitted to full Roman citizenship. The integration into the legions of the Italian *socii*, men who had little cause to love the Senate or the old constitution, meant that no longer did an army under Roman command flinch from marching upon the city itself. The active intrusion of the army into politics brought a period of almost uninterrupted civil war: by Sulla against the supporters of the dead Marius; by Julius Caesar against Pompey, who had overthrown the Sullan constitution; and by Octavian (Augustus), first against the conservative revolutionaries who had assassinated Caesar, and then against his own associate in power Anthony. The military anarchy brought no noteworthy advances in war-technique. It was, however, an age of brilliant generals, and from this galaxy it has been customary, with good reason, to single out for special consideration the generalship of Julius Caesar.

When Caesar took command in Gaul, in 58 B.C., he was in his early forties and had had military experience in Asia and Spain. By 48 B.C., ten years later, Gaul (modern France and Belgium) had become a Roman province and Caesar a military dictator. The juxtaposition of the two facts is not coincidental. Caesar was a man of extraordinary versatility, of ability amounting to genius in many fields. The thread linking his talents was a driving political ambition; his reason for absenting himself from Rome for a decade was his recognition that the shortest road to high office lay with the victorious campaigner. Even his classic account of the subjugation of Gaul, *The Gallic War,* was in large part designed as propaganda to keep his name alive at home and win fresh support. Many subsequent critics, including Napoleon, have slighted his military abilities, particularly at the tactical level, while conceding his unfailing aptitude to solve brilliantly embarrassing dilemmas caused by a slip in judgment. For example, when besieging a host of Gauls under Vercingetorix at Alesia, he allowed himself to be surrounded in turn by a relieving force; responding to this grave challenge, he caused miles of fortifications to be strung around the city, facing inward and outward, and through tenacity and inspiring leadership secured the surrender of Vercingetorix and the dispersal of the relieving army. It would have been surprising, of course, if Caesar had not defeated the Gauls, a semi-primitive people with nothing in their favor but numbers. But, in 49 B.C., near Ilerda in Spain, when he was faced by a numerically superior army of Pompey's Roman legionaries, through a series of strategically memorable marches and countermarches coupled with adroit political propaganda, he won its surrender without fighting a battle. As Caesar put it, "It was no less worthy of a general to conquer by the wisdom of his decisions than by the force of his arms." Above all else stand Caesar's qualities as a leader of men. In an age when Roman soldiers felt no strong pull of allegiance to the state, Caesar won the loyalty of his troops through oratory and force of personality, a loyalty increased by victory and the rewards that went with it. This mixture of emotional attachment and self-interest enabled Caesar to ask a great deal of his troops; indeed, it was the devotion of the famed Tenth Legion which brought him to the highest political pinnacle of the Roman state.

The task of reorganizing the government was left to Caesar's great-nephew, Augustus, and the monument to his work was the *Pax Romana*, the longest period of peace and stability that the Mediterranean world has experienced. Although Augustus preserved much of the old republican constitution, in essence the new imperial order hinged upon himself; its main prop, the imperial army of defense, was under his authority as *Princeps* and commander-in-chief.

The key elements in the Augustan military policy were consolidation of the frontiers and provision for their future security. It is not proper to say that the empire "went on the defensive." Rome had no potential enemy of the same stature. Moreover, Augustus himself annexed five new provinces and attempted to conquer Arabia and Ethiopia. He then abandoned an expansionist policy, partly because he required a period of peace in which to effect his imperial reconstruction, partly because of a deep warweariness that had gripped the empire's population, but chiefly because a further expansion could bring no tangible benefits to Rome while subjecting the state to a greater military and administrative strain than it could bear. After the disaster of the Teutoburger Wald in A.D. 9, when three legions were ambushed and cut to pieces by

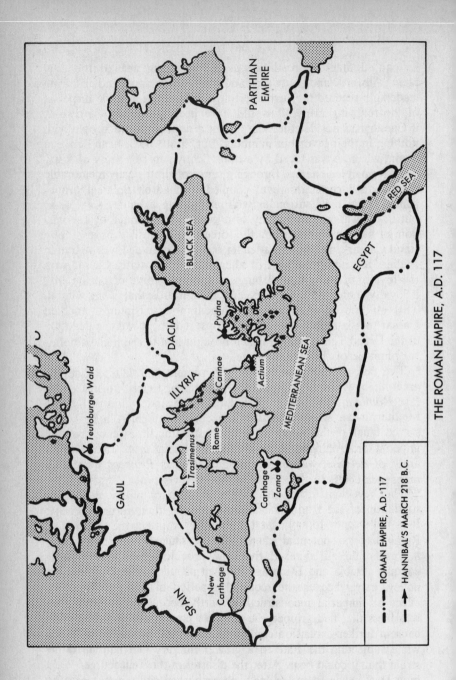

THE ROMAN EMPIRE, A.D. 117

PARTHIAN EMPIRE

RED SEA

EGYPT

BLACK SEA

Pydna

DACIA

Teutoburger Wald

ILLYRIA

Cannae

Actium

L. Trasimenus

GAUL

Rome

MEDITERRANEAN SEA

Carthage

Zama

SPAIN

New Carthage

••••• ROMAN EMPIRE, A.D. 117

⟶ HANNIBAL'S MARCH 218 B.C.

German tribesmen, Augustus and his successors were content to regard the Rhine (and Britain) as the northern limit of the Roman *imperium*. The only substantial additions to the empire after the first century were those made by Trajan (A.D. 98-116) who annexed Dacia as a buffer for the Danubian frontier and conquered Armenia, Mesopotamia, and Assyria. The latter three provinces were relinquished by his successor, Hadrian, as too costly and extensive to defend.

The Augustan army reform followed the same trend, an emphasis upon stability and security. The legions continued to be recruited from Roman citizens, whether Italian or provincial, but non-Romans were also recruited and were given citizenship upon enlistment. All soldiers now swore to serve the full sixteen years (after A.D. 6, twenty years), thus making law what had been practice and ending turbulent agitations for discharge. On discharge, the soldier was granted a gratuity by the state, so ending his dependence on generals for land. The auxiliary units of cavalry and lightly armed troops were raised from the non-citizen residents of the provinces; they were paid less and served longer than the legionaries, but received the prize of Roman citizenship upon discharge. The great bulk of the imperial army was based along the frontiers, the chief exception being the Praetorian Guard, the household troops of the emperor. The total strength of this frontier army was upward of 400,000 with a little more than half being auxiliary units; it was strung out, in numerous small garrisons and encampments, along the 10,000 miles of imperial boundary. Until the middle of the third century, this relatively small force, although a heavy financial drain on the state, efficiently performed its function of policing the boundary and maintaining peace in the provinces. Changes in its organization during this period were minor. The chief development was the large-scale application of Roman engineering techniques to strengthen the crust of the empire by permanent fortifications like Hadrian's Wall on the Scottish border, and a tremendous system of roads in the rear of the army.

The imperial army was, however, more than a dependable outwork. Its permanent camps became centers of urban development and Roman civilization; the centuries of security it granted allowed Graeco-Roman culture to take root so deeply that the barbarian invaders were unable to dislodge it.

An element often overlooked in the Augustan defensive policy was the imperial Roman navy. Augustus, who owed his position

to the decisive naval victory of Actium (31 B.C.), was the creator
of the permanent imperial fleet. Its two major bases were at
Misenum (near Naples) and Ravenna on the Adriatic. Together
with subsidiary provincial squadrons, the fleets based at these
points policed the Mediterranean so successfully that no other major
naval battle was fought until the time of Constantine, although
piracy, despite imperial propaganda, was by no means eliminated.
Other squadrons were maintained on the Danube and Rhine and
in the English Channel and Black Sea. The value of the latter
squadrons, which were integrated with the army in border defense, was evident to the Roman; it was the misfortune of the
Mediterranean fleet that once the initial task of clearing the sea
had been performed, its worth was less apparent. Unlike the army,
it had no battles to fight. The close connection which sea power
always has with commercial prosperity meant little to a state in
which legislation to promote private business was unusual. Lacking
an interest in private commercial enterprise, Rome characteristically
failed to appreciate the significance of sea power in relation to
general prosperity. Yet the Roman Empire was, after all, a Mediterranean trading community. Augustus had designed the navy as
insurance against emergency. When that emergency came, the navy,
which had survived for two centuries, had been dispensed with as
a measure of economy.

Shortly after the middle of the second century, migrant peoples
began to assault the frontiers of the empire; by the middle of the
third century their numbers had multiplied vastly and their attacks
had become almost continuous. Such terrible external pressure
inevitably brought revolutionary changes in a state already well
advanced in decay. The great defensive structure of Augustus had
been designed for a wealthy empire well able to bear the cost; but
by the beginning of the barbarian onslaught, as part of that decline whose complexities have been probed by so many historians,
the empire had passed through a period of economic stagnation
into one of actual retrogression, accompanied by a decrease in
population. This meant that the state, in order to obtain the revenues required to support the bureaucracy and army, had to resort
to even harsher taxation policies. Successive emperors, caught
between the protests of the civilian population and the urgent military needs of the state, came more and more to adopt the maxim
given by Septimius Severus (193-211 A. D.) to his sons: "Be united,
enrich the soldiers, and scorn the rest," until the armed forces,

once the servant and protector of the government, engulfed it.

The third century, particularly the latter half of it, was a very dark period in the history of the empire, a period of anarchy during which the Praetorian Guard and the provincial armies contended to place their respective candidates upon the imperial chair, the office of emperor being auctioned off to the commander making the most bountiful promises. Behind the bitter conflict were irreconcilable social cleavages. The army, by this time consisting almost entirely of soldiers from the less civilized parts of the empire, was in violent opposition to the urban middle classes that had provided leadership in the Augustan empire. The struggle was one between a barely Romanized army and the civilian, more nearly Roman, elements of the population which were attempting to deny to the army the fruits of its enhanced status. The situation was further complicated by a military reform of Hadrian now making itself felt. He had made each frontier legion responsible for its own recruiting. Inevitably the legions drew their recruits from their immediate locale or from the plentiful barbarian sources across the frontier. This system, particularly in the Gallic and Illyrian armies, produced strong regionalist tendencies instead of a common imperial patriotism and accentuated the conflict for political power in which all the frontier armies were already engaged.

Out of this century of chaos came a militarized empire, a despotism in which lip-service was paid to the old Roman traditions but in which the government was actually carried on by members of a special caste. The emperor, himself a soldier, appointed only soldiers to positions of authority in the central and provincial administrations, thus creating a purely military aristocracy constantly being reinforced by barbarian recruits. The later empire was an oriental monarchy with the trappings of a police-state, in which the citizen body no longer pursued its own ends but had become merely the exploited appendage of its defenders. There could be no turning back of the clock to the harmonized polity of Augustus: the greater the pressure exerted on the empire by the barbarian hordes, the more compelling became the justification for the extreme policies of social regimentation followed by the later emperors.

The reorganization of the empire, carried on chiefly by Diocletian and Constantine, was necessarily accompanied by a reform of the army, which had become undisciplined and corrupt during the military anarchy. Its numbers were substantially increased, mainly by the recruiting of barbarian mercenaries (Roman citizenship was no longer a prize but a tax burden). The most sweeping reform was the creation of a central, mobile field-force, largely Germanic in national origin, which could be shifted from one danger point to another along the frontier. This army was a mixture of horse and foot, with emphasis placed upon the cavalry. Its effectiveness was undeniable, since through most of the fourth century it managed to keep the bounds of the empire intact; but it bore little resemblance to the armies that had preceded it. Although the term "legion" was still in use late in the fifth century, the typical Roman soldier was no longer the heavy-armed infantryman but an armored mounted lancer, the cataphract. As for the imperial navy, it had disappeared during the third century. By A. D. 250 piracy had reappeared on a huge scale, and in 269 a war-band of invading Goths sailed unopposed through the Hellespont. Diocletian could finance only the construction of local patrol squadrons on the Mediterranean; by the end of the fourth century the imperial navy was but a memory.

It is interesting to compare the differing approaches of two fourth-century military writers to the manifold problems of imperial defense. The unknown author of *De Rebus Bellicis* saw the cause of Roman decline in the grinding taxation policy. He therefore proposed to save money by reducing the size of the army through mechanization; to this end he submitted plans and illustrations of a number of ingenious, if rather impracticable, military machines of various types. Vegetius, on the other hand, in his *De Re Militari,* found his solution in a return to ancient values and to the infantry-legion tactics which had won Rome an empire. "The re-establishment of ancient discipline is by no means impossible, although now so totally in disuse."

But the society which had held the old virtues and produced the disciplined legionary was gone beyond recall. The army of a Caesar might have coped with the cavalry masses of the barbaric Goths and Germans; it is hardly too rash to say that the infantry of the later empire, itself barbarian, was too undisciplined and uncivilized to execute the demanding tactics of the legion. Warfare was entering the long cavalry age, and no battle did more to establish that age than Adrianople. Here, in A.D. 378, a Roman army under the Emperor Valens was almost annihilated by the mailed cavalry of the Goths. It was the most calamitous defeat since Cannae. The lesson was not lost upon Valens's successor, Theodosius, who dispensed with an infantry arm that had become obsolete and engaged in the imperial service the Gothic cavalry, which had shown it to be so. With this act the corpse of the Roman military tradition was formally buried; the system that replaced it produced the Gothic warlords who supervised the dismemberment of the western empire in the fifth century.

The sickness of the western empire was nowhere more forcibly illustrated than in the disintegration of the old Roman military traditions. It would be wrong, however, to assign to the army the prime responsibility for Roman collapse. The empire was not conquered, but decayed from within until it could no longer absorb and Romanize the barbarians whom it admitted. It has often been said that the military worth of the later Roman army depended on its having as few "Romans" and as many barbarians as possible in its ranks. In this sense not only was the alteration in the composition and techniques of the army symptomatic of Roman enfeeblement, but the later army was actually an agency in that process. The gradual transformation of the army from a force disseminating and preserving Latin culture to one purely Germanic in character reflects the paralysis of a civilization of which the army had ceased to be a part.

4
Byzantium:
The Technique of Survival

When the Roman empire of the West split up into a number of Germanic kingdoms, its eastern counterpart lived on. The Eastern Roman Empire, or the Byzantine Empire, although the legatee of Roman civilization, was essentially a new departure, and one of astonishing vitality and persistence. Despite the fact that Constantine, when he founded Constantinople in A.D. 330 as the eastern capital of the empire, provided his new Rome with a senate and an exact duplicate of the imperial bureaucracy of the West, he made no effort to change its distinctive and deeply engrained features. The Eastern Roman Empire was Greek in culture, not Latin; it was the inheritor of the Hellenistic civilization diffused by Alexander's conquests; yet, the Byzantines thought of themselves as "Romans," and their chief tie to Greek culture was through the Church, to which Alexander was anathema.

It was the conjunction of its peculiar qualities with other, more fortuitous circumstances that enabled the Eastern Roman Empire to survive the passing of its western counterpart. Orthodox Christianity in the East eventually severed its ties with the Church at Rome. Eastern Orthodoxy was less universal in its appeal and much more closely allied with the state. This union of culture, politics, and religion accounts for the fervent nationalism of the East Romans, so strongly at variance with the passivity of the Romans in the West.

Less intangible, and no less important, was the economic health of the East. As the center of industrial production, the East had dominated the economy of the old Empire. Long before the collapse in the West, the traders of the East had obtained a near-monopoly of Mediterranean commerce by the export of textiles, glass, metalware, and other luxury manufactures, and had built up a flourishing trade with Persia as well. As a result the East had been by far the most populous area of the old Roman Empire. When the cities of Italy, Gaul, and Spain, which were generally administrative or military centers, were declining in size, the great cities of the East, like Constantinople, Alexandria, Tarsus, and Antioch, based upon thriving industries, were increasing. City-dwellers made up nearly half the population of the Byzantine Empire. Byzantine commercial dominance in the Mediterranean went almost unchallenged until the rise of Italian industrial competitors in the eleventh and twelfth centuries. At the same time the East was richly endowed agriculturally. The fertile provinces of Egypt, Syria, and Asia Minor fed its swarming cities. In the countryside, there were numerous large estates and great landowners; while the peasantry, although it had not fallen, like the western peasantry, into a state of subjection or even of servitude, was scarcely in a prosperous condition.

The Byzantine state never departed from the centralized, autocratic rule bequeathed to it by Diocletian and Constantine, and therefore was subject to the palace intrigue, official corruption, and naked struggles for power which an essentially non-constitutional regime invites. Nevertheless the Empire was sound in its working parts; the civil service well organized if somewhat hidebound, the aristocracy well educated and politically responsible, the imperial office occupied by more than the usual number of original and statesmanlike emperors. The Empire had need of wise leadership. Its geographical position between East and West was an economic benefit. But, since it was placed squarely in the path of invaders from the east or the north who wished to occupy the derelict lands of the West, its situation was, at the same time, a military liability. Furthermore, its wealth was a permanent temptation to outsiders. Throughout its long history the Empire was called upon to withstand countless attacks from such disparate enemies as the marauding Huns, the migrant Slavs and Germans, the fanatical Arabs, the mercenary Persians, and later, from equally rapacious West European enemies, the Normans and the Crusaders.

For this reason, the military organization of the Byzantine Empire is of great significance. To defend itself from its multitude of enemies, the empire was compelled to devote a major part of

its energies to the creation and maintenance of a military system
superior to that of any of its opponents, and far superior to the
methods employed in western Europe in the same period. During
the fifth century, the rulers at Constantinople adopted the same
dangerous expedient as the western emperors, hiring bands of
barbarian mercenaries to defend their borders. Due, however, to
the patriotic, independent peasantry of Anatolia, Isauria, and Armenia, the proportion of native to barbarian troops never dropped
as low as in the West, and it became the fixed policy of East Roman
emperors to encourage the use of native-born as against mercenary
troops, although the Empire was never able to dispense entirely with
the services of the latter. The same century marked the construct-
tion of the first of a series of huge walls surrounding the strategic
heart of the Empire, Constantinople, which rendered the city impregnable to assault until the advent of gunpowder. These sane
military policies, which testify to the inherent strength of the
Empire, made it formidable to attack; and it required only the
additional persuasion of Byzantine gold to deflect the Huns, and
then the Ostrogoths, to the more vulnerable regions of southwestern Europe.

The recuperation of the Eastern Roman Empire under the careful husbanding of its fifth-century emperors convinced Justinian
(527-65) of the possibility of reasserting the supremacy of Roman
arms in the West and of reconquering areas lost to the Empire. A
successful campaign was waged against the degenerate Vandal
kingdom in North Africa and, while the Ostrogoths showed more
spirit, substantial areas of southern and central Italy became Roman
once more. These conquests were not the result of Byzantine
superiority in numbers, for the imperial armies were invariably outnumbered, but reflected superior weapons, tactics, and generalship.
The representative soldier of East Roman history is the horse-archer,
who, like the medieval knight, was clothed in mail. There the resemblance ceased. For the horse-archer added to his mobility and
shock-power a skill with the bow which made him the most versatile
and one of the most effective cavalry soldiers in the history of warfare. Belisarius, Justinian's great cavalry general, testified to the merit
of the horse-archer: "I found that the chief difference between the
Goths and us was that our own Roman horse and our Hunnish
foederati are all expert horse-bowmen, while the enemy has scarcely
any knowledge at all of archery. For the Gothic knights use sword

and lance alone, while their bowmen on foot are always drawn up to the rear. So their horsemen are no good till the battle comes to close quarters, and can easily be shot down while standing in battle array before the moment of contact arrives." The horse-archer was supported in the Byzantine array by heavy infantry and cavalry-lancers; but it was the mounted bowmen who made the difference between the imperial army and other armies.

The small size of the expeditionary forces was one of the most notable features of the expansion under Justinian. North Africa was won with 15,000 men (6,000 horse-archers), Italy with 11,000 plus 15,000 reinforcements. The excellence of Byzantine weapons and the professional approach of able generals like Belisarius and Narses are only part of the explanation. Under Justinian, Byzantium became the premier naval power of the Mediterranean. The Roman fleet could transport forces rapidly wherever they were required, and supply and reinforce them.

Justinian's imperial offensive was a departure from the broad sweep of Byzantine military policy. His successors had to cope with the problem of territorial overextension in both its financial and military aspects; and with the reforms of the Emperor Maurice (582-602) the Empire entered a defensive phase which was to be its military outlook for the next 500 years.

The system inaugurated by Maurice took many years to reach its mature state, but the organization here described may be considered as the completion of his framework. The aim of Maurice was to provide for maximum security at a minimum of expense and at the least possible danger to the state from the political aspirations of army commanders. Generals like Belisarius had surrounded themselves with large bodyguards of mercenaries who had sworn loyalty only to them; Maurice took the power to make appointments above the rank of centurion out of the patronage of his generals and placed it in the hands of the central government. The size of the professional standing army was drastically cut down and what remained was redeployed into a central strategic reserve and cadres for the frontier garrisons. The elimination of the distinction between mercenary and native units further strengthened the control of the central government over the army. Ultimately, by granting tax relief to serving soldiers and plots of land on discharge, the state succeeded in recruiting almost the whole of the army rank and file from the dependable inhabitants within its bor-

ders. The policy of land allotments apparently did not result in the
kind of political turbulence it had produced in the days of the
Roman Republic.

The small size of this standing army was made possible by the
erection of massive defense works along the frontiers. On the line
of the Danube, for instance, protection was given the empire by
a cordon of fifty-two fortresses, strengthened in depth by a second
line of twenty-seven farther south. Constantinople was surrounded
by a sixty-foot moat, guarding a triple ring of immense walls, each
wall studded with towers at frequent intervals, and the innermost
wall reaching a height of thirty feet. To man its system of frontier
fortifications the government placed its reliance upon local militia
forces stiffened by professional soldiery.

By the eighth century, Byzantine defense had been further re-
fined, and somewhat decentralized, by a division of the empire into
a number of self-contained military districts called themes, a policy
quite similar to that earlier employed by the Roman Empire of
the West in its frontier areas. Since the Empire was open to attack
from any direction, often unexpectedly, a sudden thrust by an enemy
force might, and occasionally did, penetrate its outer crust, bringing
devastation to the defenseless interior provinces before the central
army could deal with the danger.

The theme system was the response of a government acutely
aware of the increasingly narrow margin between survival and
extinction, and of the perpetual need for watchfulness and preparedness. Each theme contained a permanent army corps, bol-
stered by local militia and commanded by a *strategos* who was also
the head of the area's civil government. Thus, just as in the Roman Empire of the third and fourth centuries, external pressure
brought the militarization of political institutions. The process was
carried further by the grant of land to peasants on the condition
that the holdings would furnish soldiers in perpetuity. The themes
were therefore firmly tied to the most stable and hardy class in
Byzantine society. The size of each theme army varied according
to its location. On the average, it probably numbered about 6,000,
with frontier themes containing as many as 12,000 troops. The
function of a theme army was to engage and blunt the momentum
of an attacking force, and so give time for adjoining theme armies
and the permanent central reserve to come to its assistance. The
theme system had the merits of an elastic overall defense. It

worked because the difficult communications problem was over-come by beacon networks, couriers, and great military roads.

The Byzantine Empire, much more than the Roman Empire, was a maritime state, deeply interested in matters of trade and industry. The military establishment made necessary by almost continuous defensive wars was very expensive; so were the re-quirements of the imperial court and bureaucracy; so, finally, was Byzantine diplomacy. It was a maxim of Byzantine diplomatists never to employ force, or the threat of it, if money would suffice, a policy which, since always backed by military power, was not so debilitating as is often the case with appeasement. Annual sub-sidies of 30,000 pieces of gold bought peace from the Sassanid rulers of Persia in the sixth and seventh centuries; at different points in her history the Empire pacified or purchased the support of Avars, Slavs, and Bulgars in the Balkans, Franks, Lombards, and Goths in Italy and Spain, Berbers in North Africa, and the rulers of Abyssinia. The very high level of public expenditure on war, administration, and diplomacy explains the existence of the pater-nalistic economic policies of the Byzantine emperors.

The importance of trade led to a preoccupation with naval affairs. It was the job of the imperial navy to control, not vast territories, but important Byzantine trading centers and the routes which connected them with foreign commercial areas. This meant controlling, either directly or indirectly, the Crimean coast, the vital water-passage from the Black Sea to the Mediterranean, the port-cities of the Adriatic, Syria, and North Africa, and the sea ap-proaches to all these areas. As early as the seventh century, there were Byzantine naval bases and shipyards at Carthage, Acre, Alexandria, and Constantinople. By the eighth century, the ex-tension of the themal organization to the navy gave the Byzantine naval system its final form. There were five fleets in the permanent navy: the imperial fleet stationed at Constantinople, and provin-cial fleets based on the southern coast of Asia Minor, Ravenna, Sicily, and the islands of the Aegean. As with the land themes, each naval district, commanded by a *strategos,* provided the major cost of the fleet assigned to it. This inexpensive, efficient, and flexible organization went far toward giving the Empire an almost unbroken command of the sea.

There were other factors contributing to the naval supremacy enjoyed by Byzantium over its competitors. The heart of its naval strength was Constantinople, with its harbor, dockyards, and arsenal. To reach the imperial capital a rival fleet had first to defeat the provincial fleets which protected the entrance to the Dardanelles, and then negotiate the narrow straits which were guarded by the imperial fleet. When the Arabs took to the sea by copying the *dromons,* or war galleys, of the Byzantines, they attempted to force the Straits on two occasions in the eighth century, but with an utter lack of success. The imperial navy possessed a decided advantage over the Arabs because it controlled plentiful supplies of naval stores and materials, particularly timber and iron, commodities which were only available in small amounts in the Arabic territories of Syria, Egypt, and North Africa. Finally, the Byzantine navy benefited from the monopoly of a secret weapon, the mysterious Greek fire, also known as "sea fire" or "wet fire." Even in Byzantine times its composition was kept a closely-guarded secret, revealed only to the initiated. Today the formula is unknown. Modern authorities have conjectured that sea fire was the result of the ignition of substances like naphtha or sulphur and quicklime. The Byzantines ejected the flaming mixture from brass tubes, using pumped sea-water as a propulsive. This weapon was used with deadly effect against an Arab fleet attempting to force the Dardanelles in 673. It was not a master weapon; but it gave a technological and psychological advantage to the superior Byzantine navy.

Enough has been said about the military methods of the Byzantine state to demonstrate that its approach to warfare was thorough and original. The disparity between the practice of war by the Byzantines and by the feudal society of the West has often been remarked. The decisive elements in western war were courage, strength, and weight. The Byzantines surveyed war with the subtle and mature intelligence of an ancient civilization, and applied to its study the same careful scholarship which distinguished their elaborate theology and elaborate public finance. But if war was not, for them, a heroic game, neither was it a merely academic exercise. It was precisely because the existence of the state hung so completely upon the capabilities of its armed forces that the study of war, so often ignored in more complacent and less threatened societies, attracted the best Byzantine minds. The Eastern Romans produced a number of military treatises for the direction of their generals, notably the *Ars Militaris* of the Emperor Maurice and the *Tactica* of Leo VI (c. 900), which were of a scientific excellence unmatched in Europe until the sixteenth century.

The prevailing tone of these writings is one of caution. The underlying premise is that the most desirable victory is that won with the least expenditure in men, money, and effort, and that fighting is something to be avoided altogether if other means will bring about a favorable result. Byzantine military thought was thus of a primarily defensive cast. War was regarded not as a temporary or unusual phenomenon but as the normal and inevitable outcome of the interaction of peoples. A state with tangible but finite resources could not permit itself the luxury of military adventures which would weaken it when the next war came along. To the Byzantine mind, war was not within the province of morality. To deceive the enemy, a general was encouraged to employ any method he thought expedient, including bribes to enemy officers, false surrenders to permit time for regrouping, and battlefield parleys as cover for ambushes. Leo VI had nothing but disdain for the chivalric code of the West, and for its exaltation of knightly courage and daring. To the Byzantine, courage was only one of the many attributes necessary to a good professional soldier, and daring usually resulted in pointless loss of life, the cardinal military sin in a society in which manpower was precious.

Military textbooks prepared a general for every conceivable situation. Explicit instructions based upon Roman military experience and, indeed, often going back to Greek manuals of the fourth century B.C. were laid down for the maintenance of discipline and training, for the entrenchment of camps, and for coping with supply problems in unfamiliar terrain. Byzantium was the only state of the period to give attention to the treatment of casualties; the textbooks reveal that the army had an organized ambulance corps of surgeons and bearers. The motivation was of course not humanitarian; the state was interested in restoring the wounded to battle fitness, and thus paid the bearers a bonus for every casualty brought in from the field.

The most impressive pieces of Byzantine military writing are those concerned with tactics and strategy. These were based on the principle that the methods to be employed must be varied according to the peoples to be fought. The Byzantines made it their business to learn everything of importance there was to be known about the methods of probable opponents, and worked out scientifically the means best suited to defeat each enemy. Leo VI, for example, observed that the most formidable feature of a western host was its initial charge, and therefore recommended that a pitched battle should be avoided. Instead, advantage should be taken of such western lack of weaknesses as discipline, careless entrenching procedure, uncertain morale, and absence of any supply organization. He recommended that western armies should be worn down by skirmishes and Fabian strategy, and by striking at their supplies. For Byzantium, this would be less expensive than great battles.

The military history of the Eastern Roman Empire covers almost a millennium. For the greater part of this immense period, its military institutions retained their original excellence and vigor, without any significant alteration in nature. During the first quarter of the seventh century the Empire fought almost continuously on two fronts against totally different peoples. In the north, migrating Slavs and Avars threatened to overrun the imperial provinces in the Balkans. Against them, the imperial forces fought an all-out war of annihilation. The danger was not from the military skill of these peoples, which was rudimentary, but from the vastness of their numbers. Therefore a ruthless policy of extermination was pursued. The struggle against the traditional Persian enemy on the east was of an entirely different character. The Sassanid rulers of Persia were in competition with Byzantium for control of the lucrative trade routes to the Far East; the struggle was therefore initially limited in aim and locality.

The strain of conducting two defensive wars simultaneously proved almost too much for the Empire. By 608 Egypt and Syria had fallen and Constantinople was menaced from the north and the east. Here Byzantine generalship and sea power took a hand, assisted by a great upsurge of religious feeling caused by the fall of Jerusalem. The Emperor Heraclius used the fleet to transport an army to the south coast of Asia Minor. Striking inland, he forced the Persians to withdraw from Asia Minor to protect their rear, and then, by marching into Persian territory, he compelled the withdrawal of Persian garrison troops from Egypt and Syria. Such brilliant maneuvering, pointless when employed against teeming hordes of migrating barbarians, was an apt strategy for use against a civilized enemy who placed great store in the maintenance of his communications and the protection of his homeland. Typically, when the war ended in 626 with a decisive victory at Nineveh, deep in Persian territory, Heraclius was content with a peace which restored the political situation as it had existed before the war. Byzantium had no appetite for indigestible territories.

Barely had the long Persian war ended when a much greater danger threatened. Countless Arab horsemen, fired with religious zeal by their prophet Mohammed (d. 632), plunged out of the Arabian wastes intent upon plunder and the conversion of the unbeliever by the power of the sword. An exhausted Persia was overthrown almost immediately. Due to bitter doctrinal dispute with the church at Constantinople, the Christian inhabitants of Syria and Egypt welcomed the Arabs, who promised toleration, as liberators. The loss of these rich provinces inflicted a heavy blow to Byzantine trade and revenue and gave the Arabs entrance to the Mediterranean. By 641 Syria and Egypt had been detached from the Empire, this time permanently. Byzantine generals had encountered raiding parties of Arabian nomads in the past, and had found that these lightly armored lancers could not stand up to their heavy cavalry and horse-bowmen. But now the Arabs were no longer raiders and their fanaticism and numbers compensated for their faulty tactics. Moreover, the Empire always labored under financial difficulties and manpower shortages, although the latter seem also to be connected with a decline in human fertility and with plagues.

It is a tribute to the high professional quality of Byzantine arms and to the latent reserves of stubbornness in Byzantine society that the Arabs, in their first flush of fury, were fought to a standstill and begged for a truce. When the struggle was resumed, each antagonist had learned much from the other. The religious fervor of the Arabs had been abated to some degree, but they had developed a political structure (the Caliphate) to embrace their conquests. They had also borrowed something of the Byzantine military organization: their lancers and horses were now as heavily armored as the imperial cataphract, and instead of throwing clouds of cavalry helter-skelter into battle, they had organized their horse into one deep, weighty line. The Byzantines, meanwhile, had countered the high mobility of the Saracen horsemen by perfecting the theme organization.

Despite the Arab switch to heavy cavalry, the Byzantines still possessed a preponderance of weight, but their leaders were not prepared to leave the issue of a battle to weight alone. During this period Byzantine cavalry tactics were developed, eventually attaining a level of performance beyond the reach of any other state during the entire Middle Ages. These tactics were strikingly similar to those employed by the Roman legion. A cavalry force was broken down into three lines, each composed of distinct units of about 450 troopers called *banda,* with other guarding units on the flanks. Such a loose grouping is as strong a testimony to the reliability and training of the Byzantine cavalryman as the maniple-legion was to the qualities of the Roman legionary. The single-line formation of the Saracens could not withstand the three successive waves of the East Roman horse. Thrown into a confusion which was exploited by the imperial horse- and foot-archers, the Arabs were usually driven from the field.

Thwarted on land, the Saracens challenged imperial supremacy on the Mediterranean. The reasons for the eventual triumph of the Byzantine fleets have already been touched on, but the contest was long, not ending until the middle of the eighth century. Because of its long preoccupation with Arabian sea power, the Empire was forced to give up most of the Italian lands won by Justinian, until by 754 only Venice and parts of southern Italy remained. At the same time the swaying fortunes of the naval war had allowed the Arabs to sweep from Egypt across North Africa and into Spain, unchallenged by the imperial navy. Spain was conquered by 717, and Arab raiding parties, filtering through the Pyrenees, probed into southern France. It was one of these parties which was defeated by a Frankish army in the desperate battle at Tours in 732. The fierce struggle of Charles Martel with one tiny tentacle of Arab power takes on a somewhat different significance from that usually attributed to it when it is remembered that what really stood between the Arabs and the more direct approach to western Europe was the double bastion of Byzantine land and naval forces. It need hardly be added that when the bulwark of Byzantium disappeared, Moslem armies striking through the Balkans were able to reach the gates of Vienna in 1529.

After the satisfactory close of the long conflict with the Arabs, the Eastern Roman Empire enjoyed nearly a century of stability and prosperity. There were, of course, numerous small wars on land and sea, but the tested formula of diplomacy, bribes, and military efficiency functioned smoothly and adequately. Naval supremacy gave the Empire a renewed mastery over Mediterranean trade. In order to retain this mastery the Byzantine state instituted a number of regulations which have been compared to the British Navigation Acts. As with London, Constantinople was the metropolis of the commercial empire; through it, and it alone, were funneled goods from East and West. The strength of the Byzantine navy compelled Moslem traders of Egypt and Syria to divert their merchandise designated for Europe to the imperial capital for transshipment. At the same time the navy also controlled the termini of the Russian and Asian trade routes on the Black Sea. The final element in the imperial trading system was Byzantine control over the western ports for eastern goods; Byzantine merchants were forbidden to deal with any cities except those expressly enumerated in governmental regulations. These few favored cities were chiefly Italian, like Amalfi, Bari, and Venice; and all were in the possession of the Byzantine state.

This closed, rigid system undoubtedly brought immediate economic benefits; but in the end it defeated its original purpose by helping to weaken the Empire. The Italian cities, having the monopoly for reception and distribution of eastern goods, soon accumulated great capital surpluses for investment. In some centers, especially Venice, part of this capital was employed in the construction of merchant fleets which gradually encroached upon the Byzantine monopoly of the carrying trade to the West. By the beginning of the tenth century the Byzantine share of the carrying trade had very noticeably declined.

For the imperial navy this process had the most serious results. The navy depended for experienced manpower upon the maritime population of the empire; but, owing to the commercial shipping depression, the impressment organization of the naval themes enlisted fewer and fewer trained sailors. In consequence the navy, upon which the whole regulatory system was based, diminished in the quality and quantity of its personnel, and therefore in its general effectiveness, and was unable to meet the rise of new Moslem sea power. The Aghlabid and Fatimid kingdoms of North Africa, shut out of the European market by Byzantium, had built their own fleets and by the early part of the tenth century had wrested naval control of the western Mediterranean from the Empire. But the Moslem victory cannot be wholly explained by Byzantine decline. There is some evidence that the Arab navies had narrowed the technological gap with their enemies by developing an incendiary weapon akin to Greek fire. Also, the Empire was in the same period beset by strong new enemies, in the Balkans by the Bulgars, and on the Black Sea by Kiev, an expanding Russian principality.

In the late tenth century the Empire underwent a spirited naval revival. The system of command was unified by placing all the fleets under a Lord High Admiral (*Drungarius classis*); the speedy *dromons* were replaced by vessels of an imposing size; and ingenious landing craft were constructed with sliding ramps, permitting the discharge of cavalry in full battle panoply. This resurgence regained much lost territory and gave at least a measure of sea control to the Empire; but the damage to her position during the naval lapse was irreparable. Although Constantinople was still the center of East-West trade, the control of the trade had passed almost entirely out of the hands of imperial citizens and into those of foreign merchants, particularly Syrians and Venetians, who had established colonies in the imperial capital. Venice was now only formally a Byzantine possession; in actuality the city was a naval power in its own right interested in maintaining the political connection because of commercial advantages.

Although the empire continued to impress its many visitors with its wealth, its prosperity was derived chiefly from revenues incidental to the trade being carried on within its borders. Foreign control of East-West trade meant that opportunities for profitable Byzantine investment were shut off, and increasingly the wealth of the monied classes was diverted into land, with disastrous consequences. The assimilation of numerous peasant holdings into large estates meant, as it had in republican Italy, the displacement of the peasant class and the destruction of the social base of the army. The attempts of several emperors of the late tenth century to arrest this process by breaking up estates and redistributing the land touched off a crippling civil war. Order was restored long enough to allow the Emperor Basil II to wage a misguided and exhausting war of conquest against the Bulgars (1004-18). When it became necessary to fight a defensive war in Italy, social disruption had proceeded so far that the Empire had to turn for manpower to mercenary forces of Bulgars, Russians, and Scandinavians to fill out its depleted armies. By 1042 it found itself stripped of its last Italian lands.

Byzantine military power never fully recovered. Shortly afterwards, in the midst of a civil war which had already spanned fifteen years and several emperors, there appeared on the eastern border an army of 100,000 Seljuk Turks, led by the Sultan Alp Arslan. The Seljuk Turks were typical nomadic horse-archers from the Eurasian steppes and, despite their numbers, they should have been no more dangerous than other eastern invaders in the past.

But at Manzikert (1071) a heterogeneous East Roman army violated one of its fundamental tactical canons: it failed to keep order during a pursuit of the enemy; and it was cut to pieces by the counterattacking Turks. Although the imperial fleet and the walls preserved Constantinople, the Asiatic themes and their peasant remnants were lost forever. By 1100, when the Crusaders had established kingdoms in Palestine, and incidentally had done much besides to weaken militarily the Christian bastion of Byzantium, Europe had made direct contact with the trade routes of the East, and the economic foundations of the Empire had disappeared as well. The Eastern Roman Empire lived on for three and a half centuries, but only the shreds of its military organization remained; it was reduced to prolonging its precarious existence by the employment of mercenary troops unschooled in the traditions of the past.

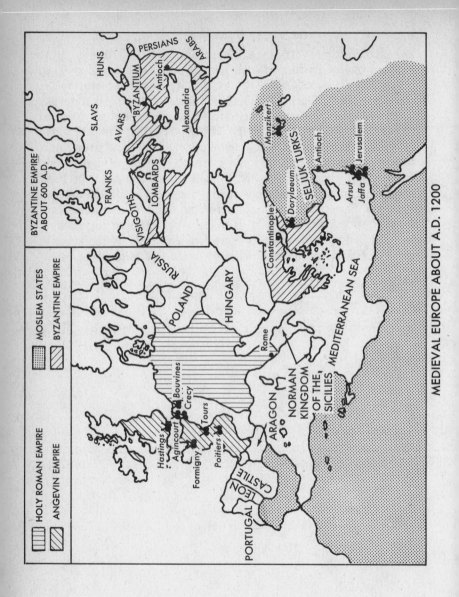

BYZANTINE EMPIRE
ABOUT 600 A.D.

PERSIANS

ARABS

HUNS

SLAVS

AVARS

FRANKS

VISIGOTHS

LOMBARDS

BYZANTIUM

Antioch

Alexandria

HOLY ROMAN EMPIRE

ANGEVIN EMPIRE

MOSLEM STATES

BYZANTINE EMPIRE

RUSSIA

POLAND

HUNGARY

Rome

Hastings

Agincourt

Bouvines

Crecy

Formigny

Tours

Poitiers

ARAGON

NORMAN
KINGDOM
OF THE
SICILIES

PORTUGAL

LEON

CASTILE

MEDITERRANEAN SEA

Constantinople

Dorylaeum

SELJUK TURKS

Manzikert

Antioch

Arsuf

Jaffa

Jerusalem

MEDIEVAL EUROPE ABOUT A.D. 1200

5
Western Europe: The Rise of the Feudal Array

The inheritors of the Roman Imperium in the West were the Franks, a Germanic group of tribes which moved slowly into Roman Gaul in the course of the late fifth and early sixth centuries from their original homeland in northwestern Europe. The German successor-states which had been created by the Ostrogoths in Italy, the Visigoths in Spain, and the Vandals in North Africa had no firm base. They were governed by a military elite which derived its authority from small armies of occupation. This Germanic upper layer was so rapidly enfeebled by its contact with Roman civilization that it could offer no great resistance to the Byzantines and the Moslems who established Eastern outposts in Western Europe. Medieval European civilization, essentially a union of Germanic and Roman-Christian culture, developed primarily in those regions where Germanic peoples settled in great numbers and merged with antecedent populations. In other words, the center of Western Europe shifted away from the Mediterranean to France and the Rhineland.

In the widespread devastation, uninhibited looting, and savage wars which accompanied the folk-wanderings of the Germanic peoples through the rotten husk of the later Roman Empire, it was inevitable that not only would the rate of economic decline in these areas accelerate rapidly, but much of what was valuable in Roman civilization would be lost, some of it never to be recovered. Among the casualties of Western Europe's Dark Ages was the Roman military tradition. We have already seen that in order to counter the mounted mobility of the barbarians, the later Romans themselves had virtually abandoned the infantry legion.

There was, however, a brief period in post-imperial military history when it appeared that the Franks might reconstitute the status of infantry. The peoples of Germany, forest fighters for the most part, had made little use of cavalry; the Goths of eastern Germany had become horsemen because, when deflected in their early migrations by the still-strong Roman frontiers, they had drifted into the south Russian steppes. The Franks, however, moved directly south into a shattered empire, and they came as infantry. They wore no body armor and carried bossed oval shields, javelins rather like the Roman *pila,* swords, and daggers. Their national weapon was the battle-ax (*francisca*), a heavy but well-balanced weapon which the Franks had learned to throw with great accuracy just before making contact with their enemy. Although little is known of their order on the battlefield, it is likely that it had progressed no further than a simple massing of warriors in heavy blocks. The primitive host of the Franks was a far cry from the supple and disciplined legion. The impotence of the Frankish infantry when faced with well-trained cavalry was demonstrated when a Frankish host invaded Italy in the middle of the sixth century. At Casilinum (554) the Franks were engaged by Byzantine infantry and cavalry and then encircled by horse-archers, who shot down the nearly defenseless warriors almost at leisure.

It was only very slowly that the Franks, in whom, as in all noncivilized peoples, the rule of custom was strong, adapted themselves to cavalry warfare. Eventually, out of the shadowy interplay between military necessity and the facts of social and economic existence, the feudal system was to emerge in the ninth century with the mounted knight as its key figure. One of the most characteristic elements in the feudal system was specialization of function according to class, with the reservation of military functions to one section of the community. Some historians have held that the origin of the feudal relationship may be traced back to the *villa* of late Roman times which was worked by unfree peasants.

Nothing could be more unlike feudalism than the social and military organization which the Franks and other Germanic tribes had brought with them in the fifth century. Their political institutions were simple. Folk assemblies, presided over by the tribal' chief, dispensed customary justice. The only other function of the chief was to lead his tribe in war. There was no distinction between status as a member of the tribe and status as a warrior; when war came, all males automatically entered the tribal host.

The *comitatus,* a military elite selected for bravery, formed the bodyguard of the chief. The Roman *villa* with its stratified society may have been an agent in the transformation of this barbarian social structure into medieval feudalism.

When, in 496, the war-chief Clovis forced the various Frankish bands in Gaul to acknowledge him as their king, the tribal host was transformed into a national levy, which the king could raise whenever required. Moreover, the duty to serve in the host of the king was not confined to the Franks but was extended to the whole population enclosed in Frankish territory, the only classes exempt being the non-free and the clergy. In practice, however, as Frankish society became stabilized and took on a predominantly agrarian character, the duty of military service became closely associated with the ownership of land. Each free household owed the service of one man with arms and equipment, an obligation that became hereditary.

The social origins of the feudal knight of later times are not to be found in the mass levy of freemen but in the *comitatus,* the circle of paladins surrounding the king and becoming the core of the Frankish nobility. Increasingly members of this small group, profiting by the lessons of battles like Casilinum, turned to the use of cavalry and body armor. Two developments furthered the rise of cavalry: the introduction of the stirrup from the Mediterranean world some time during the seventh century, and the incursions of mounted Saracens into southern France in the early eighth century. The stirrup greatly increased cavalry efficiency, since it enabled a firmly seated rider to deliver a powerful thrust with his lance or to rise in the saddle to use his sword with greater leverage. The infantry of the Macedonian phalanx and the Roman legion had never had to face such firmly seated horsemen; and the raw Frankish foot-soldiery was much less capable. Their weapons were ineffective against the armor of the horseman, nor could they now topple him easily from his saddle. Not until the time of the Swiss halberdier of the fourteenth century could infantry again cope succcessfully with cavalry on its own terms.

Yet how could the Frankish state respond to the evident need for reshaping the nature and equipment of its armed forces? The horse, lance, sword, shield, and armor of the mounted soldier represented a costly investment which was far beyond the resources of the individual freeman. Moreover, the hard struggle for existence brought about by rude subsistence agriculture denied to the freeman the time necessary to master difficult cavalry tactics. The almost complete disappearance of trade and the decay of cities from the fifth to the tenth centuries (the Dark Ages) meant that there was little or no money available to the state, nor was there in any West European monarchy an organized, literate bureaucracy which could deal with fiscal matters on a national scale. The Frankish king was expected to "live of his own" and to provide for his family and attendants from the production of his own estates. He had no surplus revenue to devote to the establishment of a professional cavalry army.

A long step toward the solution of this dilemma was taken by Charles Martel (714-741), Mayor of the Palace for one of the weak Merovingian kings. In order to meet the Saracen menace, Charles widened in scope a practice which had probably already begun. Out of the royal estates and the holdings of the Church, he gave distinguished soldiers enough land for their support. From each vassal, in return for the estate granted, was extracted an oath of allegiance by which he was bound to serve Charles as a soldier as long as he was physically able. At the vassal's death, or on breaking his oath, his benefice was transferred to another, who assumed the military obligations which the land carried. In this way Charles secured a large body of mounted soldiers who could afford to purchase their equipment, had leisure to undertake military training, and were bound to their ruler by oath and interest. It was the mobility given the Franks by the innovations of Charles Martel, and not the tenacious stand of the Frankish infantry in 732 at the battle of Tours, that won victory over the Moslems in a long struggle which did not end until 752.

The many military successes and the widely-flung conquests of Charles Martel's illustrious descendant Charlemagne (King of the Franks, 768-814) owe much to the constantly increasing proportion of cavalry in the Frankish host, although the mass levy of infantry continued to be employed. Charlemagne issued many edicts to assist the development of good cavalry. He forbade the export of armor, extended the system of vassalage to conquered areas, and defined in precise terms the equipment with which the mounted soldier was expected to appear when summoned to the host. A sweeping change was also made in the infantry levy in order to improve its quality and to ease the inordinate burden which Charlemagne's many wars placed upon the peasant. Freemen holding property below a prescribed minimum in size and value were no longer to be individually answerable for service, but were to club together in small groups to send one of their number, suitably armed. Although this reform heightened the efficiency of the Frankish army, it further narrowed the social bounds within which the military art was practised, and thus represented another stage in the slow development of the feudal state.

Charlemagne's military ability and fierce ambition resulted in the creation of an extensive empire which was bounded on the north and east by the Elbe and the Danube and included sections of modern Yugoslavia, all Italy (except Venice) to a point south of Rome, and part of northern Spain. Aside from his ambitions, Charlemagne sincerely felt it his mission to protect and expand Christianity and civilization; his empire was at once the legatee of Roman civilization and the political expression of the whole of Christendom, as was symbolized in his coronation as Emperor by the Pope in 800. Under his rule there was a great revival of learning; the last heathen Germanic tribes, the Saxons, were converted; there was even a momentary economic upturn.

The concepts of the twin unities of Christendom and the Holy Roman Empire remained strong and influential throughout medieval times, but Charlemagne's great political creation did not survive long. As a method of imperial government Germanic monarchy was too simple, too close to its tribal origins, to embrace the huge extent of the Frankish domain. The circumstances of imperfect communications, diverse populations at radically different levels of civilization, and the absence of a common citizenship and of relationships transcending the personal were compounded by civil strife resulting from the division of the empire among Charlemagne's three grandsons and by the terrible invasions of heathen marauders. Together, they brought in the ninth century a crystallization of West European society into the structure known as feudalism.

The reasons for the incessant raids of the Vikings in the ninth century and the Magyars in the late ninth and tenth centuries are obscure. It has been suggested that the Vikings represented a violent overflowing of areas of limited resources in which population had suddenly risen greatly; and also that the attempts of Scandinavian kings to bring order to their countries drove out the turbulent elements. The Magyars, on the other hand, were a people of Turanian origin from the eastern steppes; as with other nomadic peoples their movements were determined by the proximity of good grazing lands and the chance of easy plunder. Whatever the explanation of their sudden onslaught, the military problems posed

by the appearance of these twin scourges were the same. The Magyars, swift horsemen, were exponents of the hit-and-run attack; the
Vikings had the mobility and freedom of action afforded by sea
power. Wherever the Vikings landed, they scoured the countryside
for horses to mount their infantry. Since their object was loot, not
occupation, they avoided centers of possible resistance and, if cor-
nered, slipped away to their ships. The slow-assembling, slow-
moving Frankish infantry levy could not cope with either invader.
The heavy cavalry, however, was almost invariably successful if it
caught up with a raiding party; and castles built by the lords provided secure bases for offensive and defensive operations.

The anarchic conditions of the ninth century, and the absence of
organized central government, placed a premium upon the protective services of the cavalry soldier and also forced the people of
every community to fly for help, not to the monarchy, but to the
local lord in his castle. Everywhere landowners granted benefices,
or fiefs, to soldiers in return for protection, and everywhere smaller
landowners placed themselves and their feudal vassals under allegiance to a more powerful lord. In this way the great feudal ladder was formed, a progression from the knight below to the great
feudatories and the king above. The core of the feudal system was
the contractual relationship which existed between lord and vassal at every rung of the ladder. The knight received his fee, com-
prising enough land and servile labor to support himself and his
family, no longer as a revocable grant but in perpetuity, as long as
he and his descendants fulfilled their contractual obligations to
their lord. Petty barons yielded up their estates to great magnates
and received them back under conditions which obligated both
themselves and their vassals. The purpose of the contract, at whatever level, was essentially military. The lord was pledged to protect his vassals, while they were pledged to serve in his mounted array. In a larger sense, feudalism was not only a set of military relationships but the ordered response of a society seeking to avoid
anarchy. No summary so brief as this can indicate either its growing
complexity through time or its creativity in the realm of political,
social, and economic relationships.

In this system, and under the conditions which brought it forth,
there was little place for the freeman. Either he became a knight or,
more often, he surrendered his holdings to a local lord powerful
enough to give him protection, and received the land back as a
tenant owing dues and labor services to his lord. In time, as a

result of such transactions, the status of the peasant was greatly lowered, and although many communities contained freemen who held their land of no one, the majority of European peasants were depressed to various conditions of servitude. The development of the seigneurial system accounts in part for the disappearance, except in England, of the national levy of freemen. We have already seen, however, that this military institution was inadequate to the demands made upon it, and that the growth of the feudal system was brought about, in part at least, by the inefficiency of infantry.

The feudal system, then, embodied the supremacy of cavalry over infantry and the substitution of the castle for the infantry phalanx as the base for cavalry operations. In feudal eyes, no other event established this supremacy more convincingly than the conquest of England by the Normans.

English military institutions, although having the same roots as those of the Frankish kingdoms, had not developed at the same rate or in quite the same way. The Teutonic peoples who invaded Britain in the fifth and sixth centuries relied, like the Franks, upon the unarmored infantry supplied by their tribal levy, or *fyrd,* and it was upon this system that the military power of the several kingdoms of early Anglo-Saxon England depended. The ninth-century assaults of the Danish Vikings brought several modifications which owed as much to the pressure of circumstance as to the genius of King Alfred. Because of the constant fighting, the *fyrd* was divided, one part serving for a set period while the other continued in peaceful occupations. As on the continent, many stockaded forts, called *burhs,* were constructed, to act as centers of protection for the inhabitants of the surrounding countryside and as points of resistance against the Vikings. Perhaps Alfred's most notable contribution was the creation of an English navy as an outer wall of defense which, if not maintained unimpaired by his successors, certainly established the English naval tradition. The Danish invasion in force in the eleventh century, which resulted in the elevation of Cnut (Canute) to the kingship, added to the English military structure the housecarls, a professional bodyguard for the king, equivalent to the Frankish *comitatus.* By 1066, all the great aristocratic houses had such bodies of retainers, who represented the peak of English military attainment. The *fyrd,* at least in theory, was still the core of the English army. In fact, however, between the time of Alfred and the coming of William, there was a tendency to reserve military functions to a particular class, a trend toward something not unlike continental feudalism. A member of this class, known as a thegn (thane) was above an ordinary freeman in status but below the small circle of aristocrats. He owed military service directly to the king, not in exchange for any land he held, but because of his social position.

The host that King Harold the Saxon marshalled atop a hill to meet the invading Norman army on the morning of Hastings was drawn partly from the ill-armed ranks of the *fyrd,* but its nucleus was the body of housecarls and thegns, armed with the ponderous Danish battleax, and protected by steel caps and chain mail. The most significant fact about the English army, that which caught the attention of the feudal world, was that it was wholly infantry, and trusted for protection against cavalry to its solidity behind a wall of kite-shaped shields.

The leading element of Duke William's Norman army, on the other hand, was its feudal cavalry. The Normans were the descendants of those Northmen to whom the French monarchy, convinced that the best defenders against Vikings were other Vikings, had granted the Duchy of Normandy in the tenth century. In time, they had been converted to Christianity and absorbed into feudal society; their abilities as cavalry soldiers were held in high esteem. The invading army also contained archers and infantry.

The victory of the Normans at Hastings was regarded in the Middle Ages as establishing beyond doubt the superiority of cavalry over infantry. Actually, the Saxon shield-wall remained unbroken after repeated charges of the Norman horse. William won because the two wings of the Saxon army, the local levies, were drawn away from the strong hill position by cavalry feints and cut to pieces. Harold's heavily armed housecarls were not overcome until a concentration of missile fire aimed in high trajectory broke up their ranks and made them vulnerable to cavalry assault. The simplified medieval view of Hastings as a victory of cavalry over infantry is a demonstration of how military insight can be blunted by non-military considerations. The mounted knight was no longer merely a soldier; he was by the eleventh century the member of an exclusive class which owed its social and political power to its control over the instruments and conduct of war and which could neither afford nor tolerate competition from below. Neither Norman England nor any other European feudal state utilized to any significant degree the real lessons of Hastings, the solidity of well-armed infantry and the decisive effect of missile weapons. Balanced armies, like those of the Eastern Roman Empire, were foreign to, and indeed incompatible with, feudal society.

England, under the Norman monarchy, became a feudal state similar in nature to other European countries but one in which the crown retained a greater degree of power. As in continental Europe, the conversion to a feudal military system meant the construction of a great number of castles as bases for cavalry forces and as citadels of feudal power. Within a century after the coming of the Normans, there were about 1,200 castles in England, the earlier mounds and stockades soon giving way to great square stone keeps like the White Tower of London. Yet alongside the feudal cavalry army, the national military organization of Saxon England continued to exist. William retained the *fyrd* partly as a defense against his own barons: a national levy of English infantrymen was employed to quell the baronial rising in 1075. Although one of the results of the Conquest was to reduce many Anglo-Saxon freemen to the level of the unfree, and thus in turn reduce the number of those eligible for the national levy, this ancient system never entirely dropped out of sight. With some modification it was continued to become the militia in later times.

For a period of roughly three centuries, from the defeat of the Anglo-Saxon axmen in the eleventh century to the rise of effective Swiss and English infantry in the fourteenth, the cavalry soldier reigned as the dominant figure in warfare. The cavalry age coincides with the full development of feudalism as a mature form of political and social organization, common to much of Europe. It was therefore natural that the mounted knight, the individual representative of this system, should be regarded as the ideal soldier and the true backbone of an army. Conversely, the infantryman was held in contempt, partly because of his social inferiority, partly because the conditions for the development of efficient infantry forces did not exist.

Infantry did not disappear completely from medieval battlefields. Levies of peasants or townsmen usually accompanied their mounted lords to battle, but the role assigned them was insignificant. Poorly and variously armed, with no internal or tactical organization, medieval infantry was incapable of withstanding cavalry assault, had little or no influence on the outcome of a battle, and was usually exposed to indiscriminate slaughter when its cavalry was routed. There are exceptions to this general picture: the infantry of Boulogne, for example, at Bouvines (1214) demonstrated great discipline and tenacity before succumbing eventually to repeated French cavalry attacks. Occasionally, too, as at Tinchebrai (1106) or the Battle of the Standard (1138), knights dismounted and fought on foot. This was an expedient growing out of the lack of versatility of cavalry; it was usually adopted either because the terrain was unsuitable to a cavalry engagement, or because a weaker army, trapped and forced to give battle by a stronger foe, recognized the deficiency of cavalry when acting on the defensive and chose to fight as infantry.

The medieval period has often been described as one in which the development of European civilization was arrested, as a long interval of slumber between the collapse of Rome and the outpouring of energy with the Renaissance, as a time when society was stratified into a number of fixed castes. Similarly, military historians have viewed the art of war in the Middle Ages as stagnating because it was monopolized by a single class interested in preserving a mode of combat suited to its own abilities and position. There is much superficiality, and even gross inaccuracy, in these interpretations. Ignored is the vast change in European life which took place over the thousand-year span of the Middle Ages, the wonderful flowering of high culture and learning in the thirteenth century, and the fact that the "feudal pyramid" was never the neat, ordered structure described by lawyers and theologians but rather a crazy patchwork of conflicting loyalties and obligations, in which private war and struggle for power were endemic. In military affairs, even in the cavalry age, development went on, chiefly in the elaboration of fortification, armor, and the techniques of siege warfare.

Nevertheless, medieval thought was not concerned with "progress" but with stability and order, and medieval institutions reflected this conservative resistance to change. Once established, the feudal system, with military power and gathering custom to support it, was difficult to shake off; peasant risings were invariably and ruthlessly crushed, the better to emphasize the permanent gap between those who ruled and those who served. In war, as in other departments of life, the feudal class refused to allow any encroachment by social inferiors upon what was regarded as its peculiar preserve, or to tolerate any innovation which might threaten its monopoly. The castration of some South German peasants for taking up arms in support of the Emperor Henry IV in 1078 and thus infringing on knightly prerogatives is an illustration of the lengths to which the feudal warrior was prepared to go to defend his position.

The chief guarantor of stability in medieval Europe was the Church. Its influence, of pre-eminent importance in fashioning conduct and social attitudes in an age of almost universal faith, was placed upon the side of established order partly because the existing gradations appeared to reflect the differing capacities and purposes of man, partly because it taught the irrelevance of this life except as preparation for the next, and partly because, in every feudal state of Europe, the Church was the largest single land-owner with the possible exception of the king. It was not surprising that the Church should come to the aid of the knightly class by banning the use of weapons inimical to cavalry warfare. An example of this attitude occurred when the eleventh century saw the replacement of the short bow, firing wooden shafts, by the crossbow. The latter weapon, consisting of a metal bow super-imposed on a wooden stock, with the bowstring drawn back by a winch and released by a trigger, fired metal bolts which could penetrate the best chain mail. Missile weapons "which know not where they strike" were despised as unchivalrous by the mounted knight; the crossbow in particular was feared as a threat to the dominance of cavalry. In the eleventh and twelfth centuries a series of papal anathema proscribed the use of the crossbow, and its refinement, the arbalest, except against pagans and infidels.

The attempts by the Church to prohibit or restrict the use of such commoners' weapons as the crossbow were not very effective. By the thirteenth century most feudal armies had their quota of Genoese or other expert crossbowmen. The Church had rather more success in achieving its main objective, which was the limit-ing of warfare, both in frequency of occurrence and in the way it was conducted. Feudalism in essence had meant the assumption, in the absence of any centralized authority, of the functions of defense and order by local lords. Even before the last threat of external attack disappeared in the eleventh century, it was inevitable that feudal magnates, their semi-independent status assured by strong castles and having at their disposal their own private armies, should turn to fighting among themselves. Throughout the later medieval period Germany was a jungle of feudal powers which the strongest emperor could not unite. In other parts of Europe conditions were scarcely much better. Even in England, where the king possessed a potential authority unique in the West, the combination of a weak monarch and a disputed succession threw the country into the disastrous anarchy of Stephen's reign (1135-54).   In most of Europe, the sole authority overriding the crude appeal to arms was that of the Church, and in the hands of vigorous popes like Gregory VII and Innocent III the threat of anathema, interdict, or excommunication could be an influential moral weapon.

It was not the intention of the medieval Church to eradicate war, which it regarded as an irrepressible evidence of man's sinfulness. Moreover, some wars were regarded as just, and their outcome as the divine verdict of where justice lay. The Church could lend itself to the encouragement of such wars, notably the Norman invasion of England to deal with Harold the oath-breaker, or the holy wars of the crusading period. Religious sanction could also be given to the judicial trial by combat, until clerical revulsion against the sacrilege in so putting God to the test led the Fourth Lateran Council in 1215 to forbid the participation of priests in such trials (an event which, incidentally, furthered the system of trial by jury in England).

Generally, however, the Church tried to curb the prevalence of war and soften its nature. Beginning in the late tenth century, in the French provinces of Aquitaine and Burgundy, churchmen anathematized those who broke the "Peace of God," who despoiled church property and brought misery and death to non-combatants. Slightly later, excommunication was visited on those who broke the "Truce of God" by fighting at any time from Thursday night to Monday morning. Although these strictures of the Church might not have been given more than lip-service, they did operate as a brake upon the more vicious and indiscriminate forms of feudal warfare; the right of sanctuary and the inviolability of church property were generally respected by the feudal conscience. When, in the twelfth and thirteenth centuries, the Church reached a peak of prestige and power, it was able to intervene in European diplomacy and war with considerable effect. The papal legate became a frequent arbiter in the settlement of international and internal disputes.

In a broader way, Christianity had much to do with the formulation of the code of honor known as chivalry. The ideal Christian knight, *sans peur et sans reproche,* was the pagan hero softened by Christian virtues, Grettir the Strong become Sir Galahad. The chivalrous knight was one who joined to bravery and the passion for adventure qualities of courtesy, truthfulness, loyalty, and mercy toward the weak and oppressed. Perhaps the individuals who met this lofty standard were few, and the number of those who aspired to it not much larger, but the mere existence of such a code raised the level of conduct in war, even if this only meant better treatment by the knightly class for other members of their international caste.

The chivalric urge for adventure and glory, whenever it could not be satisfied by war, was met by the simulated warfare of the tournament. This lethal sport, which seems to have begun in France during the eleventh century, was immensely popular and undoubtedly was of some value in enhancing the skill of the feudal man-at-arms, but it was frowned on by the Church as a needless shedding of blood. In 1139 a decree of the Second Lateran Council forbade it, but without effect. In 1179, therefore, the Third Lateran Council denied Christian burial to those slain in such combat. This move did not halt tournaments, but it was sufficient to bring about the use of blunted weapons and eventually to reduce these events to opportunities for pageantry and relatively harmless display.

The clearest demonstration of the influence of the Church upon the military class is to be seen in the crusades. The promise of material reward and the hope of adventure found in the crusaders cannot be distinguished from spiritual motives. But the crusades are significant for another reason. Under feudalism, for the first time since the decay of Rome, Europe was powerful enough to take the offensive against the East, and in the process sack its former defender, Constantinople. The First Crusade (1095- 99) saw the winning of the Holy Land and the establishment of the crusading kingdoms; subsequent crusades, which ended in the late thirteenth century, were in the main directed toward maintaining the existence of these kingdoms.

The crusading armies were different from the usual feudal array in two respects: they were composed of volunteers, and they were even more incoherent because of their multi-national origins and the rancor and jealousy of their leaders. Yet, despite some memorable disasters caused by stupidity and recklessness, the success of the crusaders against the Moslems was on the whole pronounced, chiefly because they were compelled to employ tactics radically different from those of the cavalry melee they were accustomed to. At Dorylaeum (1097) a Turkish army allowed itself to be trapped and crushed between two wings of heavy cavalry. After this, Moslem armies, composed of lightly armored mounted lancers and bowmen, never closed with crusading forces but harassed them from a distance with missile fire. Finding their horsemen powerless to cope with a more mobile enemy, the crusaders soon realized the necessity for infantry support. Bowmen were required to counter the Saracen missiles (a bowman on foot could outrange a mounted archer); heavy infantry were needed to offer shelter for cavalry after a charge, and also to tempt the enemy cavalry to come within reach. Just such a combination of arms gave the crusaders victory at Antioch (1098) and won Jerusalem for them in the next year. These balanced tactics, so unwelcome to feudal class prejudice, had to be learned over and over again by successive crusading armies. Richard I of England applied them brilliantly against the able Saracen ruler Saladin at Arsuf and Jaffa (1191) in an unavailing effort to recover Jerusalem, lost by extreme mismanagement in 1187.

The last European foothold in the Holy Land disappeared in the late thirteenth century. Military ability was not lacking; but the crusader principalities were without adequate permanent armies and were isolated from a Europe which was becoming increasingly concerned with more profitable projects. Warfare in the West drew little benefit from the experiences of the crusaders. The chief lesson, the advantage of a combination of arms which included infantry and bowmen, was too distasteful to be accepted by feudal chivalry. What developments there were tended only to strengthen certain aspects of feudal warfare. Quilted clothing, worn under armor, was a protection against missiles. Surcoats over it provided an added opportunity for heraldic display. The major result was to accentuate the already marked defensive nature of war, through developments in the art of fortification. Feudal magnates, impressed by the great castles of the East, returned to build similar structures, of which Richard I's Chateau Gaillard, built 1197-8 to guard the approaches to Normandy, was among the first and most notable. The new castle-builders developed "concentric" fortifications, throwing out high curtain walls studded at intervals with round towers, and eliminating square corners which had proved easy to breach.

Despite the flowering of the chivalric ideal and the building of many bigger castles, by the thirteenth century feudalism as a political and military system was actually in decline. The justification of feudalism had been the order and security it brought to society during a period when central governments were weak, and in a broader sense, its preservation of the European religious and cultural heritage. This justification no longer had the same force. New forces were now uniting to dislodge the feudal aristocracy from the seat of power.

6

The Breakdown of Feudal Warfare

Even when knighthood was in its full flower, there were basic weaknesses in feudal warfare which foreshadowed its replacement whenever a more efficient method should be evolved. Although the Middle Ages have an unmistakably martial flavor, there were remarkably few battles fought. The raising of a feudal army by a king or magnate was an arduous process, lengthened by bad communications and fractious nobles. Once raised, its life was short: the usual term of service demanded of a knight was only forty days a year, and the campaigning season was sharply restricted. In England, the magnates objected to overseas service; on the continent, lords refused to serve outside the bounds of their particular state. In 1205, King John had to cancel a campaign to recover Normandy because his barons refused to cross the Channel.

A feudal army in the field was an indescribably undisciplined force. Many tenants-in-chief would take orders only from their immediate overlord, the king; therefore an effective chain of command was impossible. There was a superabundance of courage which tended to aggravate rather than to relieve the normal disorder. Long centuries of control of the art of war by one class, the exaggerated concentration upon cavalry warfare alone, and the absence of any provision for group training except in a restricted fashion in the reformed tournament meant that the study and practice of organized tactics had all but vanished. A vestigial remnant of tactical organization can be seen in the division of the feudal host into three "battles" or massed lines; but once the battle was joined all semblance of order disappeared, and the struggle became nothing more than a confused melee of hundreds of individual encounters. The practice of taking prisoners for ransom instead of fighting to the death placed a positive pecuniary incentive on breaking ranks and making a fortune by private enterprise.

The same inability to achieve swift decision because tactical finesse was lacking is to be found in the broader aspects of war. So little attention was paid to strategy, or to such fundamental questions as supply and knowledge of the terrain and of the enemy's movements, that opposing armies often searched fruitlessly for each other without being able to come to grips, or used up the campaigning season in looting the countryside in order to maintain themselves. Moreover, although cavalry is the arm of the tactical offensive, it lends itself in a strategic sense to the defensive. No commander who felt himself weak need give battle; he had simply to retire with his force to the safety of the nearest stronghold. The art of fortification kept ahead of the revival of the Roman siege train and techniques. The primarily defensive nature of medieval war was preserved, as was the security of the petty baron against centralizing rulers.

Monarchical dissatisfaction with the limitations placed upon royal policy by the deficiencies of the feudal levy brought early attempts to break the military monopoly of the feudal classes, usually through the employment of mercenaries. Twelfth-century rulers did not have the financial resources to employ professional soldiers on any large scale, but by various expedients they could raise enough money to hire a few. Such an expedient was the English system of scutage, which was used by Henry I in 1125 and may have been even older. In its matured form it was a device through which the king, by assessing his tenants-in-chief a flat rate for each of the knights they had enfeoffed, was able to dispense with at least part of his feudal levy and buy the services of mercenaries who would fight as long as there was money to pay them. King John got into difficulties with his baronage because, among other reasons, he was more ingenious than his predecessors in using scutage and other feudal dues to squeeze money from them. Although the great age of mercenaries was yet to come, by the early thirteenth century they were a not insignificant part of every army. Richard I and John hired large numbers of Welsh foot, or reached across the channel for infantry from Brabant; the Genoese crossbowman was ubiquitous; and everywhere landless knights formed an obvious nucleus for a mercenary company.

The two great institutions of the Middle Ages were the feudal system and the Universal Church. The transformation of dissension-ridden feudal states into strong national monarchies and the breakdown in the temporal authority of the Church were due primarily not to military developments but to vast social and economic movements. At the same time, however, the art of war was divested of most of its medieval trappings and entered an age of rapid change. The new forms of war then became a vital element in the process which was altering the face of Europe.

One of the chief agencies in hastening medieval Europe into modern times was the great increase in wealth which began to be noticeable about the middle of the thirteenth century, primarily because of the revival of international trade. International commerce had never died but until the eleventh century had been largely concerned with such high-priced luxuries as spices, silks, furs, and especially slaves. The prosperity that came to Venice through its connection with imperial Constantinople and its naval power has been noted in a previous chapter; the crusades enhanced its wealth and importance, and were instrumental in the rise of such mercantile centers as Genoa and Pisa. In the twelfth century the Low Countries became the most prominent cloth manufacturing region of Europe and the Rhine a highway of trade; just as in northern Italy, trade and industry brought the rise of cities like Bruges, Ghent, and Ypres. England, as the principal source of raw wool for Flemish industry, gained greatly in wealth and also in urban development. In the same period, cities of North Germany like Lübeck, Hamburg, Magdeburg, and Danzig became the land carriers of Europe, uniting the economies of Scandinavia and the Slavic East with Italy. The weakness of the imperial government in Germany led these cities to form independent leagues, the most important of which, the Hansa, was founded in the late thirteenth century. By 1300 the Venetian galley-fleet had made the first of its annual trading voyages to England and Flanders, meeting in both countries Hansa merchants, a meeting which signified the completion of a trading economy that embraced the whole of Europe.

The new trade was not merely the exchange of the raw products of one region for those of another. It involved manufacturing, and the wealth stemming from it produced a demand for the importation or home production of luxury goods. Cities like Florence became famous for fine weaving and dyeing, Milan and Nurnberg for metalwork, Marseilles and Venice for metal and glass wares. Hand in hand with the flourishing of commerce went the emergence of an urban middle class engaged in business and manufacture and subdivided according to occupation in the specialized guild organizations. The appearance of a wealthy, numerous middle class had important consequences. The old simplicity of peasant, lord, clergy, and king was gone, disrupted by the addition of a dynamic class which was profoundly anti-feudal in character. In countries like Italy and Germany, where the central government was weak, growing towns shook off the hold of adjacent lords and became in effect independent city-states. In England, however, and to a lesser degree in France, where the feudal duchies were strong, the towns became allies of the crown against the feudal aristocracy. Moreover, the growth of urban population and the spread of a money economy associated with trade had a strong impact upon the life of the countryside. Urban demands for food and raw materials made farming for profit possible; rising prices and a more plentiful money supply gave the peasant the means to purchase his freedom or commute his labor services for a money rent. In England, for example, enfranchisement and agricultural prosperity created a rural class of small farmers, the yeomen, who filled the ranks of English armies in the later Middle Ages.

One of the prime effects of the economic revolution was to enlarge the financial resources of the state, and therefore to expand its military power beyond the old limitations. Merchants with surplus capital soon turned into the bankers of royalty. During the Hundred Years' War, Italian banking houses lent money indiscriminately to both France and England; and the Hansa merchant, Tiedemann of Limburg, financed the early campaigns of Edward III. During the later years of this war, each country produced its own merchant-capitalists. Henry V reached the field of Agincourt on sums borrowed from men like Sir Richard Whittington, Lord Mayor of London, and the subsequent French recovery was in part made possible by immense loans from the famous merchant-banker Jacques Coeur. Increased revenue was also reaped directly from trade by customs duties; export duties on raw wool leaving England or wines leaving France swelled the royal treasuries. Of the utmost political consequence was the extended use of methods of general taxation, for in order to tax the new middle classes, European rulers found it wise to obtain their consent. At approximately the same time the characteristic representative institutions of late medieval Europe appeared: the Spanish Cortes and the German Reichstag in the late 13th century, the Estates-

General of France in 1302, and the "Model Parliament" of Edward I in 1295. In all these assemblies the burgesses of the towns and the prosperous gentry of the countryside were represented, and it is interesting to note the close connection, particularly in England, between the monetary needs of the king in time of war and the growth in power of these middle-class institutions. The origins of the House of Commons as the central arch of the English constitution cannot be divorced from the history of the Hundred Years' War. Through its control of the vital power of taxation, the Commons was able to extend its competence to high matters of state and even, in 1399, to include the nomination of a king, Henry IV.

By the late thirteenth century the monarchs of England and France had virtually extinguished private feudal war in their immediate domains. No longer was a castle an unconditional guarantee of baronial independence; the king, with his new-found wealth, could hire mercenaries for long sieges which would overcome the wealthiest and most obstinate lord. In both countries, royal control was cemented by the building and maintenance of royal castles, commanded by a seneschal, a mercenary captain who was more likely of middle class than aristocratic origin. Thus were established the two strongest monarchies of late medieval Europe.

There was, however, an important difference between the two. In France, the kings had used their wealth and power to harness their feudal nobility but the feudal military system continued to exist intact. In England, not only was the baronage severely curbed, but the old military society was withering at its roots. Agricultural prosperity brought about sub-infeudation, or the breaking up of the unit of military service, the knight's fee, into smaller parcels of land. It was obviously impossible to apportion military service fractionally, and so the many holders of a single knight's fee paid a fraction of its scutage instead. On the other hand, knights who continued to hold land by virtue of military service found that while their services as soldiers were rarely demanded, they were being loaded by successive kings with more and more onerous (and unpaid) duties of local government. In Henry III's reign (1216-72) the English knight was required to serve on juries, conduct inquests, administer the king's forests, determine land boundaries, and occasionally to sit in Parliament. For these reasons many men who held knight's fees refused to acknowledge themselves as

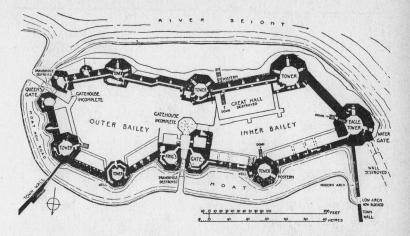

PLAN OF CAERNARVON CASTLE, a concentric castle built by Edward I of England. —(From Sidney Toy, *The Castles of Great Britain,* Heinemann, London, 1954.)

knights; and at the same time that they rejected their civil functions they ceased to provide themselves with armor and the other paraphernalia of knighthood. Edward I (1272-1307) attempted to shore up the feudal military system through a series of proclamations ordering those who held land above a certain value to assume the rank of knight and provide themselves with equipment. But no legislation of that kind could be effective. The last summons to the feudal levy of England was issued in 1385.

The Hundred Years' War (1337-1453) brought the complete discrediting of feudal methods of warfare and of the armored, mounted knight. Ever since the introduction of the crossbow, the feudal warrior had become increasingly concerned with strengthening his defensive equipment. Chain mail had been replaced early in the thirteenth century by much heavier and more expensive plate armor for horse and man. The only response the mounted knight could make to the new military techniques was to burden himself with heavy protective covering until, in the fifteenth century, he was virtually immobilized. Already, before the outbreak of the Hundred Years' War, French chivalry had received a damaging blow to its prestige on the field of Courtrai (1302). Count Robert of Artois, disdaining to wait until his Genoese crossbowmen had

A TREBUCHET, throwing a dead horse into a besieged town. —(From
Leonardo da Vinci's "Il Codice Atlantico," reproduced in Sir R. Payne-
Gallwey, Bt., *Projectile-Throwing Engines of the Ancients,* Longmans,
Green, London, 1907.)

"softened up" an infantry army of humble Flemish journeymen,
launched a cavalry charge across a bog. When the French were
hopelessly ensnared in the wet ground, the Flemings, who were
armed with pikes (a type of long infantry spear) and fired by a
sturdy local patriotism, plunged to the attack. Seven hundred gold
spurs were recovered as trophies from slain French knights.

That the French failed to learn from Courtrai (and other battles
like it) brought calamity when they encountered the armies of the
English. As we have seen, the place of the feudal levy in the
English military scheme was one of steadily diminishing importance. Following the reign of Edward I, English armies were professional in nature, and troops were raised by indenture. The king
contracted with well-known commanders to supply him with men,
their number and time of service to be determined by the amount
of money that changed hands. The type of troops required was
always stated in the contract and usually consisted of a mixture

of mounted men-at-arms, infantry, and archers. The introduction of the wage system and the dependence of the professional soldier upon his commander meant that the indentured companies had a degree of discipline unknown to previous, purely feudal armies. Another, though less important source of English manpower was the shire levy or militia, a lineal descendant of the ancient *fyrd*. The Assize of Arms of 1181 had laid down that every freeman between sixteen and sixty should provide himself with suitable weapons, according to the value of his land. In 1285 a statute of Edward I confirmed the Assize and also declared that the long-bow should be the basic weapon of the shire levy. Occasionally during the Hundred Years' War part of this militia was employed on overseas service, its expense being shared among the remainder.

Mention of the longbow turns attention to the weapon which has become identified with the Hundred Years' War. The English seem to have encountered it in their wars with the South Welsh in the late twelfth and thirteenth centuries, and were so favorably impressed that by the close of the latter century it had been adopted as their national weapon. The longbow, six feet in length, was pulled to the ear and was therefore very much more powerful than earlier bows. It was also superior to the crossbow because of its higher rate of fire, greater range, and the fact that in wet weather the bowstring could be more easily protected. Its power of penetration was great, although exaggerated by the legends which have since surrounded it. Its clothyard arrow could not pierce the best plate armor, but easily penetrated mail or the inevitable chinks in plate armor, and was deadly when employed against horses. The strength to draw the bow to the ear and the accurate use of the weapon required years of training. The longbow remained very nearly the exclusive speciality of the unique class of English yeomen.

In wars against the Scots the use of the bow was perfected and a genuine system of balanced tactics of horse and foot was built up around it. At Falkirk (1298) the archers riddled selected portions of the Scottish schiltrons (heavy infantry columns) and the English cavalry smashed into the gaps. With slight variations, these were the tactics which were to prevail in future English battles with the Scots, from Halidon Hill (1333) to Flodden (1513). The English were defeated at Bannockburn (1314) because Edward II failed to make proper use of his archers. He opened the battle with a cavalry charge which degenerated into confusion.

Then the archers, who were stationed in the rear, were ordered to fire, but probably hit as many English backs as Scottish breasts. Moreover, the bowmen had been left without any protection whatever, and were therefore easily dispersed by Scottish cavalry. By the time of the French wars, it had become customary to protect the archers from cavalry by placing stakes in front of their positions, and by intermingling their ranks with dismounted men-at-arms and foot soldiers armed with spears and bills. The bill was a six-foot cutting and thrusting weapon with a hook-shaped blade designed to unseat horsemen.

The causes of the Hundred Years' War, which were chiefly dynastic in nature, are not of great moment here, but the effects of the war upon military development and upon the history of the two nations which engaged in it were fundamental. The first and most apparent was the shock which French chivalry experienced at Crécy (1346) and Poitiers (1356). At Crécy the smaller army of Edward was divided into the usual three battles, each with a center of dismounted men-at-arms and wings of archers and spearmen. The French thrust forward their Genoese crossbowmen who, outranged and outshot by the English archers, were speedily routed or ridden down by their own cavalry. Throughout the rest of the day, charge after charge by the French knighthood withered against the solid phalanxes of dismounted English men-at-arms while from the flanks a hail of arrows took a heavy toll. When the defeated French retired at nightfall, more than a third of their number had been killed, the majority by missiles. At Poitiers the English were drawn up in much the same defensive formation, this time sheltered by a thick hedge. The French responded with tactics of such unbelievable fatuity that the only explanation can be their inability to credit the decisive contribution made at Crécy by plebeian archers. Believing that he was adopting the tactics which had given the English victory at Crécy, King John dismounted his knights and then launched them in three ponderous battles against the enemy position. Long before the struggling knights reached close quarters, they had been demoralized by English arrows. A flanking attack by men-at-arms led by the Black Prince, and another by a small cavalry force held in reserve, completed their route. The French king and his son were among the many prisoners who fell into English hands.

The military disgrace of the monarchy and feudal nobility at Poitiers was directly responsible for widespread political disorder in France. For a time Paris was virtually independent, the Estates-General demanded sweeping powers, while the provinces were convulsed by the bloody peasant rising of the *Jacquerie*. From Poitiers to the later years of the war the country was never to be free of the horrors inflicted by the "Free Companies," ravaging bands of mercenaries from all over Europe, whose contracts had expired and who owned no master.

Yet it is significant that the English were unable to capitalize greatly either from their victories or from French dissension and misery. Crécy and Poitiers were defensive battles in which the enemy had been beaten but not crushed; Edward III and the Black Prince were fine tacticians who did not rise above the general inadequacy of their times in strategic conceptions. Moreover, there were two insuperable obstacles in the way of large-scale conquests in France: the problem of supply, and the unaltered dominance of the castle. The sole result of the victory of Crécy was the capture of a base, Calais, after a long siege; but then English generals had to live off the country by loot and pillage and could not undertake prolonged investments. Poitiers was fought only because the Black Prince could move no faster than his wagon train of loot, and was unwilling to give it up.

After 1370, the tide of war turned for a space in favor of France. England was hampered by the passing of her outstanding leaders, the Black Prince in 1376 and the aged Edward III in 1377; by the succession of a minor, Richard II; by the rural unrest which culminated in the Peasants' Revolt; and by a political crisis which brought the deposition of Richard but did not end domestic troubles. In the Constable of France, Bertrand du Guesclin, King Charles V discovered a general with real ability, and not another rash feudal incompetent. Du Guesclin realized that it was not necessary to fight the English army in the field to regain French territory; the key to the retention of any area lay with the combatant who held its strong points, the castles. There was nothing of the chivalrous or the romantic in him. His refusal to consider the pleas of the feudal *noblesse* for yet another test of strength with the English removed them temporarily from the war and into their castles, out of harm's way. Using almost exclusively the professional soldiers of the free companies, du Guesclin and his successors fought a war of harassment, surprises, ambushes, sudden assaults, and slow sieges, which reduced piecemeal the English holdings in France.

CROSSBOWMEN. —(From the Roy MSS., British Museum, reproduced in John Hewitt, *Ancient Armour and Weapons in Europe*, Parker, Oxford, 1860, III, 521.)

Du Guesclin's brilliance was wasted on his contemporaries. On the field of Agincourt (1415), the chivalry of France showed that it had "forgotten nothing and remembered nothing." The army of Henry V numbered only 6,000, of whom about 5,000 were archers; it was drawn up in the old way in three battles with cores of dismounted men-at-arms and wings of archers, and with the usual careful attention to terrain, its flanks being protected by woods and its front by almost a mile of sodden, freshly ploughed fields. The French constable, Albret, a pupil of du Guesclin, was unwilling to attack an English army so securely positioned, and wished to starve it out. His slight authority could not withstand the exuberance of the nobility, confident in the knowledge that they outnumbered the English at least three to one. The rash formula of Poitiers was disinterred for the occasion. The French knights dismounted, sent their horses to the rear along with the crossbowmen and, in full panoply, began to plod through mud rising above their ankles toward the English lines. And the armor of 1415 was much heavier than that of 1356. The English archers, after easily repelling a minor cavalry assault, directed their fire against the slow-moving mass of French "infantry." By the time the French, greatly depleted in numbers, reached the English lines, they were so exhausted that they fell easy prey to the unarmored English yeomen, who abandoned bows for axes and swords. More than 4,000 French nobles and knights lost their lives in this crushing blow to feudal warfare; the losses of the English have never been estimated at more than a few hundreds.

The ultimate French victory in the Hundred Years' War stemmed chiefly from two factors: the creation of a professional standing army, and the rise of the imponderable spirit of French nationalism. The war has been called the first modern national war; from the start the armies of England were almost wholly English in personnel, though professional in character. It was inconceivable, however, that a nation of two millions, no matter how patriotic, should permanently triumph over one of sixteen; and when the mute antagonism of the mass of the French population was given expression in the inspiring figure of Joan of Arc, the days of English occupation became numbered. At the same time English enthusiasm for the war was being killed by heavier taxes, since it was becoming harder and harder for an English army to maintain itself in a hostile and thoroughly looted countryside. Moreover, livery and maintenance, an abuse of the indenture system of raising troops, had given rise to a bastard feudalism. The growth of private armies, unrestrained by an imbecile king, weakened the national effort; and internal divisions culminated in the Wars of the Roses (1455-85) two years after the close of the French war.

In 1445 the first regular standing army since Roman times was organized in France by direction of Charles VII, partly to end the scourge of the free companies. Mercenary companies, now *compagnies d'ordonnance,* were taken into the royal service on a permanent basis, giving France a professional army of some 6,000 men. Each company, composed of men-at-arms, pikemen, and archers, was commanded by a noble who gave his name to it. The campaigns conducted by the French during the last years of the war are distinguished by a professional touch; in other words, by caution, good sense, and discipline. There were no more foolish attacks on a ready and waiting English army, but instead sudden assaults on marching English columns which allowed the enemy no chance to draw up his lethal defensive battle-order.

When technical developments brought artillery to a state of

reasonable effectiveness, even the defensive superiority of the English disappeared. From 1450 to 1453 an artillery train organized by the brothers Bureau methodically blasted the English out of their castles in Normandy and Guienne. At Formigny (1450) an English army, drawn up in traditional fashion, was enfiladed by two culverins placed on its flank. When the tormented archers broke ranks in order to seize the French guns the *compagnies d'ordonnance,* no longer wary, closed in and cut up the English in a desperate hand-to-hand encounter. The English defeat at Formigny was as one-sided as their previous victories had been; and its verdict was confirmed at Castillon (1453) when an English army under the veteran John Talbot, Earl of Shrewsbury, relinquished the old tactics and attempted unsuccessfully to storm an entrenched line bristling with artillery.

The Hundred Years' War is in a sense an epitome of the revolutionary changes taking place in the art of war and the nature of society. Before its close the feudal principle had been replaced by the professional principle; aristocratic dominance had yielded to a democratization of the manpower and weapons of armies; the one-sided emphasis upon cavalry, and the tactical ignorance which accompanied it, had been gradually broadened until armies became combinations of all possible arms, tactics were restored, and new tactical departures encouraged; the new financial and political power of the state had widened the scope and lengthened the duration of wars, and had corroded the moderating restrictions of the Church; and finally, the appearance of efficient artillery gave a hint of new revolutions to come.

In another part of Europe during the same period, the Swiss, although employing tactics utterly different from those of the English, produced a similar upheaval in the nature of warfare. Indeed, they went further than the English, for they demonstrated conclusively the earlier lesson of Courtrai, that well-trained, well-armed, patriotic infantry could take the offensive against mailed cavalry and win. The Swiss Confederation, formed in 1291, was an alliance of the Forest Cantons of Uri, Schwyz, and Unterwalden, whose people were free peasants, against the feudal domination of the Austrian Habsburgs. As early victories solidified the virtual independence of the Confederation, the alliance was widened to include free towns like Lucerne, Zurich, and Berne. The underlying reasons for the emergence of Swiss military power were the compact, rugged, and defensible character of their country, the violent

MEDIEVAL ARMS.

patriotism induced in a free people by the constant threat from a powerful external enemy, and in consequence so positive an accent upon military preparedness that training and service were compulsory for all above the age of sixteen.

Swiss military development at an intermediate stage is illustrated by the battle of Morgarten (1315) at which the mounted array of Duke Leopold I of Austria was lured into a trap in a mountain pass. Powerless to maneuver, the Austrian cavalry was hewn to pieces by Swiss infantry armed with the halberd. The halberd, like the bill, united three weapons and as many functions on an eight-foot shaft: it was tipped with a spear point, had an ax-blade that could shear through armor, and a hook below the tip to pull a rider from the saddle. The halberd, however, was primarily an offensive weapon; before the Swiss could deal with cavalry in country less favorable than their own mountain fastnesses, two problems had to be dealt with: how best to receive the shattering impact of a charge by heavy cavalry, and how to prevent gaps from occurring in the ranks of their infantry which would permit cavalry to break up their formation.

The Swiss solution combined the methods of the two great infantry powers of antiquity. The standard formation was the phalanx; the standard weapon of defense the pike, an eighteen-foot shaft with a three-foot iron shank which prevented the spearhead from being lopped off by a sword-stroke. To charging cavalry, the Swiss phalanx presented the same hedgehog appearance as had the Macedonian; the first four ranks levelled their pikes in an impenetrable barbed wall to the front, while those to the rear kept pikes upraised, ready to fill a gap left by a fallen comrade. Long training, discipline, and the patriotic feeling which made subjection to discipline possible gave the Swiss phalanx the steadiness required to maintain solidity in the face of cavalry attack. But, like the Romans, the Swiss were not content with mere defensive passivity: they thought in terms of attack, and shaped their tactics to suit the offensive. Swiss troops wore no body armor except steel cap and breastplate; the extraordinary swiftness this innovation gave them was schooled into order by tight discipline on the march. (They were the first modern troops to march in step to music.) There was little time consumed in marshalling their forces for battle: the Swiss marched in battle-order of three columns in echelon. Their solidity and speed enabled them to attack bodies of horse; after the first push of pike the way was paved for the halberdiers to do their deadly work.

The ability of the Swiss to meet and defeat cavalry on open and level ground was demonstrated at Laupen (1339) when the feudal nobility of Burgundy, unable to breach the pike wall or withstand the halberd, was driven from the field. The supremacy of Swiss infantry over feudal cavalry remained unbroken until the knight disappeared from the battlefields of Europe. In the great campaign in 1476-77 Charles the Bold of Burgundy challenged Swiss invincibility by adding to his feudal levy mercenaries from many parts: archers from England, pikemen from Flanders, German arquebusiers, Italian men-at-arms. The Burgundian army, though formidable in appearance, lacked the unity and confidence of the Swiss veterans. The campaign brought defeat to Burgundy and death to Charles.

The reputation of the Swiss was so high that mercenary companies of this warlike people fought for nearly every European state. (A notable survival of the esteem in which they were held is the Swiss Guard at the Vatican.) Their ultimate downfall was due in part to their unwillingness to change their tactical formula when its victims, the feudal horse and ragged medieval infantry, disappeared; from their weaknesses in the realm of strategy; from their over-confidence; and from their curious and unsatisfactory custom of electing officers. It was also due to the improvement of field artillery. At Marignano (1515) the Swiss were brought to halt by repeated cavalry charges, and then smashed by concentrated French artillery fire. Even had gunpowder not deprived the Swiss of their margin of superiority over their opponents, the soldiers of other nations were pondering the ascendancy of the Swiss phalanx and developing answers to it. The German *Landsknechte* copied in every particular the pike and halberd tactics of the Swiss and at La Bicocca (1522) in a furious push of pike managed to defeat them.

Warfare in Italy during the later medieval period followed lines not duplicated anywhere else in Europe. The citizen militia of the rich cities of the north had thrown off the yoke of traditional feudal lords in the twelfth and thirteenth centuries. Inevitably wars against the feudality were replaced by incessant wars amongst the newly independent city-states. Because it was not possible to make perpetual demands for service upon citizens whose industry created the economic well-being of the community, the employment of mercenary forces became the primary method of making war. At first mercenaries were hired from the "free companies" of Germans, Frenchmen, and Englishmen who overflowed into Italy whenever there was a cessation of martial activity during the Hundred Years' War. Soon, however, native bands of *condottieri* were available in large numbers, attracted by the high market value placed upon military services by centers like Venice, Florence, and Milan.

The wars between Italian cities were almost purely economic in motive, and it is therefore not surprising that the mercenary captain should have governed his actions in accordance with strict business principles. It was found most economical, both for the *condottiere* and his employer, to restrict both the number and the type of troops hired. For this reason, infantry and bowmen were neglected, and the Italian wars of the fourteenth and fifteenth centuries were fought by armies of heavily armored horsemen, curious carry-overs from the feudal past. Moreover, since a victory could end the usefulness of the *condottieri* as swiftly as a defeat, the mercenary captains (often by collusion) tended to avoid battle and drag out campaigns to the limits of their employers' patience and pockets. Innovations, particularly firearms and artillery, were shunned as threats to military commerce; instead, soldiers protected their personal investment by increasing the thickness and weight of their body-armor so greatly that at Zagonara (1423), according to Machiavelli, "no deaths occurred, except those of Ludovici degli Obizi, and two of his people, who having fallen from their horses were smothered in the morass." The *condottieri* were military anachronisms, soon to be brushed aside by the modern army with which Charles VIII of France invaded Italy in 1494.

The English and the Swiss brought about the demise of the mounted knight as a power on the battlefield, and thus assisted in the complex process which was ending his political and social dominance as well. Yet once the worth of their military systems had been established, both nations rested on their arms. It was left largely to other states to develop the weapons which administered the final *coup* to the inner defense of feudalism, the castle, and to the infantry of England and Switzerland as well.

The development of weapons using gunpowder, after its reputed discovery by Roger Bacon in 1249, was exceedingly slow. Crude artillery made its appearance in the fourteenth century but, aside from the usual reluctance of soldiers committed to the prevailing weapons to accept a new one, it suffered from many technical defects. There was a distinct element of danger in the career of artillerymen, for the behavior of early pieces was at best unpredictable. Frequent confusion as to the mixture and handling of gunpowder, a very slow rate of fire, the lack of aiming devices, and the ineffectiveness of early solid shot against stone walls contributed to the minor role which gunpowder played in the wars of the fourteenth century. Froissart noted that the three cannons displayed by Edward III at Crécy served only to frighten the horses; as late as 1418 Henry V, despite his possession of artillery, took six months to capture Rouen. The employment of field artillery was long hampered by its immobility; the early culverin, a field-piece with a one- to three-inch bore, was mounted on clumsy wooden sledges until about the middle of the fifteenth century, when wheels were substituted. The French were able to bring their culverins into play at Formigny only because of the stationary position taken up by the English. An interesting attempt to lend mobility to the new arms was conceived by the Hussite general, John Ziska, who mounted artillery in armored carts and employed these rudimentary tanks with considerable success against the armies of Catholic Germany (1420-30).

The most important single effect of the introduction of gunpowder during the later Middle Ages was in the sphere of siegecraft. Improvements in the casting of barrels, growing experience in the use of gunpowder, and the appearance of professional civilian artillerymen meant a higher level of gunnery and a heavier weight of shot. John Ziska's weapons included great bombards which threw stone or metal projectiles up to one hundred pounds in weight; by the end of the century more ponderous shot was not uncommon. The new artillery rendered obsolete the stone castle, and with it the last shreds of military prestige enjoyed by the medieval knight. In forty days in 1453, Turkish artillery destroyed the immense walls of Constantinople, walls that had remained impregnable for a millennium. Many lesser fortresses throughout Europe suffered the same fate in the same era. The costliness of the new weapons meant that of necessity they would find their widest employment in royal hands, and so gunpowder became yet another factor assisting the rise of centralized national monarchies. It was the alliance of gunpowder with the other resources of the national state that was to produce the recognizable beginnings of modern warfare in the sixteenth century.

7

The Beginnings of Modern Warfare and Modern Armies

In 1494, King Charles VIII of France led an army of 30,000 men across the Alps into Italy. His professed aim was the capture of Naples in preparation for a crusade to the Holy Land. This wild venture marked the beginning of a new military era in which crusading, like all other medieval forms of war, had no place.

In the beginning, the march of the French down the peninsula was a military parade. Italy was hopelessly divided; her soldiers had no patriotic spirit; and the French had superior weapons. The Italians were stricken with awe by the great French train of horse-drawn bronze cannon which could keep up with the infantry on the march and in battle. Their own iron cannon, dragged laboriously by oxen, were much more cumbersome. But they were even more horrified by the military practices of the French. The "barbarians" from across the Alps fought to kill. The *condottieri,* and the cautious operations which they had substituted for real fighting, were shown to be more fit for comic opera than for the drama of war. On their march south, the invaders cowed the Italian armies; and if the French campaign ended ingloriously a year later, the victor was disease rather than the Italians. In 1495, at Fornovo when the French were fighting their way back, the Italian men-at-arms were routed by the French mounted *gendarmerie* and the French artillery. The next day, the Italian commander, the Marquis of Mantua, coming to ransom his friends and relatives, found to his horror that they had all been killed in battle. A new age had dawned.

Charles VIII's Italian escapade demonstrated clearly the power of new forces operating in society and in war. The French, through the use of improved artillery, had a decided technological advantage; but gunpowder had thus become a decisive element in warfare just at a time when a socio-political revolution was occurring. The Italian city-states, for all the wealth and culture they had garnered from their trade with the East, were no match for the new political organism, the nation-state, which had slowly evolved from feudal monarchies in England, France, Spain, and Portugal. In these new states, the centralization of power in the hands of the king had placed at his command the growing wealth of the new middle classes as well as of the old feudal landowners. In the course of the sixteenth and seventeenth centuries great merchants like the Fuggers in Germany, Burlamachi in England, and de Geer in Holland were prepared to manage royal financial transactions and to lend large sums on the credit of the state; men with financial experience in commerce served in royal treasuries and introduced new methods; new forms of taxation funnelled wealth into the coffers of the state; monarchs like Henry VII and Elizabeth of England and Isabella of Castile and Spain and first ministers like the Duc de Sully in France showed themselves fully aware of the power of a full royal treasury and of the value of a busy commerce and a flourishing agriculture. Columbus's discovery of America had preceded Charles VIII's invasion of Italy by only two years; and Vasco da Gama brought the first spices from India by sea three years after it. The superiority of the modern nation-state over the late medieval city-state had been demonstrated even before the opening of oceanic sea-routes transferred economic power from Italy to Portugal and Spain, and later to France, England, and Holland, and greatly increased the paramountcy of the rulers of those countries.

The real nature of the new forces operating in society and of their effect on warfare was clearly expressed for the first time in the writings of Niccolo Machiavelli (1469-1527), who became the Secretary of the Council of Ten of the city of Florence soon after the French invasions. In his book on the *Art of War,* and even more in his work entitled *The Prince,* which has sometimes been described as the first book on modern political science, Machiavelli was the first man to write about the significance of modern warfare and to portray it accurately. Machiavelli discussed the new weapons and the problems arising out of their use, though on the details of weapon development he was often wrong. Thus he believed that artillery would never be of more use than to scare peasants, that the day of cavalry was over, that infantry would always be used in large units, and that the sword would replace the pike. These mistaken opinions are explained partly by his lack of actual military experience; in his youth he had seen the clumsy field-pieces of the *condottieri* and despised them. They are also partly explained by his passion for classical models and all things Roman; like many another modern writer on war, he was a disciple of Vegetius. But his errors in forecasting trends in tactics and weapon development merely show that even the most acute observer may be wrong in such details. They do not detract from his stature as the first interpreter of the nature of modern politics and war.

Machiavelli's aim in his writings was twofold. In the first place he wrote his book *The Prince* for the deliberate purpose of ingratiating himself with the rulers of Florence, the Medici, to regain his office, which he had lost in a revolution. Secondly, he wished to see Italy restored to independence and power, and he believed that this could be achieved only by the unification of the country under a prince. Disgusted with the behavior of mercenaries, he advocated the recruiting of a national army of citizens, and he declared that only a powerful monarch, of the kind already found in other states, could revive Italy's glory.

It was this search for the secret of political power which led him to his revolutionary discoveries about politics, the nature of the state, and the significance of war. Whereas medieval writers had stressed that political affairs were subject to overriding moral considerations, Machiavelli divorced politics from morality altogether and claimed that success was based on force. Peace within the state was maintained by police power; and war was a natural condition in the relations between states. "A prince ought to have no other aim or thought than war." He comprehended the nature of the sovereign nation-state and argued that its existence must depend, in the last resort, on strength in war. He poured scorn on the limited warfare of the Italy of his day and showed that when states fight for their existence there can be no limitation. Nor could the Prince be limited by any moral consideration, either in his relation with other states or with his own people. Expediency must be his sole guide.

Machiavelli's ideas denied the existence of a universal Christian political society and hence were shocking to men whose whole intellectual background was based on the premise of such a society. Machiavelli, a child of humanism, believed that humanistic scholarship based on the interpretation of history could shape policy. He correctly diagnosed that the national state was largely independent of any external control; and he also provided a textbook for princes, autocrats, and dictators which seemed to imply that success had no relation to morality. His direct influence on rulers in the following centuries—for instance, on Henry IV of France, who is said to have had a copy of *The Prince* on his person when he was assassinated—has often been noticed. His contribution to the growth of despotism is thus generally recognized but, although succeeding generations saw him as a wicked influence, today he is more often regarded as one of the first amoral realists among political thinkers.

Machiavelli drew his conclusions from a study of the political society to which he belonged. His realization of the strength of the nation-state came from actual contact with the new monarchies when on diplomatic missions. His understanding of the fundamental principles underlying international relations he obtained from his knowledge of the relations among the city-states of Italy. It was not without significance that his ideal prince probably was modelled on Cesare Borgia, one of the arch-scoundrels of history. Thus, Machiavelli was recording, as well as reflecting, the decline of public morality. Two years before his death there occurred a shocking event, the sack of Rome, the chief city of Christendom, by the troops of the Emperor Charles V, the nominal head of Christendom. Here was a dramatic symbol that the older order had passed and that in the new day the old standards and the old authorities would be lost. War threatened the very foundations of western culture.

The imperial army that sacked Rome in 1527 is said to have included many Germans who had already accepted the doctrines of Luther. The Protestant revolt that split medieval Christendom in the sixteenth century did not create the modern national state and modern international strife; but it undoubtedly expedited them. The assumption of a fuller control over religious and ecclesiastical affairs rounded out the omnipotence of national monarchs. In England, Henry VIII became supreme head of the church and an example for Protestant rulers everywhere; but even in countries which remained within the fold, monarchs began to assume a greater power to interfere in the affairs of the Church.

The Reformation, directly or indirectly, ensured that the sovereignty and independence of national states was subject to no external or internal limitation.

Meanwhile events had been drawing all parts of Europe into international conflict. The French king, Charles VIII, and his successors strove until 1559 to conquer parts of Italy, first Naples and later Milan. Their persistent determination inevitably brought them into conflict with the Austrian Habsburgs who, as Holy Roman Emperors, had traditional claims to suzerainty over northern Italy, and also with the monarchs of the newly created kingdom of Spain, who had inherited interests in Naples. When all these dominions became united under Charles of Habsburg, who was elected Holy Roman Emperor Charles V in 1519, the Franco-Habsburg struggle enmeshed nearly all Europe. For Charles not only ruled lands which encircled France, but also aspired to lead Christendom as his medieval predecessors once had done.

The French hunger for Italy, and Charles's dream of empire, had important consequences in the history of warfare. In the fifteenth century wars had been fought in different parts of Europe, between the French and the English, among the various Iberian states, among the Italian city-states, among the Czechs, Germans, and Hungarians, between the Turks and their Christian neighbors, between the Danes and the Swedes, and between the Swiss and the Emperor, but all these conflicts had been insulated from one another. In the sixteenth century, war became pan-European in its impact. Hence, the various types of troops which had developed in relative isolation in various parts of Europe--the Swiss pikemen, the German *Landsknechte* trained by the Emperor on Swiss lines, the Italian *condottieri,* the light horse "genitors" and the sword and buckler infantry of Spain, and the heavy mounted *gendarmerie* of the *compagnies d'ordonnance* of France—were thrown together into conflict just at the time when national antagonisms, made more bitter by religious differences, were ensuring the extension and prolongation of warfare. At the same time, the use of gunpowder in artillery and in small arms was creating new problems for the tactician which could only be settled in the crucible of war. Continual warfare made the sixteenth century a period of trial and experiment in which weapons developed rapidly and in which tactics changed with them, no one arm having primacy.

The basic problem to be settled was how gunpowder would affect the relative importance of the various military arms and how it could best be employed. During this century and the next, methods of combining the firepower of shot with the defensive strength of the pike phalanx were worked out; cavalry tactics were adapted to the new warfare; artillery began to play a more important part in both the field and the siege; defensive works were adapted to meet new conditions; and the "new monarchies" experimented with professional standing armies which could serve them more efficiently than older military organizations.

The battles in the first quarter of the sixteenth century proved that firearms would dominate future battlefields. Although Fornovo (1495) was won by Charles VIII's heavy cavalry and Novara (1513) was a victory for the old-style phalanx of pikes, at Marignano (1515) the Swiss echelon of pike columns was brought to a halt and to defeat by a combination of cavalry charges and artillery bombardment. It is probable that the artillery would have triumphed on the latter field even without the aid of cavalry charges. La Bicocca (1525) was won by arquebus fire from entrenchments. At Pavia (1525), after both sides had been dug in for three days, a surprise Imperialist flank attack drew both armies out of their trenches and Charles V's arquebusiers shot down the French cavalry as they came piecemeal to the attack.

However, as is usual, the lessons of war were by no means so clear then as they are in retrospect. The adoption of firearms was therefore comparatively slow, partly because of their cost, partly because of the conservatism of soldiers whose pride in traditional weapons is an important source of morale and therefore of fighting strength, but also because the older weapons still had a part to play. While the French had led in the development of artillery, they were strangely slow to adopt the arquebus. This was a handgun with a crook, or butt, for the shoulder, which was fired by a slow-burning match fixed to a cock and trigger and which, when light enough to be easily handled, fired a bullet of less than an ounce for about 200 yards. French kings preferred to recruit Swiss mercenaries trained for pike warfare. Only after Pavia did they begin systematically to increase the number of "shot" in their infantry.

The English, whose traditional weapons were the bill and the longbow, were even slower to turn to firearms and the pike. Henry VIII (1509-47) recruited Swiss pikemen for his continental wars, presumably because the eighteen-foot pike was better than the bill for holding off cavalry. But it was not until 1595 that

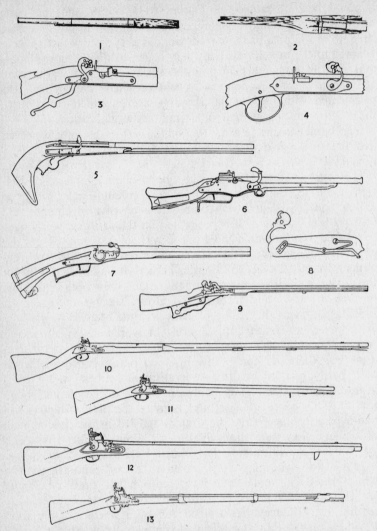

EARLY FIREARMS—1. A hand gun of the fifteenth century. 2. A hand cannon of the same period. 3. & 4. Matchlocks. 5. & 6. Sixteenth-century arquebuses with matchlocks. 7. Wheel-lock arquebus, *ca.* 1590. 8. The trigger mechanism of the matchlock. 9. Snaphaunce gun, *ca.* 1610. 10. Long-barrelled flintlock gun, *ca.* 1660. 11. English "Brown Bess" flintlock musket. 12. A late-eighteenth-century flintlock with a recoil block beneath the barrel for firing from a wall. 13. The continental type of flintlock musket.—(From Major H. B. C. Pollard, *A History of Firearms*, Geoffrey Bles, London, 1930.)

a Privy Council ordinance finally declared that the longbow was not a suitable weapon for the English militia. This delay was not merely due to empty conservatism. When handled by an expert, the longbow was superior in range and penetrating power to the arquebus and much less dangerous to the user.

It was the Spaniards who, at the beginning of the century, led the way in the use of the arquebus. Gonsalvo of Cordova, *El Gran Capitan,* first worked out tactics in which "shot" in field entrenchments played an important part against cavalry. However, influenced by the prevailing interest in classical studies, Gonsalvo also attempted to recreate the Roman legion by introducing sword and buckler men, a step which his contemporary, Machiavelli, heartily approved. But this development was short-lived. Only pikes could hold off cavalry charges. Although most men preferred the arquebus to the pike, the "shot" were defenseless in the open when enemy horsemen were at hand. The big problem for the tacticians, therefore, was to work out a combination of pikemen and shot which could operate together. Swiss experience had shown that the secret of using the pike was a tight, heavy formation and thorough drill. Introducing shot among the pikes weakened this formation. Tacticians therefore at first placed the arquebusiers on the wings or in front of the great phalanx of pikes. They could retire behind or beneath the pikes when threatened.

In the sixteenth century, mercenaries were usually recruited in companies which varied, according to time and place, from 100 men to 250. As early as 1505, the Spaniards began to group four or five companies together under a colonel, although at first only for organization and administration on the march. By 1534, they developed the *tercio,* a tactical unit of 3000 men armed with pikes and arquebuses, which was a sixteenth-century Spanish variation of the fifteenth-century Swiss pike phalanx. About the same time, the French introduced a "regiment" of similar size. These massive formations came to dominate the battlefields of the mid-century.

The French continued to rely for their infantry chiefly upon hired Swiss mercenaries, while Spain, although following the sixteenth-century practice of building up armies by hiring men from different countries to use their traditional weapons, at the same time developed its own infantry. Recruited from the mass of the Spanish population, paid for by American gold, and trained and disciplined much like the Swiss, the Spanish infantry developed a morale and a prestige which gave it mastery. The story of the triumphs of small numbers of Spanish infantry over much larger numbers of Dutch during the revolt in the Netherlands (1568-1609) is a vindication of the combination of professional training and patriotic morale. Spain dominated the sixteenth century because she was enormously wealthy and could maintain during wartime a great professional army.

During the second quarter of the century, generals became more cautious and resorted more frequently to siege warfare. Thus there was ample opportunity for siege and defense methods to be adapted to the new weapons. In the previous century, the fall of Constantinople and the expulsion of the English from their castles in Guienne had seemed to spell the end of strongholds and walled towns. But in the sixteenth century the engineer got his revenge on the gunner. The science of fortification developed rapidly. Since high walls could be easily battered down by heavy artillery, fortifications went into the ground. Low walls, shielded by a ditch and a glacis and backed by earth, became the rule. Italian mathematicians took the lead in working out angles of fire; heavily gunned bastions gave a maximum cross fire. Medieval city walls were replaced by this type of defense. The castle gave way to the fort. For a time artillery was checked by the more rapid development of the art of fortification.

In the second half of the sixteenth century, society and warfare were alike dominated by the shattering impact of the Reformation. The dynastic struggles between the Kings of France and the Habsburgs of Germany and Spain had hardly been brought to a halt in 1559 by the Treaty of Cateau-Cambresis when religious wars, which had already raged in Germany, broke out like a rash all over Europe. The intensity of the passions which religious fervor aroused embittered international antagonisms. Religion was often a basic cause of conflict and was as often a cloak for other motives. Ideological warfare meant that all restraints were cast off; in the name of sacred causes war became more ruthless and "unlimited." At the same time men who would not normally have been engaged in war took up arms in defense of their beliefs. The most important groups affected in this way were the middle classes in the towns whose commercial interests usually engrossed their attention. Religious strife, and to a lesser extent patriotic nationalism, swelled armies with elements very different from the normal type of mercenary soldier. When the religious wars ended and the fanatical citizen-soldiers returned to their homes, professional soldiers were left to fill the new armies which the religious wars had created.

The most important of these religious upheavals were the long civil wars in France brought on by the weakness of the sons of Henry II and the determination of the Mother-Regent, Catherine de Medici, to protect their patrimony against ambitious nobles who threatened it in the name of religion. A little later the patriotic and religious revolt of the Netherlands against the grim rule of Philip II of Spain began a long-drawn-out struggle that did not end until 1609, by which time geography and military engineering had decided that the northeastern portion, which could be defended by water, would become Protestant and independent Holland, while the southwestern half, now known as Belgium, would remain Catholic and be for two more centuries subject to Habsburg rule.

Sixteenth-century armies continued to include large numbers of mercenaries, but there was a strong tendency toward the standardization of tactical methods and of army organization. In place of massive formations like the Spanish *tercio* and the so-called regiment of Francis I, the true regiment began to appear, and within each of its four or five companies there were pikes and arquebuses. The shot were no longer attached as ancillaries to great phalanxes of pikes. Tactics were worked out by which pike and arquebus gave each other support; and the proportion of shot steadily increased. Gradually the arquebus was seconded by the more efficient musket, a heavier weapon that had to be fired from a rest but that could project a missile as heavy as two and a half ounces. For a long time the musket was not popular because it was heavy to carry and took fifty-six drill movements to reload. After the piece had been fired, the musket-rest was an embarrasment for which the musketeer really needed a third hand. But the musket was so much more effective than the arquebus that it was inevitable that it should replace it. Maurice of Nassau (1561-1625) used pikemen and musketeers in formations of about 250 men ten ranks deep, with the musketeers on the flanks. After each man had discharged his piece, he retired through the ranks to reload.

As Machiavelli noted, cavalry was declining in importance at the beginning of the sixteenth century; but it had regained some of its former importance before the century closed. The growing use of muskets among the pikes made cavalry shock charges even more hazardous operations than they had been against the Swiss phalanx;

CAVALRY AGAINST INFANTRY. —(From *Instruction des Principes . . .
de la Cavallerie,* Zutphen, 1621.)

so cavalry also began to use firearms. The firelock was difficult to
use on horseback but the invention of the wheel lock, a gun with
a revolving wheel which struck sparks against a piece of metal to
explode the charge, gave the horseman a satisfactory weapon. The
wheel lock was too delicate an apparatus to be used on the infantry musket, but in the sixteenth century it was widely adopted
for cavalry pistols, two of which the horseman could carry in hol-
sters with sometimes a third in his boot-top. The result of the
introduction of pistols was that cavalry began to avoid shock
action and to rely on a tactical device known as the caracole, in
which the horses fought in heavy columns instead of *en haye* (in
line) in the traditional fashion. The front rank of the column, when
near enough to the enemy, discharged its pistols and retired to
reload. Each rank in turn followed suit. Thus, while cavalry declined in importance as a shock unit, it continued to be a valuable
auxiliary. It also continued to be used for reconnaissance.

Perhaps the most significant development in armies in the latter
part of the sixteenth century was the appearance of a modern rank
structure and chain of command and of the ranks that have now
became familiar. The basic unit, the company, was commanded

by a captain. His lieutenant, or second-in-command, took his place when he was a casualty or absent. The command of several companies went to a colonel, who had a lieutenant colonel under him, usually one of the senior captains. The sixteenth-century "sergeant major" was a regimental officer, senior to the captain, and was responsible for the ordering of the regiment in battle array. As the title "sergeant major" was already associated with non-commissioned rank, the first part of the name was soon dropped and the sergeant major became a major. Sergeants and corporals also appeared in the sixteenth century within the company. In charge of the army as a whole there was a lieutenant general who deputized for the sovereign who was, in theory, the commanding general. The lieutenant general had a deputy who was known by the peculiar title of "sergeant-major-general," later abbreviated to major general. He was responsible for drawing up the army in battle order and thus performed the same function as the "sergeant major," but at a higher level.

By the end of the sixteenth century, captains were usually "commissioned" by the sovereign and there thus appeared the nucleus of an officer corps. But the army was still far from being a "national" army in the fullest sense. Its pay was irregular and its food supply was at the mercy of greedy private contractors. Part of its clothing, powder, and rations were deducted from the soldier's pay. Often, as in Queen Elizabeth's expeditionary forces, the company was run by the captain as if it were a private business concern. If the captain were dishonest he could make a fortune at the expense of the state and of his men by returning false musters or by trafficking in their necessaries. Armies were recruited for single campaigns; but disease and desertion, even more than casualties, often decimated them long before the campaigning season ended.

The Thirty Years' War (1618-48) saw further steps in the development of the art of war and in military organization. It began as a renewal of the religious warfare in Germany, but it rapidly drew in many of the great powers of Europe and soon became another round in the great struggle between the kings of France and the Habsburg rulers of Spain and Germany. Thus, although this war had its roots deep in the bitter religious conflicts of the past, it was in fact a naked struggle for European empire and power. Catholic France, led by a Cardinal, Richelieu, was allied with the Protestant Princes of Germany and the Protestant King of Sweden against the Holy Roman Emperor. The motives of the contestants rapidly became divorced from any real religious feeling, but the ruthlessness and ferocity which went with ideological warfare remained. The sack of Magdeburg in 1630, with the slaughter of 30,000 Saxons, was the most savage of many similar incidents. The combination of Machiavellian politics and religious fanaticism seemed likely to bring the destruction of society. After a generation of such conflict in Germany, which was the battlefield of Europe, that country was left devastated and large areas were completely depopulated. The Thirty Years' War, and the deep wounds it inflicted, increased German disunity. Germany, like Italy, was only a geographical expression until the nineteenth century.

Such was the nature of the war which saw the emergence of what is often claimed to be the first modern army. It came, not in one of the more advanced and wealthy states of the Atlantic seaboard, but in Sweden. National spirit, generated by the winning of freedom from the kings of Denmark in 1523, by the decline of the Hanseatic League's control of Baltic trade, and by Protestantism, was responsible for the rise of Protestant Sweden in the early seventeenth century. But the greatest factor in bringing Sweden to the fore and in maintaining her place as a great power was the ability of King Gustavus Adolphus and some of his successors. Gustavus was a pioneer in military technological development and was at the same time able to take full advantage of the national and religious fervor of his subjects. He not only was a great tactician and a capable strategist; he also realized how to fashion a new army in keeping with the developments of his time. He built up a cohesive and fervent fighting machine of a modern type in place of the customary collection of companies of hired mercenaries and palace guards.

Sweden had retained the medieval *levée en masse* which had virtually died out on the continent of Europe. Gustavus used this national obligation of military service for defense as a means of building up an army for overseas campaigns. He thus adopted a technique by which Elizabeth of England before him had used the militia to recruit ne'er-do-wells for overseas expeditions. But he did it much more thoroughly. Elizabeth's companies were collected by the Lords-Lieutenant and the Justices of the Peace in the various counties; but once transported overseas the companies lost all identification and connection with the county of their origin and became attached to professional captains, who might well be from distant parts of England. Gustavus, similarly, recruited his armies for the invasion of Germany on a territorial basis, but he also arranged that they should be fed regularly with reinforcements from the same source. Thus, although lacking the deep purse which had enabled Philip of Spain a generation earlier to maintain his *tercios* for long periods in the field, Gustavus fashioned a fighting machine which was more permanent.

While the Swedes still made use of foreign mercenaries—for instance, Irish and Scots—these served as individuals. Foreigners were absorbed into Swedish units and were no longer hired in companies with professional mercenary captains. Foreign officers were, for convenience, usually employed in units that held a number of their compatriots. But the army which Gustavus led into Germany was a national professional standing army. Its virtues were revealed in its discipline and in the proportion of fighting men which it contained. Whereas most armies of the day included hordes of camp followers who sometimes far outnumbered the soldiers, the Swedes marched without them; as a result, their efficiency on the march and in war was greatly increased.

Gustavus's genius showed itself in every aspect of war. He further increased the mobility of his armies by reducing the weight of the weapons which the soldier carried. The heavy wooden rest, which had long encumbered the musketeer, was replaced by a lighter iron spike. The musketeer was thus enabled to carry a sword. When attacked he could now defend himself with the sword and also, if necessary, with his rest. Eventually a lighter musket was introduced and the rest was abolished altogether. A paper cartridge had been introduced earlier. Gustavus made it standard equipment. As the musketeer simply bit off the end of the cartridge and rammed it home, the movements necessary for reloading were greatly reduced in number and fire power was proportionally increased. As a result, battle-drill was altered. Instead of the old ten-rank formation, the Swedes introduced a three-rank formation in which all three ranks fired together. The front rank knelt and the others stood upright. Sometimes a second set of three ranks was stationed immediately behind in close support. Thus the Swedes were responsible for perfecting the technique of those deadly volleys which were to advance infantry to primacy on the field of battle by the eighteenth century. While the smoothbore musket was accurate only at the short range of about fifty yards, the bloody carnage caused by the volley at close quarters was frightful.

One significant result of the increase of infantry fire power was the decline of the pike. The weapon itself was shortened and the proportion of pikemen among the infantry was greatly reduced. Hence the great pike phalanxes which had been a feature of all armies since the great days of the Swiss pikemen in the fifteenth century began to disappear from the order of battle. But until the end of the seventeenth century groups of pikemen were still diffused among the musketeers.

Another significant change was the abandonment of armor. Iron corselets gave too little protection against the increasing effectiveness of muskets and increased the extent of wounds. It is said that the Swedish musketeers began to go into battle without their armor because Gustavus himself, finding that his armor hurt an old wound, had abandoned it. Only the pot-helmet, the predecessor of the modern steel helmet, was retained. As a result, the musketeers gained greatly in mobility. Nevertheless, pikemen and cavalrymen continued for a long time to wear the cuirass or breastplate, partly through conservatism, and partly because their close tactics gave them more need of such protection.

Gustavus also made reforms in his battle array. The small company of a hundred to two hundred men had long existed as an administrative unit. In battle, companies had usually been joined together into an inflexible phalanx like the Spanish *tercio* of three thousand men. Gustavus split his forces up into "divisions" (more properly battalions or battle-groups) of four or five hundred men. These formations could be maneuvered more freely; and they were less vulnerable to artillery fire.

At the same time Gustavus revitalized the cavalry so that it became once more a decisive force on the battlefield. He insisted on resort to shock attacks with the sword and on the use of the pistol only at very close quarters. Thus he revived the use of cavalry as shock troops and checked the prevailing tendency to resort to the caracole. Furthermore, he introduced the first dragoons, mounted infantry who served as light cavalry in the attack but reverted to infantry in defense.

Gustavus greatly simplified the artillery, which at that time included a confusing number of types, by adopting three standard guns, siege, field, and regimental. The weight of the guns was reduced. The regimental piece, a four-pounder four feet long, was a thousand pounds lighter than those used in other armies of that day. Gustavus also introduced the first artillery cartridge and thus not only made the handling of ammunition much safer but actually made the artillery rate of fire higher than that of the infantry. His regimental gun was mounted on a gun carriage and could be dragged by a single horse. Although the gunners were still civilians, they were placed under army officers. Lastly, the proportion of artillery in the Swedish armies was greatly increased.

Gustavus's reforms were justified at the battle of Breitenfeld (1631) when he defeated the Imperial general, Tilly, largely because of the superior mobility of his new battle-groups of musketeers and pikemen, which he coordinated very successfully with artillery and cavalry. But his greatness as a tactician must not be allowed to obscure his ability as a strategist. Greater mobility gave him an advantage in this sphere also. Before embarking on his great campaign to destroy Catholic power in Germany, he first secured a firm base in Pomerania on the coast of the Baltic, opposite Sweden. Once that was done he marched rapidly, sought battle eagerly, planned his line of march and of attack with a view to future operations, and endeavored to coordinate the operations of armies in different parts of the country. It is possible that, if he had not been killed at Lützen, Gustavus's military genius, and his new type of army, might have enabled him to conquer for Sweden the greater part of Germany. As it was, the Baltic became a Swedish lake for a century. His methods, and especially his army organization, were admired and promptly imitated throughout Europe.

When civil war in England broke out in 1642, after the constitutional and religious dispute between the King and Parliament, English and Scots soldiers of fortune carried Gustavus's ideas to Britain. In the first year of the war, both sides relied on calling out the county militias which were little better than rabbles. King Charles I had an initial advantage because the landowning nobility provided him with the nucleus of a mounted force. The Royalist cavalry was entrusted to Prince Rupert, a young man with experience in the Thirty Years' War, who trained his men to break into the opposing forces before using their pistols.

But Parliament held London and the southeast the richest part of the country and the most predominantly Puritan. The trainbands of the City were the most nearly efficient militia forces in

England at the outset of the war; and the citizens were prepared to fight what they believed were Romish tendencies in royal ecclesiastical policy. The flourishing gentry of the Eastern Counties had likewise been strongly influenced by continental Protestantism. One of these was Oliver Cromwell, who trained a Parliamentary cavalry force, the Ironsides, to overcome the hard-riding cavalry of Rupert. He was not a professional soldier and had nothing like Rupert's experience in war; but at Edgehill (1642), where he had seen the Royalist cavalry drive the Parliamentary horse from the field, he realized that courage and the aggressive spirit were not enough to ensure victory. Discipline and tactical training were needed as well. He therefore insisted upon rigorous training for the horse which he raised for Parliament in the Eastern Counties.

The wealth of the City merchants and of the sheep-farming gentry provided Parliament with funds to raise a long-service professional army called, significantly, the New Model. This, like Cromwell's Ironsides, was driven by religious enthusiasm which gave it a morale superior to that of the Royalists; and yet it was at the same time a highly disciplined force. How far the New Model drew upon Swedish precedents is not clear. All the Civil War armies adopted foreign, and especially Swedish, battle formations; they all employed officers who had served as mercenaries on the continent; but the vital principle of long-service enlistment which was adopted by Parliament may have been an innovation caused by the pressure of circumstances. Whatever its source, the effect was important. The greater military efficiency of the New Model Army defeated both the Royalists and the Scots. Cromwell, as Protector, was the first ruler of England to conquer the whole of the British Isles. His new armies laid the foundations of the British army of the future. Indeed, the Coldstream Guards traces its history directly back to the Puritan armies of the Commonwealth. The traditional scarlet of the British soldier was first worn by the armies of Cromwell. The foundations of a permanent standing army had thus been laid in England by the circumstances of the Civil War.

The victorious Puritans had taken up arms against Charles I's pretensions to rule by "divine right," a political theory derived from medieval precedents but which had been used to bolster a most unmedieval absolutism. One of the irritants which had led to the Civil War was the quartering of royal soldiers in civilian billets, a practice intended to relieve the King of financial worries by avoiding the necessity of resorting to Parliament for funds. However, the New Model and other Puritan armies, raised to defend constitutional liberty, soon in fact destroyed it. They were the armies of a fanatical minority which used them to overthrow Parliament and to force its religious and moral ideals upon a largely unwilling community. When Cromwell divided the country into districts ruled by major generals, the perils of stark military dictatorship were brought home. The country soon yearned for the return of the son of the king it had so recently executed. The restoration of Charles II in 1660 was, however, possible only because the Puritan army had its own unsettled grievances—namely, arrears of pay. The military organization which Cromwell had fashioned had not been fiscally sound. Certificates given to the rankers in lieu of arrears of pay had been bought up at a discount by some of their officers who became war profiteers and parvenu landlords. Thus, an important reason why the military dictatorship collapsed was failure to pay its chief source of support, the army rank and file. Since the end of active warfare, the citizenry had gone back to their shops and their farms, leaving the armies of the Protectorate to purely professional soldiers. Pay was the bond which tied these to the state. When they were not paid the regime fell. When the restored monarchy paid them off, they went peacefully to seek civilian pursuits.

On the continent the growing military strength of monarchy based on permanent royal armies had already shown itself able to withstand any such debacle as the Stuarts experienced. For instance, although weakened by minorities and regencies, the French house of Bourbon had gained in strength and had been able to crush a dangerous revolt, the Frondes (1648-53). Nevertheless, the army was still in need of reform. Its system of supply was riddled with corruption, its regimental organization was chaotic, its pay was irregular, its discipline harsh and capricious.

During the minority of Louis XIV, the Secretary of State for War, Michel le Tellier, set about the reform of the army. Later his son, the Marquis de Louvois, Louis's War Minister, created a civil administration for the affairs of the army and thus gave it a firmer and sounder place within the framework of the state. Through the minister of war the king now exercised as firm a control over the army in peacetime and in winter quarters as he had formerly exercised through his generals while it was on campaign. These developments were in line with the contemporary growth of bureaucracy in other spheres. The seventeenth century saw much expansion of national civil services. The intendancies and the *noblesse de la robe* in France, the Admiralty, customs, and colonial civil services in England, and the civil service in Prussia were all expanding in this period.

At the same time Louvois introduced important reforms within the army itself. Battalions were integrated into permanent regiments and brigades; the grosser swindles in supply were checked; a quartermaster general's department was set up; white uniforms were made standard; the troops were taught to take up stations by word of command instead of having to be laboriously put in place by the sergeant major; a system of inspection established uniformity and obedience throughout the army; and the name of one of the royal inspectors, Martinet, became a byword for rigid discipline. Louvois cut the pattern for the regular army of the future and thus provided the support for the despotic monarchies of the next century.

But Louis could never have fashioned his great armies or fought his many wars had he not been served faithfully by another great minister, Colbert, who put his finances on a sounder footing and, following mercantilistic theory, fostered trade, industry, agriculture, internal communications, colonies, and shipping to increase the wealth of the state. Mercantilism had had its origins in the sixteenth century, when the acquisition of gold- and silver-producing American colonies had brought great wealth and strength to Spain. Money was said to be "the sinews of war." The first mercantilists were "bullionists" who taught that power flowed to princes who discovered mines of precious metals in their own territory or in overseas colonies. Later arrivals in the competition for overseas empire sought always for gold. When they could not find it they often resorted to thinly disguised piracy, as did the Elizabethan sea dogs who preyed upon the galleons of King Philip II of Spain. But economic thinkers soon realized that gold could be accumulated within a country by a favorable balance of trade and by the acquisition of colonies which could produce the exotic staple products now in demand throughout Europe. Hence the power of the state was used to protect industry and agriculture, to control the flow of trade, to acquire and govern colonies, and to foster merchant shipping. The latter policy, of which the English Navigation Acts are the best example, had a closer connection with military strength than other mercantilist regulations as it provided ships and sailors for the navy. But all mercantilist policies were designed deliberately to build up the wealth of a country and pay for standing armies and navies.

It has been argued that the growth of armies and of military organization in this period had a very special bearing on the fashioning of western society. The beginning of large-scale metal industries, without which all material and technical development would have been impossible, has been ascribed to a large extent to the demand for cannon; and the growth of financial enterprises like that of the Fuggers in the sixteenth century and of the great Jewish banking houses of the seventeenth century has been attributed to the demand for loans for military purposes. It has also been suggested that the large-scale military undertakings of the seventeenth century were the first examples of the kind of organization later to be followed in commerce and industry; that the qualities of the military adventurer were those of the "entrepreneur"; and that the "military virtues" of order and discipline were akin to the spirit of the new capitalist world.

Many of these generalizations have been denied. For instance, it has been said that it was the medieval demand for church bells, instruments of peace, and not for bronze cannon, which stimulated mining and metal-working. It must nevertheless be admitted that war, and the preparation for war, was a powerful incentive, even though perhaps not the only one, for the growth of modern industrial, commercial, and financial organization. Gustavus, Louis XIV, and Peter the Great of Russia all founded arsenals which were among the first examples of the factory system. The funding of the national debt and the establishment of the Bank of England, fundamental innovations in state finance of the most profound importance, were direct results of the need for providing ample capital to fight Louis XIV.

By the second half of the seventeenth century, the military systems of the new national states of Western Europe were being fashioned into efficient machines. Long before this time European military superiority had expanded European influence and power into the four corners of the globe. The geographical discoveries of the fifteenth and sixteenth centuries had been made possible by inventions like the mariner's compass, the astrolabe, and ocean-going caravels; but the conquest of overseas territory was only possible because the Europeans had superior weapons and superior military and political organization. The power of the national state, exercised either through viceroys or through chartered trading companies, governed large empires in Asia teeming with native races only a little less easily than it penetrated empty forests and plains in America. In turn, the possession of colonies brought wealth to Western Europe, and to the colonial powers in particular, wealth which could be converted into military strength. Hence, at the time when the states of Europe had been unified, usually by a monarchy, and when their military weapons had been tempered for use, colonial and commercial rivalry was pushing nations into conflict and taking the place of religion as one of the great causes of international strife.

8

The Beginnings of Western Sea Power

The story of the Viking raids provides a prologue, or false dawn, for the history of sea power in the West. In 734 Charles Martel, better known for his triumph over the Moorish vanguard at Tours, crushed the Frisians, who had been the leading maritime people of northern Europe for the previous two centuries. Thus the door was opened to the pagan Scandinavian seafarers at a time when social and population pressures among them encouraged the undertaking of what was to be the last wave of the great Germanic invasions.

One branch of the Vikings drove southeast from Sweden to establish Russia, to lay siege to Constantinople (865), and to penetrate even as far as the shores of the Caspian. But our concern is with the Norwegian and Danish Vikings who concentrated their sea-borne raids on the British Isles and the littoral of western Europe. During the century following the first mention of them in the Anglo-Saxon Chronicle (787), their expeditions increased in size, frequency, and range. Utrecht and Antwerp were burned, Cadiz and Seville sacked, Paris besieged, Ireland overrun, and the centuries-long conflict on English soil launched. At least two major raids extended into the Mediterranean, where cities of southern France, northern Italy (Pisa and Luna), and Morocco were captured. Before the invading Northmen were finally absorbed by the Christian peoples of Europe in the eleventh century, they had wandered far afield to colonize Iceland and Greenland and to fight the Red Indian in the New World.

From such sources as the epic *Beowulf*, the Norse sagas, and archeological findings, scholars have been able to reconstruct the warrior civilization of these people. Though notoriously fierce in battle (they contributed the word "berserk" to the English language), the Vikings contributed nothing to the development of land warfare. Their unique place in history rests on the special advantages that they gained through the use of the sea. Their ships and their seamanship made them the scourge of the West, for their numbers were small. Only at the siege of Paris is a force as large as 40,000 men and 700 ships mentioned, and those numbers are now generally believed to be grossly exaggerated.

The typical Viking warship was an open boat of lapstreak construction about eighty feet long, propelled by sixteen pairs of oars and a square sail on a single mast amidship. In 1893 a replica of such a ship made speeds up to 11 knots under sail while crossing the Atlantic. With her high dragon bow and fine lines, she proved an excellent sea boat. According to the sagas, the largest Viking ship of them all, the Long Serpent, was a 165-foot vessel capable of carrying about 400 men. That was a great king's ship; but smaller vessels, assembled in fleets of a hundred or more, transported the major Viking expeditions.

Plunder was the immediate incentive for the original Viking raids, probably single-ship expeditions conducted by exiled petty nobles and their thanes. One successful raid led to others; richer goals, better protected, required the joining together of raiding groups; blood feuds led to foreign colonization by the more discontented or the more ambitious. Their only major sea fights were among themselves. These battles were forthright and primitive infantry engagements afloat. Their naval tactics had not developed to the skillful maneuvering and ramming practised by the Greeks and Romans. The Vikings simply lashed their ships together, side by side, in one large platform for defense and, when on the offensive, relied on boarding tactics against the flanks of a formation similarly constructed. They met little opposition at sea. According to early English accounts, King Alfred had larger and better ships built and beat back the invader. The subsequent history of Viking successes makes clear, however, that Alfred enjoyed no more than a temporary naval success which the English lacked the power to follow up, for after Alfred's death the Viking raids continued unabated.

Viking navies represent a false dawn of sea power nonetheless, for the Northman's ship, though a good sea boat and resolutely manned, was primarily a vehicle for the transportation of land forces and an adjunct of land warfare. The Vikings did not control the sea in the modern sense of that phrase; rather, by means of their ships, they enjoyed the advantages of a cavalry of the sea, tactical surprise and rapid movement of a limited raiding force. At length, both at home and in the lands they had plundered, the feudal system enveloped the Christianized Vikings in the mainstream of European civilization. The progressive development of medieval sea power in northern waters derives not from the Vikings but from the conversion of the seaworthy, decked merchantman sailer into a man-of-war. For example, and by contrast with the long, fast, open galley-type Viking ship, the fifty-seven vessels which the English Cinque Ports furnished the king under their feudal agreement in the thirteenth century were "round-ships" with a length-to-beam ratio of about 2:1. They were slow, difficult to maneuver, driven by sail, and built and maintained as merchantmen, except as the king might modify them while in his service. At such times, when they had lightweight sterncastles and forecastles added to make them men-of-war, these ships provided superior fighting platforms for the king's crossbowmen and archers. They were, in fact, floating castles, stoutly built for good sea-keeping characteristics and able to withstand the weapons in use in that day.

The Battle of Dover (1217) illustrates the major features of the medieval sea battle. In this encounter a force of sixteen large and twenty lesser English warships—i.e., temporarily converted merchantmen—under Hubert de Burgh, Governor of Dover, fell upon a force of seventy small craft and ten warships carrying 900 troops and supplies to reinforce the French in London. The English came downwind, throwing lime to blind their opponents and raining crossbow bolts. Thus gaining the upper hand, they boarded, cutting down the French sails and trapping the crews under them. The contest was then decided by hand-to-hand fighting. Fewer than a score of the French vessels escaped. Besides being the first naval victory of the English over the French, introducing 600 years of intermittent war at sea between them, the battle provides noteworthy examples of basic principles of naval tactics and strategy. Tactically it was a melee, but so conducted by the English as to wrest victory by the exploitation of an upwind position. Strategically, it suggests an awareness of the potential of sea power. By assailing the enemy's sea-borne communications, de Burgh forced the French to abandon their holdings in England, thus accomplishing with ships what English land power had failed to do.

This pattern of naval warfare continued through the Hundred Years' War with certain refinements, as in the Battle of Sluys (1340), on the Flemish coast. There Edward III with a force of about 20,000 men in 250 ships attacked a French force of equal size. The English enjoyed a slight superiority in the number of heavily armed soldiers and crossbowmen otherwise the two forces were evenly matched. Against a triple French line, the English King advanced with his best ships in the van so arranged that those carrying men-at-arms for boarding could forge ahead between those carrying the crossbowmen, after the latter had engaged from a distance. This combined use of long-range weapons and heavy shock troops exactly paralleled the King's land tactics in method, and with equal success. Edward's strategy in using sea power to take the battle to the enemy revealed the offensive aspect of the naval component in the overall defensive policy of a maritime nation. Englishmen then, like Americans later, learned the advantages of doing their fighting on the other fellow's shores.

Medieval navies in northern European waters departed somewhat from typical feudal organization in two particulars. The first concerned the ships, and the second their crews. Arms could be stored for future use, but a ship cost so much and, when laid up, deteriorated so rapidly that it had to serve a continuing purpose in peace. Thus, as long as warships were converted merchantmen, a country's normal activity determined the size and quality of ships available for naval service in time of war. A king would maintain only a few ships for his own transportation and diplomatic errands; they were his personal property; otherwise he was dependent on levies from his merchant marine. Hence the king granted rights and privileges in order to encourage the merchant class and their trade so that he could obtain more and better ships for his occasional use. Thus, as England was dependent for economic well-being on the wool-trade with the Low Countries, she enjoyed an important advantage in comparative sea power. The second difference arose from the warship's need for experienced shiphandlers as well as fighting men. Unlike the peasant who could drop his plow, obtain his familiar arms from his lord's arsenal, and be off to the war, the ship's officers and the sailors were professionals performing the same duties in peace as in war. Thus it came about that the medieval warship was commanded by the king's representative, a noble, and fought by his men-at-arms, but sailed by the professional merchantman, a "boatswain," and his non-military crew. The weapons were those of land fighting and so were the tactics. As we have seen, battles were won on sea as on land with crossbow artillery and the soldier's spear and sword. Since the warship was a floating, miniature castle, siege weapons and techniques were also adapted for naval use. Of many ingenious contrivances, none was sufficiently successful, however, to challenge boarding as the decisive tactic in sea battles.

Concurrently in the Mediterranean the distinction between sail-propelled merchant ships and oar-propelled warships, dating back to the ancient Greeks, had led to the evolution of the dromon as the standard fighting ship of the Byzantine navy. A typical dromon was about 100 feet overall, with fifty oars to a side arranged in two banks and a single large sail amidships.   There was a sterncastle and a forecastle. On the latter was a bronze tube for throwing Greek fire. These ships, sometimes built much larger, were successful in turning back the Saracen naval attacks on Constantinople, but by the time of the crusades they were being replaced by the galley, a type which continued in limited use as late as the eighteenth century.

Galley warfare constitutes the peculiarly naval part of the story of the Italian Renaissance. The galley type, with oars all on one level, was developed by the Italians and was used by them to convey the treacherous Fourth Crusade which sacked Constantinople (1204), to protect their expanding commerce, to conduct their internecine wars, and finally, in the great battle of Lepanto (1571), to smash the Turkish bid for mastery of the whole Mediterranean.

From its inception as a major fighting ship, the galley, 130 to 160 feet in length, was equipped with a great "spur" extending forward like a bowsprit and intended to break the enemy's *aposti,* or outriggers for the oars, rather than to ram the hull in the fashion of the ancients. At first the rowers were free men or mercenaries; later they were more frequently criminals and slaves, chained for life to their benches. With 100 men or more at the oars, the galley could make a top speed of about 7 knots for a short time; with her great lateen sails, usually two on the larger ships, she might make 12 knots under ideal conditions.

The battle of Lepanto reveals galley warfare at its ultimate stage, influenced by the introduction of gunpowder but otherwise little changed from the land-fighting-at-sea of earlier naval engagements. The opposing forces were almost equal, the Turks being superior

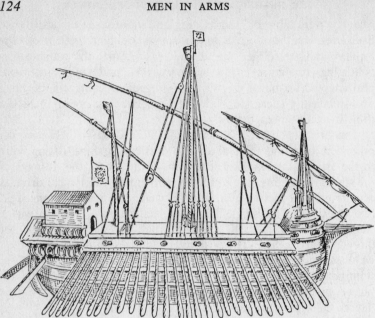

THE GALLEASS, with heavy ordnance superimposed on a modified galley
hull, used at Lepanto (1571), but a dead end in warship design.

in number of ships and men, the Christians in the weight of armor
and armament.

The Christian fleet consisted of about 200 galleys, half of them
Venetian with free men at the oars and the others Spanish ships
rowed by criminals and slaves. Counted as Spanish were the Sicil-
ian, Neapolitan, and Spanish royal galleys as well as 25 mercenaries hired from *assentiste,* the naval equivalent of the *condottieri.* Galley armament included five bow-guns, a 36-pounder
flanked by 9-pounders and 4½-pounders, as well as three 4½-
pounders on each broadside. For hand-to-hand fighting the galleys
carried large numbers of heavily armed and armored infantrymen,
many of them supplied with arquebuses. The rowers were protected
while going into battle by light wooden sideworks (*pavesades*)
and, especially if free men (as on the Venetian galleys that carried
fewer troops), were also supplied with weapons. There were also
six Venetian galleasses, which deserve special mention. This was
a new type of warship built to carry guns. It differed from a galley
in being wider, heavier, and higher of freeboard, with a gun-deck

over the rowers. The armament consisted of 6 guns firing ahead, 6 astern, and 18 on each side, for a total weight of shot of 326 pounds. These ships had fifty oars and required seven men on an oar. At Lepanto, with only four men to an oar, they had to be towed into position. Under the command of Don John of Austria, brother of the King of Spain, the combined Christian fleet carried a total of approximately 70,000 men.

The Turkish fleet numbered 210 galleys, many of them of the largest size, and forty galliots, a somewhat smaller galley type, rowed by Christian slaves. They were armed with only 3 bow-guns, did not use *pavesades,* and carried few arquebusiers, for the Turks had supreme confidence in the more rapid fire of their archers. Their entire force totalled 75,000 men, of whom 25,000 were soldiers. The Christian slaves at the oars were a potential liability, welcoming an opportunity to revolt when a Turkish galley was boarded.

With the two great fleets drawn up in line abreast, the encounter developed much like a land battle of center to center and wing to wing. Ali Pasha, the Turkish commander, took the offensive, sending his ship directly against that of Don John. The force of the Turkish charge was less effective than usual, however, because the Christian leader had placed the galleasses well forward between the opposed battle lines, two each at the center and the left and right wings, like forts around which the Turks had to detour. He had also cut the spur from his ship, as did many of the other Christian leaders, so that the bow-guns could be depressed to fire directly into the oncoming enemy. Although the overwhelming Christian triumph was finally won by hand-to-hand fighting, it is reasonable to conclude that Christian superiority in adapting new weapons to sea warfare supplied the margin of victory.

The course of events immediately after Lepanto illustrates two complementary principles of naval warfare: like fights like, and the proper object of a fleet is the enemy's fleet. The first was illustrated in 1572 by the attempt of the Christians to use twenty-four sailing ships (nefs) to supplement their galleys in an action with the Turkish fleet. The sailing ships with their guns were too formidable for the Turkish galleys to attack and, in turn, too slow to support an attack by the Christian galleys. Future naval fighting in the Mediterranean proved that the galley could usually escape the nef by rowing upwind or by venturing into shallow waters, whereas the armed nef's superiority in fire power and greater weight protected her from the galley. As a consequence, the two were not likely to fight. The second principle was illustrated in a negative fashion by naval policies until 1573, when the desultory war came to an end. The Christians, more interested in immediate personal profit than in the destruction of their enemy after Lepanto, turned aside to territorial expansion. The Venetians signed a secret "free trade" treaty with the Turks; and the Spanish, now that the threat to their own Mediterranean possessions was removed, concentrated their efforts on bringing home great riches in gold and silver across the Western Ocean. The Turks, quickly making good most of their losses and also avoiding naval action, contented themselves with the defense of their land holdings. As a result the Turkish menace remained.

Lepanto marked the end of an age; within seventeen years an entirely new concept of naval warfare was demonstrated in the defeat of the Spanish Armada (1588). The three-masted sailing ship had come into use in the early fifteenth century; such vessels were employed by the Spaniards and Portuguese in the great voyages of discovery. The peoples of northern Europe, quickened by the Renaissance, were the more adept in marrying ships of this type to guns in a union that was to give a new meaning to the term "sea power." The English were the leaders in this naval revolution. They had to share with the Dutch the claim for first place in seamanship and maritime experience, but their island sanctuary permitted them, and at times compelled them, to give priority to naval, rather than military, development. Under Henry VIII, who followed a course of action his father had already indicated, were born both the Royal Navy as a permanent institution, and the prototype ship-of-the-line.

Any history of the organization, administration, personnel, and equipment of the Royal Navy must begin in the sixteenth century. What was unique and also important was the evolution of the sailing warship. There had been little modification of the design of ships from the time of the battle of Sluys until the introduction of naval artillery. The first naval guns were breech-loading man-killers for use in repelling boarders. More and more were added, castles were built higher and higher on stern and bow to make more fighting platforms for guns, and the result was an unhandy, top-heavy vessel with possibly more than two hundred pieces of light ordnance. In actual tests Henry VIII proved the value of the cast, muzzle-loading "Great Gun" as a ship-killing weapon; but its installation required revolutionary changes. To use it, the English invented portholes and the gun-deck, for it was much too heavy to be installed in the castles. Once it had intruded in the cargo space, the differentiation between the functions of warships and merchant ships had an important effect on naval architecture. The length of the ship determined the number of guns that could be installed in a broadside. When gunfire was more important than cargo capacity, beam was incidental and the cumbersome castles could be reduced in size as their functions became secondary. Thus in 1513 the *Mary Rose,* with her increased length-breadth ratio and "Great Guns," became the prototype of the ship-of-the-line. England's new sailing warships, of which Drake's *Revenge* is a good example and Nelson's *Victory* only an improved descendant, combined the three great naval virtues of speed, steadiness as a gun platform, and maneuverability, because of greater length-to-beam, low center of gravity, and decreased windage.

The merits of this new ship as a weapon, and its influence on the tactics of naval warfare, were only partially revealed in the defeat of the Spanish Armada. One question, its superiority to the galley, had been answered by Drake in the spring of 1587. Instructed to "impeach the provisions of Spain," he was using his fleet in that classic role of naval strategy, striking the enemy's fleet and communications far from home. With twenty-five ships, some of them converted merchantmen, he sailed right into Cadiz harbor, spent two days destroying eighteen Spanish ships and taking six prizes, and sailed right out again. Twelve Spanish galleys protecting the port were beaten off by day and by night, whether the English ships were at anchor or under way. "We have now tried by experience these galleys' fight and I assure you," wrote Drake, "that these her Majesty's four ships will make no account of twenty of them in case they might act alone. . . ."

King Philip had had his beard singed too often to be ignorant of what the English could do at sea. The activities of the English sea dogs on the Spanish Main, a nursery of fighting seamen, was a threat to his treasure supply which he could not ignore. When he determined at last to attack England, he planned not a naval encounter but a major amphibious operation, sound in concept except that it called for a degree of cooperation between his land and sea forces, and of resolution in leadership, that was lacking. His main weapon was the famous Spanish infantryman. His soldiers were to board and capture any English ships that interfered with their passage through the narrow waters of the Channel and were then to join Parma's veterans in the Low Countries, cross to the Thames estuary under protection of the fleet, and march triumphantly upon sparsely defended London. For this task Philip collected sixty-four large ships, four galleasses, four galleys, twenty-three supply ships, and thirty-three small craft for dispatch and reconnaissance. Although manned by some 30,000, including over 8,000 sailors and about 19,000 soldiers, the Armada was short-handed, the seamen of poor quality, and the infantry diluted by raw recruits who had never before been to sea.

VESSELS OF THE ARMADA CAMPAIGN *

	English	*Spanish*
Tonnage	17,110	35,508
Men	8,171	15,235
Guns	1600	1350
Broadsides	7,000 lbs.	4,500 lbs.
Ammunition	50 rounds per gun	50 rounds per gun

* These figures have been compiled from data in W. L. Rodgers, *Naval Warfare Under Oars* (Annapolis: 1939). Figures are for the 45 most effective ships in each fleet.

The advantage in tonnage and manpower was with the Spanish, although the largest English ships were about the same size individually as any of the 14 Spanish flagships; but the advantage in armament was with the English, especially in the number of larger guns and the skill of the gunners.

The Armada entered the Channel in a multiple line-abreast formation, reminiscent of galley warfare, and reached Calais after a series of what the Spaniards called "skirmishes." Driven out of the harbor by fireships, the Armada had a final "skirmish" off Gravelines and returned to Spain by going north about Scotland. Of a total of 250 fighting ships on both sides, only thirty English and twenty-five Spanish had engaged. Total English losses in battle were sixty killed; Spanish, 600 killed and 800 wounded.

The defeat of the Armada was a complete strategic victory (the amphibious attack on England was abandoned), and, in spite of the very limited action, a landmark in naval warfare. The Spanish desired to board. The English, with inferiority in size of ships and numbers of men, kept the windward (i.e., westward) position. Taking advantage of their guns, and with their faster, better-handled ships, they were able to do so. Time and again they sailed in against the most windward Spanish ships, discharged a broadside when well beyond grappling range, wore about, came back to discharge their other broadside, and then retreated (ran away, said the Spaniards) to reload their guns. Shortage of ammunition, the fact that most of the heavier English guns were eighteen-pounders (too light to inflict fatal damage), the reluctance of some English ships to follow the leader in attack, and finally, the slow rate of fire (probably not more than two broadsides an hour), prevented a clear-cut tactical victory. During the entire ten-day engagement only three Spanish ships were actually sunk, but the Parthian methods of the English succeeded in demoralizing the Spanish leaders and crews. Unable to close for boarding, the Spaniards were frustrated in every effort to conduct the battle to their advantage. By the time the Armada reached Calais, it was not bringing aid to Parma but asking for it. The Dutch fleet kept Parma's transports blockaded, however, and the two Spanish forces never joined. When fireships drove the Armada from Calais, many ships cut their cables and thereafter lacked ground tackle to keep them off a lee shore. Finally, at Gravelines, where three ships were sunk, two others were disabled and later captured by the Dutch, and damage to hulls and rigging contributed to the loss of many others in the hard weather off the Scottish and Irish coasts. Only about half of the men and ships of the original Armada ever returned to Spain.

The English had achieved their tactical victory by making the outcome hinge upon the weapon in which they were superior. Great-gun fire, not hand-to-hand fighting, would constitute the primary effort in naval warfare in the age of sail. During the seventeenth century English naval power capitalized on the strength, and corrected the weaknesses, that had characterized Lord Howard's fleet in 1588 and in so doing led the way for all other European navies. The weapon had been discovered and it was soon perfected. Drake's *Revenge* had a single gun-deck, by 1610 the *Prince Royal* appeared with two complete gun-decks, and in 1637 the *Sovereign of the Seas* was launched, a true "battleship" of three gun-decks and one hundred great guns. As time passed, the three-deckers were customarily employed as flagships and, with the two-deckers of seventy-four guns, formed the line of battle. Single-deckers of twenty-four or thirty-six guns were known as frigates and became the eyes of the fleet, supplemented by sloops which were smaller vessels with no gun-decks but with all their guns on the weather deck. Vessels became ship-rigged, with three masts carrying square sails, and a fore-and-aft sail on the mizzen (aft) mast. The structural limitations of wood set the top limit of size at about 200 feet, 2,000 tons displacement, and three gun-decks. Ordnance was standardized and the rate of fire improved, with the shot-weight of the most common ship's gun increased to 32 pounds.

The hard-fought Dutch Wars of the century resulted in the development of tactical doctrine published in the form of "fighting instructions" and culminating in the Permanent Fighting Instructions of 1691. The follow-the-leader tactics of 1588 had constituted an almost accidental line-ahead formation which brought the broadside power of the ships against their opponents. In a line-abreast formation, or galley-style warfare, sailing ships would simply mask their own most effective fire power. The line-ahead formation with ships at one-hundred-yard (half cable length) intervals assured that all would engage, particularly if the opposing lines were conterminous, *i.e.* van to van, center to center, and rear to rear. This necessity was driven home by repeated instances in the Dutch Wars, when the lead ships did the fighting and the others hung back. Two schools of tactics developed, the melee-ist and the formalist. To the former belonged those aggressive leaders and innovators of tactics, such as Robert Blake, England's greatest admiral of that century, who desired the minimum of doctrine and the maximum of freedom in making an unforeseen advantage the basis of a great victory. The formalists seemed to be more concerned with fighting in the correct way than with victory. As Charles II's brother, James, Duke of York, Lord High Admiral and later King James II, was a formalist, that school had the greater political power. Formalism was not used in the seventeenth century to avoid conflict. But when the Permanent Fighting Instructions were published, they embodied a rigidity that resulted in ninety years of frustration. The essence of these Instructions was their prejudice in favor of maintaining a strict line-of-battle formation which, in effect, penalized initiative and placed a premium upon playing safe.

The professionalizing of the naval establishment of England under the Protector, Oliver Cromwell, was a natural outgrowth of a permanent navy of specialized ships. Merchant ships might be converted into privateers, but not even a great East Indiaman was a match for a ship-of-the-line. The warship, her officers and crew, her maintenance, and her employment in forwarding the national policy could no longer be left so much to chance. A period of half-solutions was brought to an end by that remarkable diarist, and even more remarkable administrator, Samuel Pepys. The Admiralty, a political body, controlled naval policy; the Navy

Board, a professional body dating from 1546, was assigned to supply and maintain naval materiel. As a secretary to the former and clerk to the latter, Pepys contributed more to establishing proper methods for the successful direction, administration, and organization of the modern Royal Navy than did any other man.

Pepy's work came at a time when it was most needed. Through the long and uncertain course of the Dutch Wars England had defeated her most powerful maritime rival. She was strong in her insularity and now had a navy which could make sea power serve national policy on a world-wide scale. From the time of the Tudors, English statemen had realized that the fisheries were a school for seamen and had encouraged them by legislation. In the Navigation Acts, deliberately directed against Dutch sea power, she had found a means of stimulating her mercantile marine and therefore her naval strength. Through the Navy Board she had the means of maintaining and supplying a navy in peace and of commanding it in the emergency of war. The Board exercised authority over what was by far the largest industrial and commercial organization of the time. It controlled the Royal Dockyards and also the contracts for building and repairing in private yards. From 1683 supply was undertaken by a separate Victualling Board. The Master of the Ordnance, an office dating from 1546, was responsible for guns and powder. These boards and officers, only loosely supervised by the Admiralty, which was concerned with personnel and operations, lasted until 1834 and were the basis for England's sea strength over two and a half centuries.

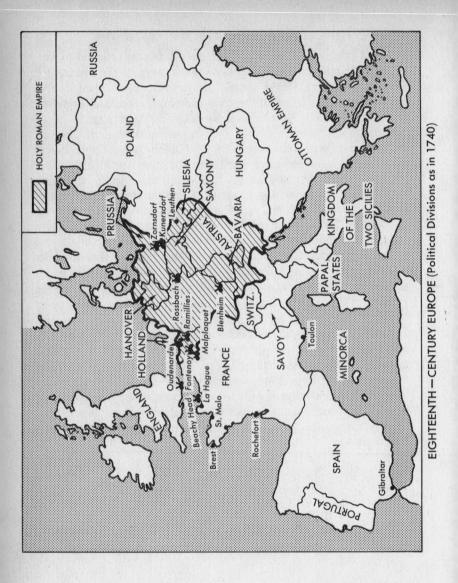

EIGHTEENTH—CENTURY EUROPE (Political Divisions as in 1740)

9

The Limited Warfare of the Eighteenth Century

By the eighteenth century a moderating trend in European warfare had come about as a result of a moral revulsion from the atrocities of the Thirty Years' War and the accompanying realization that war had so ruinous an effect upon the human and material resources of the state that, unless it were curbed, it would cease to be a worthwhile means of achieving political ends. The intellectual climate of the time favored such a moral and rational approach to the problem of war. The fierce religious partisanship which had embittered the wars of the recent past was ebbing away; the old certainties were receding before the onslaught of new, and less immediately inflammatory, ideas. The mathematical genius of Newton (1642-1727) demonstrated the relationship between the behavior of the planets and the law of gravity; and it seemed to his contemporaries that through the application of reason to man himself eternal, immutable laws governing human society could be laid bare. Rationalism was ultimately to be a revolutionary force but the early rationalist reformers were moderates who put their trust in the conversion of established rulers to a philosophy of "enlightenment." The rationalist mistrust of extreme solutions and the emphasis upon practicable and "natural" behavior was an intrinsic element in eighteenth-century life, and left its mark on warfare as it did on other activities.

The eighteenth century was an age which protested its devotion to the proprieties and its dislike of excess, but the term "limited warfare," usually applied to the conflicts of the period from the latter half of the seventeenth century to the outbreak of the French Revolution, conveys a false picture unless correctly interpreted.

It has nothing to do with the frequency of wars, which were more numerous than in the nineteenth century; nor does it refer to the size of field armies or national armies, which were larger and of a more permanent type than in previous centuries. Eighteenth-century warfare, however, was severely limited in the way in which it was fought, and in the objectives that policy-makers sought to gain by its use. In the rationalist era, the belief that all men are entitled by natural law to equal rights took firm root, at least in theory. The best society would be that in which man's natural rights are least interfered with. Hence, one of the most influential by-products of rationalist thought was the humanitarian ideal. Cruelties visited upon civilians in time of war were barbarous infringements upon the rights of humanity. At the same time, the intellectual habit of viewing mankind as a whole was deeply opposed to strident, divisive nationalism. "Patriotism," said Dr. Johnson, "is the last refuge of a scoundrel."

A combination of humanitarianism and internationalism had already led to the first modern attempt to formulate the laws which should govern the conduct of nations toward one another. The Dutch jurist Hugo Grotius, in his *Rights of War and Peace* (1625), treated states as individuals existing in a broader society, the society of nations. The law of nations (*jus gentium*) was equivalent to that regulating relations among individuals; that is, respect for the rights of others and of obligations contracted with them. Bodin and Hobbes put forward the theory of the absolute sovereignty of the state; Grotius insisted that such sovereignty must, in practice, be qualified. If the only law of conduct between nations were the Machiavellian law of the jungle, then international society would inevitably be destroyed. Hence relations among states, in war as well as in peace, must be subject to forms of law.

The legists of the eighteenth century added little to the work of Grotius. The Swiss jurist Vattel emphasized in his *Droit des Gens* (1758) that since war was unfortunately the only means available of obtaining justice, then all wars must be assumed to be just. He warned that the justice of war did not permit the use of any conceivable means to bring victory, for the essential object of war was to gain an equitable and durable peace. For this reason, noncombatants should be protected, not injured, and treaties should be moderate rather than severe.

It is obvious that since no international authority existed to enforce them, the humane and honorable precepts of international law were more a reflection of the spirit of the age than an actual code of conduct for European states. Yet the influence of the philosophers of the enlightenment on the reigning monarchs of Europe was considerable: Voltaire's friendly relations with Frederick the Great of Prussia and Catherine the Great of Russia are cases in point. To have the ear of a king was of the utmost importance, for with the exception of the parliamentary monarchy of Great Britain, the leading states of Europe had become absolute monarchies conforming to the model of the France of Louis XIV. The word of the king was law; the interests of the state were identified with those of the ruler. Royal authority was clothed in the theories of the divine right of kings to rule and of the indivisibility of sovereignty. But the real basis of power was military. The security of a dynasty was closely related to the size and strength of its standing army. The growth of continental standing armies had brought about the suppression of religious and aristocratic opposition. In the eighteenth century the "benevolent despots" ruled absolutely through control of standing armies officered by members of the aristocratic classes who had formerly led opposition to monarchical power. Everywhere, except in Holland and England, this combination of royal and aristocratic military power had ensured the destruction of forms of representative and constitutional government.

The situation in England is illuminating because of the contrast with the growth of royal military power elsewhere. From the Royalist and Roundhead armies, regiments of foot and horse had been established after the Restoration to protect the person of Charles II; but Parliament, reflecting the country's fear of a standing army, was suspicious of even these small forces. James II brought battalions of the Irish establishment to England in an attempt to bolster royal power and his Catholic policy. In the resulting crisis he was deserted by his army; and his daughter Mary and her Protestant Dutch husband, William of Orange, ruled in his stead. The terms of the "Glorious Revolution" established the principle of parliamentary control of military power. Standing armies could not be maintained in time of peace without the consent of Parliament. In time of war the machinery by which this principle was guaranteed was the passage of the Mutiny Act, which, for one year at a time, legalized the disciplinary system of the army. The annual grant of revenues to pay the army was, however, the chief source of parliamentary authority. Thus a method of providing the king with an army for defense without endangering the liberty of the subject had been worked out in England. Elsewhere royal control of the defensive forces of the realm left the crown with unchallenged power within the state.

The fundamental drive behind most of the frequent wars of the eighteenth century was the desire of absolute monarchs to strengthen their position at the expense of other states through the acquisition of territories and population. A second factor leading to wars, particularly those which involved the maritime states with colonial empires, was competition for trade to augment the wealth of the state. According to the mercantilist view, the amount of wealth in the world was constant; the only way, therefore, to increase one's share of it, other than by a favorable import-export balance, was to deprive another state of its colonies or its trade by force of arms. In Austria, Brandenburg-Prussia, and Russia, the power-motive was uppermost. In England and Holland, strongholds of the commercial classes, the mercantilist drive was a major element in foreign policy. France found herself torn between the desire for power on the continent and the necessity of protecting her commercial and imperial interests abroad; while Spain vainly endeavored to maintain her position in Europe and overseas.

The early wars of Louis XIV (the War of Devolution, 1667-68; the Dutch War, 1672-78; the War of the League of Augsburg, 1689-97) have been seen as attempts to expand France to include her "natural frontiers," or as part of a policy of bringing all French-speaking areas under French rule. Neither interpretation is supported by the documents or by events. Throughout his long reign, Louis XIV sought prestige and glory. Both for him and for his nobles, whose chief occupation was war, real glory was to be found only in military victories. Louis's bellicosity brought a succession of anti-French alliances into being. The states of continental Europe feared the rising power of France, and England could not tolerate the control of the trade of the Low Countries and of the shipping of the English Channel by an unfriendly power. The threat to the European balance and to world trade posed by the prospect of a union of the Spanish and French thrones brought the Grand Alliance and the War of the Spanish Succession (1702-13). The terms of the Treaty of Utrecht disclose the motives of the contending states: the thrones of France and Spain were never to be joined, Austria and Brandenburg-Prussia received Spanish territories in Europe, Holland was rewarded with a trade monopoly of the River Scheldt, and England won certain French colonies in North America, Gibraltar and Minorca from Spain, and the exclusive right to trade in slaves and other merchandise on a limited scale with the Spanish colonies. The later wars of the period show the same interplay of motives and interests. The War of Jenkins' Ear (1739) was a commercial struggle waged between England and Spain over the trading rights conceded in the Treaty of Utrecht. It was absorbed into the larger conflict of the War of the Austrian Succession (1740-48). This war was precipitated by the rapacity of Frederick II of Prussia, who seized the province of Silesia when Maria Theresa ascended the throne of Austria. France and Spain joined Prussia in the attack on Austria, and England, while supporting Austria with cash subsidies, took the opportunity to challenge French colonial rule in India and America. The fear of the new Prussian power drove Austria and France, traditional enemies, into alliance, a coalition joined by Russia. As usual, Great Britain benefited from French preoccupation in Europe to make gains abroad, and the result of the Seven Years' War (1756-63) was the loss of most of French India and Canada to England. Meanwhile Prussia, aided by English money, not only survived the war but received permanent title to Silesia.

The essential feature of all these wars was the relatively limited nature of the objective involved, whether dynastic or commercial. Wars were fought to achieve tangible ends which required, not the absolute destruction of an enemy, but rather a military decision favorably affecting the diplomatic bargaining to follow. Moreover, the personal ambitions of a king or the economic interests of a class did not carry the intense emotional appeal necessary to inflame whole populations. Wars in the Age of Reason, while hardly conducted in private, scarcely affected normal peacetime conditions and were participated in by only a very small percentage of the total population.

Limited participation was partly due to the social structure of European armies, which in turn reproduced the social structure of the dynastic state. Throughout Europe, society was headed by a privileged aristocracy exempt from taxation and given the chief offices of state and church in exchange for support of the monarchy. The function of the middle class in the despotic state was to produce wealth and endure taxation, and to bear without complaint its exclusion from political power. Only in England was there little distinction in function between the nobility and the middle class, because only there were the two classes nearly united in the pursuit of the same interests. Nowhere in Europe did the lower classes of town and country have political rights; indeed, in most of continental Europe serfdom was still the status of the peasant.

The sharp distinctions in society were carried over to the army. The officer corps was reserved to the nobility, while the mass of the soldiery was recruited by voluntary enlistment from the peasantry and urban unemployed. The aristocratic nature of the officer corps was the result of deliberate royal policy, for the army provided a convenient means of buying aristocratic support through patronage. This meant, however, that positions were often created to satisfy the clamoring of the nobility; and so the armies of Europe were overloaded with superfluous officers. In the army of Louis XV there were so many that commands were rotated on a day-to-day basis in order to give everyone something to do. In Prussia, Frederick William favored the landowning nobility (*Junkers*) to such a degree that at the end of his reign all officers above the rank of major were noble except three. The exceptions to this class monopoly were necessitated by the fact that a certain amount of technical knowledge was required of artillery and engineering officers. It was this necessity which led to the founding of the first engineering schools of the modern world. (Woolwich founded 1721, re-established 1741; École Militaire 1751; Academy of Engineering, Potsdam 1768). The École Militaire was at first established for sons of impecunious nobles who would submit to the discipline and hard work which a professional career entailed. It is significant, however, that under the Ancien Régime there was a strong tendency for the wealthy nobles to push their way into the college, to shoulder aside their harder-working fellows, and to introduce the standards of idleness and display for which, on the whole, their class was noted. Incidentally, the fact that the officer corps of Europe all belonged to the same caste made for the observance of an aristocratic code of honor which had direct line of descent from feudal knightly chivalry.

Military tradition and class prejudice were not alone responsible for the exclusion of the middle class from positions of command. From the mercantilist point of view, an army was necessary to protect the wealth of the state without making inroads upon it. Therefore the composition of the army was restricted to the "unproductive" classes of the state. For the same mercantilist reasons the rank and file consisted of the lower orders of society. Soldiers were enrolled by voluntary enlistment from the peasant classes and from the urban unemployed. Since enlistment could fill only part of the required quota, every army in Europe employed large numbers of mercenaries. Squads of energetic recruiting officers scoured the countryside, and even foreign countries, seeking to entice the unwary into the service of the king. One-third of the French army prior to the Revolution was German. Seldom has the military career been held in less repute. The lowly origins of the soldiery earned them the contempt of civilians and the distrust of their officers; their heterogeneous national background prevented the development of patriotic feeling. The immense social gulf between the men and their officers made impossible the group solidarity essential to high morale.

The only state to employ a draft for peace time recruiting was Prussia because, while pursuing the foreign policy of a great power, she ranked only twelfth in population in Europe. Two thirds of the Prussian army was recruited from the peasant class, artisans being exempted because their pre-eminent value to the state lay in their productive capacity. By the Seven Years' War, however, other states were also beginning to find it difficult to maintain their armed forces by voluntary enlistment alone. Russia and France resorted to the drafting of peasants only; and Austria and Spain followed suit shortly after.

The harsh discipline for which eighteenth-century armies were notorious was due in part to the untrustworthiness of the men in the ranks. Corporal punishment was resorted to as the best method of obtaining unqualified obedience. In the Prussian army, the most methodically ordered in Europe, an officer had no hesitation in striking a common soldier for the merest infraction of dress or parade regulations. It is not surprising that desertion was endemic in the armies of the period. The provision of barracks, which became almost universal, was done not because of a solicitous regard for the well-being of soldiers, but to lessen the opportunities for escape from service. Almost everywhere he went, the soldier was subjected to the strict supervision of officers and N.C.O.'s.

The nature of battlefield tactics also demanded a close attention to matters of discipline. The bayonet, which first appeared when men plugged knives into the muzzles of their muskets at Ypres in 1647, was given a permanent place in modern armies by the invention of the "ring" or "socket" bayonet in 1678. The flintlock musket, introduced at the end of the seventeenth century, sharply reduced the number of misfires to which the old matchlock had been prone and this made possible a far greater fire power. The musketeer could now defend himself against cavalry; he no longer had need of an ancillary body of pikemen. Within a comparatively short time the pike became obsolete. With the passing of the pike went the deep phalanx or column formation. The three-line formation invented by Gustavus, usually known simply as "the line," was found to be adequate even when infantry had to face cavalry attack, although it should be noted that the infantrymen of Gustavus protected themselves with the "Swedish feather" (a very long pike). For all-round defense against waves of horsemen it was quickly discovered that the "square" of "lines" was the ideal formation. Deployment and maneuver of "the line" for attack and defense necessitated rigorous training, much of which took place on the parade square. The battle drill of the eighteenth century was the origin of modern close-order drill.

There was no room in linear tactics for the exercise of individual initiative. Linear tactics were designed to exploit the new fire power to its fullest extent through the simultaneous volley upon word of command. A meticulous order upon the field of battle was of the highest importance, for if there was the least deviation from the mathematically precise line-arrangement, the musketeers would damage themselves more than the enemy. Prussian officers were reputed to "dress" their companies with surveying instruments; certainly it was not uncommon for troops advancing under fire to halt in order to re-form. Moreover, it was a leading principle of this kind of war, with weapons of very limited range, that to obtain the maximum moral and physical effect upon the enemy, the volley should be withheld as long as possible, and then followed up by a bayonet charge. For troops to expose themselves unflinchingly in the face of enemy muskets and artillery while advancing at the agonizingly slow cadence of eighty paces to the minute required discipline of the very highest kind. Because of tactical necessity and the nature of their troops, the military leaders of the eighteenth century uniformly subscribed to the maxim of Frederick the Great that the purpose of discipline was to teach the soldier to fear his officers more than he did the enemy.

The formal tactics of the line decidedly restricted the potentialities of an army in the field. To marshall an army into battle array was a slow business, and the huge frontage of the linear army required a broad and reasonably level plain. The joining of battle, therefore, could only occur by the tacit consent of two equally confident commanders, since to refuse an engagement merely involved withdrawing to wooded or rough country. Even when battle was given, it was seldom that victory was complete, since the line could not be adapted to a relentless pursuit. Moreover, so great was the fear of desertion during the confusion of a rapid advance that pursuit was officially forbidden in many armies.

Many other factors operated to reduce the frequency of battles. One of these was the heavy casualties that always resulted from the murderous exchange of volleys. In proportion to the numbers taking part, the losses in killed and wounded were much higher in this period than those experienced in other eras. At Malplaquet (1709) the victorious Marlborough lost 33 per cent of his effectives; at Zorndorf (1758) the Russians lost 50 per cent and even the Prussian victors lost 38 per cent; the next year when defeated at Kunersdorf the army of Frederick the Great lost 48 per cent of the men committed. It was natural, therefore, that generals should refuse battle unless circumstances favored them. In war of this sort, battle was the last resort. That this was so was not because heavy losses imposed an unbearable strain upon the nation itself. They did not. The army formed a very small proportion of the total population and was divorced from it. But to train a soldier to meet the exactions of linear warfare represented the work of at least two years; to find a replacement for him was a difficult task in an age when recruiting officers competed fiercely for likely candidates in every country. The professional soldier, though held in contempt as a human being, had cost his king a sizable amount in hard cash to be fashioned into a martial robot.

Not without reason were soldiers called the "toys of kings." Frederick William I of Prussia (1713-40) labored through his entire reign to fashion his army to a state of perfection, yet never once committed it to battle. Even more solicitous was the treatment accorded the "guards" regiments which adorned the military might of every European monarchy. These units, purportedly the crack regiments of the army, were actually designed primarily for show; dressed in the most brilliant uniforms, they played an integral part in the elaborate ceremonial which surrounded the despot. The most useless of these military showpieces was the regiment of "Potsdam Giants," the beloved plaything of Frederick William I. Each man in this unit was over six feet in height; Frederick William's agents toured Europe for lofty prospects; and persons seeking his favor sent him batches of outsize soldiers. Peter the Great alone despatched over two hundred tall Russians as gifts. Frederick William drilled his "Blue Boys" personally; but he could not bear to think of them in action. One of the first acts of Frederick II was to disband the 3,000 giants bequeathed him; but the "guards" tradition itself remained unbroken.

A further check upon the intensity of war was the system of supply in general use. Every command in Europe followed the practice of establishing magazines for food, clothing, ammunition, and other supplies throughout the home territory, and additional depots upon invading another country. The aim was to make the army self-sufficient, not only because the barbarities visited by plundering armies upon civilian populations in past wars offended the humanitarian spirit of the age, but because it was feared that soldiers foraging for themselves would desert in droves. The result of the system was greatly to reduce the mobility of armies. A field force was tied to the distance over which it could carry its bread. Magazines were three days' march apart. "Ovens," supplementary magazines, were set up at one-day intervals. The baggage that accompanied an eighteenth-century army was a formidable item which materially reduced the speed of march and range of action. The soldiery, largely unaffected by ideals, had to be appealed to by creature comfort; their officers had no intention of denying themselves their peacetime indulgences. When, in 1707, Lord Peterborough lost his personal baggage in Spain, it included sixteen wagons, over fifty mules, and several valuable horses, while the Duke of Northumberland proceeded to active service in Flanders with a retinue of three gentlemen attendants, one page, two footmen, a waggoner, a sumpterman, and three grooms.

Not only did supply factors hamper the movement of armies, but general economic conditions checked the size of a force in the field. Field armies were bigger than in the preceding century but circumstances limited further growth. Marshal Saxe was of the opinion that a field army should not number more than 45,000 men; greater numbers would only be an embarrassment to the general. The difficulty of maneuvering mass armies in line was only one reason for this generally held principle. The size of an army was rigidly governed by the low state of agricultural productivity and the cumbersome distribution system of the time, particularly since soldiers were no longer permitted freely to prey upon the countryside. Similarly, strategy had to conform to the dictates of the seasons. No campaign could begin until there was plenty of green forage available for the horses and the immense number of draft animals, nor could it continue in any particular district beyond the time when such forage was exhausted. Roads were so bad that, in autumn, operations had to be suspended until the late spring. The unreliability of roads placed a relatively high value upon water communications.

Almost inevitably, the Low Countries, an area of high agricultural productivity, well furnished with a network of waterways, became a favorite theater of war. The Low Countries, however, were also thickly studded with towns, fortresses, and other easily defended points. Here, and to some extent in most other regions, the necessity for securing lines of communications made inevitable the slow business of siege warfare. No general, no matter how impetuous and desirous of battle, could ignore the need for systematic clearance of his lines of supply.

This tendency toward the defensive was assisted by the state of weapon development and military engineering. It was not until the time of Frederick the Great that any appreciable advance in artillery was made. Before his day, European armies had at their disposal guns which were deficient in range, accuracy, penetrating power, and durability. Meanwhile, Louis XIV's great engineer, Vauban, and his many students had gone far to check the advantage that artillery had originally given the offensive. With emphasis upon one or another of Vauban's "three systems," engineers constructed complex defensive works designed to impede the progress of an invading army and to exhaust it in unrewarding and time-consuming sieges. Although the eighteenth century saw no radical improvements upon Vauban's techniques, forts were built to give the widest play to enfilading fire against attackers, and to provide easy methods for sudden sallies by defenders. The offensive, on the other hand, benefited from Coehorn's invention of the trench mortar in 1673, and from the perfection of Vauban's methods of attack by digging approaches and parallels and by the siting of batteries to enfilade enemy defenses with ricochet fire. The refinement of fortification and of siege methods transformed this branch of warfare into a geometric exercise, and a spectacle to delight the ladies of the court. The defense was too formidable to allow frontal assaults by irreplaceable soldiers, while unrestricted artillery bombardment of civilian houses was not indulged in, since it did nothing to assist the prosecution of the attack, and was wasteful if and when the town fell. Instead, the attack was placed in the hands of engineers, who through the precise application of mathematics brought their trench network and batteries to such a position that the defending commander, caught in the toils of Euclid, could honorably yield up his fortress.

The importance of supply and the costliness of battle imposed upon the whole conduct of warfare the attributes of a complicated game. The essence of generalship was not to force battle, for the effect of heavy casualties upon small armies would be fatal; but it was concentrated upon destroying the enemy lines of supply. The eighteenth century was the age of maneuver, of march and counter-march, of diversions and deceptions, as rival commanders attempted to menace the communications and supply areas of their opponents. The aim of the general was not necessarily to bring his enemy to battle, but to make his position so untenable through adroit movements that he would be compelled to fight at a pronounced disadvantage or else concede defeat.

The great exemplar of the war of maneuver was the French marshal Turenne, whose career bridged the dissimilar eras of the Thirty Years' War and the wars of Louis XIV. Turenne's victories, and there were many of them, were drab compared to the bloody triumphs of Gustavus or Wallenstein, but they were won with a minimum expenditure of manpower. Turenne and most of his successors regarded battle as a last resort, to be accepted with caution and then only when conditions seemed favorable. He demonstrated many times his ability to maneuver his opponent into areas of meager supply while keeping control of his own lines of communication, and to mask his movements by sudden feints which, by deceiving the enemy, permitted the seizure of desirable positions.

The generals of this age have been accused of a positive antipathy toward fighting and have often been contrasted, to their disadvantage, with the vigorous Revolutionary commanders of a later era who fought war to the hilt and who sought battles rather than avoided them. It is true that generals like Turenne, and his brilliant eighteenth-century counterpart, the Marshal Maurice de Saxe, believed that warfare, like other human pursuits, had its laws which could be discovered. Saxe, in his posthumously published *Mes Rêveries* (1756), even declared that it was not only possible, but reasonable, that a successful general might wage war throughout his career without resorting to battle. Skillful movement and close attention to logistics should bring a commander the desired results without bloodshed. Yet it is noteworthy that Saxe himself commanded the victorious French army in one of the most decisive, and bloody, actions of the age, the battle of Fontenoy (1745).

Moreover, despite the many limitations upon war, few periods have witnessed so many battles, or a more illustrious array of outstanding generals. The number of battles was a result of the many wars, which in turn were possible only because war, involving almost autonomous armies, placed little strain, other than financial, upon society as a whole. The nature of eighteenth-century warfare put a premium upon fine generalship. European armies were nearly identical in weapons, tactics, and systems of supply; military genius, therefore, became one of the chief factors in determining the outcome of war, particularly because the strategy of the indirect approach demanded a leader of high intellectual qualities, though he might lack the dash of a Condé or a Rupert. Two generals alone transcended the limitations of their age. Marlborough and Frederick the Great combined dexterity in maneuver with a strong belief in battle as the decisive element in war, an attitude not in keeping with prevailing military spirit.

One of Marlborough's major contributions to the eventual defeat of Louis XIV's bid for hegemony in Europe was the fashioning of an overall plan of campaign in cooperation with the Austrian Prince Eugene of Savoy—despite the cautious parsimony of his Dutch and English employers. Of even greater weight was Marlborough's ability to come to grips with his foe on his own terms and to capitalize on the ensuing victory. He was aided by the fact that the early advances of the French had penetrated beyond the heavily fortified border areas in the Netherlands and thus allowed him to indulge in warfare of swift movement. Thus, in the Blenheim campaign (1704), he abandoned the profitless safety of the Netherlands and, to the horror of Dutch and English politicians and to the surprise of the French generals, plunged across Europe to the Danube to deal with the French threat against Austria. Joining forces with the armies of Prince Eugene and Margrave Louis of Baden, Marlborough lured the French to attack him at Blenheim and won a hard-fought victory. As a result of this battle, Austria was saved from occupation, Bavaria ceased to be of any assistance to France, the immense prestige of French arms was destroyed, and the armies of Louis XIV were forced back on the defensive.

Ramillies (1706) was won because Marlborough was also a great tactician. During the battle, English troops were withdrawn from the allied right, passed behind the lines, and swelled a massive Dutch and Danish assault that shattered the French right. Oudenarde (1708) was an "encounter battle" in which the allied troops were committed piecemeal as they reached the field. Here Marlborough retained a steady grasp of a very confused situation and finished off the battle by taking the French in the rear with a cavalry envelopment. Yet these victories of generalship, decisive though they were, could not overcome the limitations imposed by contemporary politics. Marlborough could not carry the cautious Dutch with him in a direct offensive against Paris, nor could the Grand Alliance compel Louis to accept the exorbitant terms which it offered. When Marlborough sought to strengthen his political position by an appointment as Captain General for life, he was accused of wishing to re-establish the military dictatorship of Cromwell and was eventually removed.

The stature of Frederick the Great as a general is closely linked to the rise of the military power of Prussia, and also to the decline of French arms. The army of Louis XIV had become the model for the rest of Europe; that of Louis XV reflected the dry rot that was attacking the foundations of the Ancien Régime. The provision of commissions for the nobility had reached such an extent that the upper echelons were over staffed, and organization and discipline were breaking down. The growing practice of giving commissions by purchase added another element of disorganization by carrying over into the army the civil discord between the aristocracy and the middle class. The maintenance of too many élite regiments sapped the fighting strength of the army; even the rank and file were losing precision as the old drill regulations went unenforced.

The rise of Prussia was due largely to her army and to the fact that her rulers felt that the chief duty of a king was to be a soldier. Military ends so shaped policy that, in 1752 some 90 per cent of the budget was devoted to expenditures on the armed forces. Prussia's only claim to the rank of a great power lay in military strength, for in population and economic resources she was well down in the scale of European states. Under Frederick William I the energies of the state were directed into military channels to a degree unsurpassed in Europe. The royal bureaucracy was expanded and made more efficient, paving the way for the tripling of the revenue of the crown during Frederick William's reign. This increased revenue went to foot the bill for an expansion of the army from 38,000 men in 1714 to 80,000 by the end of the reign in 1740. The formerly hostile Junker class was firmly welded to the monarchy by reserving to its members positions of high rank in the army. In this respect, Prussian militarism was more exaggerated than that found elsewhere, since the officer caste was accorded officially a political and social precedence second only to that of the king. By intensifying the recruiting methods of his father, and by the acquisition of populous Silesia, Frederick the Great entered the Seven Years' War with an army of more than 150,000, exceeding that of the much larger Austria.

A few months after Frederick succeeded his father, he embarked upon a policy of undisguised aggression, seizing Silesia which he successfully defended against Austria (1740-48) and then against the armies of Austria, Russia, and France in the Seven Years' War. Militarily he was aided only by English gold and English-subsidized German forces.

Frederick's achievements can be partially explained by his variations from the norm of eighteenth-century strategy. His *Instructions for His Generals* paid due reverence to the strategic orthodoxies of the time, e.g., that "hunger exhausts men more surely than courage" and he stressed the importance of starving the enemy (troops, not civilians) by maneuvering them away from their sources of supply. Yet he saw also that maneuver alone could not bring a decisive verdict. "War is decided only by battles and it is not decided except by them"; Frederick's willingness to give battle, savoring strongly of the Napoleonic approach to war yet to come, was what set him off from other leaders of his age. In a time of limited war, he gained early success because he was different: he was prepared to take risks, to commit to battle, whenever advantageous, soldiers for whom, as persons, he had only contempt.

A thirst for battle would have been suicidal if Frederick's men and armament had been inferior to, or even equal to, those of his antagonists. But the Prussian emphasis upon drill and discipline had produced soldiers who could march faster, change from column to line more rapidly, and load and fire more swiftly and effectively than any other troops in Europe. The mobility and precision of Prussian troops meant greater scope for generalship, since Frederick could make unprecedented demands upon his armies with a reasonable assurance that his orders would be fulfilled. It was mobility alone which made possible Frederick's frantic struggle on several fronts during the Seven Years' War. Ringed around by enemies and deficient in numbers, Frederick taxed the endurance of his troops to the utmost by a series of speedy marches unequalled until the Napoleonic Wars. To fight Rossbach (November 5, 1757), Frederick marched 170 miles in less than two weeks, a feat beyond the capacity of his baggage-laden enemies; after defeating the French, he had immediately to retrace his steps to crush the Austrians at Leuthen (December 5, 1757).

Frederick's superiority in armament was of crucial importance in beating the Austrians. The Prussians employed the iron ramrod (and had done so for over forty years); the Austrians, in company with other European armies, still relied upon a wooden ramrod liable to warp. The combination of better ramrod and practiced loading and firing drill meant greater Prussian infantry fire power, and it was the steady volleys of the Prussians that won the decisive battle of Möllwitz (1741). In the Seven Years' War, Frederick's opponents sought to counter Prussian mobility and fire power by the use of more big guns, and Frederick, although this meant placing a grave strain upon the treasury, was compelled to match them. Characteristically, however, he made original departures in this phase of military technique. In keeping with his attention to mobility, Frederick had his guns drawn by four horses in file, so that artillery could shift position during battle. He was also the first commander fully to exploit high-angle fire; one third of his artillery were howitzers.

There have been wide differences of opinion respecting Frederick's abilities as a tactician, now and during his own lifetime. Most arguments center on his perfection of the tactical device known as the "oblique order," which involved a flanking thrust by one wing of his army while refusing the other. This stratagem arose because the Prussians found themselves chronically outnumbered. The oblique order gave local superiority at one point, and as fresh battalions arrived on the scene in column of march and then wheeled meticulously into line, the enemy was rolled up from the flank. Although the oblique order was employed at Leuthen, Zorndorf, Torgau, and, disastrously, at Kunersdorf, Frederick himself (and Napoleon, a student of his campaigns), gave the credit to his big guns, "the most to-be-respected arguments of the rights of kings."

Is Frederick, because of his strategy of the offensive, to be regarded as the precursor of Napoleon? Napoleon was to disregard

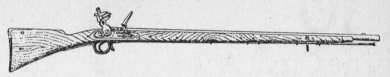

THE "BROWN BESS," used in the British army from 1690 to 1840.
—(From Charles J. Ffoulkes, *Arms and Armament,* London, Harrap, 1945.)

entirely the complicated sparring over supply depots and communications which retarded the pace of warfare before his day. For him, maneuver was a necessary prelude to battle, and battle meant the total concentration of force to obtain, not merely the defeat, but the annihilation of the enemy. Napoleonic strategy was feasible because of the vast resources the Emperor could command, but Frederick had no such blank check on human lives. He took the offensive for precisely the opposite reason. Forced to fight a war on several fronts, yet being hardly equal to any one of his three opponents in money and manpower, he had to shuttle from point to point of his kingdom, dealing a series of offensive blows to prevent a fatal junction of the armies opposing him. That he succeeded is a tribute to his energy and strength of mind, and to the capacities of his men and arms. He was not fighting a Napoleonic war of annihilation, however. Annihilation or total victory was beyond his resources. (It is noteworthy that he lost half of his sixteen battles). He fought a defensive war within the guise of the offensive. It is significant that after the glorious year of 1757, Frederick resorted increasingly to the war of maneuver and to the use of fortifications to ward off his enemies. He gave battle only when other alternatives were exhausted. In later life, rendered cynical and prematurely broken by his tremendous exertions in the field, Frederick discarded not only his youthful doctrine of the efficacy of battle but was echoing Voltaire's bitter attacks on the barrenness of war.

Just as the Prussian state was an extreme version of eighteenth-century absolute monarchy, Frederick the Great was the supreme example of eighteenth-century generalship. Wider scope was given to his talents in the field chiefly because he, as king and general in one person, could exercise an unparalleled authority over the lives of his subjects.

10
The Great Age of Sail, 1689-1815

The great age of sail, covering a century and a quarter of almost constant conflict between France and England, illustrates the profound effect on warfare of the new, permanent, professional navy with its fleets of stately ships-of-the-line. Study of the naval component of this long struggle is particularly worthwhile because of the light it throws on the part that sea power played in determining French and British foreign policy, on the way that sea power expanded warfare between European powers into global, or worldwide, conflict, on the means by which England achieved tactical superiority in naval warfare, and, finally, on that supreme test of sea power versus land power in the age of sail, the British struggle with Napoleon.

The wars between England and Spain in the sixteenth century, and between England and the Netherlands in the seventeenth, had been essentially naval, sea power versus sea power. Queen Elizabeth's navy had demonstrated its worth in the defense of the island state. The English depended absolutely upon it. Probably neither at that time nor at any time since would it have been possible for England's army at home to repel such an invasion as her enemies had the military, but not the naval, power to stage. The English had found the weakness in Spain's national policy. Spain's commitments in the Mediterranean and in the Low Countries made her dependent upon wealth garnered in her colonies. Therefore, the English ships that threatened the galleons bringing treasure from the New World endangered Spanish operations and interests everywhere, not merely those directed against England. So was it also in the Dutch Wars. The Netherlands was dependent upon her fisheries and her revenues as a commercial carrier; without those resources the Dutch could not protect their land frontiers. Thus the Netherlands proved as vulnerable as Spain to the kind of attack that could be made by the ships of the Royal Navy.

But the emergence of France under Louis XIV presented a much more difficult problem. A relatively self-sufficient land power, France was not so susceptible to naval attack as Spain and the Netherlands had been, and when France became a sea power as well, she threatened England's maritime supremacy. Under Colbert, Louis XIV's great controller of finances (1661-83), the French pursued a full-scale mercantilist policy. Colbert encouraged the growth of all forms of business activity, especially those centered in French trade and possessions overseas. French naval architects soon proved themselves the finest in Europe, surpassing the Dutch who had led in most of the seventeenth century. Colbert was able to build a navy adequate for his projected commercial program. The interdependence of commerce and naval power, long recognized in England, justified Colbert's naval expenditures and also a system of *inscription* to man the warships. Before long, a superior French fleet lay at anchor in its newly developed base at Brest where it outflanked the English fleet in the Channel and challenged for control of the North Atlantic.

France did not have to wait long to test her new sea power. The Glorious Revolution brought William of Orange to the throne of England in 1689 and involved him in a double struggle with the French; in Ireland, where he had to fight for his crown against James II whom Louis supported, and then on the continent, where French armies had invaded the Netherlands. Here was an opportunity for decisive French naval action; none was forthcoming. Louis himself had allowed William to sail unopposed to England because he thought that James II had grown too independent and needed a scare. The next year the French admiral, Tourville, did nothing effective to interfere with William's campaign in Ireland, where James was defeated in the Battle of the Boyne (July 12, 1690). One day earlier, Tourville had routed an Anglo-Dutch fleet off Beachy Head in the Channel and had gained supremacy at sea for the time being; but it was too late to influence the decision in Ireland. The French made little effort to use their control of the sea, largely because Louis's attention was directed to his continental campaigns. On the English side, Admiral Torrington had acted upon the policy of maintaining a "fleet-in-being" to keep the superior French fleet in check. Two years later, a superior Anglo-Dutch fleet defeated Tourville off La Hogue and regained control of the Channel. The naval war then developed into a stalemate, after certain inconclusive efforts by the English fleet in the Mediterranean. The main campaigns were fought on land, and naval power was not aggressively employed by either side.

Thus it was that England's minister of finance, Lord Godolphin, asking King William for "speedy directions" in the employment of "our great useless fleet" against the French in 1696, posed a question that struck at the heart of the matter: of what use is a navy? Or, more inclusively, of what use is sea power against land power? The answer to the question, of course, varied with the particular circumstances of time and place, with the resources available to each of the opponents, and above all, with their national policy. Those elements which are the constant determinants of sea power were, however, empirically arrived at by the opening years of the eighteenth century. At the same time, from the experience which France and England gained from their first struggle in modern times there were evolved the broad policies which were to govern them in a hundred-odd years of conflict and which are applicable to warfare between a maritime nation and a land power with maritime ambitions.

England found in an alliance with continental powers—in this instance the Grand Alliance, of which, among others, Sweden, the Netherlands, and Spain were members—a possible answer to Godolphin's question about sea power versus land power. King William in his conduct of the war had pursued a "continental policy," making England's primary effort the support of her allies in a land campaign on the continent, while the fleet played a secondary, almost incidental role. English statesmen who objected to the continental policy were aided by the skilled pen of Jonathan Swift in advancing a "maritime policy" as the more effective method of employing the island's resources in the war. In its extreme form, Swift's argument was for maritime isolation, cynically leaving the ally to do the land fighting, while England enriched herself with conquests overseas and the ruination of the enemy's commerce.

In practice, a middle course became the guiding principle in the eighteenth century. Under such a policy pursued against Louis XIV, King William's "useless fleet" would have been directed to undertake the screening and support of amphibious operations against French naval and privateering bases, since the French fleet refused to come out and fight. Such vigorous action was beyond British resources, however, as long as the country's primary commitment was to a continental land campaign; further, it necessitated wholehearted cooperation between army and navy for which neither one was at that time adequately prepared, mentally or physically. Amphibious operations in the West Indies were notoriously productive of disputes between commanders.

As time passed England's maritime policy became in essence a proposal for answering the sea power versus land power question by the indirect approach, concentration on economic (or "strategic") warfare directed against the enemy's sea communications and overseas resources, with only secondary expenditures of British resources to support their ally's land campaign on the continent. A modification of the maritime policy, important because it proposed consignment of a major British military force to continental fighting, is frequently referred to as the "Low Countries policy." It was an exception which arose from the fact that England must prevent the seizure of Antwerp and the mouths of the Scheldt by any major maritime power. That strategic area lay athwart British communications with the Baltic, could serve ideally as a base from which to launch an invasion of the British east coast and up the Thames, and was a serious rival of London's position as the European depot of world-wide trade.

England's first participation in a continental alliance had demonstrated both the need for allies when she was at war with a power of the magnitude of France and the necessity for a national policy realistically based on the best employment of the means available. As a maritime nation, England could not afford to isolate herself and risk the domination of Europe by a single major state. She must follow a balance-of-power policy, taking pains that her primary contribution in an alliance would be sea power supplemented by land power, not vice versa. The strength of that sea power would be limited by her national wealth, in large part directly attributable to her merchant marine, by the size, condition, and tactical skill of her navy, by access to strategic materials (which in that day were primarily Baltic naval stores) for the upkeep of the fleet, and by the possession of bases from which the fleet could operate in strategic areas. Whether she possessed these four "elements" of sea power in sufficient magnitude was dependent upon the wisdom of the British government.

England's merchant marine, the first element, flourished despite great losses to French privateers and commerce raiders. During the long struggle against Louis XIV the French merchant marine was swept from the oceans. Mercantile interests were generally well represented in Parliament. The Navigation Acts were in effect a subsidy which encouraged the building of sound types, as well as large numbers, of merchantmen. Trade with the colonies was monopolistic, of course, and conducted so as to produce the maximum possible benefit. For example, tobacco from the American colonies was imported to England exclusively in British bottoms, and then ninety per cent of it was exported to the European countries, again in British bottoms. Britain's wealth, her merchant marine, and her colonial empire grew simultaneously.

England did less well by her navy, the second element, which had seemed an onerous financial burden ever since the "ship money" days of Charles I. The situation in 1701, when only half of Britain's 130 capital ships were seaworthy and not even those could be manned, may be considered typical at the outbreak of a war. Manning the fleet became increasingly difficult throughout the eighteenth century. About half of the sailors were "pressed" into service from merchantmen, a quarter might be volunteers (including foreigners), and the final quarter might be undesirables, unemployed, debtors, the dregs of foreign waterfronts and riff-raff generally. Decay of the fleet in peacetime became, indirectly, a cause of the next war, for British unpreparedness unquestionably influenced French decisions to resort to war. Shortage of ships tended to discourage aggressive naval action, a tendency fortified by the formalist tactical strait jacket of the Permanent Fighting Instructions, with the resultant danger, often apparent during the first half of the eighteenth century but never quite realized, that the fleet might be considered an end in itself and not an instrument of war.

Access to strategic materials, the third element, was clearly comprehensible to an island people. Even while the British let their fleet rot "in ordinary" (laid up in reserve), they would become highly incensed by the possibility of being shut off from overseas markets. Dependence on Baltic naval stores was a problem as acute then as dependence on oil from overseas is today. Foresight had so far assured a supply of English oak for hulls; spars, pitch, and tar had to be obtained from the Baltic. Special legislation was passed as early as 1704 to develop North American naval stores; but Sweden remained England's principal source for years to come. To safeguard itself, the Royal Navy sent fleets to the Baltic for seven consecutive years beginning in 1715, and subsequently as necessary.

Even in sailing-ship days, the ability of a fleet to maintain itself in any given area arose from the propinquity of good bases, the fourth element, which were more likely to be obtained by war than by peaceful diplomacy. On the continent Lisbon alone was usually a friendly port adequate to meet the needs of the fleet. William III put a fleet into the Mediterranean on a year-round basis, but England did not have a base there until 1704, when Rooke captured Gibraltar. Four years later, urged on by Marlborough's strategic genius, the English also occupied Port Mahon in Minorca. The Royal Navy could then challenge the Mediterranean nations and exercise a remote but powerful influence on European strategy generally.

By comparison with the British, French naval power was less an absolute necessity than a luxury. When the expensive fleet inspired by Colbert's mercantilism failed to achieve a decisive victory against England, some French statesmen concluded that theirs was the truly "useless" fleet, a drain on resources that they could ill afford because of the demands of continental land campaigns. For a while they hoped that the use of privateers and naval commerce raiders, by *guerre de course*, would be cheaper and more effective than a fleet. Their one truly aggressive naval officer of that day, Jean Bart, advocated *guerre de course* as valuable in itself and as a means by which England's naval strength could be dissipated. Bart's many successes led such a military authority as Vauban to urge the entire abandonment of the ships-of-the-line navy and the concentration of all maritime effort against English commerce. Before peace was negotiated in 1697 some 4,000 English merchantmen had been captured. Even so, the French policy was only superficially successful. England was not defeated, and her commerce expanded even during periods of war.

The principles actually determining French naval policy before the Revolution were those of any ambitious nation which possesses valuable overseas colonies, but is not dependent on sea power for survival. Colonies became hostages to sea power. Time and again France's continental victories would be forfeited at the peace table in payment for colonial possessions that had been lost to the British fleet. Even when France conquered Flanders itself, she had to relinquish that prize in order to retrieve Louisbourg and other New World colonies. French pride and ambitions, if not survival, were vulnerable to British sea power. *Guerre de course* had to be supplemented by as large a battle fleet as French finances could afford. When that fleet was too weak to challenge the British directly, then at least as a fleet-in-being it might hold enough of the British navy in home waters, perhaps enough to keep French colonies safe while French commerce raiders drove English merchantmen from the high seas.

The Seven Years' War (1756-63), the climactic conflict of the age of mercantilism, proved how false French hopes were and how much British sea power could accomplish when directed with understanding and intelligence. Hostilities, begun as a North American border incident, had become a true world war. Seriously concerned with the financial drain of another war with England, some French statesmen had advocated maintaining peace on the continent and concentrating their undivided effort against England in a maritime war; but the possibility of defeating England in Germany, by making George II's Hanover a hostage to French continental power, was too tempting to let pass. British statesmen, on the other hand, hurriedly found a continental ally in the King of Prussia. Nonetheless, the first round went to the French. They diverted British attention by massing barges on the Channel, as though for an invasion, and with that feint screened a successful campaign for the capture of Minorca. The British fleet was forced to withdraw from the Mediterranean; and to direct the war the British government had to bring in the leader of the opposition, that staunch advocate of a maritime policy, William Pitt, later Earl of Chatham, who tailored his aims to the available resources.

"Pitt's system," as it is frequently called, was based on the cardinal principle of making the war turn on the weapon, sea power, in which the British were superior. Pitt waged war against continental France by subsidizing his German allies and by amphibious raids on the coast of France to interfere with the proper concentration of French armies; he waged war against French resources by means of the "Rule of 1756," which prohibited neutrals from taking over French colonial trade in time of war from which they were restricted in peace (i.e., before 1756), by direct attacks on French colonial possessions in America and in India, and by blockading the French ports. Except for the German subsidies, Pitt's system was an offensive extension of sea power; even the subsidies were possible only because of Britain's maritime sources of wealth.

The successful implementation of Pitt's policy saw the development of a new force in modern warfare, what the eighteenth century called a "conjunct expedition." Joint operations by military and naval forces, most brilliantly displayed in Wolfe's campaign against Quebec, made possible the conquest of Canada and of the choice French sugar islands of the Caribbean, contributed to Clive's victories in India, and led to the capture of Havana and Manila (after Spain entered the war). The experience for these successful amphibious operations was first gained on the coast of France where, however, the raids were tactically bungled. In September, 1757, Pitt had the first conjunct expedition organized. This was a joint force, with a battle fleet covering 9,000 troops in transports, directed against Rochefort, a naval and shipbuilding center on the Bay of Biscay. After exasperating delays and a demonstration of the effectiveness of naval gunfire against land positions, the expedition returned to England without attempting to assault its major objective. Lack of operational planning, indifference to achieving tactical surprise, and absence of an aggressive spirit had resulted in humiliating failure. The next June, 13,000 troops were skillfully landed on the flank of the Channel port and privateering center of St. Malo. After eight days ashore it was decided that an assault on St. Malo's prepared positions would be too costly and the force withdrew, but not until 100 privateers had been burned and the entire countryside alarmed. In August, 1758, came the third and most successful of the conjunct expeditions which captured Cherbourg by means of a well coordinated amphibious assault aided by the use of special landing craft that might have served as prototypes of some developed in World War II. Unfortunately for the British, their successful troops got entirely out of hand and were badly cut up before they could withdraw, their failure arising from the violent French reaction to their initial victory at Cherbourg.

The surprising fact is that these raids were strategically successful. Not only did they destroy French shipping and divert troops needed against the Prussians, but they proved such a nuisance that the French resolved on a counterattack, if they could concentrate their fleets in the Channel. France always suffered in its naval conflicts with England because French naval power was normally divided between a Mediterranean fleet based on Toulon and an Atlantic fleet based on Brest, with a British fleet based on Gibraltar overlooking the only route by which the two French fleets could concentrate. The Toulon fleet escaped from the Mediterranean but was caught off the coast of Portugal and destroyed as a fighting force. Shortly afterwards, the British Admiral Hawke caught the Brest fleet in the Bay of Biscay and smashed it in the overwhelming victory at Quiberon Bay.

The Peace of Paris, 1763, found England with more extensive domains and greater power than ever before. The entire east coast of North America from Key West north beyond the St. Lawrence was hers; and increasingly the great wealth of India poured into her coffers. Her navy numbered almost 150 ships of the line and more than 100 frigates. The key to her success had been the exploitation of control of the sea through amphibious operations; and an amphibious doctrine was evolved. But what had been painfully learned was quickly forgotten. Possibly the stultifying effect of the Fighting Instructions on so many naval encounters had made British officers wary of doctrine; but more likely there was a general failure to recognize that amphibious operations are a special art of war and not amenable to casual improvisation.

The results of Pitt's brilliance were soon jeopardized by subsequent British naval policy. As usual the Royal Navy fell into disrepair, but the French, under the energetic direction of Choiseul, spent large sums on their fleet and welcomed the opportunity that the American Revolution gave them to challenge British sea power again. Stretched thin, the Royal Navy temporarily lost control of the seas. Perhaps we should say, forfeited control, for De Grasse's victory off the Chesapeake Capes, which resulted in the surrender of Cornwallis at Yorktown and all its consequences, was a tame affair as battles go.

Throughout the eighteenth century naval tactics had followed a formalist pattern, perhaps appropriate to the age, but not the begetter of decisive victories. The French, usually on the defensive and unable to outmaneuver the British, preferred to fight from the leeward where the elevation and range of their guns was increased by the heel of the ship. Their objective was to disable the enemy by shooting down his spars and rigging; then they could escape from a superior force or eventually overtake and destroy an inferior one. The British preferred the weather gauge. Being upwind, they could control the battle, attacking when they chose or retiring if outnumbered. Gunfire was so inaccurate that they strove for a large volume of fire at short range and found that decisive results might be attained by bearing down to within pistol range and pouring their broadsides into the enemy's hull. In practice, however, the British suffered from the doctrine of the conterminous line and the limitations placed on command decisions, both by the Fighting Instructions and by the inadequate communications system. Not until 1776 was there an official Signal Book, which arranged the signals logically, for an entire fleet, and not until 1790 was there a single Signal Book for the entire Navy which made possible an unlimited flexibility in the orders issued by fleet commanders. Naval encounters between the French and the British, though often strategically advantageous, were tactically indecisive until a means was found for regaining tactical concentration by breaking the enemy's line and by thus restoring the melee as the crisis of the battle. Theoretically, a ship passing between two ships of the enemy's line could rake each with a broadside fire, but throughout the approach the enemy himself could deliver a raking fire; and if he fell off to leeward somewhat he could draw out the attacker's approach and defeat his purpose.

The battle which probably did most to break the stranglehold of conterminous-line fighting was Rodney's celebrated victory over De Grasse in the Caribbean at the Battle of the Saints (1782). The French admiral was engaged in the preliminary stages of a Franco-Spanish campaign against Jamaica when the British fleet caught up with him and, after several days of maneuvering, forced the battle. Rodney had an advantage in the number, size, and speed of his ships; he had more three-deckers and more ships that were copper-sheathed to prevent fouling. The French sailed down to windward from the north on a light easterly wind, their line of battle rather ragged as a result of maneuvering for position. Rodney's fleet sailed on a parallel and opposite course, to leeward. Just as the two fleets were approximately conterminous, the wind veered to the southeast, forcing the French ships to alter course toward the British line and tending to carry the British ships into the French line unless positive action were taken to avoid it. And so, largely by chance, Rodney broke the line, captured De Grasse in his great three-decker, the *Ville de Paris,* and decisively defeated the French fleet.

Much of the credit for the victory must be given to Sir Charles Douglas, Rodney's captain and a gunnery expert. He had worked effectively on improving both accuracy and rate of fire. His improved methods enabled gunners to train their pieces as much as 45° right or left for "oblique fire" and, under ideal conditions, actually pound the enemy with three broadsides in two minutes, as compared with Douglas's own hopes for two rounds in three minutes.

The enemy's rate of fire rarely exceeded 50% of the standard British performance. These improvements were achieved through training and through certain technical devices. Douglas replaced the old linstock with a flintlock which ignited a goose-quill of powder specially prepared for firing the gun; he introduced flannel powder cases which, unlike silk used earlier, did not leave a smoldering residue that had to be wormed from the barrel; and he controlled recoil by forcing the guns to roll up an inclined plane and fastening them by steel springs as large as ten inches in diameter. Thus gunnery became safer and faster, and the general adoption of Douglas's technique made the sustained rate of broadside fire in the battle fleet of the Royal Navy vastly superior to that of an enemy. At the Saints, part of this superiority was gained through use of a new, relatively short-barreled gun, the carronade, which could be easily handled and was capable of throwing heavy shot at short range with a light charge of powder. For the British style of pistol-range gunfire this cheaper, lighter weapon became very popular. Its severe limitation in range could be disastrous, however, when it was pitted alone against the standard long gun, as both sides were to discover in the famous frigate actions of the War of 1812.

Aside from these improvements in gunnery, the capital naval vessel of 1800 was scarcely changed from that of 1700. The ships themselves were long-lived, Nelson's *Victory* being in its forty-sixth year at the battle of Trafalgar. The organization and manning of the fleets remained basically the same, even after the mutinies of 1797. But as England became embroiled in the Napoleonic Wars, British sea power was called upon for more prodigious accomplishments than ever before.

The aristocratic Royal French Navy had been a natural target for Revolutionary reform. The officer class was virtually wiped out and even ships' gunners, the aristocracy of the sailors, were not spared the levelling process; they were dispersed ashore or diluted by new recruits aboard ship. The French fleet put to sea with former merchantmen as captains. But improved morale was cancelled by loss of skill, as Lord Howe demonstrated in the battle of the Glorious First of June (1794). Here the French claimed a strategic victory, for their action had saved a large grain convoy from America whose arrival was sorely needed in France, but the French navy never completely recovered from that engagement, even under the later proddings of Napoleon himself.

The British, on the other hand, had never made bolder use of their fleets to further political objectives. By 1796 Trinidad, the Cape of Good Hope, Ceylon, and various spice and sugar islands had

A TYPICAL SHIP-OF-THE-LINE OF THE AGE OF SAIL, ship-rigged, with two gun decks and a main battery of 74 guns. —(From Henry B. Culver, *The Book of Old Ships,* New York: Doubleday, 1928, p. 153.)

been occupied. Napoleon's Italian campaign drove the Fleet out of the Mediterranean, but only temporarily. In good part because of Nelson's tactical skill, Jervis trounced a numerically superior Spanish fleet in the Atlantic off its own coast; and the next year in the Battle of the Nile Nelson all but annihilated the French battle fleet that had convoyed Napoleon and his army to Egypt. This last battle had far-reaching strategic results. British exports to Turkey quickly rose to £150,000 annually and imports from Turkey to £200,000. French prestige in the entire Mediterranean suffered. Likewise, Nelson's victory at Copenhagen, claimed by some to have been his greatest, was an important precedent for the use of naval power against the neutrals in the long economic war between Napoleon and England.

Finally, the French dictator, like his continental predecessors and successors, contemplated invasion of the British Isles as the one sure method of defeating England. But his armies were collected on the Channel coast in vain, for the French admirals could not mass their naval power in the face of the British fleets blockading the French coast. The French Toulon fleet, after dashing to the Caribbean and back, was finally caught off the Spanish coast while making a final effort to return to the Mediterranean to support Napoleon's land campaigns there. The defeat at Trafalgar (1805) meant the practical end of Napoleonic sea power. Thorough indoctrination of his officers had enabled Nelson to employ his fleet in flexible divisions, in full confidence that each ship captain would improvise as necessary. His success called for a high order of professional skill, one which was far beyond the means of his opponents. It is worth noting, however, that Trafalgar came a full decade before Napoleon was finally exiled to the South Atlantic.

During those last ten years British sea power was never seriously challenged but around the world exerted economic pressure on Napoleon's allies and supported British military efforts. After various misguided efforts, it once again supported amphibious and diversionary operations on the continent, of which the Peninsular campaign had certainly the most tangible results. With great difficulty the fleet was maintained at a strength of slightly over 100,000 men. Desertions were widespread, especially to the American merchant marine, and the British Orders in Council, directing economic retaliation against Napoleon's Continental Decrees, were particularly resented by the neutrals, especially the United States and Denmark, who profited most from the war. England's economic war was not aimed at starving France into submission, an unrealistic goal, but in arousing discontent among Napoleon's often unwilling allies.

In the United States,where more bad blood was stirred up by President Jefferson's embargo on shipping, another form of economic pressure, than by the well-publicized incidents of British impressment, anti-British feeling ran high in the backwoods. The sea ports, having quintupled trade with England during the war, knew full well where their profits lay. After all, English sea power had already forced Napoleon to give the United States the greatest real estate bargain of all time, the Louisiana Purchase. It was the Canada-hungry trans-Appalachian states and not those on the coast that swung the United States into war with Britain. Although Americans take pride in their frigate victories, they should remember that in 1814 the Royal Navy blockaded the entire coast, tied up trade, and landed troops to burn Washington. However, in the lake campaigns on the Canadian border, the victories of Perry on Lake Erie and of Macdonough on Lake Champlain retrieved the American army's blunders. But in a strategically important area, the failure of Commodore Chauncey to fight Sir James Yeo to a finish on Lake Ontario left British communications open to the Niagara peninsula and beyond and denied Americans the likelihood of obtaining any decisive victory.

Without a single ship-of-the-line, the United States had not been able to oppose a British fleet in battle; but her resources for shipbuilding and in unemployed sailors had produced a formidable number of privateers which preyed upon Britain's world-wide trade. At the end of the Napoleonic Wars, when the Duke of Wellington was asked what force would be required to defeat the United States, it was American sea power on the lakes that made him place his estimate far too high for the British government to pursue the matter.

The days of the square-rigged ship-of-the-line were numbered. The great age of sail, as we have seen, was the great age of British sail. To protect itself and its commercial interests, an island of rather modest resources had built, manned, and maintained a navy and then had employed it with sufficient courage and wisdom to create the greatest empire the western world had ever known. British naval policy had been the product of a constitutional state in which the merchants possessed great influence. British success had not been owing to any great technical advantage. Apart from improvements in naval artillery, the French usually were ahead in naval architecture and usually had ships, especially frigates, that sailed better than those of Britain. But, even during the age of formalism, the Royal Navy had built up a tradition of sea service and of vigorous action that was superior to that of the French. Therein lay the key to victory on the ocean and to world empire.

11

War in the New World, 1492-1783

The relative ease with which Europeans established themselves in America after the great discoveries should not be allowed to obscure the magnitude of their accomplishment. The Spanish Conquistadores subdued, not primitive tribes, but civilized Indian empires. The domain of the Aztecs in Central America contained a population which has been estimated at 15,000,000; its capital, Tenochtitlan (Mexico City), was a city of some 300,000 people; and the Aztec ruler Montezuma also exercised uncertain control over a number of other peoples. The Peruvian empire of the Incas, although not so populous (perhaps 6,000,000 people) was a centralized despotism. Cortes overthrew the Aztecs with a tiny army of 600 men and a few pieces of artillery, partly because he was supported by Indian dissidents; Pizzaro seized power in Peru with the incredibly small force of 183 men simply by eliminating the apex of the centralized Inca state.

The most obvious military reason for the collapse of the Indian civilizations was the immense technological superiority enjoyed by the Spanish invaders. Although both Aztecs and Incas had developed metallurgy to at least as high a standard as that of contemporary Europe, their work was done in precious metals. Their armament, however, was little better than that of Stone Age man. They used javelins, bows and arrows, and wooden clubs with stone blades; they wore armor of brine-soaked quilted cotton and carried wickerwork shields. Against the steel and shot of the Spaniards such equipment was useless. However, the Spaniards won not so much because of the number of casualties they could inflict, but because of the terrifying effect of firearms and mounted men. The Aztec and Inca societies had not developed the complex military organization which had accompanied the rise of civilization in Europe. Aztec warfare was largely an extension of religious ceremonial, and was not the occupation of any special class or group of individuals. The only Indian advantage was numbers, and this was far outweighed by Spanish armament, organization, and disciplined tactics.

In North America, the conquest of the Indians was a process which paralleled the western push of white settlement ending, in recent times, with the disappearance of the frontier. There was never any likelihood that the Indians would drive the Europeans back to sea, or even wipe out an established colony. Their numbers were too few; they were broken up into many tribes, united only at rare intervals by the abortive flickering of "Pan-Indian" nationalism; and they were immeasurably inferior to the whites in the tools of war and in the social and economic organization which sustained and effective fighting requires.

By 1641 there were 50,000 English settlers on the Atlantic seaboard of what is now the United States; less than fifty years later there were 200,000. The surge to the interior which resulted from population growth was accompanied by the consequent dislodgment or extermination of indigenous Indian groups. The basic occupation of the colonists was agriculture; it was the prospect of land which had brought many of them to the New World. To the colonist, the semi-nomadic Indians, who required extensive lands to support tribal life with hunting and crude agriculture, were wasteful obstacles. The strong aggressive drive which land-hunger exerted was heightened, especially in New England, by Protestant zeal. America was the New Canaan, a promised land set apart by God for his elect. The Indians who encumbered it were pagans "of the cursed race of Ham"; the Reverend Richard Mather, on hearing of the Pequot massacre, rejoiced that "on this day we have sent six hundred heathen souls to hell." The Pequot Wars (1637-44), King Philip's War (1675-76), and the near-extermination of the Susquehannock tribe which accompanied Bacon's Rebellion (1676) cleared the North Atlantic seaboard of most of its aboriginal population; the last substantial coastal group, the Delaware, was deprived of its Pennsylvania lands and forced across the Alleghenies in the 1740's.

Except in regard to the most formidable Indian power in eastern North America, the Iroquois Confederacy, the relations of New France with its Indian neighbors were different. The Iroquois, or Five Nations, by virtue of their relatively large numbers, more advanced political organization, and commanding geographical position on the Hudson-Mohawk waterway between New France and the English colonies, were able, unlike their weaker Indian brethren, to bargain with the whites on nearly equal terms. For the most part, their aims coincided with those of Albany businessmen who wished to siphon off the cream of the French western fur trade; the Iroquois therefore concentrated their efforts against that French economic lifeline. In the middle and latter part of the seventeenth century, the Iroquois, through their fierce depredations, held the tiny French colony on the St. Lawrence in the grip of fear for years at a time. Indeed, not until this unique confederacy exhausted itself through too-constant war could the French relax their vigilance.

The relations of the French with other tribes were much happier. The economic base of the colony was the fur trade, in which Indian assistance and cooperation was indispensable. Moreover, French Catholics regarded the Indians, not as pagans eternally damned, but as benighted souls to be rescued from hellfire and guided to salvation. Eventually almost all the tribes of the St. Lawrence, Ohio, and Mississippi basins were bound to New France by economic necessity and missionary effort. It was the unswerving policy of the government in Quebec to reinforce the Indian connection by annual and lavish distribution of gifts, partly to maintain control of the fur trade, but also to enlist the Indians as allies, in face of the ever-widening disparity of strength between New France and the English colonies. In view of the vast difference between English and French attitudes and policies, it is not surprising that an overwhelming majority of Indian tribes supported the French against the English who menaced their homelands. In the same way it was natural for the Indians to ally themselves with the British during the American Revolution and the War of 1812. Encroaching American settlement, and not British officialdom, was destroying Indian culture.

Confronted by American conditions, both French and English soon shed the accoutrements of the battlefields of Europe—armor, pikes, swords, and heavy cavalry. But it should be noted that armored English colonists of the seventeenth century were far more effective against primitively armed Indians than were their eighteenth-century successors against Indians armed with guns and iron tomahawks. The formal tactics of the Old World were replaced by forest tactics which approximated those of the Indians themselves. In the ambush, lightning attack, skirmishing, and sharpshooting from cover of small war, the European eventually surpassed the Indian. But frontier society did not become Indian; far from it. The exigencies of frontier life placed a premium upon qualities produced in a mature, civilized, highly organized society. The discipline and command structure of the whites, plus their superior technical knowledge, made 'possible a level of bush tactics to which the Indians, who rarely rose above the imperative urge of self-preservation, could not aspire. The Indian war party was merely a collection of individual warriors attracted by the fame of an eminent war chief. The chief customarily had no power of command over his braves; after the initial brush, an Indian force lost coherence, since each warrior fought for himself. Indians were always unwilling to attack prepared positions of any kind; with the possible exception of Pontiac's inflamed tribesmen at Detroit, no Indian war party ever attempted a sustained siege.

Until well on in the eighteenth century, both French and English colonies in America relied for defense primarily on their respective militias. In the English colonies, the militia structure stemmed from the old English system. The militia was a compulsory levy of the male population which drilled a certain number of days a year and could be summoned in emergency. As with other aspects of colonial life, the control of the home government over military affairs was slight and each colony therefore developed its own version of the militia. Exemptions from service (which were extensive) varied widely; the size of the unit, whether trainband of infantry or troop of horse, differed from colony to colony; the geographic basis of recruitment for the unit might be the village, the town, or the county; in some colonies, the election of officers was the rule; in others, officers were appointed. Enthusiasm and the sense of urgency necessary for the development of an efficient force were directly related to the likelihood of hostile attack; however, even in relatively exposed Massachusetts, the amount of compulsory drill had been reduced to four days annually by the late seventeenth century.

Unlike the English colonies in which "salutary neglect" allowed the development of considerable local initiative, the colony of New France, at least after the coming to power of Louis XIV, was closely supervised by the home government. The execution of policy was in the hands of a governor, who was also the commander-in-chief, and an intendant; representative institutions did not exist. The colony, according to the tenets of Colbertian mercantilism, existed solely to provide raw materials and a market for the mother country; as an investment, it must be defended, but as cheaply as possible. The result was that the militia system was established as a uniform, centrally directed organization in keeping with the authoritarian politics and graded society of this American extension of the Ancien Régime.

The militia was under the direct control of the governor at Quebec, who commissioned the captains of militia in each parish. A populous parish might have more than one company. Due to the much inferior military position of New France, there was a far more decided appreciation of the value and function of the militia than in the English colonies. Exemption from militia service was almost impossible to obtain. The French *habitant* was provided with arms, not issued them for an occasion; he was drilled in musketry at least once every two weeks. In contrast to the Thirteen Colonies, where the militiaman was bound to serve only within the limits of his own colony, the Canadian militiaman was liable for duty wherever his governor ordered.

It was inevitable that French and English should fight one another in North America, but not merely because their mother countries were so often at war. In contrast to that waged in Europe in the same period, warfare in North America was punctuated by atrocities caused by deep antagonisms between the two white groups. Economic rivalries abounded—the clash of interest in the fur trade, in the Atlantic fisheries, and eventually in the rich heartland of the Ohio. To these differences was added religious hatred. The French colonists were products of the Catholic Reformation, and remained zealous even when chill winds of scepticism blew from the mother country. The people of New England, who had the closest contact with the French, were fiery Calvinists unalterably opposed to Catholicism.

Neither side hesitated to employ Indian auxiliaries. Neither had much compunction in borrowing the barbaric practices of their savage allies. The Iroquois, incited to take the warpath by their friends at Albany, massacred the inhabitants of Lachine, near Montreal, in 1689; in 1690, in reprisal, a band of French militia and Christian Iroquois slaughtered many people at Schenectady, while other groups of militia and Abenaki Indians raided and killed in New Hampshire and Maine. In 1704, another French and Indian raiding party surprised the sleeping village of Deerfield, Massachusetts, killed fifty-three persons, and carried off 111 others to captivity in Canada. This barbaric strain, present in American warfare almost from the beginnings of European settlement, was to culminate in the excesses which marked the Seven Years' War and the American Revolution.

For the most part the French militia were more effective in forest warfare than their English opponents. Because New France devoted much more of its energies to the fur trade and made more extensive use of Indian allies than did the English colonies, the French militia had a much broader knowledge of terrain, Indian methods of transport, and the technique of living off the country for long periods. Although the men of Virginia and Kentucky, and units like Rogers' New England Rangers, were quite the equal of the French in bush tactics, the English colonial militia was usually ill-trained. In fact, so far were they from fitting the popular picture of sharpshooting backwoodsmen (most of them were peaceful farmers who dwelt far from the frontier) that the British army actually had to detach men from its own regular regiments in 1757 to learn woodcraft and forest-fighting. The regiment so formed, under the command of Lt. Col. Thomas Gage, was the first light infantry regiment in the British army.

French superiority in the techniques of small war availed little. Incessant border raids in the period 1690-1713 were only pinpricks, designed to keep the English off balance and disguise the paucity of French resources. The inexorable truth was that the French were only staving off ultimate disaster. The economy of the Thirteen Colonies was much more diversified and healthier than that of New France; the disparity in population was great. (By 1754, there were 1,500,000 English and 60,000 French in North America). Moreover, the flourishing merchant marine of New England gave the English colonists a formidable weapon, for New France was vulnerable to sea-borne attack. The two greatest efforts of New England against New France were combined operations. William Phips failed in 1690; Quebec was too hard a nut for the militia to crack. The capture of the great French fortress of Louisbourg in 1745 was almost entirely a triumph for colonial military and naval arms (supported by four ships of the Royal Navy); its return to France by the Treaty of Aix-la-Chapelle was much resented in the colonies.

However, the full measure of English colonial superiority in numbers and resources was never exerted. Each colony was so jealous of its own authority, and so unable to see that the danger to one colony might well become a danger to all, that the possibility of coordinating effort either defensively or offensively was slight. In King William's War (1689-97), only New York and New England took part, because none of the other colonies felt themselves menaced by the French. In Queen Anne's War (1701-13), in order to preserve Iroquois neutrality, the French did not attack New York, which thereupon allowed New England to bear almost the whole burden of the war against the common enemy. Many prominent Americans saw the necessity of a common approach to the problem of defense but, because of the strength of local feeling and the suspicion of the political and financial power that any central body in charge of military affairs would have, their proposals came to nothing. Thus Franklin's Albany Plan of Union (1754), which provided that a "Grand Council" of the colonies should "raise and pay soldiers and build forts for the defence of any of the Colonies, and equip vessels of force to guard the coasts and protect the trade on the ocean," was rejected by all the colonial legislatures.

The European regular did not loom large in American war before the middle of the eighteenth century. English regiments were despatched to the colonies at intervals; for example, in 1676 troops were sent out to help quell Bacon's Rebellion in Virginia. During the conflict from 1689 to 1713, small numbers of British troops were stationed in America, particularly at New York, while a large expeditionary force was used in the disastrous Hovenden Walker attempt on Quebec in 1711. As for New France, regular troops had made their appearance as early as 1665, but thereafter during the Ancien Régime in Canada there was no permanent garrison of French regulars, only the colonial regulars of the *Troupes de la Marine*. Not until the Seven Years' War did European concern for American empire warrant the posting of large drafts of troops.

The history of military techniques in North America has often been portrayed in terms of the different practices of the native-born militiaman, whose tactics were fitted to the environment, and the rigidly orthodox European regular, who was contemptuous of the indisciplined skirmishing of the colonial. In both English and French America the dislike between the "colonials" and the representatives of the mother countries was an inevitable result of profound social differences; in North America distinct societies had been created, different from those of the homelands. This social cleavage, when carried over into military affairs, was accentuated by the contrast between European and American methods.

The Seven Years' War and the American Revolution brought these differences into the open. The Seven Years' War began (unofficially) with a clash between French and American militia in the Ohio Valley and the rout of George Washington and his Virginians. Until 1757, although the Marquis de Montcalm had at his disposal large numbers of French regulars for some time before the English arrived in great force, a heavy part of the military load, on both sides, was carried by native-born troops. Braddock was overwhelmed near Fort Duquesne by colonial troops and Indians firing from cover, in part because European regular forces did not know how to adapt their tactics to forest warfare, but mainly because the British column had not observed conventional marching procedure and discipline. Nevertheless, Braddock has become a classic example of the inflexibility of the European commander.

Yet the defeat of Braddock is the sole victory of any importance that irregular or provincial troops of either side could claim during the whole war. Increasingly, as the two mother countries became committed more heavily to the colonial struggle, the professional took over from the amateur, the regular from the militiaman. The replacement of Governor Shirley of Massachusetts as Commander-in-Chief in America by the Earl of Loudoun in 1756 signalized this change. When William Pitt, as Secretary of State for the Southern Department, took the direction of the war into his own hands and roused the latent nationalism of the English people, the pace in America quickened, because Pitt believed that the war was to be won overseas. During the first years of the war, the British government had attempted to recruit regulars in America; but largely because the provincial governments were offering high bounties for service in the militia regiments, the British were not able to fill their establishments. This policy was therefore dropped for one of requisitioning men, money, and supplies from every colonial government; but the traditional colonial unwillingness to cooperate remained. Only Massachusetts, Connecticut, and New York met their quotas, actually contributing 70 per cent of all the troops raised in the Thirteen Colonies. By 1758 the British had 20,000 regulars in America. The war was developing into one of orthodox operations and sieges for which the provincial corps were ill-suited.

The war was to be decided by regular troops; and reinforcements from Europe depended upon sea power. New France, deficient in

population and industry, incapable even of producing enough food
to supply her own people, was desperately in need of assistance.
This assistance was not forthcoming. The naval blockade established by Pitt, and the supremacy of British naval power conclusively demonstrated by the victories of Lagos and Quiberon Bay
(1759), prevented all but a trickle of men and supplies from reaching Montcalm in his extremity. In that critical year he received only
a bagful of decorations and promotions and a corporal's guard of
three or four hundred men; his request for a diversionary operation
against the southern colonies was completely ignored.

Professionalism of European standards marked the final campaigns of the war. In 1758 Louisbourg, a formidable example of
military engineering, had fallen to an army of British regulars under
the command of General Jeffery Amherst, in an expertly conducted
orthodox siege. With the St. Lawrence gateway opened, the way
was then clear for a final assault on the heart of French power. In
1759 the British made a three-pronged assault upon New France.
Prideaux attacked Fort Niagara, the key to the West; Amherst cautiously moved up the Hudson-Richelieu gap toward Montreal;
General Wolfe and Admiral Saunders ascended the St. Lawrence to
Quebec. Montcalm was thus compelled to split his meager defense
force. The decisive battle was fought on the Plains of Abraham.
Its nature was indistinguishable from engagements in Europe; but
the regiments that fought for France on the Plains of Abraham had
been brought up to strength by infusions of half-trained militia who
could not fight a stand-up battle in the European manner. The volleys at very close range fired by Wolfe's highly trained troops were
among the most effective in history.

The American Revolution marks, indeed, an important transi-
tional step in the history of warfare. The professional military
methods of the eighteenth century, which had come to be predom-
inant in the Anglo-French struggle in America by the time of the
Seven Years' War, were more important in the Revolution than
popular legend admits. At the same time, the war was a portent
for the future, pointing toward conflicts quite different from those
of the dynastic quarrels of eighteenth-century Europe. This was
partly the outcome of military experience on American frontiers
since the time of settlement; but, more important, it was the result
of a spirit and an attitude on the part of individual Americans which
led many to take up arms for a cause. True citizen armies re-

appeared in western warfare, anticipating the change that came in Europe with the French Revolution.

The Revolution was a war between societies which had grown apart. That of Great Britain was stable and relatively rigid; one in which birth and status counted for much. That of America was much more fluid and democratic. The British military system, although constitutionally controlled, was essentially that of any European state. Commissions in the army were reserved mainly for the aristocracy and gentry, and were obtained through political patronage and purchase. The rank and file came from the lower orders, were voluntarily enlisted, and were professional, long-service soldiers armed and trained according to the prevailing European mode. The military tradition of the Thirteen Colonies, long sheltered by the British fleet and army, was that of the militia, a levy of citizens unschooled in European tactics or standards of discipline.

Yet the Revolution was not won by victories of free citizen-militia over rigidly disciplined British and German mercenaries. It is true that Washington and his generals could not have done without the state militias and the short-term soldiers who accepted a bounty, served for as little as three months, and then went home, often with their army-issued muskets. In the early months of the war, the militia was the only force available; its exploits at Boston and in Canada were remarkable. Generally, however, the militia was used only in an emergency. It was shown again and again that militia were unreliable in the face of an assault by regular forces; General Anthony Wayne declared himself satisfied if he could get three volleys out of them before they ran. Therefore, despite its early successes, the young Republic soon found that in order to grapple on even terms with the enemy, a long-service, professionally trained army was essential. As Washington said, "Regular troops are alone equal to the exigencies of modern war, as well for defense as offense, and whenever a substitute is attempted it must prove illusory and ruinous."

Late in 1776 Congress authorized the recruitment of men for three years or the duration of the war in an attempt to build a trained army of veterans. But not until 1778, at Valley Forge, did the Continental Army receive any systematic tuition in battlefield drill. A former Prussian officer, General von Steuben, introduced exercises in the tactics of the line, a training that became uniform throughout the army and gave the Continental regulars the cohesion needed to stand up against the British. Steuben recognized, however, that the time was too short to apply fully intensive drill of the kind imposed upon Prussian troops; moreover, it did not suit the independence of the Americans. Precision was therefore sacrificed in favor of swiftness of execution in order to bring American marksmanship quickly into play; for the Americans, as Lafayette and others noted, always aimed at an individual target, even when volleying. The crack regular troops of the Continental Army, generally about 10,000 in number, were one of the major elements in the eventual American victory.

It is sometimes suggested that the superiority of the American rifle over the British Brown Bess musket made a significant contribution to American fortunes. The long-barrelled weapon of Daniel Morgan's sharpshooting riflemen was certainly superior in accuracy and range to the short rifle used by the Hessian *Jägers*. It took less time to load because the frontiersmen had developed the technique of wrapping the ball in greased cloth before ramming it home. Undoubtedly, too, Morgan's men were the best marksmen of the war; at battles from Boston to Saratoga, they and their like took a heavy toll of brilliantly clad British officers. But riflemen were relatively few. Most of the Americans were armed with muskets. Moreover, the rifle was not equipped with a bayonet, and its rate of fire was much slower than that of the smoothbore musket. At Brooklyn Heights (1776), riflemen firing from cover were bayonetted by British and Hessians who drew their fire and then rushed them before they could reload. Morgan himself conceded that rifles were effective only when supported by muskets and bayonets. His corps was broken up after Saratoga and its members were used against raiding Loyalists and Indians along the frontier. The day of the rifle was yet to come; but the weapon, and the skirmishing tactics which went with it, made a strong impression upon some British and French officers, and were to have an important influence on war in the future.

With the American Revolution ideological conflict was reintroduced into warfare. In the bitterness which arose out of an irreconcilable struggle over the issue of independence as against the coercion of the colonists back into their old allegiance, the controls that restrained war in the eighteenth century were weakened. Between the regular armies, although no atrocities were committed, the European military code of honor was frequently ignored; the conventions regarding uniforms, the treatment of prisoners, and the rights of non-combatants were largely abandoned, particularly because it was difficult to determine, as when patriots posed as Loyalists at Bennington in 1777, who was a soldier and who a civilian. Excesses were more frequent in the fierce encounters between state militias and Loyalist units. Along the great arc of the frontier, outside the main theaters of the war, American frontiersmen, Loyalists, and Indians waged a savage war of barbarity.

As a result of the ideological issues in the conflict the protagonists wooed public opinion with a flood of pamphlets. In this propaganda battle, the Americans were much more successful than the British. *Common Sense* and the Declaration of Independence had an immeasurable influence on international opinion and in forcing fence-sitters to commit themselves. The heat of the battle of words, and the extreme nature of the issues at stake, drove politicians to utterances quite out of keeping with prevailing moral attitudes. Lord Suffolk, a member of the British government, defended the use of Indians, since "it was perfectly justifiable to use all the means that God and nature put into our hands" to crush those who rebelled against properly constituted authority.

On neither side, however, was there a total preoccupation with the war effort like that later brought about by intense modern nationalism. At the same time, there was on both sides of the Atlantic a division of opinion on ideological grounds which cut across national feelings. In Great Britain, the justice of the war was a party question, with the Whigs supporting some form of conciliation. There was little popular enthusiasm; public opinion tended to split along party lines. The war was fought in the old way by the regular army supplemented by German mercenaries, 18,000 of whom saw American service. The British political system of the eighteenth century functioned efficiently in the prosecution of war only when, as with the elder Pitt in the Seven Years' War and with the younger Pitt in the Napoleonic struggle, it threw up a great war leader or prime minister. This occurred only when national interests aroused widespread support. In the War of American Independence, Lord North was merely the political manager of the House of Commons whose principal job was to deliver majorities through influence and patronage. With these duties, no ordinary British prime minister had time for war leadership. For England the war was therefore very like the dynastic struggles of the century.

In the American colonies, nationalism was weakened by state loyalties and by the fact that the Revolution was itself directed against central authority in the name of local autonomy. The American population was not of one mind about independence. At the beginning, at least, convinced revolutionaries were outnumbered by the Loyalists and those uncommitted, undecided, or apathetic, but the Tories' failure to organize themselves effectively and the rapid polarization of sentiment in favor of the colonial cause soon left the Loyalists in a decided minority in most areas. Congress, consisting of delegates from the thirteen "sovereign" states, lacked the vital financial powers necessary for the direction of such a struggle. Every state but one boasted its own navy; every state had its militia defense force which was only occasionally made available to the national command; every state conducted a private war with the enemy. The Continental Army reflected the tug-of-war between the urgent need for a unified policy and the antagonism of the states toward centralization and standing armies in general. It was not a truly "national" force, despite the fact that its general officers were appointed by Congress, but a composite army in which the troops of the states retained their identity. The regimental officers of the state "lines" or regiments were named by the state legislature concerned. Owing to the inability of Congress to tax and thus to raise revenue for support of the army, in 1778 it directed the states to issue supplies to their own lines. This increased internal division within the army, because states like Pennsylvania supplied and equipped their regiments much more generously than did others. Despite its lack of consolidation, however, the Continental Army was the chief expression of rising American national feeling.

The extent of popular participation belies a simple nationalist interpretation of the war. In 1776 approximately one man in every eight of military age saw service against the British; in the years following the proportion dropped to one in sixteen, far below modern standards. Of course, it must be remembered that about one third of the population was Tory. It has been estimated that men engaged in privateering at sea exceeded those in the armed forces in every year except 1776. The only means that Congress had to attract men for long service was to offer bounties. Even here the states often outbid Congress; many men trafficked in bounties; and galloping inflation made civilian life more attractive by reducing the value of the bounty. On two occasions, Congress went to the length of authorizing Washington to draft men, but this was ineffective in the face of state and popular resistance. Despite the war, and in part because of it, the American economy flourished, yet the army was grudgingly supplied by the states and was victimized by profiteers. It maintained a sufficient amount of arms and equipment only because of French help.

The Revolution began with Great Britain holding the advantage over the colonies in almost every respect. Only a few years earlier she had been victorious in a "world war" in which she had no ally but Prussia. Her economic power alone appeared decisive. But during the Revolution eighteenth-century strategical precepts were severely shaken. The British found that it was not enough to menace the supply lines of an American army, or even to defeat it in the field. Once away from the security of their coastal bases, they discovered that not only had they to counter the Fabian strategy of Continental forces but, wherever they passed, the bulk of the civilian population transformed itself into an army of irregulars of a kind unknown in Europe. Although the Americans might not flock to join the army of Congress, they would fight to defend their own states, and thus the British were exposed to the novel experience of engaging the mass of the population.

The Saratoga campaign (1777) was the clearest example of this new qualification upon strategy. Upon Burgoyne's "magnificent armament" rested the hopes of the British administration. Striking south from Montreal, down the Richelieu, Lake Champlain, and the Hudson, Burgoyne's forces were to take Albany and thus, acting with the army under Sir William Howe, cut off New England, the center of rebellion, from the rest of the colonies. His army consisted of 6,500 British and German regulars, more than 1,000 Canadian and Indian auxiliaries, much more artillery than he needed, and all the paraphernalia of a typical European army, including camp followers, servants, and 600 wagons to carry supplies. Moving at a ponderous pace (at one point, twenty miles in twenty days), Burgoyne pushed the outnumbered Continentals from Ticonderoga back across the Hudson. But as his lines of supply stretched to the breaking point, the Americans prevented him from living off the country by methodical devastation along his line of march. Short supply alone did not bring him to a halt. His snail-like progress allowed thousands of militia from New York and New England to concentrate against him. By the time he had reached Saratoga, the original Continental force of 4,000 had been swelled by militia to perhaps 17,000 men. Enveloped by weight of numbers, his own force denuded, and with Howe's army involved in the Philadelphia campaign, Burgoyne surrendered. The mass citizen-army of Saratoga has no eighteenth-century precedent; its counterpart is to be found in the armies of the French Revolution.

British armies in North America were severely handicapped by operating at the end of an extremely long line of supply. For this reason, the first concern of British strategy was with the seizure and maintenance of ocean ports, like New York, Philadelphia, and Charleston, which acted as magazines for the armies in the field. When France entered the war in 1778, British communications at once became vulnerable to naval attack, and land operations suffered accordingly. The war became world wide and Britain faced Spain and Holland, as well as France, in Europe. The American war was but a single theater in a world conflict. The disaster of Cornwallis at Yorktown was due to a failure in the use of British sea power. When the French Admiral De Grasse won control of the Chesapeake, Cornwallis, cut off from New York supplies or the hope of evacuation, could do nothing but surrender. Sea power had determined the issue.

12

The Nation in Arms and the Napoleonic Wars

The eighteenth-century professional standing army was as efficient as was possible within the limitations imposed by the political and social structure of the contemporary state. But even while it flourished, some men had realized that it did not represent the ultimate development of military strength. The principle of allowing the defense of the state to become the responsibility of hired professionals was convenient in so far as it led to expert efficiency in arms; but it was a source of weakness in that it did not utilize the full resources of the national man power. Some of the *philosophes,* the leaders of the eighteenth-century intellectual world, had seen this clearly but were puzzled to find a solution. Voltaire had criticized the contemporary military system, scoffing at the fact that the defenders of the state were recruited from the poorest human material. But, typically, he had no other suggestion than that the armies should decide issues by "fighting it out in a field." This was not a solution but was, indeed, exactly what was happening.

Other *philosophes,* critical of the rigid class structure of contemporary society and of its reflection in the "irrational" army of their day, had argued that in an emergency the man power of the nation should be called out to fight as a militia and should be disbanded when the crisis passed. Montesquieu saw a citizen army as a defense against arbitrary rule; in a republic, he thought, the army must be the people, as in Roman times. Rousseau had carried this a step beyond the normal thinking of the eighteenth century by suggesting that the citizen had a responsibility to fight in defense of his country, an idea which was logical for a democratic form of government but not for the autocratic monarchies that prevailed in Europe. Switzer-

land, where Rousseau lived, had such a militia. Elsewhere it might
have endangered the regime.

Some military thinkers had put forward similar ideas. Guibert,
who died in 1789, the year of the French Revolution, preached a
war of movement and proposed the recruiting of a citizen army. He
had criticized the limitations of the contemporary supply system and
had suggested that the army should be freed from the restrictions
which the magazine system imposed and should march with a
minimum of baggage through the enemy's territory, living off the
country. He believed that a nation which was sound in government
could create such an army and would be able with it to dominate
its neighbors. He thus forecast the great revolution in military
organization which began soon after his death. But he apparently
did not realize that it could not take place until a political revolution had occurred.

The effect of a political revolution on military organization in
America has already been discussed. In France the same thing happened in rather different circumstances. The monarchy had an
antiquated fiscal system which, failing to utilize the full resources of
the French nation in the wars of the eighteenth century, had bank-
rupted the state. The Estates-General, which met in 1789 in an
attempt to solve the financial tangle, recommended constitutional
changes which would have sharply curtailed the power of the Crown.
Ensuing crises led to mob violence, and the royal armies, their rank
and file unpaid and disaffected, could not be used safely. Of the
whole army, the real prop of the despotic state, only the Swiss
Guards could be relied on in emergency. The constitutional regime
set up by the men of 1789 was terminated by the consequences of
the French declaration of war on Austria in 1792. The war thus
launched was not only a preventive one against counterrevolu-
tionary intervention by the great powers but also an ideological
crusade for the liberation of other peoples. Within a few months,
the French monarchy was overthrown and a Convention summoned to design republican institutions. Under the Convention,
foreign invasion, internal counterrevolution, mob pressures, and
economic problems led to the establishment of the "Terror" by
the radical Jacobins, a dictatorial regime intended to crush counter-
revolution. It was this regime which established the citizen army,
large-scale war production, mass indoctrination, and economic regimentation characteristic of modern states in wartime. Nevertheless,

the old structure of "privilege" in the state and of an hereditary absolutism was gone, and the republican principles of popular sovereignty and of "liberty, equality, and fraternity" were henceforward to be powerful forces in French politics. A state in which the people, and not a monarch, seemed to hold supreme power had won the hearts of the masses.

When the Revolution occurred in France and unhinged the state, a new type of army emerged. The most obvious sign of the change was a vast increase in the size of the military forces resulting from the conscription of the citizenry in 1793. But the new army was not merely a citizens' militia. It was rapidly to take upon itself the efficiency of professionalism. Even so, it did not become merely a larger version of the eighteenth-century standing army. As a result of the circumstances of its creation it remained different in kind as well as in size. The "nation-in-arms," the "armed horde" as it has been well called, was born of the Revolution and reflected that fact in its morale. It was moved not only by discipline but also by ideological and patriotic fervor. The vote and national military service were corollaries. The people had, in theory, seized control of the state from the dynasts and now had to defend it; and the new form of state had harnessed public opinion to the machinery of national defense, with the result that its military power was vastly increased. Generals of the French Revolution and, later, Napoleon showed that these forces could be used for aggression. They thus fulfilled Guibert's prophecies.

It must be noticed that in addition to this sociological explanation of the new might of the revolutionary state, there is also a technical explanation which some writers have suggested as the real one. During the long period of wars in the eighteenth century, military efficiency had been increased by improved weapons, by new forms of military organization, by greatly improved communications, by better map-making, and by the growth of productive capacity. One technical development in particular is most frequently mentioned as a cause of the revolution in warfare at the end of the eighteenth century, namely, the further development of artillery. The French had attempted to regain the military prestige lost by their final defeat by England by greatly improving their ordnance. Inspector General Gribeauval had introduced a series of changes after 1763 which have been described as the foundation of the military achievements of Revolutionary and Napoleonic France. Guns were made with interchangeable parts for mass production; carriages were built to a standard model; the mobility of the guns was improved by harnessing the horses in pairs instead of in file; hardwood axles replaced heavy iron ones; and accuracy was promoted by the introduction of a "tangent sight", a graduated brass measure which enabled the gunner to "lay" the gun on a target. The greater mobility of the guns made possible divisional formation, which was to become a feature of the warfare of the Revolutionary age.

At the same time the building of roads and canals, which had gone on apace in France and western Europe in the eighteenth century, had made possible the deployment and movement of divisions of an army in complicated maneuver. Furthermore, the development of the science of mathematics and of engineering (the latter had been chiefly promoted in the military colleges in the eighteenth century), and the great improvement in cartography (which had been made possible by greater skill in mensuration), undoubtedly contributed to the increased power of the new armies.

But these technical developments do not explain the great increase in the size of armies or their new morale. If they had been of primary importance, they would have provided the Ancien Régime with a new military strength which might have prevented the Revolution. But technical achievements were secondary to the morale factor. It is reasonable to argue, then, that although the technical developments of the eighteenth century strengthened the military power of the revolutionary state, they did not create it.

The history of the first years of the Revolutionary Wars shows exactly how the political and social upheaval affected military organization and methods. When the Revolutionary government of France first declared war on the Austrian and Prussian monarchs who thought to restore Louis XVI to power, it had to rely on armies which consisted mainly of regulars from the armies of the Ancien Régime with an intermixture of volunteers. They were far from successful. Then, in 1792, came the triumph of Valmy, the beginning of the victories of the French Revolution, sometimes said to have been won by a cannonade of massed artillery. It is true that the opposing infantry never came into contact; but the victory was not caused by a cannonade. The French won at Valmy because their enemies were weakened by indecisive command and by dysentery. However, the victory set France afire with nationalism, and, as a result, the Revolutionaries wildly invaded the Low Countries pretending to bring freedom to oppressed peoples everywhere. But once again their armies proved unequal to the task. Defeats, and the desertion of their only experienced military leader, the former royal general Dumouriez, brought France and the Revolution to the brink of disaster.

It was this crisis which produced the Terror in France and with it a complete overhauling of the military system. The Committee of Public Safety, set up to root out treason, became in effect a war cabinet with dictatorial powers. Thus was remedied one serious defect in the system of government which had replaced the despotism of Louis XVI. Hitherto, the Revolutionary state had lacked an efficient executive. Now it possessed one of the most powerful ever known. Within a few weeks there came the decree of national mobilization and then one of requisition. The effect of the enhanced power of the Revolutionary state was thus to organize the resources of the nation more fully in its service. Carnot, one of the greatest war ministers of all time, proceeded to reverse the defeats of the early years.

France soon discovered a formula whereby numbers and zeal could bring victory. Highly trained light infantry had been used as skirmishers in the eighteenth century to cover the advance of the line. By the time of the Revolution, agricultural developments had increased their value: in some parts of northern Europe open fields were giving way to enclosures, and walls or hedgerows provided greater cover for the skirmish line. Thus at Hondschoote in the Low Countries in 1793, walls and dikes prevented the enemy from forming line and maneuvering against the French.   Captain Colin shows that, although most French armies retained the capability of maneuver in the field, the Army of the North, which fought the British, lost maneuverability, because its cadres were heavily infiltrated with recruits. The French army was short of trained light infantry in 1793 and 1794 and therefore also used poorly trained troops for skirmishing.

These circumstances led to a mistaken interpretation of the tactical innovations of the Revolution. Sir Charles Oman and General Fuller have said that, as a consequence of using inferior troops, Revolutionary generals resorted to massive columns. However, after Dumouriez ordered an attack in columns-in-line at Jemappes in 1792, that formation was apparently not used for a year or two. It is also true that the raw levies of the Revolution could not have advanced far in line and would have been thoroughly disorganized by the debris of front lines falling back to the rear. But the Revolutionary generals did favor advancing in columns-in-line for attack, partly for this very reason, but even more because small columns-in-line would not mask the new mobile field artillery inherited from Gribeauval's reforms in Louis XVI's army. And artillery was the decisive factor in Revolutionary victories. It was not massive columns but swarms of highly trained skirmishers and small assault columns-in-line, with a powerful artillery bombardment, that constituted the Revolution's tactical innovation. Revolutionary zeal was also important, but perhaps not so important as a new ruthlessness. This affected foraging—not a new practice, but now carried on with greater severity. It also affected discipline and the willingness of commanders to drive their men and take risks: for revolutionary generals who failed were liable to be summarily dismissed or even shot. Furthermore, the system of conscription introduced in 1793 gave them a glut of lives to squander lavishly.

Just as the Revolution produced new tactics and tactical formations, so it also affected the organization of armies. By 1794, the French had called up over half a million men. Not since the great barbarian invasions had there been so many men in arms. Armies of that size could not be commanded and fought in the old way, as a single whole, commanded by a single general. It was imperative that they be divided into "divisions," which were portions of an army composed of all arms, able to operate either in cooperation with other parts of the army or, if need be, by themselves.

Divisional formation revolutionized strategy. Armies were now composed of detachable parts which could fight the enemy alone until the rest of the army came up in support. Divisions could also be detached to carry out encircling movements; and on the defensive, could be used to prevent them. Divisions could advance along parallel roads and concentrate immediately before making contact with the enemy. Thus generalship was made more complicated and staff work became more important. Highly detailed maps, showing natural features, were now required. Improved cartography made them available.

At the same time, the Revolutionary fervor of the conscripts caused them to operate in a manner that would have been more difficult for the regulars of the eighteenth century. They marched faster, with the Revolutionary quickstep of 120 paces to the minute; they bivouacked in the open; and since they lived on the country, they carried less baggage. They thus freed themselves from the restricting magazines which had too often held eighteenth-century war in a strait jacket.

Furthermore, there was a new spirit in warfare. When the mass citizen army became a reality, it became imperative to instill in it a nationalistic and Revolutionary zeal. Under the Convention, deliberate efforts were made to indoctrinate soldiers in Revolutionary patriotism with handbooks and manuals containing military "catechisms," inspirational stories of heroic Republican soldiers and sailors, and Revolutionary songs instead of the hymns and prayers of former days. The troops of the Revolution thus marched for a cause, primarily to defend their country, secondarily to free the oppressed. They used psychological weapons as well as physical ones. They sought to win the minds of their enemies and to turn the people against their rulers. Ideological warfare, unknown in Europe since the end of the period of religious strife, returned once more.

But it is important to realize that the Revolution had produced a greater professional skill as well as greater morale. The wild revolutionary soldiers of the early years rapidly became veterans without losing all of their early zest. Once more, as in England in the days of Cromwell, professional skill and belief in a cause were joined to produce an unbeatable combination. The Revolution had been preserved by military action; and military efficiency was therefore highly prized by the Revolutionary state. Indeed, the armies of the Revolution were vastly more effective than those of the past, not only because all ranks were united by a common enthusiasm, but because the old limitations had been broken down by a powerful impersonal state.

The political revolution brought an important revolution in military training. Ever since the coordinated operations of pikemen had overcome the individual skill and courage of knights, the importance of training and drill had been recognized; but there had been little change in the nature of the training process from the time of the Swiss phalanx of pikes down to that of the "line" of muskets and bayonets. The employment of skirmishing tactics in the era of the Revolution meant that the soldier had to be trained to operate as an individual as well as part of a group. The whole training process was thus affected; and it brought a parallel revolution in military discipline. This can be most clearly demonstrated in the British Army; but similar changes occurred in the armies of Revolutionary France, of the United States, and in due course in all armies everywhere.

Jägers and Pandours, highly mobile troops of a semi-regular nature from the woods and mountains of Southeastern Europe, had fought in loose formation in German armies in the eighteenth century. The experiences of the British in North American fighting in the eighteenth century had led to the formation of a "Rifle Corps" and of companies of "Rangers" in which a completely new form of discipline was asserted. In place of the lash, which had been used brutally to enforce discipline in the old armies, these new regiments fostered the self-confidence and pride of the men and developed a high morale. The experiment, one not popular with conservative military leaders of the old type, had lapsed after the end of the American Revolution, but during the Revolutionary Wars in Europe it was revived. In 1800 there was formed the "Experimental Rifle Corps." A little later came Sir John Moore's Light Brigade which he trained by new methods at Shorncliffe. In the words of Liddell Hart, Moore gave "a new spiritual meaning to discipline." His training methods and the new discipline were amply justified in the Peninsular War when the Light Division proved itself.

The appearance of new methods of training and a new discipline was due to a combination of technological and sociological factors. The adoption of the rifle for light infantry (which had been delayed for centuries because rifling impeded the speed of loading) was partly responsible. Much more important was the impact of the political revolution which had occurred first in America and then in France. The citizen-soldiers who composed the "rabble in arms" could be trained to fight together only under a system of discipline which was less degrading to the individual than that of the eighteenth century. Competence in the mastery of more complicated weapons and tactics could not be developed by the brutal methods of the drill sergeant; and the masses, especially those who were beginning to advance from the lowest levels of untutored ignorance, required more enlightened methods of training when enlisted into the armed forces.

The impact of the Revolution, and at the same time of technological progress, had an even more immediate and obvious effect on the training of line officers. Military engineers and gunners needed some knowledge of science, particularly mathematics, and this had led in the seventeenth and eighteenth centuries to various schemes to give formal education to potential officers. The American and French Revolutions emphasized this trend towards a professionally trained corps of officers. Neither the United States nor Revolutionary France could rely on an aristocracy for a supply of officers and each was therefore compelled to set up military academies in which entry and graduation alike depended on merit and hard work. L'École Polytechnique was founded in 1795; the year 1802 saw the birth of military colleges in France, the United States, and Great Britain which eventually became established at St. Cyr, West Point, and Sandhurst, respectively. Thus similar forces were operating in countries which had not experienced a revolution at first hand.

The social and technical revolution which came at the end of the eighteenth century had profoundly affected the nature of armies and of warfare. Along with the fuller employment of the resources and manpower of the state came a new kind of army based on a new spirit and discipline and trained more fully than ever before in the art and science of warfare. Thus, the increasing participation of the nation in national armies and in warfare did not bring an inevitable decline in military proficiency. Sounder methods of training the men in the ranks, and improved selection and training of officers, made possible a great increase in the effectiveness of military power in the nineteenth century.

The new mass armies of the Revolution were inherited by Napoleon Bonaparte who used them to climb to power in France and to perpetuate and spread the political upheaval which had overturned the Ancien Régime. The "little Corsican," a former royal artillery officer, had learned the way to power as a result of an episode on October 5, 1795. Placed in charge of the defense of the Convention against an attack by civilian insurrectionists, Napoleon used field guns ruthlessly in the streets to repulse the assault. As a result, he came to realize that an ambitious man with few scruples could use military force to dominate the state in a way that had not previously been possible. It was a lesson he was never to forget and one which was to have a profound effect on human history.

The Directory, which had now taken over the government of France, sent Napoleon to command the Army of Italy, which was ragged, half-starved, and mutinous. He was ordered to drive the Austrians back across the Alps, a formidable assignment that might well have spelled the end of his career. But the Revolutionary spirit was strong in the mass armies which the Revolution had called into being, and Napoleon at once showed those personal qualities that made him a great leader of men, and also his genius for strategy.

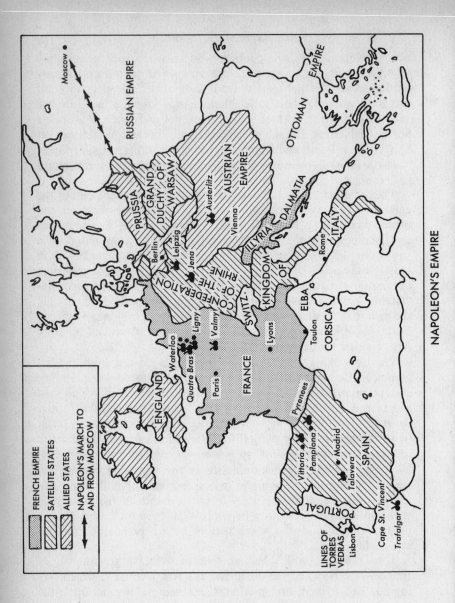

NAPOLEON'S EMPIRE

FRENCH EMPIRE

SATELLITE STATES

ALLIED STATES

NAPOLEON'S MARCH TO
AND FROM MOSCOW

ENGLAND

RUSSIAN EMPIRE

Moscow

PRUSSIA

GRAND
DUCHY OF
WARSAW

AUSTRIAN
EMPIRE

Austerlitz

Vienna

Berlin

Leipzig

Jena

CONFEDERATION
OF THE
RHINE

SWITZ.

OTTOMAN
EMPIRE

DALMATIA

ILLYRIA

KINGDOM
OF

ITALY

Rome

ELBA

CORSICA

Waterloo

Quatre Bras

Ligny

Valmy

Lyons

Toulon

Paris

FRANCE

Pyrenees

Vittoria

Pamplona

Madrid

Talavera

SPAIN

PORTUGAL

LINES OF
TORRES
VEDRAS

Lisbon

Cape St. Vincent

Trafalgar

He almost always tried to attack where he had local superiority. The ragged army followed him into Italy, forced the Piedmontese to make peace, and expelled the Austrians. At the engagement at the bridge at Lodi, he deliberately blooded his troops by a head-on assault when he knew there were fords which would have provided an easier route. By that time his personal magnetism had won the hearts of his men and they were prepared to follow him anywhere. In due course, the armies which the Revolution had created made their new leader Emperor of France and thus turned the clock back to autocracy. For nearly two decades they fought to conquer Europe in his name.

Napoleon's campaigns and battles have been studied by a multitude who have sought the secret of his genius. No one can deny him a high place among the great captains of world history as a master of the art of strategy; and his military greatness is enhanced by the fact that he inherited all his weapons from his predecessors. The arms which Napoleon's troops used were not new and therefore do not in themselves explain his achievements. The musket and bayonet of the infantryman had changed little since Louis XIV's time; Napoleon's artillery came to him as a result of the reforms of Gribeauval in the last years of the Ancien Régime and he made little improvement in it; and although he introduced heavier defensive armor for his cuirassiers and furnished more of his light cavalry with lances to overreach the bayonets of opposing infantry, his mounted troops were armed little better than those of earlier centuries. Napoleon mastered Europe with weapons available to other men before he rose to power.

Indeed, in some ways he was an arch-reactionary toward new weapons and technological progress in the materiel of war. He disbanded the balloonists in 1799. They might have shown him the direction of Blücher's retreat after Ligny in 1815 and thus have warned him that he would meet the Prussians as well as Wellington's army at Waterloo. Shrapnel had been invented by a British major of that name before 1803. It would have made short work of Wellington's squares at Waterloo, but it was a carefully guarded secret which Napoleon never learned.

There is a stronger case for saying that Napoleon triumphed through a more efficient use of well-known weapons. He was a master of strategy. His usual practice on campaign was to sleep until 1 A.M., by which time his cavalry had brought in full reports of the enemy's movements. It is significant that he made extensive use of cavalry for reconnaissance. Frederick the Great, half a century earlier, had done so only sparingly, partly because he was not able to trust his troops when too far from his immediate control. The information obtained was carefully outlined on the largest available map of the area and the Emperor's plans were then added. Frequently Napoleon himself was to be seen crawling about on the map to indicate dispositions. But the tactical handling of the battle was left to his subordinates.

Napoleon was a past master in the art of confusing the enemy and striking where he was not expected. Pierre de Bourcet, a chief of staff of the royal armies in both the War of the Austrian Sucession and the Seven Years' War, and from 1764 the director of the school for staff officers at Grenoble, had taught that an enemy could be misled by moves of different units which appeared to be disconnected but which were actually part of a connected plan. The aim was to compel the enemy to divide his forces, then to fall upon one part before it could be reinforced. This was the basis of Napoleon's strategy. He used it with signal success against the Austrians and Italians in his first campaign; and he rarely departed from some variation of this basic technique. One variation he learned by accident at Marengo in 1800. That battle was won for him by the timely appearance of a division which had failed to concentrate in time for the beginning of the battle but which arrived fresh when both the French and the Austrian armies were weary. Afterwards, Napoleon often held reserves back until the enemy forces were worn out; and at Austerlitz he deliberately repeated the strategy which had triumphed accidentally at Marengo.

As a rule, Napoleon engaged the enemy in front with a holding attack while a corps (that is, a group of divisions) swung in a wide flanking movement to fall upon the enemy's rear and threaten his communications. When Napoleon heard the guns of the detached force and so knew that it was attacking, he usually delivered a hammer blow at a weak spot in the center of the enemy's line. This blow, the decisive one, was normally made possible by a tremendous concentration of artillery fire. It was frequently delivered by a massed cavalry formation. He kept the bulk of the cavalry for use on the charge and sent only divisional cavalry with the flank attack. It was his practice to keep the heavy cavalry, the cuirassiers, in reserve until the later stages of a battle for the final shock charge. For infantry assault he always employed heavy columns, the tactical formation more properly called "column of divisions" which derived directly from the methods of the generals of the French Republican armies. Column of divisions was a formation in which the three battalions of a regiment advanced one behind the other with a front of one hundred muskets and a depth of nine ranks in each battalion. It was normally preceded by a screen of *tirailleurs* or skirmishers whose fire protected the charge until the moment of impact.

These strategical and tactical methods were not entirely his own. He borrowed them from earlier theorists and in some cases they had already been tried out in action. Mobility, divisional organization, heavy concentrations of artillery, and (according to some interpreters) a tactical formation called *ordre mixte* were the keys to Napoleonic victory. Each of these had been advocated earlier. Guibert, in his *Essai général de tactique* (1770) and *Défense du système de guerre* (1779), had stressed the need for greater mobility and had advocated divisional formations. It has been shown that divisions had been used by Marshal Saxe in the War of the Austrian Succession. Guibert had also proposed the *ordre mixte,* in which the battalions were drawn up alternately in line and in column, thus combining the shock of the column with the fire of the line. Napoleon borrowed it from Guibert but appears to have used it only for those parts of his battle line which were detailed to hold the enemy troops opposed to them. For the assault, he used his heavy columns.

It is frequently said that Napoleon won his battles by the weight of his bombardment. He was, of course, an artillery officer and had first attracted attention at Toulon in 1793 by his command of the guns. His belief was that, while the infantry was the main arm of an army, it could not stand up to superior artillery. But even here Napoleon was a borrower rather than an innovator. The Chevalier du Teil, Napoleon's superior in command of the artillery at Toulon, had urged in his *L'usage de l'artillerie nouvelle dans la guerre de campagne* that artillery be concentrated at the point of attack and not dispersed along the whole line. This practice was followed by Napoleon and he used the big guns to blast a hole in the enemy's line into which the infantry could penetrate. As time went on, and as the quality of French conscripts deteriorated, he increased the proportion of artillery in his armies and relied more and more on bombardment. In 1801, he replaced the civilian drivers of the gun teams by soldiers. Napoleon raised artillery from the status of an auxiliary to that of equality with infantry and cavalry.

Nevertheless, his use of artillery was only a contributing factor in the Napoleonic victories. It is not the sole key to his domination of the battlefields of Europe for nearly two decades.

The increase in the size of armies and the practice of operating with several detached corps or divisions greatly increased the difficulties of command. Napoleon had a chief of staff, but that officer acted more in the role of what would today be called an adjutant general. He also had chiefs of artillery, of engineers, and of the quartermaster department. Each of these officers had a large subordinate staff. But there was no organized coordinated general staff as it is understood today. Napoleon did much of the staff work, both operational and supply, himself. He was, in effect, his own chief of staff in the modern sense. It was his genius to be able to direct the operations of his armies in circumstances in which lesser men would have failed.

However, the real explanation of Napoleon's meteoric career springs not so much from his own military genius, which is unquestionable, but from the Revolutionary and nationalistic spirit inculcated by the events of 1789. His long run of victories was due to the mass armies which the Revolution had produced. As Revolutionary fervor faded, those armies were maintained by the use of the frightening power which the new "democratic" state possessed. The Revolution had conferred upon the government a power of coercion far beyond that enjoyed by the autocratic monarchs of the eighteenth century. That power was used to compel Frenchmen, and even the men of conquered countries, to fill the ranks in the armies of Napoleon as fast as they were depleted by casualties and disease. The First Empire conscripted about three million men for all arms; and few of them returned to civil life while the Emperor reigned. He said that he had an income of 200,000 young men a year and, on another occasion, that he "did not take much heed of the lives of a million men." He was apparently never aware of the danger of growing public opposition to his demands, even when he had to employ an army of troops to round up those who evaded military service. While before the Revolution field armies of 40,000 or 50,000 were large, the French Imperial armies, freed from the magazine system, grew in size until by 1809 they were over 100,000 strong, larger than those put in the field by Louis XIV and the Grand Alliance. In 1812 Napoleon took on his futile invasion of Russia over half a million men from all western Europe except Spain and the biggest armed horde seen since the time of Attila.

A secondary factor in Napoleon's military success was increased industrial production. Although, as we have seen, he made no great use of new advances in military technology, it must not be forgotten that the huge armies upon which he built his empire could be provisioned and supplied only because production and communication had greatly improved toward the end of the eighteenth century. While the full blast of the Industrial Revolution had not yet reached the Continent from the British Isles, there had already been an expansion in productive capacity. Gribeauval had learned the principle of interchangeable parts from Austria, and in 1785, Le Blanc anticipated Eli Whitney's use of it in the manufacture of arms on a mass-production scale, although still largely by hand rather than by machine. Furthermore, distribution was vastly improved by new roads and canals. The Emperor left to France the best road system in Europe, one which could be used for both military and commercial purposes. He paid great attention to problems of production and supply. When the war with England and the Continental Blockade cut him off from British industrial resources, he strove hard to further the industrial development of his Empire. But he did not understand economics and how to stimulate business, and the net effect of his efforts was insufficient to meet Britain's rapid commercial expansion.

Napoleon's reliance on masses of men and materials remedied a serious omission in eighteenth-century thinking about war. So much emphasis had been placed upon tactical and strategic maneuver by the generals of the Ancien Régime that it had become accepted that relative strengths counted for little. Napoleon, indeed, often won when he did not possess absolute superiority in numbers; but it was usually by the achievement of a temporary local superiority over a part of the enemy forces. On the whole, it is true to say that his victories were due also to the intelligent use of mass. His successes caused opinion to turn away from the eighteenth-century tendency to ignore mass and to swing to the other extreme. As the Napoleonic legend grew, the concept of the primacy of mass grew with it.

A fourth consideration in Napoleon's achievements was the ideology which he deliberately spread. Like the armies of the Revolution, those of the Empire always marched "to free the oppressed." Napoleon deliberately sought to destroy the fiber of his enemies by seducing their soldiers. In Italy, he preached liberty and the expulsion of the foreigner even while he was bringing chains and a new foreign dictatorship. After the Battle of Jena, in 1806, the people of Berlin received the Emperor with smiles and cheers. He represented liberty, not oppression. The spreading of beliefs and opinions, true and untrue, was not a new weapon in warfare, but after the political and social revolution of 1789 it had come to possess a new importance. Here again Napoleon benefited from the Revolution which he always claimed to be preserving.

As a result of the new emphasis on ideas, the very nature of warfare was changed. The purpose of war came to be the complete overthrow of the enemy instead of, as in the dynastic and commercial struggles of the eighteenth century, the gaining of a limited advantage. Whereas formerly men had fought to ensure a succession or to seize an outlying province, now the goal of war was to carve up the state by major amputations, to revolutionize it, or to drive out its legitimate government; and the ultimate aim of the victor was complete annexation. The partitions of Poland (1772, 1793, 1795) had shown what could be done to destroy a state completely. The warfare of the eighteenth century, limited both in manner of operation and in objective, thus gave way to war in which military action and objectives alike were "total."

The same factors which had made possible Napoleon's conquest of most of Europe led inevitably to his downfall. In successive wars he had defeated the Austrians and the Prussians and had conquered Spain and Italy. In 1807, he had forced the Czar of Russia, at Tilsit, to come to terms of peace which in effect recognized Napoleon's possession of most of continental Europe except the Czar's own territories. Only the British remained hostile. They had destroyed the combined French and Spanish fleets at Trafalgar (1805) and Napoleon, foiled in his hopes of invading the British Isles, had sought to subdue them by decrees cutting them off from trade with all his territories and satellites. The attempt to impose this economic policy upon Portugal and Russia aroused the forces which eventually destroyed him.

The British attacked through Portugal and Spain with an army which had been thoroughly overhauled since its defeats at the hands of the French republicans. In 1794 the British government had suddenly realized that the country, if it had to face the possibility of invasion, would be practically defenseless. In the following years the Commander-in-Chief, the Duke of York, undertook a program of reform which brought more changes in the army than had occurred in the previous two centuries. He increased its pay, improved its drill and equipment, introduced corps of riflemen, and reorganized military administration. The regimental system, the chief source of pride, tradition, and morale in the British Army, was retained; but a new method of feeding recruits into the regular army through the militia was introduced. As militia service was based on the ballot, the country had selective compulsory service for home defense until the end of the war. Led by Wellington, this revitalized army defeated Napoleon's marshals in Spain and in 1813 invaded France.

In 1812, Napoleon was compelled to retreat from Moscow, and Russian Cossacks, aided by "General Winter," practically destroyed the remnants of his army. Inspired by this, the Prussians and Austrians rose against their conqueror, and their arms were strengthened by nationalistic passion which French arrogance had stirred up. At the Battle of the Nations at Leipzig in Saxony, the peoples of Europe inflicted a crushing defeat on the Emperor. When Paris fell to the invader, Napoleon abdicated. His return from Elba in 1815, and the Hundred Days which culminated in Waterloo, were an anticlimax. The nations were aroused and in arms and even had Wellington suffered defeat instead of victory at Waterloo, Napoleon could never have regained his old hegemony in Europe.

Napoleon was struck down partly because he had become intoxicated with his own success and with his power to command armies which had actually out grown his control, but even more because the forces which had raised him up cast him down again. The nations he had conquered adopted his methods. Mass armies became used universally and were no longer a monopoly of the French. Thus when Prussia, after Jena, was limited to an army of eighteenth-century proportions, Gneisenau invented a system of reserves by which the trainees remained liable for mobilization and so available to a sudden army expansion. This device was possible only because the Prussian people, particularly the young men, were willing to accept it. Their patriotic hatred of France had been inspired in a way not possible before the Revolution. The recruiting of foreign soldiers had to be abandoned because of the poverty of Prussia. In 1813 and 1814, the *Landwehr* (a universal militia) and the *Landsturm* (a kind of *levée en masse*) were instituted. Prussia thus achieved an army of the new mass type without undergoing a political revolution herself, but rather as a result of the pressure of the Revolution in France. When Napoleon was defeated in 1814, his armies had been wasted by casualties and by shortage of conscripts to a mere 214,000 effectives, while those of the allied nations numbered more than 325,000. The "big battalions" had changed sides.

Along with mass armies, the continental nations copied French tactics. Thus, whereas the French had formerly achieved victory by hurling columns against a weak spot in the enemy line which opposing generals, following eighteenth-century practice, had spread to cover all points, the continental European armies all began to use columns covered by skirmishers and backed by concentrated artillery. A penetration no longer achieved the same deadly result.

The British army, however, had adhered to the linear formation in the belief that the new French system was fundamentally wrong and successful only against unsteady troops. Wellington, who had been employed in India after his sole meeting with the French Revolutionary armies in Flanders in 1794, went to take command in Portugal in 1808, determined to test against the French his own theories of how the "line" could defeat the French tactics which had overthrown all the armies of Europe. He was convinced that most European armies were beaten before they started and that well-trained troops, confident in their leaders, could not be defeated by the crude methods developed by the exigencies of the Revolution.

His conflicts with Napoleon's marshals in Spain, and afterwards with the Emperor himself at Waterloo, were accompanied by, and have been followed by, a long and sometimes bitter dispute about the relative merits of the line and the column. The debate has tended to oversimplify the issue and to exaggerate the difference between the tactical formations used by the two opposing sides. In particular, it has led to an erroneous belief that the French attacked with a whole army, or with whole divisions, in long narrow columns. To some extent this belief is based on the fact that occasionally a French column on the march did bump into a deployed British line before it had time to deploy into its tactical formation of columns of divisions and *ordre mixte*. The weakness of the column attack, as Wellington and the British realized, was that a battalion deployed against it in line could overlap it with musket fire on each flank. The men in the rear of the column could be shot at but could not shoot.

Wellington was never able to muster as many field guns as the French. His plans for the use of linear formation were based on the idea that the line should not be exposed until the enemy came within musket shot, that it should be protected by a skirmish line of riflemen, and that it should be flanked either by natural cover or by cavalry or artillery. His ideal position, as at Waterloo, was behind the crest of a low hill where his men could stand or lie until the enemy, toiling up the slope, came within range. Sheltered by the ground, they were out of artillery fire until the time came for them to advance over the crest and to fire deadly volleys. Thus the British retained the linear formation of the eighteenth century; but there was one significant difference. They reduced it to two ranks instead of three, to spread the effect of its fire power. Despite all the victories of the French based on column formation of nine or more ranks, the thinning of the line was the proper trend for tactical development. Heavy phalanxes had been obsolescent ever since the pike had given way to the musket as the decisive infantry weapon. Battles were now won by fire power and not by push of pike or bayonet. Napoleon himself admitted that the sword and pike of ancient times meant deep formations, but that modern firearms had made shallow formations imperative. Wellington's resolute adherence to linear formation was a sound recognition of that essential truth.

Napoleon had correctly emphasized mass, numbers, artillery fire power, and the psychological weapons given him by the new popular state; but the methods which he used on the battlefield were not really suitable to the new age. He had endeavored to drill the revolutionary mob into a massive phalanx. Such a development could not proceed far even in face of the weapons then available.

The War of 1812 between Great Britain and the United States might logically have been expected, as a result of the place and time of the conflict, to reproduce many of the features of the new mass warfare of the Old World. War in North America had never been marked by restraint; the American Revolution had anticipated many of the military innovations of the French Revolutionary and Napoleonic Wars; and the ideological bitterness of 1776 had not significantly abated. In Europe, for almost two decades, Great Britain had been engaged in a life and death struggle with France in which she had developed new methods of fighting to meet those of Napoleon.

Yet the War of 1812 was a comparatively mild conflict in which the number of participants was relatively small and the temper and pace much less extreme than that of the war in Europe. The explanation for this apparent anomaly is simple. The British were involved in a major European war; their garrison in Canada was never large, even when veterans were diverted to North American service in 1813 and 1814. Canadian militia units were never more than auxiliaries of the regular forces. For the most part, the British contented themselves with holding the Canadian border, blockading the American coast, operating against American shipping, and indulging occasionally in pin-prick raids such as the descent upon Washington in 1814.

The initiative for a major effort had to come from the United States, whose population, wealth, and resources represented a military potential far in excess of that which the British could muster in Canada. But the United States went into the war divided. British interference with neutral American vessels on the high seas, and alleged British manipulation of the tribes of the Northwest, had been seized upon by the land-hungry, nationalist "War Hawks" of the West and South as cogent reasons for war. The time seemed opportune for rounding out the Union by the inclusion of those British possessions that had remained within the Empire at the time of the Revolution. "The militia of Kentucky are alone competent to place Montreal and Upper Canada at your feet," declared Henry Clay. But to the Federalist party, whose strength lay in New England, the war was a gross error of policy, since it interfered with maritime trade, regarded as the lifeblood of that area. New England opposition to the war rapidly led to a movement for secession from the Union. While the war was a party question affecting the very existence of the nation, an all-out American drive to win Canada was impossible.

American strategy reflected the sectional origins of the war. The key to Canada was Montreal; if it fell, communications with the entire western portion of the colony would be cut off and Upper Canada could be taken bloodlessly. Throughout the war, however, American planning was directed toward the west, that is, to the Detroit and the Niagara frontiers. In part this was due to the frontier desire to eradicate once and for all the Indian menace, now captained by Tecumseh; in addition, there was a yearning for the fine farmlands of the Ontario peninsula, and the mistaken belief that the American settlers, who had been moving there in large numbers in recent years, could be counted on for help. Thus the

American effort was wasted on peripheral campaigns. Montreal went virtually unchallenged.

On both sides of the border there has persisted a legend that militia took the most prominent place in the fighting. The fact is that the contribution of the American and Canadian militia was not great, and the conduct of the Americans, as at Detroit and Queenston in 1812, was notoriously poor. The major exception, the brilliant victory of Andrew Jackson's militiamen over Pakenham's veterans at New Orleans in 1815, came about because Jackson realized his men must not be exposed on the open field. The British foolishly attacked riflemen and artillery sheltered behind strong breastworks and suffered over two thousand casualties for their pains, while the Americans lost only seven killed and six wounded. The true significance of the War of 1812 was that the American army had begun to shake off the faulty militia tradition of the American Revolution; it was regulars trained by Winfield Scott who fought British regulars on their own terms in the fierce battle of Lundy's Lane (1814) claimed by both sides as a victory.

13

The Nineteenth Century: The Illusion of Limited War

At the beginning of the nineteenth century all the signs seemed to point to an intensification of warfare and of its impact upon society. The industrial and agrarian revolutions had already made possible a greatly increased national war effort; bounding population figures had provided the manpower for larger armies; improvement of communications, even before the introduction of steam railways, had increased military mobility; and the new order of society thrown up by the political revolution had led to embittered international rivalry.

Nevertheless, after the upheaval of the Napoleonic Wars, the century settled down to a long period of peace undisturbed by major strife. For over fifty years most nations abandoned the mass armies which had grown up during the struggle against the French. For nearly a century British sea power made it unlikely, and perhaps impossible, that a minor international conflict should become an international struggle for world hegemony like those in the days of Emperor Charles V, Louis XIV of France, and the Emperor Napoleon. The nineteenth century was a time of decision in the history of human society or at least in the history of those European nations which had come, by that time, to control much of the world and whose policies therefore affected all humanity. Not until 1914 did it become certain that the forces driving man on to suicidal strife had gained the upper hand. During most of the century there was widespread hope that a way could be found to limit the impact of war upon society. Naturally these hopes and efforts became more urgent as the century progressed and small wars, the threat of greater wars, and the increasing power of destruction became evident. But these hopes and efforts were not new and were not at first caused by frightening portents. They had their roots deep in the past; they represented an alternative to the path to general strife and total war which was eventually chosen.

Two interesting but very different attempts made early in the period to restrict war must be noted: the Congress system set up at Vienna in 1815 and the Rush-Bagot Agreement of 1817. After the defeat of Napoleon, the victorious allies, to prevent a recurrence of the French threat, arranged for meetings of the great powers whenever the Vienna settlement was menaced. The Congresses soon came under the domination of the reactionary powers. They were designed to make the world safe for monarchy; they made no allowance for possible social change. But at Congresses at Aix-la-Chapelle (1818), at Troppau (1820), at Laibach (1821), and at Verona (1822), it was found impossible to obtain agreement upon concerted action against revolutionary movements which had overthrown regimes set up in 1815 in Italian and Iberian states. Austria and France, therefore, had to intervene independently. When the question of reasserting Spain's authority in her South American colonies was raised in 1823, a "Doctrine" announced by President Monroe of the United States, powerfully backed by British Foreign Minister Canning and the Royal Navy, prevented intervention and at the same time destroyed the whole system of Congresses. Spasmodically during the rest of the century, when an international war seemed imminent, the idea of a "Congress" of the "Concert of Europe" was revived. In 1878 a Congress was called at Berlin to settle the question of the disposal of the Balkan territories, which were slipping from the sickly grasp of the Sultan of Turkey; and a second Congress at Berlin in 1884-85 dealt with the fate of Central Africa. But these revivals were only a shadow of the grand scheme evolved in 1815 to rule Europe by Congresses and so to preserve peace and the *status quo*. The "Concert of Europe" had no great permanent value as a check upon war in the nineteenth century.

The second move to restrict war, the Rush-Bagot Agreement, although pregnant with possibilities for the future, had even less immediate effect on the renewal of major warfare. After the war of 1812-15, Britain and the United States, in order to avoid the expense of a naval building race in peacetime on the Great Lakes, such as had developed during the late war, agreed in 1817 to reduce their naval establishment on each lake to a single gunboat. This agreement has endured as a magnificent example of the manner in which international problems can be settled by mutual agreement; but it was an unusual case involving only two powers and in a remote area. It was limited to only a small part of the possible causes of tension between the two powers concerned. And even within the area covered by the Agreement, the land fortifications which were erected in the ensuing years and are still extant are mute witnesses to the weakness of international agreements as a means of preventing martial activity. The decline in war and in preparation for war which followed the defeat of Napoleon cannot be attributed to organizations and instruments specifically designed for that purpose.

The lull in warlike activity which marked the first half of the nineteenth century was a result of many factors. Primarily, it was a reaction against the prolonged military efforts of two decades of a war which had been the greatest conflict in western history up to that time. Men everywhere were weary of war; and the nations were physically and financially exhausted. Europe needed a long period of peace for reconstruction.

Secondly, in the minds of the legitimate monarchs now restored to power and of the upper classes on whom they depended, war was inextricably mixed up with Jacobinism and was therefore dangerous. The suppression of liberal and nationalist movements, the first requisite of their policy, might require warlike measures; but a major military action which might arouse popular enthusiasm once more was unthinkable. At all costs, a new world conflict must be avoided. International police actions, many of which were necessary up to 1849, were moves to forestall the possible rise of another militarist like Napoleon, as well as to check constitutionalism and liberalism.

Nevertheless, the political upheaval which had been spread widely through Europe by French example and French arms could not easily be suppressed. Agitation for constitutional reform and for the expulsion of alien rulers, driven underground by the Quadruple Alliance of the three eastern monarchs and France, flourished in secret societies like the *Carbonari* in Italy and flared up again in 1830 and 1848, when revolution spread across Europe with the speed of a prairie fire. As time went on, political unrest was increased by social dislocation stemming from the disruptive force of the Industrial Revolution. The condition of the new industrial proletariat eventually drove some workers to think of the seizure of political power, either constitutionally or by violence, as the only palliative. Their masters, the industrial middle classes, were also excluded from power until, aided by worker agitation, they gained political influence by violence in France in 1830 and by constitutional means in Britain in 1832. In each case the workers, feeling themselves cheated, became more restive. Elsewhere in Europe power remained in autocratic and aristocratic hands, at least until mid-century.

Industrial unrest was not a cause of war at this time. The dangers from social disturbances occupied the western nations internally. At the same time these countries were engrossed with the expansion of their industrial production. In the long run increased output would be applicable to war purposes; but not until later in the century did the competition for materials and markets become a potent cause of war. Meanwhile, the bourgeois regime of Louis Philippe set up by revolution in France in 1830, the free Belgium which threw off Dutch control in the same year, and the states of North Germany tied together economically by the Zollverein agreements negotiated between 1828 and 1834 made great strides in their industrialization and thus absorbed energies which might otherwise have been devoted to international strife. For many years after 1815, no nation threatened the interests of its neighbors to a degree likely to provoke a general upheaval.

The Napoleonic Wars had demonstrated in various ways the importance of economic factors in modern warfare. However, political philosophers and economists who often led middle-class thought were neglectful of the economic components of military strength. Adam Smith, the high priest of free trade and private enterprise, had not been guilty of this cardinal sin. Indeed, he had regarded war as the "noblest of all arts"; he had believed in the necessity of a standing army, provided there were adequate safeguards for the preservation of liberty; and he was even prepared to accept the Navigation Acts and other elements of protectionist legislation for the sake of military security. But his successors in various intellectual fields—for instance, David Ricardo, Joseph Hume, Jeremy Bentham, Thomas Malthus, and Herbert Spencer—thought of war only as a malignant disease which impeded the operation of the social laws they strove to formulate. Bright and Cobden, the Manchester Radicals who worked to put the principles of free-trade economics into practice, were pacifists. For them war was the greatest of all destroyers; they were not prepared to recognize that military preparation entailed adjustments in the national economy in peacetime. In fact, free-trade policy was eminently suited to Britain's position in mid-century, when she had a long lead in industrial production and held command of the seas. She needed cheap food and raw materials and had little use for a large army. The industrial expansion and light taxation which free-trade policies furthered were directly beneficial to her potential military strength.

One of the most powerful deterrents of war in this period was undoubtedly the prevalence of liberal ideas. Liberalism is hard to define, especially in these days when it has come to be identified in some quarters with extreme left-wing philosophies which are its opposite. In the nineteenth century, as now, liberalism implied freedom and was identified with constitutionalism and opposition to the absolute form of government which had prevailed in the preceding century. This political creed was paralleled in the economic sphere by liberal doctrines which demanded freedom for the businessman from governmental restriction and control.

Liberalism, both political and economic, acted as a powerful check upon the war-mindedness of the peoples of Europe in the first half of the nineteenth century. Economic liberalism meant free trade; and liberals, believing that trade barriers were a nonviolent form of international conflict, claimed that their abolition would make actual warfare less likely. In general, liberalism stimulated humanitarianism which regarded war as barbarous; and while not all liberals were thoroughgoing pacifists, some were active propagandists of an anti-war doctrine. One of the best examples of pacifist liberalism in action was the negotiation by Richard Cobden of the British free-trade treaty with France in 1860. Even later, when it had become apparent that a new conflict of major proportions was in the making, it was widely believed that, with the establishment of an effective system of universal suffrage, no nation would freely vote itself into a war that would bring death, maiming, or hardship to a large number of the voters. Women electors would be a majority; and it was expected that they would vote solidly against war. Education would in due course turn the minds of the masses to more civilized pursuits.

The fear which the entrenched ruling classes had for rabid nationalism and the preoccupation of the middle classes with the pursuit of wealth were reflected in the military system of the period, which in many ways was reminiscent of that found before 1789. Most states discarded the national conscript armies which had beaten Napoleon and returned to regular standing armies, limited in number, and closely attached to the regime.

After Waterloo, the British army was slashed from its strength of 685,000 to 100,000 by 1821; 50,000 of these were "hidden away" in the colonies from the economizing eyes of members of Parliament. The desire for economy was almost the only interest that Parliament took in military affairs, despite the fact that as the years wore on, the organization of the army, and the conditions of life in it, became shockingly bad. A parliamentary commission of 1837 recommended that the thirteen independent agencies of army administration be centralized under the Secretary at War as an efficiency measure; but this proposal was dropped because it incurred the displeasure of the Duke of Wellington, who felt that the Secretary at War would become a "new leviathan." Thus the British began the Crimean War with the army organization of 1815.

The army was left to the guidance of those classes who had traditionally led it, the aristocracy and gentry; it was protected from criticism by the immense prestige of the Duke of Wellington (d. 1852). There was little penetration of the officer corps by middle-class elements. Rates of pay for officers were low; only members of the aristocracy and gentry, to whom military distinction appealed, were prepared to buy commissions and expend their own money to keep up a suitable position. The rank and file of the army were even more distinct from society at large. Enlistment was voluntary, but for life; the only way to get a discharge was through remarkably good or remarkably bad behavior. The social structure of the army was thus identical with that of the dynastic armies of the previous century; if anything, discipline was stricter than before, and punishments up to 300 lashes were not unknown. The only training was of the parade-ground variety, with little practice in musketry; the guards regiments, for example, fired only thirty rounds every three years. The British army in India, "afflicted with oriental rot," outdid eighteenth-century armies in cumbrousness. At the siege of Bhurtpore (1808), General Lake's army was well supplied with meat: 12,000 bullocks on the hoof. Sir Henry Fane invaded Afghanistan (1839) with a retinue of 40,000 camp followers. The camels of his Bengal contingent alone numbered nearly 30,000. His officers' requirements were prodigious: one brigadier had sixty camels to carry what he thought necessary for comfortable campaigning.

The British army was completely out of step with the unfolding industrial might of Great Britain, but Sir Robert Peel spoke for a majority of Englishmen when he favored "husbanding our resources in time of peace" and trusting to "the latent and dormant energies of the nation."

In France, under the restored Bourbons, there was an absolute reaction from the Napoleonic army. The Charter of 1814, while preserving many of the political gains of the Revolution, sharply restricted the franchise and at the same time renounced conscription. Although the peacetime strength of the army was only 150,000, less than under the Ancien Régime, voluntary enlistment did not produce the required number of recruits. In 1818 a limited form of conscription was instituted. Out of the annual class eligible for call-up, 40,000 were selected to serve for six years. Shortly after the middle-class revolution of 1830 the size of the army was doubled and the period of service lengthened by a year; but no other important alteration was made. The only other military force in France was the civilian National Guard, a poorly trained middle-class body. Not even in 1848, when the Orleans monarchy was ousted and Louis Napoleon emerged as President, did any significant support appear for a military establishment of Napoleonic grandeur. When a motion for the restoration of universal military service was proposed to the Constitutional Convention, it was rejected by a vote of 663 to 140.

Of the great powers, only Russia and Prussia retained the principle of the mass army. In Russia, where there was no semblance of a middle class or of constitutional rule, military policy was an emanation of the czar's will. It was Czar Alexander's belief that the Russian army should always be equal in size to the armies of Prussia and Austria combined. Thus selective conscription was continued; the army was maintained at a strength of about 750,000; and this immense establishment consumed a third of the total revenue of the state. Russian power, however, although feared throughout Europe, was much less formidable than it appeared, since the Industrial Revolution scarcely made itself felt in that country until the twentieth century.

In Prussia, the reasons for the retention of the principle of the nation-in-arms were more complex and were related to her position in the German Confederation and in the European power balance. Only by virtue of military strength had she become a force to be reckoned with; in population and resources she was still far behind other major nations. Prussia's need for security abroad confronted her conservative leaders with a dilemma. They feared the revolutionary potential of the mass army so much that many of them were prepared to sacrifice a strong foreign policy in order to secure internal safety. The leaders of the left, however, were strongly nationalist as well, and desired the retention of the reforms of Stein, Scharnhorst, and Gneisenau. The result was compromise. The principle of the nation-in-arms was adhered to by conscription, but the military budget permitted the recruitment of only a third of the class. The *Landwehr,* the militia, into which the conscripts passed for completion of three years' service, was, because of its democratic tradition, kept separate from the regular army. The officer corps of both forces was virtually closed to all those whose fathers had been enlisted men, workmen, or retail tradesmen. Thus the dominance of the aristocracy was ensured. Prussian military power was very great. The regular army was maintained at a strength of 125,000; in addition, a third of the male population had received sufficient military training to enable its rapid commitment in time of war. Prussian expenditure on military matters was much higher than that of other European powers, amounting at times to more than 50 per cent of the annual revenue.

The restoration of the conservative military system of the eighteenth century in place of the mass nationalist armies of the Revolutionary era could not exclude entirely the influences of the recent past. Napoleon's genius had irrevocably transformed warfare and could not be effaced. Since he had neither set out his ideas in any complete form nor analyzed his methods, his many unrelated utterances about war tended to suggest that his victories were the result of the manipulation of the brute force of the Revolution by a prodigy, rather than of scientific military operations. In the eighteenth century men had studied tactics and administration but, as Saxe had pointed out, had not uncovered the basic principles of strategy. Not until Napoleon destroyed the eighteenth-century system of making war did military students strive to discover the principles of war by analyzing the campaigns of the master and of other leaders. The two most important studies of this kind were Clausewitz's *Vom Kriege* (1831) and Jomini's *Précis de l'art de guerre* (1836). The former, which will be discussed later, had a delayed influence leading to a new view of the nature and impact of war. The latter, on the other hand, won immediate acclaim and directed the attention of soldiers to what were really pre-Napoleonic concepts.

Antoine Henri Jomini, a French-Swiss who began his career as a bank clerk in Paris, entered the French Revolutionary army as an unpaid supply officer and attracted the attention of Marshal Ney by his agility of mind. Ney encouraged him to publish a volume in which he compared the generalship of Frederick the Great with Napoleon's. Jomini served as Ney's Chief of Staff in Spain and later transferred to the Russian army. After the war he studied the campaigns of Napoleon and became recognized as the leading interpreter of the Emperor's military methods.

Jomini analyzed and defined the various kinds of warfare and described different types of military operations. He disentangled strategy from tactics and logistics, showed the importance of strategic planning, and established its fundamental principles. He was the father of modern methods of teaching military science, setting down the general divisions of operational study and distinguishing and describing specific types of operations in a fashion that has become universally accepted.

Jomini believed that war was not merely a state of confusion out of which a leader like Napoleon arose as a result of personal genius, but was a field of human activity in which rules obtained much as elsewhere. He argued that Napoleon had simply used successfully principles which had always been applicable to war. He sought to set down those principles for the guidance of future commanders. He believed that a commander should seize the strategic initiative; should maneuver so as to impede the enemy's lines of communication and supplies without endangering his own; should concentrate the bulk of his forces against the decisive point, taking care to attack only a portion of the enemy's forces; should achieve victory by use of mobility and surprise; and should follow rapidly in pursuit of the defeated foe. In the course of his discussion he laid emphasis on such military conceptions as lines of operation and zones of operation, concentric and eccentric maneuver, and interior as opposed to exterior lines of attack. He was the first military theorist to note the distinction between interior and exterior lines; and he regarded the former as being much the more likely to bring victory.

By his emphasis on lines of operation Jomini, in effect, returned to the eighteenth-century method of approaching the study of war as a geometric exercise. He was fond of diagrams. This emphasis on the diagrammatic approach to strategy tended to depreciate the importance of psychological factors in war, even the factor of surprise which Jomini had included in his discussion. It led him also to underestimate the worth of such new military formations as skirmish order. He thought the value of skirmishers was merely to make a noise; it was the heavy columns which followed them up that carried a position.

Jomini had never fully realized that with the Revolution and Napoleon a new age had dawned in warfare. In emphasizing the continuance of traditional features he missed the things which were new. There can be no doubt that this interpreter of Napoleonic warfare actually set military thought back into the eighteenth century, an approach which the professional soldiers of the early nineteenth century found comfortable and safe.

The events of 1848-49 showed conclusively that the existing military establishments were capable of snuffing out the crude military efforts of amateur enthusiasts. But soon after the mid-century a succession of wars demonstrated that the old order was fast disappearing. The forces which had prevented a major European conflict were wearing thin. The nations had long recovered from the exhaustion caused by the Napoleonic struggle. Buoyed up by increasing industrial prosperity, they had begun to take hesitating steps to ameliorate the worst aspects of their social problems. After the firm suppression of the revolts of 1848, it was seen that the possibility of a successful rising against autocracy was remote; and while some workers took up subversive plotting in secret, more eventually turned to industrial trade unions as a solution for their grievances. A gradual increase in general prosperity took the edge off the bitterness of class conflict. At the same time international problems diverted much dangerous energy into patriotic channels. Inevitably, problems which defied settlement by other means now led to armed strife.

The first conflicts between major powers which broke the long nineteenth-century peace, although revealing some features which were in the future to bring about a revival of the great nationalist struggles of the Revolutionary era, were in the main limited wars of the pre-Revolutionary type. The first of these wars, that fought in the Crimea against Russia by England, France, Turkey, and Piedmont, was caused by the disintegration of the Ottoman Empire, which left a power vacuum in the Middle East. It is sometimes described as an "unnecessary war" because the pretext for Anglo-French intervention, the Russian invasion of the Balkans, had been removed before the fighting began. The war continued because public opinion in England and France had been inflamed and would not be appeased without bloodshed. Whether this was necessary to delay eventual Russian expansion into the Mediterranean to challenge British and French sea power is a matter of contention. But the war was limited. The contestants were too far apart for major engagements; action in the Baltic was limited to naval operations; and elsewhere Russian sea power was too weak to prevent the allies from taking the initiative. The Russians, fearing Austria, kept most of their troops in Poland. The allies made a raid to eliminate the new Black Sea naval base, Sevastopol, and found themselves in a winter campaign far from their bases, assaulting a city which had not first been blockaded. But the Crimea was equally far removed from the heart of the Russian Empire. With such obstacles, this war could only be limited in objective. There was no prospect that it would end in anything but a negotiated peace.

The Crimea exposed astonishing weaknesses in the professional armies of the great powers, rusted through long disuse. The British had had a kind of staff college for over fifty years; but 206 staff jobs out of 221 were given to men who had not taken the course. Command appointments were made on the basis of wealth and birth rather than merit, experience, or even seniority; personal feuds lessened any hope of effective cooperation between units; allied cooperation was poor; the army had not been trained to operate in any formation larger than a battalion; it had some difficulty in finding its way in the Crimea because it had no adequate maps; and tactical blundering led to one of the most famous military failures of all time, the charge of the Light Brigade. The supply organization faltered and almost collapsed. Horses were landed without adequate fodder because of shortage of transports. The British, despite their great lead in industrial engineering, had not expected to have to lay a light railway to carry supplies from the port of Balaklava to the front five miles away. They possessed no ambulances and no adequate medical supplies or organization: one hospital had only twenty chamber-pots for 1000 men with diarrhoea. Though the French had wooden barracks, better hospitals, and litters for their wounded, they were in little better condition, but suppression of the press by Napoleon hid the extent of their privations. It was only because the Russians (whom Lord Raglan persisted in calling "the French"), with no railroads south of Moscow, could not take advantage of the invaders' weaknesses that the capture of Sevastopol was ultimately attained.

There were some signs, even during this war, of change. Florence Nightingale's by-passing of senior officers, who could terrorize men but could not handle an accomplished lady of gentle birth, brought about the provision of good nursing and cut the death rate in hospitals from 42 per cent to 2 per cent. And a new feature in war, detailed reporting by which William Howard Russell sent to his paper, the London *Times,* now becoming powerful, information which army commanders described as treasonable because it revealed the incompetence of military authority, brought about the fall of the Aberdeen government and began a new era in which military commanders in remote areas were increasingly subjected to supervision by political authority.

Within a few years a second limited war again demonstrated that the restraints upon war had not yet been entirely removed. In the Italian War of Liberation in 1859 the objective of Piedmont was the liberation of Italy, an objective which was clearly total in nature. But the Italians had no hope of overcoming their Austrian oppressors without the aid that they obtained from Napoleon III of France. He plunged into the war to satisfy his thirst for glory and his vague liberal aspirations. The French Emperor found, however, that he had alienated many conservative Catholics by allying himself with the Pope's rival for authority in Italy, the King of Piedmont. Hence, after the battle of Solferino, he withdrew from the war, leaving the Piedmontese to make a peace which obtained only part of their desires.

Yet this war, like that in the Crimea, although limited in result, showed some signs of the changing forces in warfare. Napoleon III and his generals believed that they had beaten the Austrians by the weight of their columns of bayonets. Actually the attack was pushed home only because the enemy had been demoralized by the devastating bombardment of new French rifled artillery and because the columns were protected by clouds of riflemen firing from cover. Colonial campaigns in Algeria had given the French experience in skirmishing tactics which proved more effective than the traditional mass attack of the Napoleonic pattern.

By far the most important result of these two limited wars was that they brought home to many Europeans a realization that international conflict was likely to be far more devastating than the great struggle against Napoleon. It became clear that liberal ideology, when combined with nationalism, was a force which could work for war instead of for peace. In all the mid-century wars liberalism, or the frustration of it, was an important *casus belli*. The Italian war was a war of liberation. The Crimean war appeared to some people as a war between western liberalism and eastern autocracy. The American Civil War was hastened by the movement to free the slaves. The Prussian wars were skillfully planned by Bismarck to recruit liberal nationalist sentiment for his policy of Prussian expansion.

As a result there was an adjustment in the liberal attitude to the problem of war. In place of a vague belief that great wars would be impossible if liberalism triumphed, there grew up a positive and vigorous attempt to curb the impact of war upon society. The sufferings of the combatants in the Crimea, caused more by political and military bungling than by the destructive powers of weapons, had aroused the humanitarianism of Victorian England. Henri Dunant, a Swiss observer at the Battle of Solferino, seeing the dreadful effect of the new rifled cannon used by the French, wrote a famous book, *Un Souvenir de Solferino*, which was an important factor in bringing into existence the Red Cross by international agreement. At Geneva in 1864, twenty-six nations agreed to respect regulations governing the care of the wounded, the rights of prisoners of war, and the protection of medical supplies and of hospitals covered by the new Red Cross flag. About the same time, in America, rifled weapons and mass armies were producing new horrors which taxed beyond capacity the limited military medical facilities of the day. Conditions in field-dressing stations and hospitals of both Federal and Confederate armies were as bad as in the Crimea. British observers said they were actually worse. But lessons were learned in the bitter school of experience and military medical services were expanded and improved. An American Nightingale, Clara Barton, fought for better conditions for the wounded and went on to campaign for American acceptance of the Red Cross Convention, a feat accomplished in 1882.

Thus, the mid-nineteenth century wars, largely as a result of liberal agitation, led to the first of a long series of international conventions or "laws" relating to the conduct of war and designed to protect combatants and non-combatants by imposing limitations on the use of military force. These rules were introduced at the very time when wars were becoming more frequent, more bitter, and more destructive. They may be regarded, therefore, as a reaction against that trend and as an effort to curb it.

The idea that the conduct of the participants in war was subject to the control of law was not new. The laws of war are a part of "international law," the long history of which has already been referred to. Although different in kind from "municipal law" (the law of individual countries) because the latter is enforced by sanctions or penalties imposed by a superior authority, and no such superior authority exists in the international sphere, international law is, nevertheless, a real and significant force. It is derived from the writings of great international jurists, from the decisions of international courts, and from agreements between two or more states.

Modern "laws and usages of war," which have developed from these sources, are subject to several influences or principles. In the first place, it is arguable that a belligerent is justified in using any amount and any kind of force to overcome the enemy; but humanity prohibits the use of more violence than is necessary to achieve this end. In addition, a tradition that all soldiers are brothers-in-arms has served to introduce the idea that there are "fair" and "foul" methods of fighting; and a spirit of chivalry has meant that incapacitated combatants and non-combatants, especially the aged and women and children, should be given reasonable treatment. Within the limit set down by these principles, the rules of war which gained acceptance during the latter part of the nineteenth century were specifically designed to moderate the incidence of war upon society. Actions which were harmful to individuals were prohibited, subject to the overriding qualification "in so far as military necessity permits."

Generally speaking, the nineteenth-century movement to impose restrictions on warfare served to confine hostilities to the armed forces, to prevent wars of attrition, and to localize wars. Inevitably these restrictions tended to make wars short but frequent, and to favor aggressors. Hence they were on the whole acceptable to military men as well as to the liberals. The net result of the coincidence of the desires of the humanitarians and the militarists was that the movement to impose some restraints on warfare enjoyed a certain degree of success. Quarter was given in battle. As in the Middle

Ages and the eighteenth century, rules were set down for the capitulation of beleaguered fortresses in which bodies of troops were hemmed in by greatly superior forces. The parole system was regularly employed in the American Civil War; indeed, a suburb of Annapolis is named Parole because it was the site of a large Civil War parole camp. In the Franco-Prussian War prisoners were released on the condition that they should not serve again. The definition of the rules of war, however, had led to the summary punishment of those who contravened them. Released prisoners who were captured again in battle were shot out of hand. *Francs-tireurs* who fought without uniform were arbitrarily executed.

Because the rights of neutrals were more likely to be infringed as a result of naval operations, the attempt to limit warfare by international agreement had a more important, and in some ways more successful, history when applied to warfare at sea. At the outbreak of the Crimean War, in order to prevent a recurrence of the blockade which had throttled Europe half a century earlier, all belligerents were called upon to state their policies. All announced that they would not issue letters of marque to privateers. Britain stated that she would not seize enemy goods on neutral vessels, while France promised not to seize neutral goods on enemy vessels. The concessions by the western allies were severe handicaps upon their superior naval power. It is probable that they were made only because Russia was unlikely to present a real challenge at sea.

These limitations upon the methods of conducting naval warfare were originally intended only for the duration of hostilities. However, at the Peace Conference in 1856, the powers present issued the Declaration of Paris, which laid down permanent rules for the conduct of naval operations. Privateering was abolished for all time; a neutral flag was held to cover and protect all enemy goods except contraband of war; and neutral goods, except contraband of war, when carried in enemy ships were not liable to confiscation. It was also ruled that naval blockades must be effective to be recognized as legal—that is to say, they must be maintained by sufficient force to prevent access to a blockaded coast. This was a repudiation of the British doctrine and practice of "declaring" blockades which were maintained only intermittently.

The temporary renunciations made by the powers for the duration of the Crimean War, which were made only because that war was not primarily a naval conflict, were converted into general rules to limit all future naval operations. These rules were produced just at the time when steam power, iron-clad ships, and rifled guns were revolutionizing war at sea. Before long, the submarine was to appear, to assume the part formerly played by the privateer in naval strategy. It is probably safe to say that the outlawing of privateering remained effective simply because privateering was no longer considered by governments to be a useful method of making war. Other limitations upon naval operations—for instance, blockade—remained subject to dispute because of difficulty of definition and because technical developments modified the conditions of naval warfare.

The first real test of the efficacy of rules to govern naval warfare came with the American Civil War, but in circumstances which distorted the validity of the test case. Traditionally, the United States had been nurtured on the doctrine of the "freedom of the seas," even in time of war. During the Napoleonic Wars the British blockade of Europe had been strenuously opposed by the United States, whose sailors resisted British claims to search American vessels for enemy goods and for deserters. When the Civil War broke out the roles were reversed. British vessels were engaged in trade with Southern ports blockaded by the United States. American statesmen were now put in the position of having to justify the search and seizure of neutral British vessels, thus reversing the roles the two countries had had during the Napoleonic Wars. Both the United States and the British, however, were aware that their actions must be governed not only by the circumstances of the moment but also by the fact that precedents were being created. The British, therefore, did not give unqualified expression to the doctrine of the freedom of the seas.

Two important naval incidents during the Civil War led to diplomatic exchanges that had an important bearing on the history of attempts to limit warfare. Britain had allowed a Confederate cruiser, the *Alabama*, which later took a tremendous toll of Federal shipping, to be built in a British port. On the other hand, a Federal warship had halted the *Trent*, a British packet, on the high seas and removed two Confederate agents, Mason and Slidell, who were soon released. After the war, the *Alabama* case was submitted to international arbitration. A decision was given in favor of the United States, and the award of $15,500,000 was paid by Great Britain. This was a precedent for the enforcement of international law by the process of arbitration. It followed the settlement in the Treaty of

Washington (1871) of outstanding disputes between the United States and Great Britain and Canada, aided by the conviction that war between the North Atlantic powers was unthinkable. Neither country offered any real threat to the other's vital national interests or way of life.

Meanwhile, efforts were being made to extend and strengthen the international codes restricting war both by land and by sea. On December 11, 1868, the Declaration of St. Petersburg, signed by seventeen states, forbade the use of explosive charges in projectiles under fourteen ounces. The cannon shell was not to be matched by the explosive anti-personnel bullet. In 1874, following upon the horror inspired by the siege of Paris by the Germans, an international conference at Brussels agreed that the bombardment of towns should be prohibited. All civilized peoples approved this restriction. However, during the following decade, a group of French naval officers known as the *Jeune École* argued that sentimental restrictions should not stand in the way of any method by which a war might be brought to a speedy conclusion. Therefore, sea powers should be allowed to bombard seacoast towns or hold them to ransom. Continental naval powers began to include mock bombardments in their maneuvers. As this practice appeared to favor superior naval power, Britain followed suit. Hence, when the bombardment of open undefended towns came up again for discussion at the Hague Conference in 1899, bombardment from land guns was prohibited, but the question of bombardment from the sea was referred to a future conference.

Other rules of naval war which needed clarification were the arming of merchantmen and the nature of blockade. After the abolition of privateering, it was generally accepted that the state could acquire and arm merchant vessels and operate them as cruisers. But this still left unsettled the difficult problem of when such a vessel could be converted. Thus, during the Russo-Japanese War, two Russian merchant ships passed through the Dardanelles (which were closed to warships by international agreement) and through the Suez Canal, and then declared themselves to be warships and seized neutrals carrying contraband. Clearly, if vessels could change their status at will, no rule could be effective. A second problem came during the First World War. By international law, merchantmen which were unarmed were protected against attack but must submit to search in proper form. When German submarines sank merchantmen, sometimes without any formal warning, the British began to put guns and gun crews on merchant ships for their protection.

The problem of blockade was similarly affected by changes in weapons and in ships. In the days of sail, neutrals and weaker sea powers alike had claimed that, to be legal and effective, a blockade must be "close." Right up to 1914, the French actually argued that the blockading ships must be anchored in such a manner that vessels entering the port could not safely pass. However, with the development of long-range coastal guns, of submarines, and of torpedoes, a "close" blockade of this type became manifestly impossible, and, indeed, some naval authorities argued that blockading was gone forever. What actually happened was that a new technique of long-distance blockade was evolved, operated sometimes from the home ports of the blockading fleet. Such a blockade, created by declaration, was of doubtful legality under former rules. But as a result of the changing nature of war this difficulty was overcome by the wide extension of the list of goods classified as "contraband of war."

At the end of the century, a Polish banker, Ivan S. Bloch, wrote a book forecasting the nature of warfare with the new weapons which technology had made available. The Czar of Russia was so impressed by the horrors portrayed that he proposed that the nations should limit armaments, mitigate the horrors of war, and provide a system of arbitration for the settlement of international disputes without resort to war. He summoned a conference of the nations which met at the Hague in 1899. No support could be found for the proposal of arms limitation; but some progress was made in other respects. However, the decisions on which agreement was most easily reached were those which, in fact, provided loopholes for evasion of any rules that might be laid down. Thus, it was agreed that the laws of war applied only when both sides were parties by ratification to the particular international agreements concerned; and it was agreed that reprisals were permissible in retaliation against enemy breaches in the laws of war. A second conference was held at the Hague in 1907, when dum-dum bullets (with soft expanding noses) and poison gases were outlawed. An attempt was also made to forbid the use of projectiles or explosives from airplanes. The only really important result of the Hague Conferences, however, was the establishment of an international panel of justices for the settlement of disputes; and even in that sphere the achievement was limited. Recourse to this International Court was optional and not obligatory. Codes to define the rights of neutrals by land and sea were discussed in 1907, but were not accepted by Great Britain, the power most likely to resort to blockade in the event of war. Accordingly, another conference, held in 1908-9, produced the Declaration of London to govern blockade, contraband, and the rights of search. By 1914, no power had ratified its terms.

Throughout all these endeavors to restrict, restrain, or abolish war, it was evident that no nation was willing to tie its hands in any way that would limit its freedom of action. All paid lip service to the general principle of preventing or mitigating the horrors of war; all issued manuals to their troops outlining the international law of war as they saw it. But every step taken toward limitation of war invariably appeared to one or more of the nations as a potential danger to national security. Any attempt to prohibit a useful weapon was difficult to enforce.

Much of the initiative had come from Russia which was not one of the most advanced or liberal of the great states. It is not unlikely that one reason why the Czar took the lead in measures to limit war was his belief that Russia was less able than the other nations to fight a modern war successfully. The more "progressive" powers, for instance the United Kingdom and the United States, which might have been expected to support schemes to check the barbarism of war, were at least as cautious as other powers. Thus, British caution had rendered ineffective the agreements made at Brussels in 1874. The United States did not accept the Geneva Convention of 1864 until 1882. Captain Mahan of the United States, at the Hague in 1899, voted against a motion to prohibit poison gases. At the same conference the British opposed the abolition of dum-dum bullets on the grounds that such bullets had stopping power much greater than that of ordinary bullets and that this was necessary against a rush of uncivilized tribesmen. The plain fact was that the western democratic nations were wary of subscribing to measures which might limit the potential military value of their superior industrial organization. Measures to restrict and limit the impact of warfare in the century between the Great Wars of Napoleon and of Kaiser William II thus failed, primarily because national sovereignty prevented any real possibility that adequate restrictions would be adopted or, if adopted, would be effective. Many other nations expressed surprise at a statement in a German military manual of 1904 that the "law of necessity" would justify breaches of the international laws of war; yet, in dire emergency, any belligerent power would probably take any action deemed necessary to win a war or to prevent defeat.

A similar fate met the preaching of minority groups who held pacifist views and called for the abolition of war. After the middle of the nineteenth century, the industrial workers of Europe had been organized into labor and socialist parties whose aim was to obtain for them a greater share of the wealth they produced. One of the basic tenets of socialists, whether gradualists like the Fabians or revolutionaries like the Communists, was that the real enemy of the worker was the bourgeois capitalist employer against whom all the workers of every nation had a common cause. Socialist parties were therefore opposed on principle to imperialist wars between nations. The most outspoken group to take this stand was the German Socialist Party, which seemed to be sufficiently powerful to be a real obstacle to any warlike plans the Kaiser might concoct. The strongest socialist literary indictment of war was produced by an English writer, Norman Angell, who attacked imperialism and argued that colonies were a financial burden and that the conquest of colonies did not pay.

All these minority movements against war proved singularly ineffective in 1914. When war came the German Socialists abandoned their former principles and fell into line with the nationalists. In England, sincere conscientious objection to fighting was allowed as a reason for exemption from combatant service; but the number of conscientious objectors was not large enough to hamper the war effort. Everywhere, despite all the prophecies of the horrors of a modern war, the crisis of 1914 was greeted by scenes of popular enthusiasm. Public feeling against war was shallow. Democracy showed that it could be as belligerent as autocracy. The carnage of 1914-18 had to take place before there was really effective popular support for movements to restrain warfare.

14
The *Pax Britannica*

At the peace conferences which terminated the Napoleonic wars, British statesmen, adhering to a maritime policy, had abstained from acquiring territory on the continent and so avoided continental commitments. By supporting the creation of the Kingdom of the United Netherlands in order to ensure that Antwerp and the Scheldt were not possessed by a major power, they had found a satisfactory solution for an old problem which had frequently embroiled Britain in continental wars. The revolt of Belgium in 1830, and its establishment as a separate, independent kingdom ruled by Queen Victoria's uncle and guaranteed in its neutrality by the powers was, for Britain, an even happier solution. In 1837, the accession of Victoria brought an end to the personal union with Hanover (in which the succession followed the Salic Law of male descent) and removed another source of entanglement in European wars, one which, however, had already ceased to have any real importance.

At Vienna in 1815 the British attitude toward acquisition of territory outside Europe was governed by the prevailing doctrine that colonies were, as Disraeli said later, "millstones around our necks" costing far more to administer than their trade was worth. All political parties and groups in Britain in the first three-quarters of the century were influenced by this disenchanted view of empire. The Whigs and Manchester Radicals were confident that British industrial supremacy made tariffs, and the closed imperial commercial system that accompanied them, obsolete; the Tories, although clinging until the 1840's to a policy of agricultural protection, were convinced Little Englanders who saw dependencies as political and military, as well as economic, liabilities. It seemed to most that the ultimate destiny of the white colonial empire was independence; the bitter lesson of the American Revolution seemed to be confirmed by the abortive rebellions in the Canadas in 1837-38; it was this attitude which made possible the Confederation of Canada in 1867 and its evolution as an autonomous nation within the Empire.

Therefore, after the Napoleonic Wars, colonies seized by British fleets during the war were returned to their former owners at the conference table; but there were certain important and significant exceptions. The British realized that the war had been won by "those far distant, storm-beaten ships upon which the Grand Army never looked [but which had] stood between it and the dominion of the world" (Mahan). They therefore retained those places which, as strategic bases, controlled the world's sea lanes: Heligoland in the North Sea, Malta in the Mediterranean, Mauritius in the Indian Ocean, the Cape of Good Hope (for which the Dutch received compensation), the South American settlements which later became British Guiana, and Ceylon.

With Sir Stamford Raffles's acquisition of Singapore in 1819 Britain was to be found astride every major sea lane except the Dardanelles; and during the remainder of the century she continued to pick up supplementary naval bases throughout the world. Her most important additional acquisitions were Aden (1839), Hong Kong (1841), and Cyprus (1878). Control over the Suez Canal (opened in 1869) was obtained by the purchase of the Khedive of Egypt's shares in 1875 and by the establishment of a protectorate over Egypt in 1882. In the nineteeenth century Britain, and Britain alone, possessed the far-flung bases essential to world maritime predominance.

Other factors contributed to the increased importance of sea power as opposed to land power and hence to the British hegemony. Three centuries of European expansion had augmented the relative weight of overseas possessions in the balance of power; with the American Declaration of Independence there had appeared the first of the non-European powers to have influence in the modern world, and others followed later; sea power, exerted to bridge the oceans of the world and to exploit distant resources, became proportionally more significant. The Industrial Revolution, by increasing productivity, by intensifying the quest for markets and materials, and by improving the means of communication, including those across the oceans, made control of the seas imperative to a power with imperial possessions. British industrial leadership implied maritime leadership as well. Finally, the revolutionary upheavals and Napoleonic Wars had weakened the continental land powers. Trafalgar had thus left the Royal Navy supreme in the world at a time when sea power was of increasing moment and when Britain was the only power able to wield it.

For nearly a century after Trafalgar she had no dangerous rival upon the seas. France was unable to repeat what she had done after the Treaty of Utrecht when she had rapidly built a new fleet of wooden ships and had soon been able to re-challenge British sea power. Her task had now become more difficult because the design of warships, which had changed little since the sixteenth century, began in the nineteenth to undergo a process of rapid transformation; and her industrial capacity was really inadequate to challenge the British in the new types of war fleets. Russia, whose land power was unreasonably exaggerated and feared from 1815 to 1914, was locked up in the Black Sea until 1871. The United States, whose sailors and merchant marine had been a valuable part of British naval strength when the Thirteen Colonies were British, led the world for a time in the design of merchant sailing ships, those beautiful clippers which represented the climax of sailing-ship development; but, as a result, America lagged behind in steam.

The United States assigned small squadrons to protect her flourishing trade against piracy in the Far East, the Caribbean, and the South Atlantic; in 1845 she established the Naval Academy at Annapolis, Maryland, to give the professional and essentially engineering education that technological change was making desirable for naval officers; in 1846-48 she employed her naval forces extensively in the Mexican War, which brought California and Texas into the Union and showed the advantages of steam auxiliary power in a number of amphibious operations in the Gulf of Mexico; and in the next decade she used naval power to back her diplomacy with China and Korea and in the opening of Japan. All this American activity between the War of 1812 and the Civil War was made possible, in large part, because of the Royal Navy's control of the seas but was on such a relatively small scale that it constituted no challenge to British naval supremacy. American naval power greatly increased during the Civil War. Then, for a full generation, it fell into the doldrums. National energies were devoted to reconstruction, domestic economic expansion, railroad building, industrial growth, heavy immigration, and opening up the interior of the continent to agriculture.

During the century most British governments were influenced by the numerous disciples of Adam Smith who taught that free trade was the best way to commercial greatness and argued that wealth did not depend upon the possession of empire. The Navigation Acts, upon which British mercantile and maritime strength had formerly depended, were repealed. These artificial props were no longer needed. Such was the margin of Britain's lead in industry, trade, and shipping that her merchant marine and commerce continued to expand. Despite the coolness of her governments the flag followed trade. The British Empire grew from 20,000,000 people in 1,500,000 square miles in 1800 to 390,000,000 people in 11,000,000 square miles in 1900. Its foreign trade in the same period grew from £80,000,000 to £1,467,000,000. This phenomenal development was in part the product of quietly pervasive strength upon the seas.

British leaders were conscious of their heritage of sea power and of Britain's position as keeper of the seas. After the United States had given the lead by standing firm against the exactions of the Barbary pirates and by defeating an Algerine fleet off Cartagena (June 20, 1815), an Anglo-Dutch squadron commanded by Lord Exmouth bombarded Algiers and put an end once and for all to this scourge of peaceful trade in the Mediterranean. After the slave trade was abolished for British subjects (1807), Britain worked for international cooperation to suppress it altogether; and the task of policing the seas fell largely upon the Royal Navy. The Lords of the Admiralty regarded the oceans of the world so much as a British concern that they undertook the task of surveying and charting them, excluding only the north coast of Africa, which was left to the French, and the east coast of North America, which was done by Americans (many of whom were West Point graduates).

The influence of sea power was exerted without major campaigns or battles and its most important effect was the negative one of silently preventing the conflicts of continental land powers from developing into world-wide wars. But it was also exercised deliberately to further British policies by the direct use, or the threat, of force. The South American colonies of Spain and Portugal won their independence largely through the work of the British Admiral Cochrane commanding South American squadrons (1808-25). The Monroe Doctrine (1823), proclaimed by the United States to forestall the plans of the Holy Alliance to aid Spain in reconquering South America and against Russian penetration down the west coast of North America as far as San Francisco Bay, was effective to a large extent because it was openly backed by the Royal Navy.

The Greeks gained independence from Turkey when Britain, cooperating with France and Russia, annihilated a Turkish fleet at Navarino Bay (1827). Sixty-five out of eighty-one Turkish ships were destroyed, and Moslem power was checked for a century. British sea power ensured the independence of Belgium (1830), bombarded Acre (1840) to prevent Mehemet Ali from conquering or dismembering Turkey, and blockaded the Piraeus (1850) to compel the Greek government to compensate a Gibraltar Jew, Don Pacifico, who had claimed protection as a British subject. Sea power made possible the invasion of the Crimea (1854-56) and was more effective than the land communications within Russia upon which the defending armies depended. Sea power watched benevolently over the unification of Italy from 1860 and forestalled a Russian advance upon Constantinople (1878), compelling the Russians to negotiate the disposal of the disintegrating Ottoman Empire. Throughout the century, in less spectacular places, when British traders were threatened on their lawful occasions by unruly elements or by hostile, anti-foreign regimes, the despatch of a gunboat was the usual, and the effective, method of restoring peaceful commerce.

Most of these examples show that British sea power was exercised to foster British trade, but that it also frequently acted in the name of liberty. Small powers, and national groups seeking freedom and independence, often found comfort under the guns of the Royal Navy. The Disraeli-Gladstone debates about the Eastern Question, in which Britain had to choose between supporting the territorial integrity of the "unspeakable Turk" or aiding independence movements of Balkan Christians who, being Slavs, might fall into the Russian orbit, dramatically illustrated the strength of feeling in Britain that her navy should be used in the cause of liberty. This association of sea power and freedom was not illogical, for navies differ from armies in that they can less easily exert influence within the territories of subjected states beyond the reach of their guns. Sea power can pervade the oceans, but can only occasionally operate in the interior of continents where rivers are navigable. Only by the use of supplementary military forces can sea power be translated into an oppressive imperial power; and Britain's concentration upon the navy limited the size of her military forces. In these circumstances it is not surprising that the second British Empire, built up after the collapse of the first in 1776, was, like its predecessor, remarkable for the growth of autonomy for white colonial settlers and also for the relatively liberal treatment of native races.

The *Pax Britannica* could be enforced as long as England, the greatest industrial nation of the century, could retain her naval supremacy through the flood of revolutionary technical developments in naval warfare that separated Trafalgar from Jutland. The Royal Navy was conservative by nature, and not without reason. Trafalgar had confirmed British confidence in her maritime prowess; and the Nelson tradition was a source of naval strength. Having proved itself in the superior handling of the square-rigged ship-of-the-line, the Navy was reluctant to encourage any change which might make its greatest ships obsolete. (Lord Melville, the First Lord of the Admiralty, wrote in 1828 to the Colonial Office that "steam was calculated to strike a fatal blow at the naval supremacy of the Empire.") Nevertheless, the British had to counter every innovation by a possible enemy. Because of the growth and efficiency of Great Britain's heavy industry based on excellent coal and iron resources, and because for decades the cheapest iron production, the best engines, and the most skilled engineers were all British, effective response to challenge was long possible.

Among the nations which strove to overtake Britain's lead upon the seas, especially the French, the Americans, and the Germans, naval inventiveness sometimes found greater stimulus. The outcome of this naval rivalry was a tremendous revolution in the nature and design of warships—from the three-decker sailing ship like the *Victory* (1759) to the first iron-hulled, armored steam warship, the *Warrior* (1861), and thence to the first battleship of the World War I era, the *Dreadnought* (1905). Unprecedented changes affected the architecture of the ship, its hull and power plant, and its armor and armament. New naval weapons were developed, such as the mine and the torpedo. These developments sprang from advances in technology; and they led from new ships and weapons to changes in tactics and in the composition of fleets, and to important alterations in the strategic role of sea power.

Within the half-century after Trafalgar improvements in ordnance and in steam propulsion eventually made the square-rigged ship-of-the-line obsolete. The first steam warship, Robert Fulton's *Demologos* (1814), built for the United States Navy to break the British blockade of New York, was something of a freak. It was a catamaran with engine in one hull, boiler in the other, and paddle-wheel between the hulls. Armed with thirty heavy 32-pounder guns protected outboard by extremely thick wood sheathing, with two

100-pounder submarine guns which fired under water, and capable of a speed of six knots, it might have achieved the purpose for which it was built had the war not ended before it could be put to the test. Not a sea going vessel, and with a small fuel capacity, the *Demologos* drew attention to, rather than solved, the problems of adapting steam power to the fighting ship.

Early engines were large and heavy, low in power and high in fuel consumption. Paddlewheels were obviously vulnerable; and their installation replaced a good part of the ship's broadside battery; early boilers were dangerous and a liability in combat; and fuel was so quickly exhausted that the steam engine was long used only as an auxiliary to sails. For these reasons steam was at first adopted only experimentally for tugs and special craft. When an effective screw propeller was invented (1836), it at last became feasible for the three-deckers to use steam as auxiliary power. Tests in which ships were matched in a tug-o'-war demonstrated that the screw was more efficient than the paddlewheel. The first propeller-driven warship was built by the United States, the frigate *Princeton*, in 1844. With no paddlewheels to obstruct the line of fire, she had full broadsides, and with her engines protected by being placed below the waterline and coupled directly to the screw, she was a more serviceable auxiliary steam warship than any of her predecessors. In 1840 the Royal Navy had only 29 steamers; but by 1849 this number had increased to 121 out of a total of 460 ships.

Meanwhile, hoping to challenge British sea power once more, the French had developed a new weapon, the Paixhans shell gun (1824). Its horizontally fired explosive shell threatened to make unarmored warships obsolete. By 1837 the Paixhans shell had been adopted by the French navy; and within two years the English and Americans also armed their ships with shell guns. The 8-inch shell gun took its place alongside the old 32-pounder as the standard heavy naval weapon. By 1840 British ships were also armed with a 68-pounder; and many other experimental weapons were appearing, such as the 12-inch wrought iron guns of the *Princeton*. The explosion of one of these, named the Peacemaker, killed the American Secretary of State and the Secretary of the Navy and thus tragically demonstrated that further progress in ordnance depended on improvements in metallurgy. These were not actually forthcoming until the Bessemer process of steel manufacture, invented in 1856, had been sufficiently improved to control the content of carbon.

The first operational test of the changing navies was provided by the Crimean War. At the battle of Sinope (1853) a Russian fleet proved the efficacy of the shell gun by blowing a Turkish fleet of wooden ships out of the water; but when the British and French fleets arrived in the Black Sea, the Russians offered no further naval resistance. Russian admirals were understandably unwilling to match their ordnance against the heavier guns and greater volume of shellfire of the Allied fleets and their softwood ships against oak and iron. Of equal importance was the fact that the Crimean War demonstrated conclusively the operational superiority of the steam auxiliary. In both the Black and the Baltic Seas mixed Allied forces found that the sailing ships could be left behind while the steamers went forward about their business. More dependable and more maneuverable, the steam warships were outstanding in the bombardment of Odessa, circling about so as to present a more difficult target to the Russian gunners. They were also used to tow sailing ships into position for bombarding the naval base of Kinburn, where armored French gunboats first revealed the ability of the ironclad to withstand bombardment.

Great Britain now found that her world-circling naval bases were of much greater importance than she had expected because her steamships depended upon them as coaling stations; and her lead in the iron industry soon was seen to be the true fount of naval power. When France launched the *Gloire* (1859), the first sea-going armored ship, England countered with the iron-hulled *Warrior* (60 guns), protected by 4.5-inch side armor. England's shortage of ship timber, the structural limitations of wood, the increasing weight of ordnance, and the increased displacement necessary to float an armored ship, its ordnance, and its coal bunkers, all combined to make the iron-hulled ship inevitable. The *Warrior* was of such great size, 420 feet over all, that she could not have been built satisfactorily of wood. But wooden hulls persisted for some time, particularly for use in tropical waters, where a copper-sheathed wooden hull would not foul so rapidly as iron, and for smaller ships, especially those of the United States where there was an abundant supply of wood.

The iron hull, however, not only solved major constructional problems but gave Britain an additional advantage. Iron ships were built by private contractors; and thus the skill and facilities of her great merchant shipbuilding industry were made available to the Royal Navy. The Royal Dockyards, where England's wooden navy had been built, became merely maintenance bases for the fleet. Orders for warships from foreign nations brought further profits to British shipbuilders and made British designs and methods prevail throughout the lesser navies of the world. Later in the century Britain's shipbuilding industry was to retain its world leadership, even when her iron and steel production had fallen to third place. A further change, once again to Britain's relative advantage, was the rate at which warships became obsolescent after 1859. The *Warrior* was launched in the exceptionally brief period of two years after keel laying, but within that short time improvements in ordnance had made a more heavily armored ship desirable. Each decade required a new fleet, an expensive program, which Great Britain could afford more easily than her less wealthy competitors.

The American Civil War provided the next operational test of machine-age sea power. In that conflict the agrarian Confederate states were severely handicapped, for they had been dependent on the Northern states and Europe for almost all their manufactured goods; and the South had neither merchant marine nor navy. Northern naval strategy was accordingly based on an "Anaconda policy" of economic strangulation of the Confederacy; but could such a blockade be maintained effectively against steam-propelled blockade runners? It became immediately apparent that the long Southern coastline and its many inlets could not be closed unless the Federal fleet possessed conveniently located coaling stations and operational bases. Thus arose the strategic necessity for the capture of Port Royal (between Charleston and Savannah) and of New Orleans, the recapture of Norfolk and Pensacola, and, finally, the seizure of Fort Fisher guarding Wilmington, N. C., from which supplies moved by rail directly to Richmond. The completion of this ring of bases, isolating the South from all important foreign aid, contributed indirectly, but significantly, to her defeat.

The Confederacy's efforts to break the blockade were concentrated in a few heavily armored ships capable of demolishing the wooden ships of the Union navy. A first effort was made by the *Virginia,* an iron-casemated ram improvised on the razed hull of the former frigate *Merrimac.* Little more than a floating battery, she demonstrated again that shell guns could destroy wooden ships and so discouraged a naval attack on Richmond; but her encounter with the Union ironclad *Monitor* left the impression that ironclads could not destroy one another. If the Confederate gunners had been prepared to use solid shot instead of shell, it is possible that they could have destroyed the *Monitor*; and if the Union gunners had known that their 11-inch Dahlgren guns were capable of taking twice the weight of powder charge used, they could certainly have destroyed the ram. Neither ship was a true sea going vessel and neither contributed much to the progress of naval architecture. The revolving armored turret of the *Monitor* was the single feature which was to be incorporated in the modern warship. From this and later engagements with Confederate ironclad rams, the obvious lesson was learned that only armored ships could defeat armored ships. This was not a new discovery in England and France, each of which had warships much superior to those used in the Civil War.

The Confederacy also experimented in shallow rivers and harbors with mines which sank more Union ships than did gunfire, and with primitive submarines and spar-torpedoes. Vastly more significant were the successes of her steam-auxiliary commerce raiders. One of them, the *Alabama,* came uncomfortably close to sweeping clipper ships from the seas; and another, the *Shenandoah*, decimated the Union whaling fleet. Even fewer in number than the German surface raiders of World Wars I and II, Confederate cruisers had no measurable influence on the outcome of the war. While the American merchant marine was much diminished and never again regained the place it had held during the first half of the century, it was more for economic reasons than as a consequence of Confederate commerce raiding.

By contrast, the naval support of the Union armies in their Mississippi Valley campaign materially shortened the conflict in the up-river fighting. Ironclad gunboats maintained water-borne logistic support, provided heavy artillery fire for the troops, and contributed to Farragut's capture of New Orleans by drawing Southern military power away from this greatest Confederate port. Then the fresh-water and salt-water navies joined in continued support of the land campaign. The result was that the Confederacy was split apart and the way was prepared for Sherman's great wheeling movement which contributed greatly to the final victory.

In the year following the American Civil War, the Battle of Lissa (1866) again illustrated the relative invulnerability of ironclads to gunfire. An Austrian fleet under Tegethoff steamed in wedge formation right through an Italian fleet of superior armament and put it to flight, having sunk one ship by ramming. This return to galley tactics led to a mistaken emphasis on the ram which temporarily influenced all navies. Actually Lissa had no clear lessons to teach. A wooden ship, the *Kaiser*, withstood as much punishment as the ironclads. Only one ship was sunk by ramming, and that was stationary at the time.

As armor was thickened, guns were made more powerful. England's development of the Armstrong built-up gun, of Whitworth's armor-piercing projectile, and of the Franco-American "interrupted screw" breech mechanism kept the great gun as the primary weapon of naval warfare. In 1873 the Royal Navy commissioned the *Devastation,* the first mastless, armored, turreted, screw warship. She had a waterline belt of foot-thick armor and carried four 35-ton muzzle-loading rifles protected by 14-inch armor plating. In 1881 the *Inflexible* carried 24-inch side armor, the thickest ever used, and 16-inch guns. From that point on armor was improved in quality and reduced in thickness. A temporary peak in gun size was reached three years later when some English ships actually carried 16.25-inch guns weighing 111 tons each. A reaction then set in against size in ordnance. During the 1880's, when slow-burning powder was introduced, it became possible to fire projectiles from long-barrelled naval rifles with far greater range and velocity. The naval engagements at the end of the century in the Sino-Japanese War (1894) and the Spanish-American War (1898) emphasized gunnery and the need for methods of improving accuracy and range. It was recognized that a practical balance between armor and armament in any particular ship must be determined by the overall fighting functions for which its type was designed.

Behind these technical developments lay constantly expanding industrial capacity and wealth from commercial enterprise. The opening of the Suez Canal in 1869 was a prelude to the new imperialism of the 1880's and 1890's. Great Britain, isolated from European conflicts, remained neutral even during the Franco-Prussian War of 1870. In Europe, favoring maintenance of the *status quo*, she regarded her fleet as essentially defensive. Elsewhere, she sought new outlets for her products and led the imperial penetration of Africa and Asia under the revised slogan "trade follows the flag." As late as 1889 Russia and France were still her only important rivals in sea power. In that year her "Two Power Standard" was officially adopted and announced, by which the

Royal Navy was to be kept at a strength to match the combined strength of the next two maritime powers.

A new surge of imperialism in the form of world-wide colonial and trade rivalry among the European powers induced continental states to undertake expanding naval programs and these of necessity produced larger appropriations for the Royal Navy. It was then, when she seemed to be at the peak of her power, that Britain lost first place as the leading industrial nation. Her wealth was greater than ever; but her share of world trade was relatively less than before. German industrial capacity was increasing rapidly and in direct competition. The United States in 1890 took over England's position as the world's greatest iron producer. In the Orient, Japan was developing a textile industry that would lead to a further challenge to England's commercial supremacy.

All the world's ambitious maritime nations were stimulated in the 1890's by the publication of an American's analysis of British success in an important work, *The Influence of Sea Power upon History, 1660-1783*. In this and subsequent books Rear Admiral Alfred Thayer Mahan set forth a philosophy of naval warfare which, by setting up naval power as the key to imperial success, was powerful "big navy" propaganda. His work was only one feature of an intellectual renaissance occurring in the United States Navy. After the post-Civil War doldrums, the navy had been reinvigorated by a group of officers led by Admiral Luce who had reformed the education of enlisted personnel and in 1884 had founded the Naval War College for the advanced instruction of officers. Mahan had been appointed its first President; and his studies of the influence of sea power had been delivered there as lectures.

Mahan discovered nothing that was not already known. The British had been putting his theories into practice for a long time. Hitherto naval history had been written merely as a series of thrilling episodes; no one had set down the principles of naval warfare in popular, yet scholarly, form. Mahan described the operation of sea power, analyzed the elements upon which it was based, and examined critically various kinds of naval strategy. He taught that sea power worked silently to build great empires. It was in England that Mahan first attracted the imagination of the general public. Mahan put into words what Englishmen had long subconsciously realized, and gave a plausible explanation of British supremacy. Nevertheless, by stirring up interest in sea power in other countries, including his own, Mahan furthered the growth of rivals to the Royal Navy. His work was translated into many languages and had great influence upon naval development in Germany, Japan, and France.

Everywhere popular interest in naval strength was on the increase. The new imperialist rivalry for trade and colonies was paralleled by competition in naval-building programs. Before 1890 the general public had little knowledge of naval affairs, even in Britain which depended so much upon sea power. In the ensuing decade, through magazine articles, through the new penny press, and through propagandist organizations like the British and German Navy Leagues, popular interest in naval affairs was stimulated. Thus was prepared the ground for the dramatic Anglo-German naval building race which preceded the First World War.

At this time American naval men were usually admirers of things British. The British government, for its part, regarded the United States as a friendly rival, omitted to take account of the United States Navy in its "Two Power Standard," and cultivated good relations with America. Meanwhile America's own brand of the prevailing imperialism made itself manifest in the annexation of the Hawaiian Islands, Guam, the Philippines, and Puerto Rico, and in the so-called Roosevelt Corollary to thé Monroe Doctrine, under which the United States policed the Caribbean states, and, with the help of the navy and the marines, acted as debt collector where necessary. Theodore Roosevelt encouraged the building of an ocean-going navy second only to Britain's. Later the satisfactory settlement of the Panama Canal question with Great Britain ensured the continuance of amicable relations between the two countries. The net result was that the United States assumed the responsibility for policing the Caribbean area. Britain withdrew some naval units from the West Indies and thus was reinforced in European waters without endangering Central American interests.

In Europe, alarmed by the expensive naval race and the prospects of war, the Russian Czar had proposed an international conference to consider naval limitations, restrictions on war, and arbitration. The resulting Hague Conference (1899), as has been seen, accomplished a little in every category except that of naval limitation. Neither Mahan nor Admiral Sir John Fisher of the Royal Navy was surprised at this failure, for to each it was clear that the growing rivalry on the seas could be resolved only by world acceptance of England's dominant position or by England's accept- ance of a relatively weaker position. In the atmosphere then prevailing neither alternative was realistic. The spirit of the times was better illustrated in the German Naval Bill of the very next year, by the passage of which Admiral Alfred von Tirpitz obtained a "risk fleet," a naval force so powerful that Britain would be able to accept the challenge of Germany only at the risk of weakening her naval strength to the point where she could be defeated by the third naval power, presumably France.

The British reaction to these events was vigorous, if reluctant. During the 1890's, by comparison with energetic American, German, and Japanese naval leaders, the British Admiralty had seemed at times complacent. A myth about remarkably accurate shooting by American ships in their war with Spain (the fact was that, under almost ideal conditions at Santiago, less than 4 per cent of the shots were hits) aroused interest in gunnery. Interna- tional censure of Great Britain during the Boer War, coupled with an invasion scare, likewise caused the Royal Navy to look to its laurels. Beginning in 1901 came an era of reform. Instead of ex- pending ammunition by throwing it overboard, as one critic alleged was done, the fleet turned seriously to gunnery practice. In Captain Percy Scott it found an expert who, like Captain Douglas in the eighteenth century, proved that much more could be done with modern naval guns than most officers had realized. His idea of "continuous aim" was followed by the development of the director system for salvo gunfire. By that system the accuracy of naval guns at ranges of 10,000 yards was to be improved tenfold by the time of World War I. The German, Japanese, and American navies were making comparable improvements on their own account with equal success.

In the field of weapons the improvement of the self-propelled torpedo—designed as early as 1860 by Robert Whitehead—and its use as the offensive weapon of the submarine, extended naval warfare into a new element. Although the idea of the submarine was ancient, the practical development of a submersible ship was not achieved until almost the end of the century. By 1898 French submarines took part in maneuvers. Two years later the American Holland submarine was purchased by both the United States and Britain. In tests both the submarine and the torpedo boat appeared

capable of revolutionizing tactics and of giving a lesser sea power
a weapon which could force a major fleet to take up a purely
defensive strategy. The fast torpedo-boat destroyer was developed
in reply; but only in actual warfare could the relative merits of
these vessels be properly tested.

After the Boer War, Britain's diplomatic relations improved with
every nation except Germany. In 1902 a treaty with Japan balanced
Russian naval strength in the Pacific. Less than three years later an
entente with France gave England a free hand in Egypt and
effected a general reconciliation, possible in large part because the
French had dropped from the naval race by default.

The Russo-Japanese War demonstrated what twentieth-century
naval power could do. For Mahan the war was a show piece of
naval strategy, illustrating the dangers of a divided fleet and of
confusion in objectives. The Russian fleets at Vladivostok and Port
Arthur were eliminated in detail. When Admiral Rozhestvensky's
Baltic fleet, burdened with coal and convoying supply ships, arrived,
it was overwhelmed by Admiral Togo at Tsushima (1905), a naval
victory comparable with Trafalgar. For Fisher, the vigorous newly
appointed First Sea Lord at the British Admiralty, a man of great
prescience, the tactical aspects were of immediate practical interest.
Both sides had scored hits at up to 10,000 yards with the heaviest
guns doing the most effective firing. Neither the torpedo nor the
submarine had played any conspicuous part, although mines had
been employed elsewhere in shallow waters with considerable success. In every engagement in the war superior speed had permitted
the Japanese to control the course of the action.

Of speed Fisher said, "It is the 'weather gage' of the olden days.
You then fight just when it suits you best." He proposed a fleet of
21-knot battleships, 25-knot cruisers, 36-knot destroyers, and 14-
knot submarines. In his view, with such ships, and holding the five
keys that lock up the world, Singapore, the Cape, Alexandria,
Gibraltar, and Dover, Britain would be secure. As a result of the
experience of Tsushima the main instrument of his new navy was to
be the "all-big-gun" ship, the first truly twentieth-century battleship,
and the prototype of all battleships built since. With a displacement
of about 18,000 tons, Fisher's *Dreadnought* carried ten 12-inch
rifles in five turrets, three on the centerline and one on each beam,
giving her a fire power equal to that of any two other battleships
afloat at the time she was launched. When the improved director
system was installed, her guns could score hits at ranges up to

20,000 yards. Her eleven-inch armor belt was two inches thicker than that of other battleships, and the first battleship turbines drove her at 21 knots, two knots faster than any foreign battleship building or afloat. Extensive watertight compartmentation and facilities for burning oil or coal (oil would give one third greater cruising range) marked her as the most advanced warship built up to that time. Fisher's innovations revolutionized naval warfare and readied Britain for war.

The tactical developments of World War I, culminating a century of experimentation, were clearly envisaged by Fisher; and his views were shared by the most competent leaders in all the world's major navies. The backbone of the fleet was the battleship which would, for maximum gunfire concentration, be fought in line-of-battle but at great distance from the enemy. It would be supplemented for scouting and special duties by the battle cruiser, a ship with the high speed and relatively light armor of a cruiser, but with the guns of a battleship. Cruisers would be the eyes of the fleet or could be detached like the frigates of the days of sail. Destroyers would screen the fleet from attack by submarines and torpedo boats and would use their own torpedoes as offensive weapons. The submarine, Fisher believed, would revolutionize fleet actions. However, while the submarine extended offensive operation even into the anchorage of the battle fleet, the mine and the torpedo gave weapons to the defensive.

Great changes had come also in the field of strategy. Close blockade was no longer possible, but "distant surveillance by the main fleet in well defended bases" could be supplemented by mine fields, submarine pickets, and aerial observation. The vulnerable flank was sea-borne commerce; for no modern western nation was self-sufficient. Allied exclusion from the Baltic and Black seas was to contribute to the defeat of Russia just as surely as Germany was herself to be brought to defeat by the Allied blockade. Hence as long as the elimination or control of all neutral channels for supplies was possible, close blockade was not necessary. In a war of attrition, a lesser power, through its submarines, could strive to deny the use of sea communications without itself being able to obtain positive control. Technology had added a new negativism.

But it was not technology that brought the *Pax Britannica* to an end. Tirpitz's Navy Law of 1898, giving Germany a fleet to challenge Britain in the North Sea, was "applied strategy." Many Germans had come to believe that two great commercial rivals could not coexist in peace.

After the challenge of German sea power was definitely accepted in 1905 by the laying down of the *Dreadnought*, and by the concentration of the Home Fleet in the North Sea as a result of the entente with France, the *Pax Britannica* was for the first time seriously endangered. Germany responded by laying down several *Dreadnought*-type battleships; Britain replied that she would build two ships for every one. British policy in building the *Dreadnought*, which made every other type of battleship obsolete, was sharply criticized on the grounds that it scrapped the advantage Britain already enjoyed in numbers; later this criticism was countered by the argument that battleships of her great size delayed the German menace because they entailed the deepening and widening of the Kiel Canal. But the most important feature of the bitter Anglo-German building race was the antagonism which it revealed. The British simply could not understand why Germany, with little coast-line and with relatively few overseas colonies, desired to enter into a maritime armaments race unless she had ulterior motives.

The end of the *Pax Britannica* cannot be attributed solely to the naval-building race which was only a manifestation of world-wide economic competition and imperial rivalry; nor was it due to the failure of England's maritime policy. Germany had taken the place held by France in the eighteenth century; but her industrial might and larger population made her a greater menace and increased the magnitude of the resultant war.

However, the power which ultimately upset the century-long balance was the United States. In wartime neither England nor Germany could accept the American doctrine of the "freedom of the seas". The seas had never really been free, a fact learned and forgotten by the United States in her cooperation with the Royal Navy in the quasi-war with France (1799-1800), in her wars with the Barbary Pirates (1803-05), and in her war against England (1812-15). During the *Pax Britannica* the freedom of the seas had served the interests of Great Britain and had been enforced by her sea power. When war came in 1914, if the United States wished to keep the sea lanes open for her own trade, she must either seize control of the seas herself or enter an alliance which had the ability to control them. The American policy of isolation, and of avoiding entangling alliances, had become incompatible with her own economic interests. After the First World War Wilson's policy,

THE U.S.S. *IDAHO* (1919), as built at the close of World War I. Rebuilt with modern tripod masts, *Idaho* fought at Saipan, Iwo Jima, and Okinawa in World War II.—(From Edwin Tunis, *Oars, Sails and Steam,* Copyright 1952 by Edwin Tunis, New York: World Publishing Company, 1952, p. 61.)

expressed in 1916, of building an American navy "incomparably the greatest navy in the world," was to create a naval situation entirely different from that of the nineteenth century, one in which Britain would accept American equality on the seas and in which the United States would be content not to use her superior industrial power to achieve the maritime preponderance which was within her reach. But sea power would then operate in a much more unstable world than that of the nineteenth century and one in which its function was complicated by the development of air power, a new world created by the vast social and technological changes which had occurred during the nineteenth century

15

Approach to Total Warfare

The intellectual link between the warfare of the Revolutionary-Napoleonic era and the total warfare of the twentieth century is to be found in the writings of Karl von Clausewitz, a Prussian general who fought against the French in both the Prussian and Russian armies and who served under Scharnhorst, Blücher, and Gneisenau. Clausewitz was appointed the Director of the Military School in Berlin in 1818, and found that his position gave him ample time for the study of military history. He spent so much time in private reading and contemplation that he was suspected of secret drinking. His *magnum opus, On War,* was still unfinished when he died of cholera in 1831, but it was given to the world by his widow.

Whereas Jomini had attempted to distill from Bonaparte's campaigns the pure essence of Napoleonic strategical and tactical doctrine and in so doing had actually reverted, to some extent, to eighteenth-century concepts of warfare, Clausewitz, although missing some of the essential points of Napoleonic strategy, grasped the new spirit bred into warfare by the political revolutions. He wove his conclusions into a philosophy of war as well as a guide for action. His book was a study of the nature of war though still, to some extent, a text for operations. Since its conclusions are largely unaffected by changes in the nature of weapons, his work is applicable in all ages; and by revealing the foundations upon which strategy must be built, he has come to exercise a powerful influence upon strategic doctrine in the modern world.

According to Clausewitz, "War is nothing else than a continuation of political transactions intermingled with different means." The core of his teaching is that these different means entail the full utilization of the moral and material resources of a nation to bring about, by violence, the complete destruction of the enemy's means and will to resist. He declared that warfare must always tend to become "absolute," by which he meant the use of the utmost violence to achieve complete annihilation; but he was well aware that absolute warfare was only an abstract concept and that, in practice, war must fall short of it.

Clausewitz held that the destruction of the enemy's armed forces is the first aim of generalship and that the best method of bringing it about is by direct attack. He placed great emphasis on the battle as the ultimate goal of strategy and wrote, "Let us not hear of generals who conquer without the shedding of blood. If bloody battle is a horrible spectacle, then it should only be a reason for treating war with more respect . . . ." He emphasized the importance of mass and concentration in Napoleon's methods, but missed the significance of elastic deployment which was an equally important part of the Emperor's technique. His disciples carried this distortion of Napoleonic strategy still further to the point of undue reliance upon numbers and weight.

Clausewitz demonstrated the weaknesses of those eighteenth-century theorists and practitioners of war who had sought to achieve victory without fighting; and he disagreed with thinkers like his contemporary, Jomini, who sought to discover the laws of the science of war. The greatest contribution which he made to military thought was to show that there can be no single tactical pattern or strategic system by which victory can be ensured. The moral factor, and the element of chance, cannot be reduced to law. Nevertheless, in the future, Clausewitz was accepted as the prophet of a strategic doctrine as rigid as any which he had challenged.

On War was actually a delayed-action time-bomb. When it was first published, Jomini held the field as the recognized interpreter of Napoleon's genius. Clausewitz was known only in Prussia until the elder Moltke applied his ideas against France. The French army "discovered" *On War* in the 1880's. By the beginning of the twentieth century Clausewitz's phrases had found their way into the thinking and writing of the general staffs of all the great armies of the world, even in Britain, where, however, officers still studied strategy on Jomini's lines rather than war with Clausewitz, although an English edition of *On War* had appeared in 1873. Responsibility for the bloody slaughter in the "mausoleums of mud" on the Western Front in the First World War has been attributed to Clausewitz by many authorities, including the British military writers Liddell Hart (who coined the phrase) and General J. F. C. Fuller.

As Liddell Hart has pointed out, much of the blame must really fall to those military leaders who read Clausewitz's startling sentences out of context and without the qualifications that invariably accompanied them. The passage in *On War* which most fully expresses the idea that war is a continuation of politics by other means is actually directed toward showing that the beginning of a war does not mean the end of political relations between the belligerent nations, since war in itself is a form of political transaction. Thus that vital passage, the key to all Clausewitz's doctrines, should be interpreted as an argument for the supremacy of political over narrowly military policies and for the exercise of moderation once victory has been ensured. Instead, it has too often been used to justify the very opposite policies; according to Clausewitz, when this occurs, "we have before us a senseless thing without an object."

Just as Clausewitz carried over the doctrines of totality in war from the Revolutionary era into the twentieth century, a contribution to the achievement of totality was being made by thinkers in non-military spheres. In countries which did not enjoy a guaranteed security and prosperity, men were searching for a formula for national power and wealth. They found it in the reiteration of a simple truth which the mercantilists had emphasized a century earlier, namely, that military strength is, in part, a product of economic forces. Thus, in 1791 in the United States, Alexander Hamilton turned his back on Adam Smith and advocated the protection of infant industry for the avowed purpose of increasing national security. Against the sentiments of most of his fellow-countrymen he also favored a standing army and navy. In Germany, members of the "Romantic-Nationalist" school, which included Müller, Treitschke, and Fichte, likewise rejected doctrinaire *laissez-faire* economics and espoused autarchy, or self-sufficiency, as a means of providing strength for war. The German economist Friedrich List preached the economic union of the Germanies as a step toward political unity, which in fact was borne out by the success of the Zollverein, 1834. Fully realizing that they could probably not be carried out without war, he advocated programs of unification and expansion for Germany. For some members of this German school, the warlike spirit was itself a vital element of national strength and efficiency. They inaugurated the worship of the state and nation as a philosophy of life.

These nationalist arguments, calling attention to the close connection between economic and social forces and military strength, received powerful, but unsolicited, support at mid-century from the founder of Communism. In 1848, in *The Communist Manifesto,* published to rally the workers to support widespread insurrections against autocracy, Karl Marx issued a call to arms. The fundamentals of his argument as elaborated in his massive work *Das Kapital* (1867-94) were that political power must inevitably pass to the proletariat which, through its labor, was the creator of wealth; but, unlike earlier socialists, he believed that violence would be necessary to effect the transfer of power.

Marxian theory appealed strongly to the lower classes whose lot had been made desperate by the harsh conditions created by the Industrial Revolution. But the Industrial and Agrarian Revolutions had a much more direct and immediate effect upon warfare than that resulting from Marxist propaganda. They provided the material, and some of the techniques, by which the impact of warfare was greatly increased and total warfare became possible.

In the eighteenth century, English farmers had pioneered improved methods of animal husbandry and tillage. A few years before the Revolution of 1789, Arthur Young, an English agricultural journalist, while touring rural France, had noted that French agriculture was backward by comparison with English. The Revolutionary leaders propagated his ideas of improvement; but it was not until the early nineteenth century that improved agricultural methods began to be adopted on a wide scale on the Continent. Increased yield per acre in Europe was accompanied by the opening up of the continents of America, Australia, and Asia for the production of food. McCormick's reaper, invented in 1831, and Appert's perfection of the art of canning were responsible for making available a greatly increased supply of grain and meat for industrial workers in time of peace and for armies in time of war. The use of citrus juices and potatoes to prevent scurvy, introduced into nautical diets at the beginning of the century, was equally important in land warfare to prevent that decimation of armies on campaign and in sieges which had often resulted from this debilitating disease. By the mid-nineteenth century, it was possible to provision armies far larger than those of the Napoleonic era and also to keep them in healthier condition.

At the same time the Industrial Revolution made possible the production of many forms of goods on a vast scale, including, of course, uniforms, weapons, and other military supplies. The application of power machinery, of capitalist organization, and of

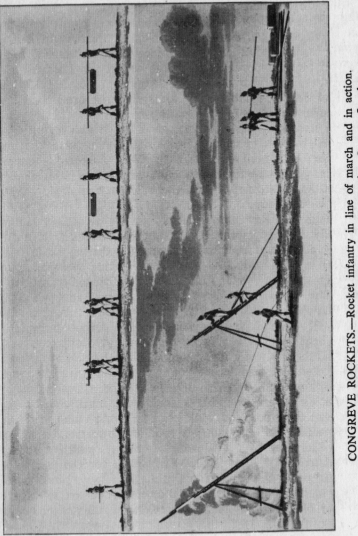

CONGREVE ROCKETS.—Rocket infantry in line of march and in action. —(From Colonel Congreve, *The Details of the Rocket System*, London: Whiting, 1814, plate 5.)

the factory system to manufacturing processes had first appeared in the sixteenth century, but made no significant impression on warfare and society until the late eighteenth and early nineteenth centuries. A remarkable series of inventions in the English textile industry between 1733 and 1785 enormously increased the output of cloth; Eli Whitney's cotton gin (1792) furnished vast supplies of raw cotton to the mills; and from 1800 steam power and iron machinery in great factories poured forth an ever-increasing flood of cheap cotton and woolen goods into the markets of the world. Elias Howe's invention, the sewing machine (1845), clothed and shod the great armies of the second half of the nineteenth century.

For military purposes, the revolution in the iron industry was even more important. The development of the technique of using coke instead of charcoal for smelting iron ore had been perfected about 1750, just in time to prevent a serious shortage of metal in England in the Seven Years' War. At that time Britain produced only one third as much iron as France; but by 1840, because of the proximity of British iron mines to coal fields, the ratio had been reversed. Meanwhile methods for producing artillery by mass production had been worked out in Woolwich Arsenal in England, in the Carron Ironworks in Scotland, at Le Creusot in France, and elsewhere, and had made available the great quantities of ordnance used in the wars at the end of the eighteenth century. Specific military and naval demands stimulated important new technical processes in the manufacture of iron. In 1784 Henry Cort, a purchasing agent for the Royal Navy, patented the reverberatory furnace and "puddling" in order to purify and toughen iron, and the rolling mill to work it more easily. In 1854, on the outbreak of the Crimean War, W. G. Armstrong offered to the British War Office his method of making guns built up from cores of steel; and this made possible more accurate boring, rifling, and breech-loading. The Bessemer steel process was introduced in 1856 in answer to a request by Napoleon III for a steel capable of with-standing the new explosive shells. The Bessemer, open-hearth, and Gilchrist processes of steel manufacture greatly lowered costs of production and led to the general use of steel, in place of iron, for heavy artillery by the last quarter of the nineteenth century.

Similar improvements had been made in the manufacture of small arms. Whitney had introduced the principles of interchangeable parts and division of labor in his Connecticut factory for the manufacture of firearms. This technique was applicable to industry generally and was the basis of all future mass-production methods. The percussion cap, invented by a Scots clergyman in 1807, made practicable a breechloader. In 1830 the "sugar loaf bullet" was introduced in the United States and, while it still required the use of the greased cap, it simplified loading the weapon. In Britain Captain Norton (1842), and in France Captain Minié (1833), perfected the cylindro-conoidal bullet which, in rifled barrels, increased the effective range of small arms to 1200 yards. By the middle of the nineteenth century a revolution in armaments had been inaugurated. Thus in 1840 the Brown Bess musket, which had been the standard small arms weapon of the British infantryman since 1690, began to be replaced by the rifle. Gatling's machine gun (1862), used on a small scale in the Civil War, pioneered automatic small arms which were to have enormous importance in future warfare. But the massed fire of American riflemen had already begun to revolutionize tactics.

The Industrial Revolution affected strategy as well as tactics, principally by the improvement of transportation. The steam engine, in addition to increasing production by driving textile mills, operating steamhammers and boring tools, lifting coal from deep shafts, and pumping water from mines, was belatedly applied to locomotion. Watt's first efficient stationary engine had appeared in 1768; but Fulton's first practical paddle-wheeler steamed up the Hudson only in 1807; and Stephenson's first passenger locomotive did not begin operation between Stockton and Darlington until 1825, and then only at walking speed. The realization of the military importance of steam locomotion came much more quickly than the locomotive itself. By 1833 a German, Harkort, had calculated that strategic passenger railways could save much time in the transportation of troops and would bring them into battle unfatigued by the march. Nine years later a scheme had been worked out for covering Germany with a network of railways which a French deputy described as "aggressive." List's plans for German union were based partly on the building of strategic railways which would not only unite the country but would reverse its historic role as the battlefield of Europe by permitting German military power to move outwards. In 1846 the Prussian VI Corps, with all its equipment, was moved 250 miles in two days, a journey which hitherto had taken ten days to two weeks. Within a few years of the running of the first passenger train, clear-sighted men had compared the effect of the invention of the steam locomotive upon society and war to that of printing and gunpowder.

One important result of rail travel, and of another associated development, cheap postal services, was the binding of nations into more tightly knit communities. The railway made possible the opening up of the United States, Canada, and Russian Siberia; and the railway and steamship transported their products to world markets. At the same time the railway marked the beginning of a greater mobility of the national populations; and the railway and post office maintained family ties which might otherwise have been severed. Thus, Prince Albert's Great Exhibition in London in 1851 attracted thousands from the North of England by cheap excursion trains. This invasion of the metropolis by northern "barbarians" was feared at first as a possible source of disorder, but proved to be a merry, peaceful occasion. Everywhere the age of railway building led to closer national unity and greater national strength.

Only the continuation of peace prevented steam locomotion from having an earlier effect upon military operations. Even so, Russian troops were moved by rail to suppress revolution in Austria in 1849; steam transports took British troops to the Crimean War in 1854; and the French made use of railways in the Italian campaigns in 1859. In the last case, although the French thereby gained a temporary advantage, it was lost because they failed to organize the transportation of adequate supplies for the troops and horse moved quickly by train. Hence it was not until proper techniques were worked out for their use in the American Civil War and the Prussian wars of the following decade that railways played a really significant part in military operations.

Along with the great increase in the supply of material for war and the greater mobility furnished by the railway and steamship went an unprecedented increase in the populations of the countries of Europe and North America, brought about by the improvement in methods of production and by better hygiene and enhanced medical knowledge. During the nineteenth century the population of the United States increased fifteenfold; but a large part of this was the result of immigration from Europe. In the same period, however, the increase in England, Scotland, and Wales was more than threefold; and the population of Europe as a whole grew from 185,000,000 to 400,000,000. With less than a quarter of the area of Asia, in 1800 Europe had a third of Asia's population; by 1900 the population gap had been narrowed to one half.

One result of this great increase of European peoples was to provide the manpower for the frequent wars which marked the century beginning in 1850. Secondly, the fact that some countries increased their population by natural and other causes more rapidly than their rivals led to a disturbance of traditional balances of power. The rise of Germany and the decline of France during the nineteenth century are partly explained by the inferior French birth rate.

The increase in populations was accompanied by a re-distribution of people into new or different areas, for instance into the Middle West in the United States, and into the North of England and away from the South. It also led to the growth of great urban centers. It was in the new areas of the West and the new industrial cities that movements for the extension of the franchise were strongest. Manhood suffrage had been achieved in most of the United States by 1827 (for whites), in France by 1848 (although only as an empty form until 1871), in Prussia by 1850 (subject to constitutional impediments), in the German Empire by 1871, and in Britain by 1884. Even when not accompanied by real representative government, the democratic franchise carried with it an obligation upon the citizen to share in the defense of the community. Therefore, in the latter part of the century, conscription became the rule on the continent of Europe. But socialists preferred a militia, and in 1915 Jean Jaurès' *L'Armée Nouvelle* made that the basis of the Leftist concept of national defense.

Moreover, the democratic franchise implied the necessity of general public education. Compulsory universal elementary education had appeared in Prussia as early as 1794. It was introduced in the United States between 1852 and 1880, in France in 1882, and in England between 1870 and 1880. Widespread literacy was an important preliminary step in the education of young men for modern war.

The concept of popular sovereignty had been re-introduced into Europe by the revolutions of 1848 only to be checked in France by Louis Napoleon, not by the use of artillery in the tradition of his uncle, but by manipulation of the ballot in popular plebiscites. Similarly, in Prussia, the constitutional movement of 1848 was betrayed and dissolved by being diverted into patriotic channels. In both countries, war was used, in part at least, to divert the masses from domestic constitutional problems: by the Crimean and Italian campaigns in the case of France and by the wars with Denmark, Austria, and France in the case of Prussia. One point of close connection between war and the growth of the "popular" but undemocratic state was thereby made apparent. In 1859 in England, fear of the rise of Napoleon III and of a second French attempt to establish hegemony in Europe led to the organization of "volunteer corps" by middle-class citizens. War, and preparation for war, was not a monopoly of autocracy.

A few years later, the American Civil War clearly demonstrated many of the features which were to mark the warfare of the age of democracy and pseudo-democracy. It was the first great war to be fought in the era of the Industrial Revolution and so it showed the effects of technological advances in industry and agriculture which were to revolutionize warfare. It showed also the growing importance of economic factors in modern warfare, in that in a struggle between two different types of economy, agrarian and industrial, the ultimate result was a victory for the power that was stronger industrially and financially. Although in the territories of both combatants there were large dissident minorities, the Copperheads in the North and the Unionists in the South, the Civil War was an ideological conflict, a struggle of rival "nationalisms" and cultures. Abolitionist sentiment acted as a powerful stimulant in the North, and propaganda was a useful weapon. This was not a war simply of hostile armies, but of hostile peoples, in which both sides were equally convinced of the absolute justice of their cause. The North was fighting for the preservation of the Union, the South for independence. Emotions kindled by the slavery issue intensified the bitterness. For both sides the objective was total. There could be no treaty, no compromise, no argument, no terms except unconditional surrender or separation.

The Civil War, the first great war to be fought by modern democratic states, raised many of the problems which trouble a democracy at war. The North, believing in democratic liberty and freedom of the press, fought the war in a blaze of publicity which endangered military security. The problem of command was even more difficult. Whereas in autocracy civil and military power is centralized, democracy cannot adopt that easy arrangement without endangering the sovereignty of the people. Democracy at war needs to produce a political leader as head of the state whose grasp of grand strategy enables him to guide war policy. The Constitution of the United States, and after it that of the Confederacy, by making the President the Commander-in-Chief of the armed forces, ensured that the higher direction of the war was a civilian responsibility; but it was difficult to draw a clear line of demarcation between major policy decisions in grand strategy to be made by the President and the planning and carrying out of military operations which must be the task of professional soldiers.

In the Confederacy a solution was found by choosing a President with much military experience. Believing himself to be a great military leader, Jefferson Davis would have preferred a military command. But he lacked the ability to get on with men over whom he had no disciplinary control.

Davis was much less successful as a war leader than Lincoln, who had fewer obvious qualifications for the task, but who had a flair for human relations and was able to learn from experience. At first, Lincoln concerned himself in the direction of the war at all levels. But he was continually seeking military leaders whose ability he could trust, and also a suitable system of command. He found the ideal solution in March, 1864, by appointing Grant as General-in-Chief of the army with Halleck as his Chief of Staff in Washington. Halleck thus served as interpreter between the President and the leader of the army. Although the United States did not actually evolve anything quite like a modern general staff during the Civil War, it did create a system of command which proved efficient in practice.

It was inevitable that Congress should seek contact with the army in order to obtain information on military affairs about which, through its legislative powers, it was compelled to make decisions. Therefore it created a Joint Committee on the Conduct of the War. Opinion has differed about the value of Congressional interference. Most of the Committee's activity took the form of legitimate enquiry and of suggestions and advice; but democratic control of the military effort also brought some intrigue.

The armies on both sides in the Civil War, although largely composed of volunteers, were a reversion to the democratic principle of the nation-in-arms. The Confederacy numbered about five and a half million whites. Only about five hundred of the regular army of the United States, most of them officers, left to join the South. The Confederate government therefore had to build an army from the bottom up. It called for quotas of volunteers from the states, men who were enlisted at first for one year and, later, for three years or the duration of the war. Conscription acts in 1862 and 1864 required the registration and enlistment of every fit man between seventeen and fifty. In all, some 900,000 whites were enrolled, with a maximum in 1863 of something less than half a million.

The North, which was more than four times as populous as the South, began the war with the regular army of the United States of about 15,000 men and supplemented it by volunteers levied by quotas upon the states. In 1863 it also resorted to conscription to fill out quotas not completed by volunteers. Throughout the war it recruited about 2,375,000 men, with a maximum strength in April 1865 of a little over a million. Thus nearly twenty per cent of the total population in the South, and over ten per cent in the North, was recruited for military service, either voluntarily or by conscription. Individual armies often ranged from 60,000 to 130,000 men.

At the outset of the Civil War, some troops still had smoothbore flintlocks, but the basic infantry weapon was a muzzle-loading rifle, a Springfield or an Enfield; and toward the end of the war a breechloader was introduced. A magazine rifle and a primitive machine gun also made their appearance. Field artillery included a smoothbore 12-pounder "Napoleon" gun and the 3-inch rifled Parrott gun. Casualties were high. At Gettysburg, where 81,000 Confederates fought 100,000 Federals, the killed numbered 20,451, while the wounded and missing numbered an additional 23,059. And Gettysburg was only one, although one of the biggest, of some 150 major encounters in less than five years. These casualties were evidence of the resolute behavior of the soldiers of democracy given what was, by European standards, a negligible amount of military training.

Heavy casualties, and the employment of amateur soldiers, hastily recruited and trained, led to important innovations in tactics. Prior to the war American army manuals described various formations, but commanders preferred attacks with regiments of about a thousand men on a narrow front of two companies in column. In the war these mass tactics gave way to attacks in two-rank line with a frontage of perhaps a thousand men. Experiments were made with skirmishers thrown out ahead of the attack, and with leapfrog rushes in which half of the attackers provided covering fire before rushing forward in their turn. One difficulty experienced in these tactics was caused by the necessity for the soldier to stand while reloading his muzzle-loader. In addition, it was sometimes difficult to induce men to advance from the prone position. But as the war went on, and as the amateurs became seasoned veterans, the *élan* of the troops on both sides grew. They pressed home attacks with a resolution that astonished foreign observers who, nevertheless, commented adversely upon the Americans' lack of precise formation. Attackers and defenders alike relied heavily upon fire power. Indeed, so little use was made of the bayonet that according to a later authority that weapon was often thrown away as a useless encumbrance. In summary, the American Civil War revealed the growing importance of fire power and the folly of the traditional close-order charge in the conditions of modern warfare. It showed that the infantryman was destined to seek shelter in trenches from the devastating power of rifled weapons. The spade and the ax had become major weapons of war. Breastworks and rifle-pits were already widely used in the field.

Cavalry tactics were similarly affected by the greater killing power of weapons. Foreign professional soldiers noted that the American horse failed to carry a charge home with the sword and believed that this was due to inadequate training. What they did not see was that rifled weapons were making the old kind of cavalry warfare impossible. American cavalry acted as mounted infantry, using their horses to carry them rapidly to the scene of an action and then dismounting and taking cover to use their breechloading carbines, weapons which, although not equal to the infantry rifle, were much superior to the musket. Thus cavalry was used to prevent the stagnation in tactical mobility which was fast developing. Independent cavalry raids deep into enemy territory, strategic operations of a kind which Frederick the Great would never have dared to use and which Napoleon never contemplated, exploited opportunities created by the dependence of the armies on the railroads.

But the most important way in which mobility was retained in the Civil War was by the strategic use of railways. The theater of operations was enormous, as large as the whole of Europe, and thinly populated. Railways had been laid down in both territories, although on a much greater scale in the North than in the South; but in neither case had they been built for strategic purposes. The use of railways for war on any important scale was unprecedented. The commanders of the Civil War had to work out principles and techniques for the military use of the railway. Most of the problems connected with the use of railways for military purposes were solved in this war; and the intelligent use of the rails was an important factor in the ultimate victory of the North.

It was found that the railway made operations possible at great distances from supply bases, that troops and materials could be carried quickly to threatened points, and that a great increase in the fighting power of troops in the line accrued from the correct use of railways. Special corps were created for the restoration, operation, and destruction of railways. Hospital trains and armored trains appeared, and cuttings, embankments, and railway lines generally became tactical objectives, often more important ones than the natural features of the ground.

At first, Herman Haupt, a West Point graduate who had civil experience in railroading, was appointed in the North to supervise the construction of railways and the transportation of troops and supplies and was fairly successful. But difficulty in coordinating the activities of rival private companies led to the appointment of Daniel M. McCallum, a railroad man, as Director of Railways with full power to requisition. He employed civilian railway personnel. Some of his feats of transportation in this war were remarkable. In September, 1863, 23,000 men with artillery and road vehicles were moved 1200 miles in seven days to save Rosecrans after his defeat at Chickamauga. This operation would have taken three months on the march. Thus the North worked out a technique of operating the railways under the full authority of the state but by making use of the experience of civilian railwaymen.

The failure of the South to organize its railways as effectively for war purposes was a factor in its defeat. To some extent this was unavoidable. The South lacked the industrial capacity to maintain and extend its lines and rolling stock. Early in the war Jefferson Davis ordered the completion of a vital link to maintain the armies on the northern front; but no leading man saw the necessity for a thorough railway policy and administration. The South was deeply committed to the principle of *laissez-faire*. Left to themselves the railways, which had mainly been built to carry goods from the interior to coastal ports, languished while waiting for the breaking of the blockade. Their lines and rolling stock might have been more advantageously employed to supplement the work of the railways running to the war fronts in Virginia and Tennessee. Not until February, 1865, did the Confederacy take over control of the railways and thus end suicidal private competition; and by that time it was too late. The railways were worn out. Lee's army in Virginia starved because, although there was food in Alabama and Georgia, it could not be moved to the troops.

While the Americans had been pioneers of the use of the railway in war, their experiences had not had a revolutionary effect on the structure of military command. It was in Prussia that the realization of the importance of railways in war contributed to the perfection of the General Staff system to plan and direct the great mass armies of modern times.

France under the Ancien Régime had had a general staff for the collection of military information and the preparation of war plans; but it had been abolished in 1790. Napoleon had felt no need for aid from such an institution. However, the growth of armies, the use of divisional formation and of improved field artillery, and the evolution of skirmishing tactics in place of the traditional line of battle meant that command must be exercised from a distance rather than by visual oversight. Plans must be prepared on a map; orders must be given in writing, instead of orally; and the telegraph, perfected by S. F. B. Morse in 1844, made possible even more remote control. In Prussia, the Quartermaster General's Department of the seventeenth and eighteenth centuries, which had been made responsible for survey and cartography, was reorganized in the early nineteenth century by von Massenbach and Scharnhorst. It consisted of the Great General Staff and the General Staff with the Troops, both under a single Chief of Staff. The former collected and collated information for planning, and the latter acted as adviser to the commanders of armies in the field. Staff colleges were set up to train staff officers. The reason for the growth of general staffs was not merely the necessity of creating a system of command capable of handling mass armies, but was also a result of the experience of the Napoleonic period that inadequate preparation for war might bring national extinction. Prussia, because of her relative weakness, had the most need of planning. As her king and his family held field command by law, a general staff provided necessary expert assistance.

Von Moltke, appointed Prussian Chief of Staff in 1857, saw that railways had made possible much more precise and reliable calculation of the movement of troops and supplies, with the result that accurate and detailed planning for the mobilization and commitment of the armed forces to war could now be undertaken. He therefore set up a railway sub-section of the General Staff in 1864, in time for use in the Danish War of that year.

In 1866 the sub-section became a separate Railway Section of the Great General Staff, a recognition of its importance. The lightning mobilizations of the Prussian army which struck down Austria in 1866 and France in 1870 were almost completely done by rail under the supervision of this section of the General Staff. There were mistakes, even in the war against France. In their enthusiasm, railway officials, supply officers, and contractors sometimes rushed goods forward in excess of requirements with the result that lines and stations became choked. But Austrian and French plans for the use of the railways were, by comparison, ill-contrived and defective; and there can be no doubt that Prussian exploitation of the railway was one of the most important weapons of victory.

Seeing the Prussian victories, other nations quickly adopted the general staff system, although not necessarily in exactly the same form as in Germany. Some form of the capital staff system was set up in Russia in 1863, in France in 1874, in Austria-Hungary in 1875, in Japan in 1879, and in Italy in 1882. Everywhere these general staffs changed the functioning of military command. They enabled a chief of staff to supervise and coordinate the operations of armies in several different theaters; and within each theater of war, the staff system provided a method by which armies of great size could be controlled. Whereas in the eighteenth century a force of about 40,000 had been about all that could be conveniently handled by a commander, in the Franco-Prussian war the Germans mobilized and committed 480,000 men at the outset. Moltke saw that the general staff system, coupled with improved methods of transportation, made possible huge concentric movements and thus gave the advantage to external lines of operation, in place of the inner lines favored by Frederick the Great and even by Napoleon.

At the same time, the growth of capital staffs inevitably affected the relationship between civil authority and military command. General staffs, possessing a corporate entity and planning for future eventualities, came to exercise a powerful influence over national policy to the disadvantage of hereditary autocratic rulers, and even more of democratic institutions. In Germany under Kaiser Wilhelm II, the general staff came to rival the civilian executive and legislature as a formulator of policy. The urgent nature of its task, the security of the state, made it the ultimate arbiter in emergency.

The Prussian victories were the result of other factors besides the railways and the improved system of command. Even without the advantages derived from the scientific use of railroads, the Prussian system of mobilization was superior. While France and Austria had to organize their army corps when war was imminent and thus lost valuable time, the Prussians had maintained the corps organization first set up during the great wars of liberation. What is more important, the Prussians had never completely abandoned the concept of the nation-in-arms which Scharnhorst had established by the army reforms after the disastrous defeat at Jena. In 1862 Bismarck had obtained appropriations to extend conscription by overriding the constitutional powers of the lower house. Hence, within two weeks of the beginning of hostilities in 1870, the Germans raised 1,180,000 trained men as against France's 330,000. While military experts in France and elsewhere were convinced that a smaller army of long-service veterans which had seen recent service in North Africa, in the Crimea, and in Italy would prevail against a horde of short-service conscripts, quantity proved on this occasion to be superior. It must be said, moreover, that the Prussian officer corps was superior to the French in morale, ability, and training, and this probably compensated for any deficiencies of the rank and file. The strength of Prussia, which so surprised European opinion in 1870, was thus based upon a retention of principles discarded by other nations after 1815, and also upon the militarist traditions of the Prussian monarchy in which popular clamor for constitutional government had been transformed into patriotic zeal for German unity and power.

In addition, the Prussians had the advantage of superior weapons. In the war with Austria, the Prussian infantry had a breechloader, the needle-gun, which not only had a more rapid rate of fire than the enemy's muzzleloader but also could be fired from the prone position. The Austrian infantry, having to stand up to reload, presented good targets. Realizing the importance of this advantage in weapons, the French hurriedly introduced the *chassepot* which, with a range of more than 1200 yards, was twice as efficient as the needle-gun. As their troops had not had enough practice with the new rifle, the advantage of a superior infantry weapon was lost. The German breechloading artillery was superior to the French muzzleloading rifled cannon, was more numerous, and was better handled. The French hoped to counter this superior-

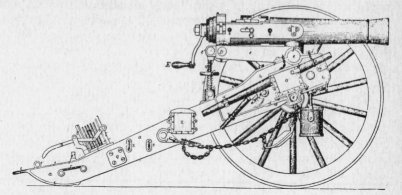

THE FRENCH *MITRAILLEUSE* OF 1870. — (From a pamphlet by Lieut-Com. W. M. Folger, U.S.N., 1873.)

ity by the *mitrailleuse,* a machine gun with thirty-seven rifled steel barrels which fired simultaneously. It looked like a field piece and was misemployed by being used as one instead of as an infantry weapon; but at close range with good cover it was effective. The Germans also possessed rifled siege artillery, which fired shells up to four miles, and howitzers.

Although Moltke had learned something about the value of rail power from the American Civil War, he learned little else. He described this struggle as a contest in which huge armed rabbles chased each other around a vast wilderness. European soldiers generally were convinced that the American conflict had little to teach. As a result, the Prussians and French alike learned the effect of new rifled weapons in the bitter school of war and were compelled to modify their tactics under fire. The French infantry, relying on their superior rifles, made use of rifle-pits and exacted a heavy toll from German infantry attacks in column. Under stress of battle, the Prussians deployed into skirmish order. They also adopted, probably not by direct borrowing, the American system of attack by which one half advanced while the other provided covering fire. Whereas the Americans, using muzzleloaders, had been able to employ this form of attack only when the ground provided some shelter for the covering parties who had to stand up to reload, the Germans with their breechloaders could fire from the ground. The Franco-Prussian war showed that all infantry must fight as skirmishers, that cavalry could no longer charge unshaken infantry, that the bayonet attack was an anachronism, that positions must be carried by fire power, and that the full power of concentrated artillery must be used in every battle. The last fact meant that, ultimately, industrial potential would be all-important in a major war.

The Prussian military victories in the 1860's, and the political results which followed, led many European nations to inspect their armories and re-examine their military organization. In Britain, ever since the Crimean War, it had been realized that the army needed a more thorough overhaul than that which had been achieved during that short sharp conflict. But military inertia blocked this until Prussian military might cast a sudden shadow over the continent. The British army was then reorganized and centralized under a political head responsible to Parliament; the iniquitous system of the purchase of commissions was abolished; military training and military education were investigated and improved; and regiments of the line were associated with the militia units of particular districts to foster recruiting and to combine those twin fountains of morale, regimental tradition and local pride. Garrisons were withdrawn from overseas colonies, like Canada, which could now stand alone, and the Cardwell system (named after Edward Cardwell, Secretary of State for War, who was responsible for many of these reforms),by which the battalions of each regiment alternated in home and overseas duty, provided forces to guard the expanding British Empire in an age when international tension was manifestly increasing.

Bismarck had given the lead to his generation by using war deliberately as a tool of policy. The most important outcome of the premeditated wars with Denmark, Austria, and France was the unification of Germany under Prussian leadership. This provided wider scope for industrialization and Germany shortly became a major industrial power. At the same time, two other new industrial powers appeared on the scene, the United States, where industrialization had been greatly furthered by the triumph of the North, and Japan, which had undertaken a conscious program of westernization including industrialization and the creation of a western-type army and navy. Production figures for coal and steel show the way in which British industrial predominance, which had been one pillar of the *Pax Britannica* of the nineteenth century, was overthrown.

Coal—Percentage increase in production 1893-1913*

United States	210%
United Kingdom	75%
Germany	159%

Production of Steel (in thousands of tons)

Year	United Kingdom	Germany	United States
1890	3579	2195	4275
1896	4133	4745	5282
1900	4901	6260	10188
1908	5300	10900	——

* Figures in these tables are compiled from R. C. K. Ensor, *England 1870-1914* (Oxford, 1941).

Germany, by dumping and subsidies, built up her steel industry in peacetime to an uneconomic position. When war came, its huge capacity proved an invaluable military asset.

The spread of the Industrial Revolution during the latter half of the nineteenth century meant increasing competition among European powers for raw materials and markets. Africa and China alone remained as major fields for exploitation. Discoveries in tropical medicine, and the invention of canning, made possible the opening up of the heart of Africa, partly by traders in search of gold, ivory, and tropical products, and partly by missionaries seeking to carry the Cross to the heathen Negro. The Dark Continent was divided among the European powers. China, narrowly escaping reduction to colonial status, was compelled to grant special rights to western powers and was partitioned into spheres of interest. The scramble for Africa and China in the last quarter of the nineteenth century was accompanied by a revival of imperialism among European peoples, a sentiment which was intensified by the growth of democracy. The newly enfranchised industrial classes evinced a powerful desire to see the map painted with their own particular patriotic color. At the same time the building of empire provided jobs for soldiers, traders, and administrators and richer investment for the capital of the middle and upper classes. The period was marked by the growth of emotional imperialism; in England this phenomenon was called Jingoism, from the words of a music-hall ditty.

Competition for colonies increased the friction arising among the European powers on various other grounds. It has been suggested, particularly by socialist-pacifist analysts, that this friction was actively provoked by certain interests which desired to profit by the sale of munitions to rival governments. The iron and steel industry in Europe and America had been greatly stimulated by the Prussian and American Wars. While in the United States the steel industry found outlets for its increased productive capacity in railway expansion and in steel construction for buildings, rivals in Europe found other markets. Certain armaments salesmen earned the suggestive epithet "merchants of death." Culpability of individuals and corporations in the deliberate kindling of war is difficult to prove. Undoubtedly some small wars and insurrections all over the world were deliberately provoked by unscrupulous arms salesmen. But responsibility for the great conflagrations of the twentieth century is another matter. Arms races certainly increased international tension; but the arms manufacturer could claim that he was performing a patriotic service by ensuring that his own country was adequately prepared against the danger of an attack which the unsettled times seemed to threaten. At the same time he was pushing his wares abroad.

Thus the nations of Europe prepared themselves for a major conflict. The French dreamed of *revanche* against Germany. Germany sought colonial equality and challenged Britain's naval hegemony. Russia and Austria were competitors for the spoils of the disintegrating Ottoman Empire. Britain, holding tightly to its economic and political hegemony of much of the world, clashed with almost every other power in some corner of the globe. Armed with the weapons furnished by the new industrialism, the massed forces of nations-in-arms were prepared for war by military leaders who had absorbed Clausewitz's theories. Total war had become both possible and likely. The Crimean War and the Austro-Prussian War were the last of the limited wars fought by great powers in Europe. The Franco-Prussian and Russo-Turkish wars (1878) showed signs of a new age, even at the tactical level. In the American Civil War and the German wars there was increased use of firepower and also dispersion and flexibility in the field. The use of entrenchments in America recurred both in France (1870) and at Plevna (1878), thus anticipating the Western Front of World War I.

16
Total Warfare Begins

By the end of the nineteenth century, there were many signs of Armageddon. Perhaps the clearest were in the writings of Ivan S. Bloch, who published in St. Petersburg in 1897-98 a six-volume study of war in which he made a remarkably accurate forecast of the nature of the First World War. This work was translated into German in 1899. Bloch declared that in the event of a great war in Europe, the technical development of weapons, coupled with the increased possibilities of harnessing the political and economic organization of the state to war, would make a stalemate inevitable between the fighting forces of the contending nations. As a result, civil populations would be subjected to a fearful war of attrition. He declared that the victor would suffer as much as the vanquished and that the ultimate result would be the collapse of social organization.

Bloch's book influenced the Czar, who called the Hague Conference, actually because Russia could not afford to modernize her artillery. But Bloch's warnings went largely unheeded by military men, perhaps because he was not a professional soldier. Moreover, in his last volume, the only one to be published in English and French, he suggested that technical developments had made traditional war all but impossible; he thus diverted attention from the horrible truths about future wars which his brilliance had uncovered. In most countries military men who might have found ways to prevent fulfillment of the prophecy failed to respond. Only the Germans, who had recently integrated their field and foot artillery, and who had increased the proportion of machine guns as a result of observing conditions at Port Arthur, were prepared for the kind of war that emerged after the Marne. The others modified their training, organization, and equipment after siege war had occurred on a huge scale.

Yet there were other signs nearer at hand which were written in the kind of language the military understood best—namely, in actual warfare.Three wars at this time gave a foretaste, each in its own way, of what the century was to produce. These were the Spanish-American War, the South African War, and the Russo-Japanese War. At first sight they appeared to prove Bloch wrong, but this was because all were "limited wars" in so far as they were restricted in objective or in locality or by the inability of the contestants to engage the whole of their national strength. Actually, taken together, they made up a picture which portrayed the total warfare of the future, the kind that Bloch had forecast would occur when modern European nations went to war.

A significant lesson of the Spanish-American War was that the new "democratic" state was vastly more powerful in war than any earlier political organism. The Spanish-American War might not have occurred if it had not been for the new "yellow press" which played upon the mixed feelings of liberalism and nationalism in the United States. Sensational reports of the cruelty of the Spaniards whipped up a fever which made war inevitable. This war showed that democracies were not immune from the fever of aggressive war. In the hands of autocracy, the press obviously could be used for nefarious purposes. Furthermore, the state had, in the cheap newspaper, an organ of propaganda which greatly increased its control over its people. Public opinion could be molded at will; and nations could be inspired to endure hardships far beyond anything known in earlier centuries. Future wars would be long and bitter. But democracies were poorly prepared for them.

The South African War, fought by Britain against the two small Boer republics, was mainly a war of movement; but this was principally because relatively small forces were being employed in a huge theater of operations. The Boer War, as it was popularly called, taught lessons which had already been made clear during the American Civil War. The Boers were hardy farmers who were excellent marksmen with their Mauser rifles. They were not hampered by traditional military methods. In their own country, which they knew intimately, they were a stubborn foe, even for a nation with the wealth and resources and military tradition of Great Britain. It was found that the magazine rifle and smokeless powder had made frontal attacks more costly for infantry and that cavalry using swords (the traditional *arme blanche*) had become a mere relic of the past. However, as the Boers were mounted riflemen—a kind of soldier for whom European cavalrymen had hitherto felt nothing but contempt—an excuse was provided for the retention of mounted troops for a generation, long after they had outlived their usefulness. Trenches dominated tactics.

A second lesson of the war in South Africa was taught by the bitterness of the struggle. Britain had begun the war badly, largely because of inferiority of numbers. In due course, she was able to put enough men in the field to overcome the organized forces of the enemy, but the Boers resorted to guerrilla warfare on a broad scale. Here was the concept of the nation-in-arms carried out to the limit. This wholehearted national resistance was not overcome until Kitchener had cut the country up by blockhouses and barbed wire, had gathered the women and children of the "burghers" into concentration camps, had burned the farmhouses which gave shelter and provided supplies for the partisans, and had swept each section of the country free of warriors. Inevitably, in the improvised conditions of the camps, many women and children died of disease. The revelations of Miss Emily Hobhouse, an English humanitarian, shocked Britain and led to a softer peace than the military victory portended.

The third war of this period, the Russo-Japanese War, was fought between two great powers, and gave even more indication of what was to come. Perhaps only the fact that the contestants were separated by a continent crossed by a single railroad prevented this from becoming the first total war of modern times. It had many features which were to reappear in Flanders a decade later. Both sides had modern rifles; the Japanese had Hotchkiss machine guns and eleven-inch howitzers; and the only defense against these weapons was to dig in. The entrenchments protected by barbed wire around Port Arthur resembled the Western Front of the future. Heavy concentrations of artillery dominated the field of battle and frontal attacks were unprofitable. Neither Russia nor Japan could afford a long war, but, when the way to victory by turning a flank became impracticable, a stalemate rapidly developed.

A final lesson to be drawn from these three little wars was that Mahan's recently expressed doctrines of sea power appeared to be vindicated. Although widespread and unwarranted popular fear of the bombardment of the east coast of the United States by a Spanish squadron led at first to faulty deployment of the American fleet, it was sea power that eventually ensured the defeat of Spain, both in Cuba and in the Philippines. In the South African War, British victory of Tsushima destroyed Russia's naval power and the possibility of her cutting the shorter Japanese supply lines. Thus the three wars which ushered in the twentieth century provided plenty of indications of the nature of the warfare of the future; and they also reinforced the lesson that, in a major war, the command of the sea might well be the decisive factor.

One direct effect of this preliminary period of small wars was that both of the two great western democracies geared their military machine more firmly to the state by the adoption of a form of that system of military leadership developed in Germany and France. In both countries there had long been strong opposition to the creation of a general staff, partly because both British and Americans had been satisfactorily successful against primitive peoples and in Britain because the Queen's cousin, as Commander-in-Chief, had resisted it. On the other hand, in both countries there were strong supporters. In England, Spenser Wilkinson, an Oxford professor, wrote *The Brain of an Army* in 1890, which had great influence in bringing about the ultimate adoption of a general staff system for the British Army. Civilian authority was preserved by the creation of an Army Council. The office of Commander-in-Chief was abolished, and many of its functions were taken over by the new Chief of Staff. A Committee of Imperial Defence, established in 1901, and the Imperial General Staff, as it was called by 1909, were used to coordinate the defense plans of the United Kingdom with those of the self-governing British dominions. The dominions, however, retained independent control of their own armed forces.

The structure of the army was revised. Weaknesses in mobilizing adequate forces early in the Boer War had shown that if war with a great European power were to break out, the country would be virtually defenseless. Hence, the Cardwell system, created to provide a garrison for the far-flung empire of the late nineteenth century, was replaced by the Haldane system, a combination of regular and "territorial" (or reserve) forces, designed to provide an army for operations on the continent of Europe. As a result of Haldane's work, when the First World War came Britain was able to put fifteen divisions on the continent within a few months of the outbreak of hostilities.

The new British general staff was significantly different from its German counterpart. It was not a separate corps, and therefore it did not become distinct from the regiments. At the same time, it was subordinate to a civilian member of the cabinet and so was in no position to act independently in the making of policy. Even so, contemporary with the reorganization of the army and the creation of the general staff, the Foreign Secretaries, Lansdowne and Grey, authorized staff talks with the French without informing the whole cabinet. The result was that Britain was, in effect, committed to come to the aid of France in the event of a German invasion. At a time when European alliances were hardening into two bitterly hostile groups, this secret military arrangement, which was kept from the Cabinet from 1904 to 1912, was of great importance in making war certain.

Similarly, largely through the work of Elihu Root, Secretary of War, 1899-1904, a general staff was created in the United States. Although consciously modelled on the German system, it was, like the British general staff, subordinate to civil authority. The constitutional powers of the President as Commander-in-Chief were left untouched, and Congress kept a tight hold on the purse strings. However, the new policy permitted a more cohesive organization of the United States army to band together scattered units which, in the nineteenth century, had effectively policed the plains. Hence, when the United States became involved in a major war, the incorporation of the National Guard divisions and a rapid general expansion of the army were facilitated.

But perhaps the most significant lesson of the three small wars which preceded the First World War was that new powers had appeared to upset the old balance of power and therefore to threaten world peace. That Britain had such difficulty in coping with a small colonial people like the Boers suggested that her century-long hegemony over subject peoples was ended. Japan's defeat of a great European power forecast a serious challenge to white supremacy in Asia. Most important, the American defeat of Spain, which marked the "coming of age of the United States," led to the acquisition of Caribbean bases, of the Philippines, and of other Pacific possessions and was followed by the start of the Panama Canal in 1904. Popular agitation for a United States navy "second to none" indicated that domestic support was growing for a more positive foreign policy. Meanwhile, however, as a result of distaste for the growing antagonisms of the Old World, the United States held back from major involvement in world affairs.

The growth of national armies in the nineteenth century and of a competitive arms race, the Anglo-German naval rivalry, the development of techniques of mobilization which, once started, were

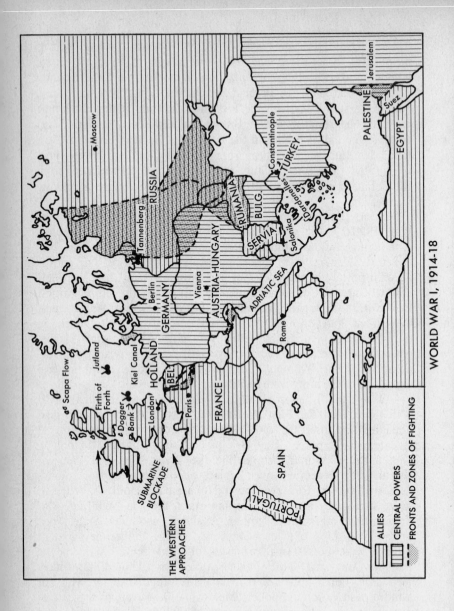

WORLD WAR I, 1914-18

Moscow

RUSSIA

Tannenberg

Jerusalem

Constantinople

PALESTINE

Suez

TURKEY

EGYPT

RUMANIA

BULG.

SERVIA

Salonika

Dardanelles

Berlin

GERMANY

Vienna

AUSTRIA-HUNGARY

ADRIATIC SEA

Rome

Scapa Flow

Jutland

Firth of Forth

Dogger Bank

Kiel Canal

HOLLAND

BEL.

London

Paris

FRANCE

SPAIN

PORTUGAL

SUBMARINE BLOCKADE

THE WESTERN APPROACHES

ALLIES

CENTRAL POWERS

FRONTS AND ZONES OF FIGHTING

difficult to stop, all pointed to the likelihood of a major European war in the event of some particularly critical "incident." The fact that many of the European powers were rivals for overseas empire, the existence of alliances with non-European powers like Japan, and the certainty that a long war would raise the vexing question of the freedom of the seas for neutral trade, made it likely that a major European war would encompass the world. The resources and armies which could be conscripted and committed forecast a conflict of unprecedented magnitude. Shortly after the war began, Germany had mobilized and deployed nearly 2,500,000 first-line troops and Austria about 1,500,000; on the Allied side Russia had sent approximately 3,000,000 men to the front and France nearly 2,000,000. Britain delayed conscription until 1916, but eventually mobilized 5,000,000 in her armed forces. Among the other great powers, the total forces raised were: Germany, 13,250,000; France, 8,000,000; Russia, 15,000,000; and the United States, 4,700,000. By the end of the war, 65,000,000 men of all nations had borne arms.

Yet it was at first expected that the war would be short; both sides hoped for a quick victory. Germany, which took the initiative by violating Belgian neutrality to which the powers had agreed in 1839, relied upon a plan drawn up before 1914 by the then Chief of Staff, Count von Schlieffen. The purpose of the Schlieffen Plan was to avoid a long war on two fronts, which the Franco-Russian Entente seemed to threaten. As the vast area of Russia seemed to make a quick decision in the Eastern theater unlikely, Schlieffen argued that it was imperative that Germany should knock France out before Russian mobilization was completed. To achieve this end, he planned to invade France through Belgium, to weight the right of his armies for an overwhelming blow, and to lure the French to attack on the Rhine while the German armies on the right were sweeping around to accomplish an encirclement as effective as that at Cannae. By 1914 Schlieffen was dead and the control of the German military machine was in the hands of a nephew of the great von Moltke who replaced a strategy of expedients by a hard plan. Moltke, fearing that a French invasion in Lorraine might cut his communications and that the railways could not support the full attack on his right, strengthened his center. Furthermore, the rapid advance of the great German armies led to confusion and loss of contact which no amount of staff planning had been able to foresee and overcome; and an unexpectedly early Russian offensive caused von Moltke to draw divisions from the West for use against the Russians. Hence the Cannae on the Western Front was not achieved, the German invasion was halted at the battle of the Marne in September 1914, and the invaders withdrew to the Aisne to dig in for a long war.

The failure of the adulterated Schlieffen Plan was the immediate cause of the great stalemate on the Western Front, which was to last for more than four years; but the real cause of the stalemate was the fact that developments in technology had led to a predominance of the defensive and had not yet been adapted to the offensive. This was most evident on the Western Front where both sides could concentrate their biggest forces and where defeat would be decisive. The great railway network in this thickly populated industrial area, built with an eye to strategy as well as to commerce, made it possible to rush huge armies to the frontier within a few hours of a general mobilization. A new invention, the gasoline engine, made it possible to haul supplies of ammunition and food from the railheads to maintain huge armies deployed from Switzerland to the North Sea. Strategical considerations on the Western Front came to be subordinated to tactical possibilities measured by the difficulty of capturing German trenches in different localities.

Tactics on the Western Front were reduced to suicidal infantry assaults in formations which were theoretically skirmish order but which were sometimes so thick as to be almost the shoulder-to-shoulder lines of the eighteenth century, though without their drilled rigidity. The chief variation on these tactics attempted by the military leaders on both sides was to increase the amount of preliminary artillery barrage, to achieve suspense in its employment, to vary its use by such techniques as the creeping barrage behind which the infantry advanced, the box barrage which isolated a section of enemy trenches, and the saturation barrage in which the concentrated fire of all available arms was poured on a small area to obliterate it. In the battle of Verdun (1916), artillery dominated the battlefield and the infantry then came to hold the ground cleared by the shells.

The ammunition required by the artillery for this kind of warfare was on a scale which no one previously had contemplated. Military leaders on the allied side were peculiarly slow to realize that vigorous measures must be taken to obtain it by gearing the great industrial plants to war production. When French, the British Commander-in-Chief in France, was sending daily demands for

also the departments occupied after the German inva-
The gist of Foch's teachings had been an emphasis on
ce of morale. "The purpose of discipline is not obe-
make men fight in spite of themselves." There could
ry without fighting" and "to make war always means
A battle won is a battle in which one will not confess
n." Colonel de Grandmaison had developed this morale-
ing into a rigid doctrine of the *offensive à outrance*
arly brought a French defeat in 1914, when Plan XVII
take account of German numbers and flexible strategy.
the war went on the generals on both sides developed
ified and somewhat illogical doctrine of morale and
which stated, in effect, two contradictory things: "su-
rs will win," and "superior morale will win." From a
f these they developed the principle that whatever the
it was correct to attack. This was almost their only
great predominance which the rifle, the machine gun,
ents had given to the defensive.

ar progressed, continuous entrenchments became
crete was added to earth and sandbags; and when the
ed to a new defensive line, the Hindenburg Line, in
it was hailed as impregnable. Its plan was based on
f defense in depth, using concrete pillboxes, which
ad developed from experience at Verdun and on the

ctics developed slowly during the war. The principle
place of a general assault in line had been suggested
ar by Captain Laffargue, a French officer; but the
tle attempt to model their offensives on it, relying on
bombardment, later supplemented by the infantry
un, in 1916, the Germans used combat groups of
en, but they did not develop this idea further until
hen the German Chief of Staff, Ludendorff, pushed
infantry forward and through the line and switched
his attack from place to place by moving troops
or bus on roads immediately behind the line. Thus
reeping painfully back into war. The great Allied
e which finally broke the German lines and appar-
Foch's doctrine of "attack" was based on a rapid
at different points, as well as on overwhelming mass
teriel.

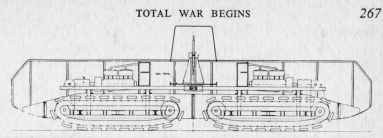

THE CATERPILLAR LANDSHIP, as submitted to the British Admiralty,
March 4, 1915. Leading particulars are as follows: total weight, 25 tons;
over-all length, 36 feet; over-all width, 12 feet 6 inches; height to top of
turret, 10 feet 6 inches; height to top of body of car, 7 feet 3 inches; turning
radius, 65 feet; pressure on ground, 12 pounds per inch. The landship was
powered by two 46-HP Rolls Royce engines.—(From Sir Murray Sueter,
The Evolution of the Tank, Hutchinson, London, 1937, p. 67.)

more and more shells, the politicians had to overrule the soldiers at
the War Office before the shells were produced. The Ministry of
Munitions, under Lloyd George, had to take over the control of war
production from the War Office.

Some attempts were made to achieve tactical surprise and the
desired breakthrough by the introduction of new weapons. For
instance, the Germans used gas shells in Poland in 1915, but with
little success. On April 22, 1915, the Germans tore a great hole in
the allied front at Ypres by the use of chlorine gas discharged from
cylinders; but they failed to take advantage of the breach and the
Canadians quickly sealed it. Gas, although "improved" during the
course of the war, failed to be a war-winning weapon because,
surprise having been lost, protective measures were introduced; and
the prevailing winds being westerly, the allies had an advantage for
retaliation. In the long run, the introduction of gas did the Germans
more harm than good because allied propagandists made effective
use of this breach of the Hague convention.

A second example of the misuse of a new weapon which might
have provided the tactical surprise necessary to breach the fortifications on the Western Front is to be found in the story of the tank.
Armored cars existed before the war began; but they were restricted
in use by the necessity of staying on hard roads. The endless track
was already available, being used on the great farms of North
America. The incorporation of the gasoline engine in an armed and
armored caterpillar tractor came just before the realization that new
weapons had forced a stalemate. In 1916 the tractor and the armored car were effectively mated by Colonel E. D. Swinton with the

blessing of Winston Churchill, the First Lord of the British Admiralty. Tanks were used for the first time on the Western Front on September 15, 1916, but not in the way their creator, Swinton, had advised. He had been overruled by Haig, the British Commander-in-Chief, and had been ordered to produce a small quantity for immediate use rather than to build up a big tank force to achieve a knockout blow. Operating on unsuitable ground and restricted in mobility, the tanks achieved a temporary success, but skeptical commanders had failed to have infantry up to exploit the breach. The great advantage of surprise was lost. However, it must be noted that the early tank was unreliable because it was mechanically imperfect.

A third technological development must be mentioned in connection with efforts to achieve a tactical superiority on the Western Front. The gasoline-powered airplane, invented by the Wright brothers in 1903, developed with remarkable rapidity under war conditions. By 1916 and the Somme virtually every future tactical use of the aircraft had been exploited operationally. The first function of the aircraft was reconnaissance; aircraft of the Royal Flying Corps played a significant role in the detection of the movements of Kluck's First German Army in 1914 and hence in the Marne counter-offensive. No longer could an army expect to move freely without detection; night movements of troops became the rule, and elaborate camouflage precautions had to be taken to attempt to disguise planned movements. From early 1915 photographic reconnaissance assumed great importance, especially in preparing trench maps and in the detection of gun sites for counter-battery work. At about the same time aircraft began to be employed to control and direct artillery fire. All these functions demanded protection. Therefore specialized fighter aircraft mounting machine guns synchronized to fire through the propellor were developed. The Fokker single-seater fighter, which appeared on the Western Front in late 1915, gave the German Air Force immediate superiority. For the rest of the war, air superiority fluctuated as one side or the other developed better fighter aircraft. The spectacular mass dogfights of the air war were, however, less significant than the mundane activities of larger numbers of aircraft used more closely with ground operations. In the last two years of the war, these activities were extended to support of infantry and tanks, and to the ground strafing of enemy rear areas, particularly in the Battle of Amiens (1918).

Air bombing on the Western Fr
in support of ground forces. At
Corps's tactical bombing program
way junctions and yards, bridges,
however, the Germans had shown
strategic, possibilities of the air a
later the Gotha and Giant bombers
and cities in England and France.
civilian morale and politics than
and they caused a major diversio
build up a home defense organiz
followed by the French and Britis
strategic bombing force, the Indep
the British to carry out raids up
Under its commander, General
ducted a bombing offensive agai
war and planned to strike at
Handley-Page aircraft capable o
pounds. Thus, in the heat of op
power prophecies of the interwa
concept of a strategic role for air
in years to come.

With these scattered except
too conservative to attempt to
produced by costly and slow exp
victory. However, they showed
tactical usage of their arms in t
prevailed. They varied the time
accumulation of supplies and t
different methods of coordinati
these variations had two comm
infantry in heavy formations in
artillery as an offensive weapon
were not impressive, except in ca

Military leaders on both side
ence that only through such at
found. In this determination the
lectures of one of their number,
some years before the war had
France was wedded to an off

Lorraine an
sion in 191
the importa
dience but t
be "no vict
attacking."
oneself beat
raising teac
which had n
had failed t
However, a
an oversimp
mass attack
perior num
combination
circumstanc
answer to t
and entrenc

As the
stronger. C
Germans re
March, 191
the principl
the German
Somme.

Offensiv
of infiltratio
early in the
Allies made
heavy artill
tank. At V
about fiftee
March 191
small group
the weight
laterally by
flexibility w
counter-off
ently justif
series of att
of men an

It must be noticed that throughout the war, although many cavalrymen were dismounted to fight as infantry, large numbers of cavalry were kept behind the lines of the Western Front for a breakthrough which never came. On other fronts, where the concentration of rifles and machine guns was thinner, the horsemen saw more action. But the value of cavalry in the West was a negative one. Large numbers of men were kept idle, and forage for the horses entailed a tremendous strain on the supply lines. Overlooking the fact that horse-drawn transport was still vitally important and used even more fodder than the cavalry, Major General J. F. C. Fuller, the British exponent of tank doctrine, went so far as to argue that if the Allied leaders had not maintained a mistaken belief in cavalry, bread rationing might not have been necessary in England.

In addition to the tactical problem of breaking through the Western Front, there was an interesting problem of grand strategy which led to strong differences of opinion. While the French and most of the British military leaders insisted the war would be won or lost on the Western Front, an important group of civilian leaders, among whom Winston Churchill and Lloyd George were prominent, argued that the Allies should make use of their command of the sea to attack the Central Powers in the rear. Most professional military opinion declared that the "Easterners," as the school which advocated this strategy of indirect approach was called, were ignorant of the logistic problems involved in supplying large forces at a great distance from their principal bases. Efforts made elsewhere than on the Western Front were usually inadequately supported, either on account of the problem of geography, or because of the lukewarm interest of the British and French military commands. Hence Turkey, which had joined the Central Powers in November 1914, defended herself successfully against Russian, French, and British attacks. The attempt to force the Dardanelles, link with the Russians in the Black Sea, and knock Turkey out of the war by an Anglo-French naval bombardment in February, 1915, was a costly failure and was followed by the abortive landings on the Gallipoli peninsula. An Anglo-French landing at Salonika (which, in the fashion of total war, ignored the desires of Greece to remain neutral) was little more successful. Not until 1917 did the British, under General Allenby, make significant advances into Turkish territory, capturing Jerusalem at Christmas of that year. It is perhaps some vindication for the Easterners' school of indirect approach that the crackup of the Central Powers came first in the

Near East and Balkans. On the other hand, the Westerners could claim that the only place where the war could be, and was, won was on the Western Front.

The great strategic dispute draws attention to the vital problem of command. Under the German system of government, the military leaders, controlling the High Command and operating through the General Staff, had a centralized control over the war effort. The only group which might have challenged military hegemony was the Social Democrats, but upon the outbreak of war their German patriotism easily overcame their socialist doctrines and they left the direction of the war effort to the traditional leaders of Prussia, the Junkers and the military hierarchy. After the dismissal of Falkenhayn in August, 1916, von Hindenburg had been placed at the helm with Ludendorff as his Chief of Staff. This pair were masters, not merely of the military machine, but of the economic side of the war effort, and continued to be in command until almost the end of the conflict.

In the democracies, the problem could not be settled so easily. The military leaders, who were appointed by the civil government and were subservient to it, were, in theory, left in complete control of all matters military. But in modern war the dividing line between military and civil matters is not easy to draw; and in any case, grand strategy at the summit is a responsibility of the civil government. In both France and Britain this problem led to bitter disputes. Control of the war effort could not be surrendered completely to the military leaders without endangering the principle of the sovereignty of the people. Hence civilians were compelled to make decisions about military policy and to encroach on the traditional sphere of the professional soldier. In several major instances their instinct was sounder than the soldiers' expertise.

Their intrusion frequently met resistance from the soldiers. Thus the Military Committee of the French Chamber was refused permission to visit the front by Joffre, who believed that civilians had no place near the battle line. Not until October, 1917, were the constitutional rights of the committee recognized by the Commander-in-Chief, and by that time Clemenceau had fully asserted civilian authority. War, he believed, was too important to be left to soldiers.

In Britain, the disputes between soldiers and statesmen over the supply of munitions and over the grand strategy of the war have already been mentioned. Lloyd George, who became Prime Minister in December, 1916, insisted on taking control into civil hands;

but he did not succeed in gaining the confidence of his professional advisers nor did he entirely rely on their professional competence. The military men accused him of acting for purely political motives, of being concerned more with votes than with the safety of the Empire. On the other hand, it must be remembered that even when the Prime Minister had doubts about the competence of his military leaders it was no easy matter to dismiss them without destroying the confidence in war leadership which had been deliberately built up by propagandists. The civil-military dispute did not become so urgent in the case of the United States in this war, partly because American armies were operating farther from their base, partly because of the constitutional position of the President as Commander-in-Chief, partly because of the personality and ability of War Secretary Baker and General Pershing, but most of all, perhaps, because the duration of American war effort, and particularly of effort in adversity, was not long enough to bring matters to a head.

One fertile source of trouble between civil and military leaders in Britain was the question of a unified Allied command. From early in the war, the politicians were convinced of the disadvantages arising from divided command on the Western Front in face of the centralized control exercised by the German High Command. Influenced by a belief in the military prowess of the French generals, and by some distrust of their own, Lloyd George and some of his colleagues, supported by General Sir Henry Wilson, were prepared to subordinate the British Army to the French Commander-in-Chief. Robertson, the British Chief of the Imperial General Staff, and Haig resisted this move grimly because they were doubtful both of the competence of Nivelle and of French motives; they used the argument that the British soldier would fight better under his own leaders. It is difficult to believe that there was not also an element of personal ambition, particularly as Haig was a strong advocate of the complete integration of the troops of the dominions, and even of American troops, in the British army or under British command.

When American forces began to arrive in France in 1917, both British and French military leaders pressed for the incorporation of American infantry into their own armies to fill the gaps caused by the awful casualties which they had suffered. They were astonished by the insistence of General Pershing that American troops would fight better as a national army; and they yielded only reluctantly and partially to this argument. However, while unity of command at the highest political level had been achieved by the creation of a Supreme War Council, it was not matched by an effective unity of military command when, in March,1918, the great German offensive threatened to drive the armies apart, forcing the French back on Paris and the British on the Channel ports. At this point, Haig, seeing the danger, proposed the appointment of Foch to coordinate the action of all Allied armies on the Western Front. President Wilson ordered Pershing to accept Foch's directions in strategic, but not tactical, operations. This was a timely solution of that vexing problem of inter-Allied cooperation, which had nearly led to defeat.

But the war was much more than a military affair in which questions of strategy and tactics, and of military command, were all-important. Far more than ever before, the nations as a whole were harnessed to the war effort. Germany, ringed about by enemies and cut off by the blockade from her former sources of supply, had to accept state direction of the whole of her economic life. In the first few months of the war, Rathenau, an industrialist, set up controls over the whole field of production. Later the General Staff sponsored the creation of a new *Kriegsamt*, or War Office, to organize war production and to produce *Ersatz*, or substitute materials, for those necessaries which were in short supply. Rationing was an inevitable part of this machinery. Other nations adopted measures of the same type, although in lesser degree.

The impact on national life and on society was tremendous. People learned to submit to state control to an extent not before contemplated. Labor was directed, taxation was increased to phenomenal heights, women went into industry, into the armed forces, and in Russia even fought, and finance and industry came under state direction. The use of substitutes led to changes in the eating habits of the household and some of them were permanent; some new inventions, like artificial fertilizer, came to stay. But the effect of such innovations on the life of the people was less important than the cumulative effect of state direction and control. While in the democracies the legal supremacy of parliament or assembly was carefully preserved during the war, the tendency to rule by order-in-council or executive order, and the willingness of the people to accept such rule, was to have far-reaching effects and to set precedents for a new kind of state control.

Only those states, whether autocratic or democratic, which were already highly developed industrially could fully reorganize themselves for this kind of war; and failure to do so spelled defeat. Imperial Russia was the first of the major states to crack under the strain. At the beginning of the war Russia, the "Colossus of the North," had been portrayed in Allied propaganda as a steamroller; and it was confidently expected that when her millions were armed she would roll over the Central Powers. Instead, when the Dardanelles-Gallipoli strategy failed to open the way for the arms she needed, Russia became a liability. The war on the Eastern Front rolled backwards and forwards much more freely than in the West, but the sufferings of the Russians were even more severe than those of the troops on the Western Front. Russia and Austria, lacking adequate industries, proved much less able to supply their armies than Germany, France, and Britain. While Austria could be propped up by Germany, Russia was too remote from her allies to be effectively sustained. Eventually her communications system collapsed and revolution broke out both among her industrial workers and in the armed forces. The net result of failure on the military and economic fronts was the communist revolution. This same phenomenon was to reappear in Germany in 1918. The economic dislocation which the war produced helped to create the communist totalitarian state.

Meanwhile, war on the economic front had included the traditional use of sea blockade, but with new weapons, new methods, and a new ruthlessness. When the war began the rival navies, unlike the armies, were already mechanized. By December, 1914, all German shipping except submarines had been swept from the seas. In that month the Battle of the Falkland Islands secured for Britain the decisive advantage of full use of the waters of the Southern Hemisphere. Yet, despite the fact that one major cause of the war was the Anglo-German race in building battleships, only twice did the fleets of capital ships meet, at the Dogger Bank action, January 24, 1915, and at Jutland, May 31, 1916, an unexpected engagement in which the British lost more heavily in ships but were left in control of the North Sea. After that battle, the German fleet did not come out to seek its opponents' main fleets until it came to surrender. Even so, both before and after Jutland, the necessity of watching and blockading the German navy tied up a large proportion of the Royal Navy in the remote bases of the Firth of Forth and Scapa Flow.

The Germans made good use of the principle of the fleet-in-being, while following the traditional policy of the weaker sea power, commerce-raiding. For this purpose they had a powerful new weapon, the submarine. When Britain proclaimed the blockade of Germany and published a contraband list that included every kind of goods which might conceivably be used in the war effort, the Germans, arguing that the remote blockade was not legal, retaliated by proclaiming all the waters around the British Isles war zones in which vessels would be subject to attack by German submarines. Because merchantmen were being armed and Q-ships were being used, the Germans sank merchant ships on sight without providing for the safety of the crew and passengers. In 1917, the rate of sinkings grew so high that Britain, dependent on imports for raw materials and food, found her economy seriously threatened. The Allies were forced to protect their trade by organizing convoys. They were short of escort vessels because of the overconcentration in the North Sea.

But the most important result of the blockades imposed by both combatants was their effect on neutral nations. The United States, by far the most important neutral, naturally became the champion of neutral rights, following her traditional policy of the "freedom of the seas." Britain's insistence on comprehensive contraband lists, the black listing of firms which "traded with the enemy," the assertion of the right of search, and the forcing of neutral ships to report at certain British control stations aroused bitter resentment among American shipping interests. However, in the long run these resentments were overbalanced by the German policy of torpedoing neutral ships without warning. It was this latter practice which played the greatest part in influencing America to enter the war on the side of the Allies.

The submarine campaign was not the only factor in deciding American policy. American financial interests had lent money to both combatants but, influenced partly by a greater sympathy, and partly by the fact that the blockade made it easier for the Allies to operate in the United States, the loans to the Allies amounted to one and a half billion dollars against 27 million dollars to the Central Powers. Although many Americans of foreign extraction wanted the Central Powers to win, there was a far greater bond of sympathy for the Allies, especially for France, with whom the United States had had ties of friendship since the early days of the Republic, and for Britain, with whom she had a common language and a common inheritance of free institutions and of law. When the collapse of Czarist Russia made the war appear more clearly as a conflict between liberty and autocracy, the way to American participation was made easier.

At the same time, it is important to realize that this element of ideological sympathy was stimulated by deliberate propaganda which both sides undertook, but in which the Allies had a natural advantage because they were able to identify their cause with the cause of constitutionalism against autocracy, and therefore of liberty against tyranny. They also proved to be more adept in the arts of propaganda. After the war, some of the deceptions of the propagandists were to recoil upon their heads. In the 1920's many Americans became convinced that the United States had been dragged into war, not so much as a result of the submarine campaign but as a result of the activities of Wall Street financiers and Allied propagandists, who had exaggerated German atrocities in Belgium, and had invented such lies as the famous story of the "German corpse factory," which was alleged to have produced fats for industrial use. The manipulation of public opinion and the deliberate use of propaganda were as important elements in the new total warfare of the twentieth century as real ideological sympathy. Even so, one of the most important causes of the ultimate Allied victory was the moral crusade preached by President Wilson. His enunciation of the Fourteen Points promising a new kind of world in which war would be banished became the basis for discussion of the terms upon which the Germans would surrender.

It would be doing less than justice to the armed forces, however, and to the material efforts of the workers on the Allied side if it were not made clear that by this time Germany had suffered severe defeat on the Western Front and was losing her allies. Undoubtedly what had saved the Allied cause was the timely appearance of huge fresh American armies backed by overwhelming material resources. By early 1918 both sides were war-weary. The German High Command had promised the German people that the United States would never be able to bring her armies across the Atlantic through the U-boat blockade. Although the Army of the United States was insignificant in size in 1917, by the middle of 1918 a quarter of a million American soldiers were landing each month in France. When this news reached the German soldier and when he saw the spirit and equipment of the American forces, the end beckoned.

17

The Modern War Lords

The World War of 1914-18 had a most serious effect on the society of the whole world. Its physical consequences alone were enough to slow the onward march of civilization and to destroy that general belief in the inevitability of human progress which had marked much of the philosophy of the nineteenth century. The material cost of the war, including property damage, has been estimated at twenty-eight billion dollars; and the number of killed and permanently disabled, military and civilian, at twenty millions. As the vast majority of the latter were young males and potential fathers, the actual loss to the world's population was much greater. Dislocation caused by direct losses was only a small part of the story. The wartime re-direction of channels of trade, the stimulation of uneconomic industries and of sub-marginal agriculture, the postwar rearrangement of political frontiers on lines of national "self-determination" cutting across well-established regional economies, the huge debts incurred by the belligerent governments, and the heavy reparations imposed on the vanquished, all placed a tremendous strain on national economies and on the balance of international payments. Currencies crashed, unemployment figures rose, unrest flourished, and moral standards declined.

For the first time in human history, the scourge of war came to be regarded by a large part of mankind as a primary evil. Some evidence of this may be found in the victors' attempts to punish "war criminals" and those alleged to have been guilty of causing the war. There was talk of bringing the Kaiser to trial and even of hanging him. While these plans came to nought, the same tendencies revealed themselves in an indictment of guilt written into the peace treaty with Germany, and in the large sums which were to be levied for reparations. The Allies were moved to a considerable extent by the desire for revenge; but these things were also indicative of a new attitude: namely, that those guilty of making war and of war crimes must by some means be brought to atone for their deeds.

Clearer evidence of this new attitude to war is found in the fact that the statesmen entrusted with the task of making the peace treaties were also charged with the planning of a system for the prevention of a recurrence of the holocaust. There obviously was a widespread revulsion against war. Many people became outright pacifists, declaring that war was a far greater evil than any other evil which it might be used to remedy; others sought to distinguish between "just" and "unjust" wars and to demand machinery for preserving peace. Hence the Covenant of a new type of political organization, the League of Nations, was written into the treaties which put a legal end to hostilities. Many people believed that mankind was entering a new era in which war would be no more.

The basic principle of the League of Nations was the new concept of "collective security." The member nations solemnly promised to refrain from recourse to war to settle their grievances until three months after other methods had failed. While no clear and effective method was established for the prevention of aggression, it was hoped that the moral pressure of organized world opinion would be a powerful deterrent. If that failed, the Covenant provided that economic and military "sanctions" could be undertaken.

From its birth, the League was weakened by troubles which were probably inevitable in a new and revolutionary political device for which the nations were not yet ready. It was quickly found that it was impossible to obtain resolute action to check incipient or actual aggression, especially when powerful nations were concerned. Furthermore, when attempts were made to define aggression and to tighten the machinery for preventing aggressive war, some nations were more anxious to limit such obligations as the Covenant had already imposed upon them; and some of those who were anxious to improve the machinery for preserving peace were at opposite poles in their ideas. Disappointed by their failure to obtain an Anglo-American guarantee in 1919, the French wanted an international army to restrain Germany; the British Commonwealth regarded the League primarily as a diplomatic meeting ground where differences could be resolved by customary British methods of discussion and compromise. As these were by far the strongest powers in the League in the twenties, little progress could be made toward more effective organization.

Furthermore, a fundamental weakness from the beginning was that the League was not universal in its membership. The United States, which had sponsored the plan at Versailles, returned to its traditional policy of isolation from European entanglements and did not join. Russia, Germany, and Japan were, for long periods, non-members. In these circumstances, the League of Nations lacked the broad base which was important for its success. It is not surprising, then, that within a few years of the creation of this world organization to ensure peace, new defensive alliances were forged (like that between France and the Little Entente of Czechoslovakia, Rumania, and Jugoslavia); and regional pacts were arranged to guarantee peace in especially dangerous areas (like the Locarno Treaties which dealt, among other regions, with the western border of Germany). These were but poor alternatives for the hopeful aspirations of the founders of the League.

The frustration of the idealists led to a new attack on the problem of war. From the United States came a proposal for a general agreement to outlaw war. By 1931, fifty-six states had signed the 1928 Kellogg-Briand Pact solemnly renouncing war as an instrument of policy. Without any provision for enforcement, such an undertaking among sovereign nations proved of little practical worth. It would be honored only as long as each of certain signatories was convinced that peace would serve its ends better than war.

Contemporary with the schemes to check aggressive war and to outlaw war altogether, there was a long-drawn-out attempt to render war unlikely by a process of general disarmament or, more accurately, by a general agreement to limit national arms. This was based on the realization that the arms race had been one of the important causes of war in 1914, and also on the belief that a nation which possessed a great and expensive military establishment was likely to be tempted to make practical use of it. The arms limitation imposed on the Germans at Versailles had been accompanied in the Treaty by a vague statement about aspirations toward general disarmament; the Covenant provided for a plan of multilateral arms reduction; and one of the first actions of the Council of the League was to instruct its Permanent Armaments Commission to explore the problem. When the First General Assembly met, it was argued by many delegates that the Council's committee, which was dominated by the military advisers of the great powers, would not really be interested in cutting the size of armies, and so the

Assembly appointed a "Temporary Mixed Commission," which included civilians, to prepare a plan for disarmament.

But still progress was very slow. There was suspicion among the powers and therefore a reluctance to lay down arms; and the technical difficulties were great. The armed strength of a state and its requirements for security are affected by the degree of its industrialization, by the literacy and technical capacity of its people, by the circumstances of its geography, and by other immeasurable factors. Proposals to scale down arms on the basis of the amount of money expended were unacceptable to those nations in which the cost of manufacturing arms was high. No convenient formula could be found by which various kinds of technical troops could be equated with infantry and with one another. Hence it was 1931 before an agreement to call a World Disarmament Conference was reached. When the Conference met on February 2, 1932, the Nazi seizure of power in Germany was only a year away. It had met too late.

Previously, as a result of the impatience of the United States at the slow progress being made toward disarmament, and more especially at the high cost of American naval programs, a conference to deal with naval disarmament had been called at Washington in November 1921. There the chief naval powers, the United States, Great Britain, Japan, France, and Italy, agreed to a ten-year "holiday" in the building of battleships and aircraft carriers, to limitations on size, and to a ratio of 5:5:3:1⅔:1⅔ among their respective fleets of these vessels, because some admirals knew that battleships were out-of-date.

But the Washington Conference achieved no comparable success in other categories of vessels; the cruiser question led to acrimonious debates between Britain and the United States about the kind and number of cruisers each should possess; the submarine problem led to trouble between France and Britain; France was reluctant to accept absolute equality with Italy since she felt that she had much greater obligations; and Japan accepted naval inferiority only as a temporary expedient. The reason for such success as was achieved was simply that the United States, which could so obviously out-build all other powers if a naval building race began, wanted to cut the arms budget; and battleships were the biggest single item in that budget.

The failure to bring about general disarmament, on which great hopes for peace had been placed, was one of the chief causes of the failure of the League. The problems of collective security and disarmament were inextricably entwined. No nation could disarm until it felt reasonably secure; but no nation would make a contribution to collective security by surrendering its freedom of action and a vital part of its sovereignty while its potential enemies were strongly in arms. Every power protested that it had only the minimum armament needed for its defense. Each power saw its neighbor's arms as a potential threat. There appeared to be no way out. When the World Disarmament Conference met in 1932, the Germans claimed equality in arms on the ground that the general disarmament, toward which they alleged the limitations placed on Germany at Versailles had been only a first step, had not been achieved. The first signs of a new arms race had thus appeared. By late 1933, Hitler had recalled the German delegations from the Conference, had announced the rearmament of Germany, and had pulled the Germans out of the League.

Actually, Germany had set out on the way to rearmament long before the rise of Hitler. Willingness to renounce war as an instrument of policy was, not unnaturally, less general among the vanquished than among those who had triumphed in 1918. War-weariness, of course, existed in Germany. But the militarists had long been all-powerful and their defeat in 1918 simply left them convinced that only by the re-creation of Germany's armed strength could the verdict of the war be reversed. By the terms of the Treaty, the German army was limited to 100,000 long-service troops for purposes of maintaining internal security; battleships, tanks, and military aircraft were forbidden; the Great General Staff was to be dissolved; and war industries were to be demolished. From the first these conditions were evaded. The Treaty army was increased by 150,000 *Schutzpolitzei,* who were theoretically policemen but were trained and armed just like soldiers. The General Staff lived on under another name, the *Truppenamt,* or Troop Office. Skillful measures were taken to impede the Allied Control Commissions in their work of supervising the demolition of war industries and of limiting the army. Illegal private armies, the *Freikorps,* were regarded by the military authorities of the *Reichswehr* with paternal friendliness; and disciplined organizations of veterans, like the *Stahlhelm,* were encouraged. Private civil flying, glider schools, and air lines, aided by government money, prepared the way for the day when military planes would be available. Troops practised for mobile warfare with cardboard tanks. After the Treaty of Rapallo, April, 1922, Soviet Russia permitted training on Russian soil with tanks denied to Germany by Versailles. Under the designation "Development Projects in Experimental Motor Boat Technology," the German navy kept its hand in in the field of U-boat design. Since some of these designs were actually built in Spanish yards for Turkey, testing was also carried out. The German army made up for its limitations in size by high standards of efficiency; and it consisted of highly trained specialists, every man a potential officer or NCO ready for the day when Germany once again would have a great national army. Furthermore, compelled by circumstances to seek every means to increase its power and effectiveness, the *Reichswehr* was more willing than most other armies to investigate new doctrines and methods of warfare.

While Germany was obliged by the Treaty of Versailles to abandon conscription, other countries took the same step voluntarily after 1919. Armies and military service were generally unpopular; economic difficulties meant that military budgets must be cut to the bone; the prospect of peace by way of collective security and disarmament seemed to make the maintenance of large military establishments unnecessary, and the experiences of World War I raised a cry of "never again." Britain quickly abandoned conscription, demobilized her armies, and returned not merely to the pre-1914 Haldane system but to something like the Cardwell army designed mainly for imperial garrison service. In the United States, universal compulsory service for a three-months' period was proposed but had to be abandoned in face of Congressional opposition. Thus the United States as well returned to the old system of a small long-service army.

Advocates of the regular army argued that it was greatly superior in efficiency to a conscript army. General Sir E. B. Hamley, British military writer, Professor of Military History at Sandhurst, and Commandant of the Camberley Staff College, pronounced in *The Operations of War* (1867), a standard textbook, the doctrine that a "regular army is immeasurably superior to an armed population," and this position was echoed by military writers with a conviction that was probably more than mere rationalization. Professional soldiers, disgusted by the warfare on the Western Front, argued that too many soldiers were as dangerous as too few because of the impossibility of maneuvering a great mass army into position for an overwhelming assault. A small, efficient, professional army and a quick victory were believed to be the remedy for the stalemate of trench warfare.

In France, the debate about the nature of the postwar army followed the same lines as in Britain and the United States, but other factors influenced the decision. In the first place, the Revolution of 1789 had left a tradition of universal service which was quite as strong as the contrary British and American fear that large armies were a danger to constitutional liberty. While the Channel and the Atlantic, and reliance on sea power, enabled Britain and the United States to avoid the implication that democracy entails the obligation of universal military service, France had no such security and so built the Maginot Line, manned by an army of *couverture* to shield an offensive force. It fostered a defensive mentality. The French debated the army question as an alternative between taxing for a highly trained, costly, professional, long-service army, and calling up young men for regular military service. There was opposition to both plans but eventually the taxpayers outvoted the recruits. With the victory at the polls of the *Cartel des Gauches* in 1924, the leftists, who by tradition supported a large national army of conscripts as against a small professional army, won out and ensured that France would retain the system of the nation-in-arms.

But it was a victory for which a price had to be paid. The term of conscript service, which had been raised to three years in 1913 in face of German militance, was reduced to eighteen months in 1923 and to one year in 1928. This meant, in effect, that apart from her army of *couverture* on the frontiers, France possessed no organized trained troops at all. The remainder of her regulars were engaged in training conscripts; and the latter, as soon as they were trained, were released. Thus, while Germany managed to create a highly efficient army of a quarter of a million, France, which was generally believed to be the most powerful military nation in the world, had little more than a militia behind the armies in her frontier defenses.

The debate about the maintenance of the nation-in-arms as against the *armée de métier* was paralleled by a related but distinct debate about mechanization. While professional soldiers generally, in their dislike of the armies and tactics of 1914-18, were almost universally agreed that there must be a return to the small regular army, not all were willing to agree that such an army must be highly mechanized. World War I had shown that the defensive had become dominant. Discussion after the war ranged about methods by which mobility and decision could be restored. The great tank battle of Cambrai, the battle of Amiens, the campaigns which had brought about the defeat of the German army in the West, and Allenby's campaign in the desert were all studied intensively. Trench warfare was generally regarded as having come and gone during the last war; but there was no general agreement on the means by which it would be avoided.

Some French soldiers, following the main line of development of the war, believed that the emphasis must be put on fire power, with the infantry taking over ground in which all opposition had been eliminated by artillery. Slow-moving heavy tanks, operating with the infantry, would help to cut down casualties. Other writers, like the Italian Douhet, the American Mitchell, and the White Russian Seversky, argued that aircraft would completely revolutionize war, that the great battles of the future would be aerial battles, that land and sea forces would be at most ancillaries to the dominant air arm, and that wars would be won by seizing control of the air and by aerial bombardment. Some writers like the German general Von Seeckt and the American historian R. M. Johnston (*First Light on the Campaign of 1918*, New York, 1920), put all their faith in small, highly trained, ground armies for a quick victory. In England, General J. F. C. Fuller, who had planned the battle of Cambrai, advocated all-tank formations. Captain Liddell Hart, the military correspondent of the *Telegraph* and later of the *Times,* while also urging the use of tanks in large numbers, taught that armies must be balanced units of all arms using aircraft and tanks to restore mobility and motorized infantry to keep up with the speed of modern war. In France, Charles de Gaulle, one of Marshal Petain's aides, who had lectured at the Ecole Supérieure de Guerre in 1925-26, opposed reliance on great conscript armies. In the United States, Chaffee and a few tank enthusiasts explored ideas about their use in future wars.

But the conservatives in all armies, many of whom were in high positions and were chiefly concerned with justifying their World War tactics, were hard to convince. An editorial in the British *Army Quarterly* in July, 1921, defended the tactics of 1916 and 1917 with the argument that their results were to be measured in terms of the exhaustion of the enemy and not of ground gained. It claimed that German losses in the battles in those years had made possible the victory of 1918 and it made no mention of the fact that the Allies had also suffered crippling losses, nor of the fact that American manpower had turned the tide. British Field Service Regulations, in 1924, asserted that "infantry is the arm which in the end wins battles" and while admitting that "to enable it to do so, the cooperation of other troops is essential," implied that infantry was the arm around which all tactics should be built. In 1932, General Fuller was retired from the army. Only 500 copies of his *Lectures on Field Service Regulations, III: Operations between Mechanized Forces* (London, 1932) were distributed in Britain, but they were known in Germany and also in Russia. Liddell Hart was influential in Germany but not at home. Although Guderian and other German tank generals were to claim later that they had been thwarted by conservative opposition, they fared much better than their counterparts to the west. The French army was trained to misuse tanks by splitting them up among the infantry; and in Britain in 1935 twice as much money was spent on cavalry as on tanks and armored cars.

To some extent, the slow development of new weapons of war, like the tank and the military aircraft, was the result of parsimonious military budgets. When their appropriations were pared to a minimum, the military chiefs had good excuse to avoid experiment, to neglect costly development projects, and to adhere to well-understood tactics and arms. However, even after rearmament began in Britain in 1935, although the navy and the air force began to plan for new forms of warfare, the tank forces were still behind the times. When the British army began to motorize and mechanize its forces, conservatism held back the construction of tanks and put greater emphasis on the tracked infantry vehicle, the Bren carrier. All armies were slow to equip their tanks with large guns, preferring to concentrate first on the development of defensive armor. But it was only a tracked, armored vehicle mounting a heavy gun that could fully restore mobility to war. The tradition that fire power was defensive only, and that the bayonet and the *arme blanche* were the proper weapons for the offensive, was dying hard.

The controversy between the conservatives and the innovators was brought into sharper focus in the discussions about the use of air power. Basically the question was whether air power should be used as an ancillary to the existing ground and sea forces or should be granted an independent and co-equal status. The former would presumably increase the effectiveness of cooperation by the preservation of the traditional principle of unity of command; the latter would permit a fuller development of the potentialities of the new arm by men who specialized in it, and would make possible the implementation of air power in a revolutionary way, by striking at the enemy far behind his protecting military and naval forces.

Toward the end of World War I, Britain had accepted the principle of an independent air force. In order to maintain it in peacetime, its leaders, exaggerating the effect of Germany's Zeppelins and of the R.A.F.'s own bombing campaign against Germany, stressed its independent role. Between the wars, British airmen built up a doctrine of air power based on what was unfortunately miscalled "strategic" bombardment. Up to 1923 "strategic" bombardment was related to close support for armies and navies. Afterwards it referred to more remote targeting which it would have been more correct to name "grand strategy."

The first duty of the air force was to destroy the enemy's air power. When that was achieved, the destruction of the enemy's economy could be undertaken. Cooperation with the army was the work of special squadrons but was limited chiefly to aerial reconnaissance and artillery spotting. The use of Royal Air Force aircraft, independently of the army, as garrison "police" forces in the deserts of the Middle East gave some justification for the theories of air bombardment. Conservatism and shortage of money slowed development. The heavy bombers to carry out this distorted role did not get beyond the drawing board until January, 1937. The deterrent striking force was therefore not in existence when the war began. Meanwhile the home-defense force had been neglected; had it not been for a privately financed RAF entry in the Schneider Trophy contest, Britain would have developed no modern fighting plane by 1939. From the Supermarine S6 came the Spitfire, and in 1934 the air ministry belatedly accepted the monoplane design. In 1939 the Hurricane had also been developed and the radar early-warning system was in operation; but the heavy bomber force was not yet equal to the tasks envisaged for it by the theorists of air power.

In the United States, Brigadier General William Mitchell had in 1921 publicized the potential of air power by reducing an obsolete battleship, anchored and unmanned, to a smoking hulk by means of aerial bombardment. Henceforth air enthusiasts in all countries argued that the capital ships of 1914-18 had become as obsolete as the mastodon. As this problem could hardly be settled with certainty by a single experiment, the conservatives prevailed; but mainly by use of the argument that as long as potential enemies built battleships they had to be matched. The Royal Navy succeeded by 1924 in establishing some degree of control over naval air power by the creation of the Fleet Air Arm. But a complicated joint system of RAF and RN command of air forces operating with the fleet continued until 1937. Hence, since there was all too little money for the Royal Navy as a whole, it was not surprising that the air service suffered. Even after the Admiralty took over completely in 1939 a few months before the war, development in naval aircraft, and in carriers, still lagged behind development in land aircraft and behind naval air services in Japan and in the United States, where the naval air arm was always directed and operated by the Navy, and where Mitchell's ideas had had some influence even though he was at first discredited.

Few other countries followed Britain's lead in creating an independent air force. In France, the air force was subordinate to the army and thus was inevitably weak. Even in Germany, when rearmament began, although the patronage of Goering gave prestige to the *Luftwaffe*, it was subordinate to the *Reichswehr*, and, although it made rapid strides in the development of good aircraft, its function was chiefly limited to cooperation with the ground forces.

By and large, it can be said that, during the peace which followed the first total war, development in arms and in methods for using them fell behind contemporary advances in science. This lag was especially true in the democracies, where there were greater hopes for the creation of an effective system of collective security, and where the voters had a more direct influence on the spending of money for military purposes. But the axiom that weapon development lags in peacetime operated even in the totalitarian states. However, while the democracies were turning their backs on things military and were wrestling with the economic upheaval caused by the last war from which many of them had never recovered, Russia, Italy, and Germany in turn began to organize the whole structure of their state toward efficiency in war. The totalitarian state was fundamentally a war state. It was World War I and its aftermath which brought the totalitarian state into full bloom, but the principles on which it was based go back far beyond the war to several different sources. The concept of the nation-in-arms, coupled with the power generated by the Industrial Revolution, was the seed bed of totalitarianism.

The communists of the mid-nineteenth century had grasped the significance of force in politics and became convinced that their plans for the introduction of socialism could be achieved only by violence. Hence they regarded the normal relation between classes as a state of war and they studied tactics for use in armed revolution. (In their political and economic jargon the communists reveal the extent of their military interest by the use of such military terms as "labor front," "battle of production," etc.) While Marx and Engels, and their successors Lenin and Trotsky, spoke of internationalism and pacificism, they also believed that the revolution could be brought about by the disintegration of the state, and particularly of the army, in war and that the revolution would have to be defended by the workers in arms. Pacifism was only a weapon to be used for the purpose of rotting the armies of capitalist states. It was not an end in itself. As long as capitalism existed, there must be, according to communist theory, a state of war even when there was no actual fighting.

After the 1917 revolution in Russia, the communists were faced with the necessity of defending themselves against a White counter-revolution and against both German and Allied intervention. They managed to buy off Germany by concessions at Brest-Litovsk, but they were compelled to organize a "Red Army" to replace the Czarist army which their two years of propaganda had dissolved. Inevitably they had to use the experienced officers and NCOs of the old army; but for a long time they avoided the term "officers," using instead "technicians," "specialists," "instructors," "commanders," or "red commanders." At first, the practice of electing officers prevailed, but that was soon abandoned. Communist theory continued to speak in terms of the nation-in-arms, or rather of the "armed workers," but in face of the danger from outside, the creation of a professional army was imperative; and this tendency toward a regular force was undoubtedly strengthened by the fact that the Communist regime was a minority regime dependent on force for its existence. Gradually the symbols of professional militarism returned: an officer class, a rigid rank structure, medals and decorations. While 75 per cent of the Red Army in 1924 were militia troops, by 1939 it was a completely professional army.

Nevertheless, the Red Army and Soviet military doctrine retained important influences from communist revolutionary ideology. Political commissars, with authority to screen a commandant's military orders for political implications and with a duty to supervise the political indoctrination of the troops, became an important part of the Russian military organization. The Red Army developed what was called "Marxist military doctrine," which combined an emphasis on offensive strategy, based on a belief in the superior spirit of the Red soldier with the use of "political warfare"—that is to say, propaganda and subversive or partisan activity behind the enemy's lines. The defensive positional warfare of the 1914-18 war was spurned, and the writings of Fuller and Liddell Hart were intensively studied.

Realizing that the weakness of the Czarist army had been to a large extent caused by the industrial weakness of the country and by the lack of social cohesion in the state, the communists introduced a five-year plan designed to build up the nation's heavy industry. The first five-year plan was followed by others, all aimed at strengthening Russia for war. In effect, in order to direct the economy from consumer goods to war production, the Soviet government imposed the kind of direction which other nations had found necessary during the last war.

Furthermore, because the regime feared a counter-revolution, it imposed a rigid control over the movements of its citizens and over their actions and utterances. Since the state had become the owner of virtually all property, it directed the whole foreign trade of the country and it used that control to implement its policies. Finally, as all political activity except that of the Communist Party was suppressed and punished by death or exile to Siberia, the Party had become identified with the state.

In all these respects, Russia went much further than the belligerent countries had gone in the war. But it is to be noticed that these measures were taken by the Soviet regime because the Communists regarded themselves as being engaged in a war to the death with all capitalist states; some precedent for all these actions could be found among the policies of the belligerents in the First World War. The Soviet Union simply carried rigid wartime controls to their logical conclusion. Total war had produced the totalitarian state.

Like the communist Revolution in Russia, the fascist revolutions in Italy and Germany were brought about by the war. In Italy, dissatisfaction caused by failure to gain the rewards promised by the Treaty of London in 1915, coupled with the industrial unrest in North Italy in the period of post war readjustment, created the conditions in which Mussolini seized power and set up a Fascist dictatorship. Like the Communists, the Fascists adopted the monolithic one-party state and used many of the same political tricks and tactics. Mussolini, having established himself as *Il Duce* in Italy, proclaimed his determination to win back the Roman Imperium over the Mediterranean area. His followers, wearing black shirts as uniforms and adopting a Roman salute, were organized in "fascisti." The Fascist state, built up on force, glorifying war, and regimenting the easy-going Italians in military fashion, shows how militaristic ideas could be imposed upon a democracy and could subvert it.

The German brand of fascism, called national socialism, was also born of war, since it was made possible by psychological factors and by the depression which was in part caused by the war. Writing in justification of his war leadership, Erich Ludendorff had advanced a theory of total war which argued that preparation for war must come before the fighting, that the military command must have unchallenged authority, that the war should be fought by the whole nation and not merely by the armed forces, that it should be fought over the whole area of the enemy territory, and that all methods of propaganda should be used to strengthen the home front, provided that the information distributed was based on truth. About 1920, a Munich professor, Dr. Karl Haushofer, discovered a lecture published in 1904 by Sir Halford Mackinder, a British geographer, which described Europe and Asia as the "heartland" around which the rest of the world was grouped. Mackinder also argued that if Russia and Germany ever united to take advantage of their interior lines of communication, "the empire of the world was in sight." From this concept, Haushofer built up the pseudo-science of "geopolitics" which declared that the forces of geography had destined Germany for world leadership. Many young Germans, driven to desperation by the shame of defeat, embraced Haushofer's theories; he had close connections with the General Staff; and, most important, he was acquainted with prominent members of the *National Sozialistische Deutsche Arbeiterpartei,* and with their leader, Adolf Hitler.

The Nazis, absorbing the cult of total war and the doctrines of conquest implicit in the theories of the geopoliticians, forced their way to public notice by screaming from the platform that Germany had not been defeated but had been "stabbed in the back," and by denouncing the "shame" of Versailles and the iniquity of Germany's indictment for war-guilt. They used the familiar strong-arm methods of the communists. They adopted from the *Freikorps* and the military organizations of German veterans the idea of organizing bands of "stormtroopers" for street-fighting; and they became masters of the art of political propaganda and of the technique of the "big lie."

When they had obtained control of the government, the Nazis followed the normal totalitarian pattern. The one-party state was ruled by use of the machine gun, by control of the organs of propaganda, and by filling the concentration camps. Although the Nazis did not abolish capitalism (perhaps because they had been aided to power by financiers like the iron and steel magnate Thyssen), they exercised a rigorous control over the whole economy by methods similar to those used by Rathenau during the war. Control of currency, production, and exports and imports, and the orientation of the economy toward making arms, techniques used by the belligerents during the war, were introduced by the Nazis in Germany in time of peace.

In part, the Nazi aim was to solve the unemployment problem, which had been the curse of post war Germany, by state-directed rearmament; and there was an immediate economic revival. But uneconomic war production could have only one end when there was no alternative means of subsistence for the German people. Indeed, as Hitler made perfectly clear in his book *Mein Kampf,* the Nazi philosophy was that peace was merely a period in which preparation could be made for total war. Following the arguments of Clausewitz, Ludendorff, and Haushofer to their logical conclusion, the Nazis made the state into a war machine tuned up for action. The distortion of the economy toward war production and the system of *autarchy* or self-sufficiency which they developed was made possible by depriving the people of consumer goods. Propaganda made the Germans accept "guns instead of butter," and those who resisted were ruthlessly dealt with by the all-powerful state. The adverse balance of trade, which could not be avoided despite stringent controls, was repaired from time to time by sharp trading practices with weaker nations and by the seizure of the gold reserves of Austria and of Czechoslovakia by "peaceful" annexation. But such methods could not long continue. The German totalitarian state born of total war rushed on inevitably to a yet greater war.

The only element in Germany which might have been able to overthrow Hitler once he had seized power and had set up his Nazi regime was the *Reichswehr*. But the army leaders made no move either to defend the republic or to seize power for themselves. They watched the Nazi rise to power with sympathy because they believed that they could control Hitler, who was promising the restoration of their chief interest and concern, German military strength. But they deceived themselves. The former corporal took over the leadership of the High Command himself; and his chosen political stormtroopers, given military arms of all types and called the *Waffen S.S.,* eventually became the elite shock troops of the German army. Indoctrinated with Nazi creeds, they were, like the men of the Red Army, typical soldiers of total war.

The German repudiation of the Treaty of Versailles, rearmament, the reoccupation of the demilitarized zone in the Rhineland, and the Italian attack on Ethiopia were the first steps toward a new world conflict. In Spain, a civil war was fought in which fascist and communist totalitarianisms were found on opposite sides, but in which the real issue and ultimate result was the destruction of constitutional government. That war, although limited to the Iberian peninsula, was an ideological conflict of the total war variety and was a preview of the Second World War. In it communists and fascists tried out their new weapons and methods of warfare. Terror and frightfulness, like the aerial massacre of Guernica, were foretastes of what was in store. And the difficulty experienced in defining neutrality in an ideological war of this kind showed how far the concept of war had changed since the dynastic conflicts of the eighteenth century.

The military doctrine of the new German army—total war and the *Blitzkrieg,* or lightning attack with all arms—was in startling contrast to the peaceful attitudes of the western democracies, where the cry of "No more blood-baths" still prevailed. Despite all the portents of the gathering storm, the western democracies maintained their belief that they could avoid war. In the United States in 1934, books and articles exposing the methods of the armaments manufacturers led to an investigation under Senator Nye, and aided the passage of neutrality legislation to insulate America from European wars. About the same time, as a result of Nazi policies, Britain began to rearm, but under the leadership of Baldwin and Chamberlain she also continued to work for the appeasement of the dictators. In June, 1935, without consulting any other power, she made a naval agreement with Germany which was a breach of the Treaty of Versailles and in no way limited German building during the next decade, for German naval rearmament had a long way to catch up. Appeasement may have delayed the war and may even, as some have claimed, have given the democracies time to make up some of their deficiencies in military strength, but it proved futile as a policy for the prevention of a war which the devastating effects of the First World War and the consequent rise of the totalitarian state had ensured. Hitler was a genius at propaganda and a charismatic leader with a remarkable sense of timing his aggressions. The German seizure of Prague in March, 1939, was followed by Anglo-French guarantees to Poland and Rumania. When Hitler attacked Poland, the Second World War began. Thus ended a long series of peacetime aggressions that had started with the occupation of the Rhineland in 1936.

18
World War II

The drift to modern total warfare had been evident from the beginning of the twentieth century. Looking back from our present point of vantage, we can see that everything was moving relentlessly in that direction. However, to contemporaries that trend was not always clear, and, when the nations came to grips in World War II, events served at first to obscure the fact that the conflict was total.

In the Orient, Japan had long been troubled by overpopulation and by a thirst for markets, resources, and empire. She had swallowed up Manchuria in 1931 and had soon moved across the Great Wall. By July 1937, her militarists had sent mobile columns to conquer China itself. The strategy and tactics of the offensives undertaken in the Sino-Japanese War are worthy of study as early examples of the new mobile warfare. Against feeble opposition the Japanese made remarkable headway. Nevertheless it soon became clear that the conquest of sprawling China was not going to be easy. China's vast spaces, and her almost inexhaustible supplies of expendable man power, offset the Japanese superiority in mobility, armor, fire power, and material. This campaign therefore provided no clue to the future of warfare.

The initial phases of World War II proper misled observers about the nature of the trends of modern warfare. At dawn on September 1, 1939, having been assured by his Russian Treaty of August 23 that he would not have to fight a major war on two fronts, Hitler ordered his troops into Poland and, in a terrain peculiarly favorable to mobile operations and without any natural defenses, the *Reichswehr* carried through a classic campaign straight from the new manuals on armored warfare. Surprise aerial bombardments destroyed the meager Polish Air Force before it could take to the air; the gallant but ineffective Polish cavalry was swept aside; and when serious resistance was met, as in the labyrinth of the city of Warsaw, terror bombardment snuffed it out.

The technique of the *Blitzkrieg* thus proved itself in practice. The Germans had about a million men mobilized, but the defeat of Poland was achieved by only seven or eight armored *Panzer* divisions which encircled and cut up a much greater number of Polish divisions. The total war potential of Germany had not been used. Poland, attacked from the west by Germany and from the east by Russia, was crushed in three weeks. Thus, although it led at once to the disappearance of Poland from the map, the Second World War began, in some senses, as a "limited" war. *Blitzkrieg*, in the Prussian tradition, had achieved as nearly perfect a limitation in time as could be desired by the most optimistic planner.

A deceptive appearance of limitation was also produced by the attitudes and behaviors of the great powers. While German radio stations, with unconsciously ironic accuracy, blared out frightful tales of "unheard of (*ungehörte*) Polish atrocities," the propaganda war in the West was singularly restrained. On the eve of hostilities the British had published information about the torturing of Jews in Nazi concentration camps; but it was prefaced by a virtual apology for the publication of hate-propaganda. In the West this tragic story was doubted; in Germany it made no impression at all; and not until the curtain was torn back in 1945 was the full extent of Nazi shame realized. Thus in 1939 the totality of the war was hidden.

While Poland was in her death-throes, her two western allies stood helplessly by and watched. They possessed neither the armored might to draw off the attackers by invading Germany, nor the air power to halt aggression by the threat of bombing. Furthermore, in both countries governments and peoples were not ready to accept the fact that all-out war must come. On September 3, 1939, up to the last minute, it was not known whether France would declare war at all; and although England had always made it perfectly clear that she would honor her pledges to Poland, the Chamberlain government was still in power and was unable to shake off the lethargy of its former policy of appeasement. American newspaper men described the second stage of the war, following the conquest of Poland, as "phoney."

While Germany and Soviet Russia digested Poland, the western powers dug themselves in behind the Maginot Line and along the Belgian frontier and, in a somewhat leisurely fashion, prepared for a war which they professed to believe would be short but which they vaguely felt might last a very long time. Conscription, an approach to the nation-in-arms, had been introduced in Britain in March, 1939. In September, when war broke out, Chamberlain had hesitatingly consented to plans for a fifty-five-division army to be ready within the next two or three years. But mechanization of the army, despite the lessons of the Polish campaign, was very slow. One skeleton armored division was sent to France; but a second was not to be equipped until the second year of hostilities.

No one appears to have fully realized that modern war between great powers would entail *both* the full mobilization of the nation's manpower and full mechanization of its armies. The long debate between those who had urged the creation of armored professional armies and those who had defended the "armed horde" had obscured the possibility that in total war both might be needed at the same time. The course to be followed if *Blitzkrieg* failed to secure a quick victory had not been properly explored, either in the West or, for that matter, in Germany.

During the first winter of the "twilight" or "phoney" war, the main weapons used against Germany were blockade and propaganda. Instead of bombs, the RAF dropped leaflets, since it was incapable of a bombing offensive and German retaliation was feared. If the Germans could not be talked out of their sins, it was hoped that economic pressure would bring them to their knees. Thus, the carried over into the war against German totalitarianism. Even here the war was incomplete and therefore limited. The 1914-18 blockade had been re-introduced in an improved form with a Navicert system, by which neutral vessels carried certificates to show they had no contraband. The point of control had thus been carried back to the port of lading. Black lists of neutral firms who traded with the enemy had been drawn up. But although the blockade of the seas worked smoothly and efficiently, the situation was actually very different from 1914. The whole of East Europe was open for German trade; and *Ersatz* products and stockpiles of essential commodities were in much greater supply. Propaganda and the economic weapon were parts of the apparatus of total warfare, but used by themselves, and in this incomplete fashion, they were practically impotent.

During this same period, Hitler also relied on economic warfare. Following the precedent of 1914-18, he proclaimed a submarine blockade of the British Isles and backed it by dropping a "secret

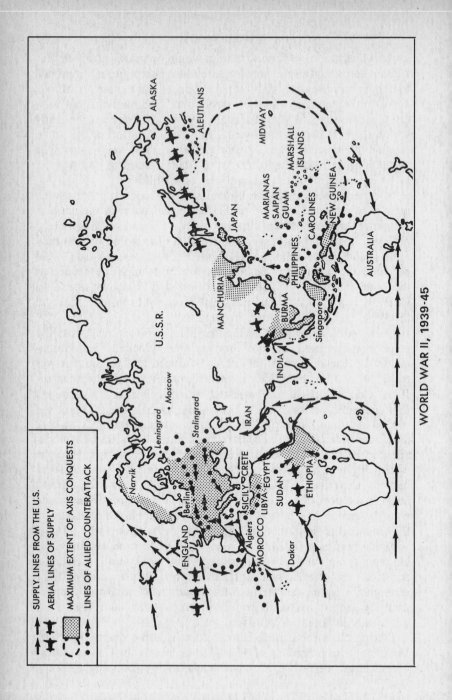

SUPPLY LINES FROM THE U.S.

AERIAL LINES OF SUPPLY

MAXIMUM EXTENT OF AXIS CONQUESTS

LINES OF ALLIED COUNTERATTACK

WORLD WAR II, 1939-45

ALASKA

ALEUTIANS

MIDWAY

MARIANAS
SAIPAN
GUAM

MARSHALL
ISLANDS

JAPAN

CAROLINES

NEW GUINEA

PHILIPPINES

MANCHURIA

BURMA

AUSTRALIA

Singapore

U.S.S.R.

INDIA

Moscow

IRAN

Leningrad

Stalingrad

Narvik

CRETE

ETHIOPIA

Berlin

SICILY

EGYPT

ENGLAND

Algiers

LIBYA

SUDAN

MOROCCO

Dakar

weapon," new magnetic mines, in the shallow approaches to the ports. German aircraft sorties for this purpose were the nearest approach to those great aerial attacks on enemy territory which the prophets had long declared would herald a new war. The Nazi aerial onslaught in the West, in the first winter of the war, was otherwise limited strictly to reconnaissance.

The third stage of the war, the renewal of *Blitzkrieg* with attacks on Denmark, Norway, Holland, Luxembourg, Belgium, and France in the spring of 1940, was, like the attack on Poland, limited war in time. Denmark fell without a blow, Luxembourg in a day, Holland in five days, Belgium in less than three weeks, and France in six. Furthermore, in the Battle of France, although the Germans had used a hundred divisions, a few armored columns won the victory. *Blitzkrieg* had again shown itself to be a method of restricting the full impact of war by the very speed of its onslaught.

The German victories in the West were won by the use of new tactics and weapons against armies which were inadequately prepared for war and whose strategy and tactics were faulty. The Nazis used specially trained parachute troops to clear difficult obstacles (for instance, a few were dropped on the Belgian fort Eben Emael), Stuka dive bombers to give close support, and tanks to probe, pierce, and fan out behind the Allied lines. They were superior in training and they exploited surprise as a psychological weapon to give them an advantage in morale. For these armies the Maginot Line, which had never been properly extended to the sea, presented no great difficulties. General Gamelin (under whose command, as a result of the lessons of 1918, the British expeditionary forces had been placed) relied entirely on a static and linear defense. When the Low Countries were attacked, the Allied armies on the left flank were ordered forward to their aid despite the fact that, because the Belgians and Dutch had sought to protect their neutrality, plans for mutual defense had not been worked out. Before a front could be formed, the Allied armies were pouring back in retreat. The Nazis had planned to repeat the strategy of the Schlieffen Plan, a thrust on the right. Instead, acting on a plan developed by General von Manstein which turned the Schlieffen Plan inside out, they thrust their armored columns through the Ardennes, which were regarded by the French as unsuitable tank country and were therefore only lightly defended. French tanks were dissipated along the whole front; and when their front was breached, the Allies possessed no "mass of maneuver" to throw against the bulge. The

Allied air forces were unable to prevent the *Luftwaffe* from dominating the field of battle; and at the crisis of the Battle of France, the British refused to transfer their metropolitan air force from Britain to French bases. It was a hard decision; but the RAF could not have turned the tide. The planes and pilots were thus preserved for the Battle of Britain.

Although the war had been limited thus far, there were ominous signs that it was moving into a new phase of intensity. Five of the victims in 1940 were neutral states which had vainly striven to keep out of the conflict but had been struck down without warning. Neutrality had been ignored because it stood in the way of the aggressor. In the First World War neutrality had been infringed upon, but only after formal warnings. Now it was breached in the night.

The aggressor was fully abetted by "fifth columnists" (the phrase was coined during the Spanish Civil War to indicate those in enemy territory who were working to soften the defenders). Major Vidkun Quisling, a Norwegian Nazi and former War Minister, by betraying his country to the Germans, gave another new term to the dictionaries of many languages. "Quislings," traitors who for ideological reasons were ready to sell their country, although not a new phenomenon in history, were now much more numerous because of the growth of social and economic cleavages within the state. Class warfare, whether real or imagined, had brought ideological disunity and had loosened some of the cement which held nations together. Total victory, leading to the complete disintegration of a defeated state, had thus become much more likely.

The internal weaknesses of Belgium and France had been cunningly exploited by the Nazis. The small amount of sabotage and subversion carried on by quislings and parachute troops was deliberately exaggerated to destroy the morale of the defenders and to soften them before the *Blitzkrieg*. Terror was spread further by the machine-gunning of refugees on the highways. By such methods the impact of *Blitzkrieg* was greatly intensified. Neutralism in Belgium and defeatism in France had sapped the strength of the defenders and had laid those countries wide open to the psychological propaganda of total warfare.

When the fall of Norway put an end to complacency in Britain, Churchill replaced Chamberlain as Prime Minister. The fall of France had a yet greater result. It convinced President Roosevelt and many other Americans that the United States could not stand idly by, watching the overthrow of Britain. Already in November 1939 Congress had revised the neutrality legislation to permit the belligerents to buy arms in the United States on a "cash and carry" basis. This legislation favored the democracies, because they could use the ocean to get the arms they needed; but America was still shielded from being dragged once again into war through financial entanglements or through the loss of her ships. When the Nazis broke through to the Channel and the Atlantic Coast and threatened to overrun Britain too, rifles, machine guns, and ammunition were hurriedly rushed across the Atlantic; in August, 1940, President Roosevelt met Prime Minister Mackenzie King at Ogdensburg, New York, and arranged to set up a Permanent Joint Board of Defense for the north half of the Western Hemisphere; on September 3 he announced the exchange of overage American destroyers for British bases in American waters. The United States was passing from benevolent neutrality into a state of passive belligerency.

Inside the United States, a vast arms program and the passage on September 3 of the selective service law, the first "draft" in the peacetime history of the country, showed an increasing public awareness that geographical isolation was no longer a secure defense. In campaign speeches both presidential candidates, Roosevelt and Willkie, while promising to keep the nation out of "foreign wars," pledged themselves, if elected, to aid those countries which were resisting aggression. After the election President Roosevelt declared that, while Britain was the spearhead of resistance to world conquest, the United States must become "the great arsenal of democracy" and proposed a scheme to make possible the continuation of aid although Britain's dollar credits were nearly exhausted. On March 11, 1941, Congress enacted what Winston Churchill later called the "most altruistic act in history," legislation by which the President could lend or lease arms and supplies to any country whose defense he regarded as vital to the safety of the United States, with repayment to be made in kind or in any other way deemed satisfactory. (Canada did not receive lend-lease aid but in the Hyde Park Agreement of April 20, 1941, arranged to dovetail her economy for war production with that of the United States. About the same time, she granted to Britain a billion dollars' credit.) Thus, to achieve an integration of defense production for total war, traditional concepts of international finance were swept aside while, as yet, the United States was still technically neutral. More than anything else, this fundamental change in American policy away from strict isolation and neutrality showed that the peoples of the democracies were coming to a realization of the danger which totalitarian aggression spelled for their way of life and to believe that, to save themselves, they must revolutionize their traditional ways and attitudes. When the United States entered the war, techniques worked out for coordination with Britain in industrial output, shipping, and food production went far beyond any degree of integration previously achieved by allied sovereign states at war.

Meanwhile, on July 10, 1940, the Germans had begun daylight aerial attacks on Britain. By September 7, however, the *Luftwaffe* had been beaten by the Royal Air Force and Goering was compelled to resort to night attacks. These soon degenerated into an indiscriminate bombardment of London. A defensive air victory of enormous significance had been won. On September 17 Hitler postponed the invasion, Operation Sea-Lion, indefinitely.

Thus began the next stage of the war which was to last until June, 1941, when the Germans invaded Russia. Although in this period the war seemed once more to be in many ways limited warfare, this was actually the time when both sides were organizing themselves for a total fight to the finish. In Europe, the victims of the Nazi conquest were ground down under German rule, and the world saw what totalitarian victory meant. The Gestapo ruled by torture; and the subject states were pillaged for the benefit of the conqueror. The total eclipse of historic nations was a sign that war had become unlimited in its objective.

Halted by the Channel, the Nazis were forced, by the very dynamics of the domination which they had created to seek further conquests. For a time they had talked with Franco about a march to Gibraltar to close the Mediterranean at the western end. Then, in March, 1941, they found it necessary to come to the relief of Mussolini in North Africa where the Italians, who had boasted that they would capture Suez, were hard-pressed.

The vital strategic significance of the Middle East had been recognized by Churchill when he sent an armored brigade to Egypt in 1940 at the time of Britain's great peril. In campaigns fought between 1940 and 1942 on the borders of Egypt and Libya the use of mechanized and armored forces by both sides led to a new degree of mobility in modern warfare. The desert, for the most part flat and trackless, was eminently suited to tank actions which resembled operations at sea. With both sides using armor, fronts became fluid. In desert campaigns in earlier wars, logistical problems had severely limited cavalry actions. They still created great difficulties and often brought promising offensives to a halt; but the essentials of mechanized warfare—gasoline for tanks, and water and supplies for the troops—could now be moved much farther and faster, and in greater quantity, than in times when fodder and water for horses had been a major item. Troops from Australia, New Zealand, India, Palestine, and South Africa as well as British and Free French forces stopped the Italians and Nazis from cutting the Suez and so penetrating to the Indian Ocean and to the threshold of southern Asia. By February, 1943, they had driven Rommel's Afrika Korps back to Tunisia.

A campaign against Yugoslavia and Greece in the Balkans delayed Hitler's real objective, a long-planned invasion of Russia, because he regarded a firm Balkan flank as a prerequisite for such an invasion, and he wished also to deny the British the chance to bomb the vital Ploesti oilfields in Rumania. From the time he had given up the idea of invading England it had been clear to him that one day he must seek a reckoning with Stalin. He could not hope to maintain his domination of Europe with great potential enemies in both west and east. The inevitable result of totalitarian victory was that the conqueror had to destroy all possible enemies.

The Nazi invasion of the Soviet Union in 1941 seemed at first likely to knock Russia out at one blow. Great encircling pincer movements cut off large pockets of the Red Army and forced them to surrender. Within five months the Nazis had reached the outskirts of Moscow, had enveloped Leningrad, and had penetrated the Crimean peninsula and the Don Valley. But this three-pronged attack, the strategy of which was dictated by Hitler himself, failed to achieve its object, the destruction of Soviet ability to resist. By December 7 it had become clear that a quick victory was not possible and Hitler announced the end of the campaign for the season, only to be taken by surprise by a Russian winter offensive for which his troops were ill-prepared.

By mid-August, 1942, concentrating on the southern front in order to seize desperately needed oil fields, the Germans reached the foothills of the Caucasus and, further north, the great industrial city of Stalingrad. This was the high water mark of German conquest in the East. By the end of the year a Nazi army was surrounded near Stalingrad and Leningrad had been relieved. The tide had been turned by stubborn Russian courage, by the building up of war production in factories carried back to safety across the Urals, and by British and American supplies sent in perilous convoys through Arctic seas or by the long route through Iran.

The war was clearly becoming total in objective, in method, and in its impact on peoples. Under the whip of totalitarianism, the whole economy of Germany was harnessed for war. Drawing forced labor from the subject territories, the Nazi war machine was able to increase its potential effort vastly. In the Todt Organization at least five million men and women labored on immense war projects, such as constructing defenses (normally a military function), repairing bomb damage, and building air fields. After the defeat at Stalingrad in January, 1943, the Nazis decreed total mobilization. Even the children were drafted for work in factories and fields.

Total mobilization for war on the home front was also adopted by the United Nations, as the opponents of fascism now called themselves. Indeed, after the war it was discovered that Britain was harnessed to the war effort to a degree that was greater in certain respects than was so in Germany. For instance, British married women were compulsorily employed in war work on a much greater scale than the German *Hausfrauen*. But in all countries the same techniques were followed. Great national armies, navies, and air forces were conscripted and trained; labor was registered, drafted, and directed; property was requisitioned; industry and production were controlled; consumer goods were severely cut and rationed; and travel and transportation were limited. This arbitrary government was rendered inevitable by the emergency. It became an offense to spread alarm and despondency or false rumors; and state-directed organs of propaganda sought to condition the thoughts of the people. All these were the tools of totalitarianism. Total war had driven the democracies to adopt some of the methods of their adversaries. But it must be remembered that all of these had first been forged in the previous total conflict.

Despite the great mobilization of manpower for war industry, the size of armies continued to increase. In the early years of the war relatively small but highly powerful armored forces had won great victories, but when peoples were fighting for their national existence great mass armies were thrown into the field. For the invasion of Russia in 1941 the Nazis had used 160 divisions, of which no fewer than 20 were armored, and in a very short time there were 9,000,000 men struggling on the Eastern Front. Even so the war did not become static as it had on the Western Front in 1914-18. Great armored offensives encircled huge pockets of resistance, defense was organized in depth, fronts were fluid, and the battle raged over great areas. As the German juggernaut rolled on toward Moscow, the retreating forces ruthlessly scorched the earth they left behind. Red Army units that were overrun either fought in pockets until all further resistance was useless or went underground to organize guerrilla warfare against the invader. In those parts of the country like the Ukraine where non-Russian peoples were to be found, many Soviet citizens and deserters welcomed the invaders and some even joined the Germans in the fight. Total war had engulfed the civilian population as well as the soldiery. Strangely enough, while the war on the Eastern Front was apparently one of fascism versus communism, and while large numbers accordingly deserted to the enemy on both sides, Stalin at the same time found it expedient to proclaim a patriotic war for the defense of "Mother Russia." Logic and truth became blurred; any weapon, and any ideology, was recruited for the conflict.

Nevertheless, fascist and communist ideologies played an important part in conditioning the armies locked in combat. The Red Army had from its birth been politically indoctrinated, and although its commissars were abolished for a short period during the war, they soon returned. The German army also included political soldiery, the *Waffen* S.S., heirs of the stormtroopers who had violently opened the way for Hitler to seize power in Germany. The *Waffen* S.S. were first created as militarized police to relieve the army of its occupation duties in the conquered territories but they soon became the elite shock troops of the German forces. Ultimately they were increased to twenty divisions, some of them armored (the *Panzer* S.S.), having the pick of all equipment and personnel.

The war became global at the end of 1941 when Japan embarked upon the conquest of the "Greater East Asia Co-Prosperity Sphere" and involved the United States by attacking Pearl Harbor. Even before Pearl Harbor, the United States had in fact been co-belligerent, giving much aid to Britain, with whom Roosevelt had made common cause in the Atlantic Charter, and also to Russia. The enormous American industrial power had already been thrown behind the democratic cause by the Lend-Lease Act; the United States had established air bases in the Danish colony of Greenland

and had also relieved Britain of the occupation of Iceland. Virtually abandoning the former decision to keep American ships out of belligerent waters, the United States navy had taken over the task of preventing enemy submarines from acting in American waters, which were now considered to extend to within 700 miles of the British Isles. In September, 1941, after several submarine attacks on American naval vessels and merchant ships, the United States navy had been given orders to shoot at any hostile submarine encountered in the neutrality zone. By November a shooting war had begun; one American destroyer had been sunk and another damaged by U-boats. This was stretching neutrality to the limits.

A most significant American contribution to the winning of the war was the enormous material aid which was put into the war against the fascist powers. In the vital shipbuilding industry alone, American shipyards built over five thousand ships to maintain the sea-communications between the industrial plants of the New World and the fighting fronts in the Old. In addition, millions of rifles, thousands of guns, and equipment and weapons of all kinds were produced for the fighting forces of the other United Nations as well as for those of the United States. American industrial power, in this war even more than in the last, made victory possible.

For all the major contestants, this war was a war of materiel. Only those nations which had great industrial plants or could build them could claim to be major military powers. Hence it was the expansion of her war industries, as much as her military contributions, that raised Canada to the status of a middle power on the Allied side. In Russia, the transference of a great part of the industrial machine beyond the Urals and out of reach of Nazi attack was a significant step toward the defeat of the invader. Even in relatively backward China, the creation of a cottage industry for war production was an essential part of the war effort. The technology front was as important as the fighting fronts.

The planning for the conversion of this great industrial effort of the nations fighting fascism into effective military power led to important discussions among the Allied leaders on strategy and grand strategy that revealed serious differences of opinion, but Roosevelt agreed with the British to concentrate upon the defeat of Germany before turning to Japan. He was anxious that American troops should be involved in the all-out fight against Hitler within a few months of the United States' entrance into the war. Although wishing to open a second front on the continent of

Europe, which the Russians had been demanding ever since they were attacked, he agreed to the invasion of French North Africa as a first step. Churchill had persuaded him that lack of shipping and of other material made a major attack on Europe impossible for the present and that the preliminary invasion of French North Africa would help clear the Axis from that continent and eliminate the serious threat to the Middle East. The President's advisers wanted to fight the Germans by a direct attack in overwhelming strength which, although costly in lives in the early stages, could conceivably shorten the war. They were suspicious of Churchill's "Mediterranean strategy" of attacking the "soft under-belly of Europe" through Sicily, Italy, and the Balkans, which seemed to them like playing the old imperialist game and which might antagonize the Russians. The British were anxious to avoid heavy initial losses which might have a dangerous effect on popular morale; and they also paid more attention to the political implications of strategy, and especially to the results that might follow the defeat of Germany if the Russians advanced too far into Europe.

In any case, the strategy of invading Europe depended upon success in the war at sea. While the war on land had remained "phoney" for seven months, at sea conflict was intense from the first hour. On the day after Britain entered the war, a German submarine torpedoed the passenger liner *Athenia* without warning, in disregard of international law. The sinking had not been planned and the submarine captain was reprimanded by Hitler; but in fact the Germans took up again the policy of unrestricted submarine warfare almost where they had dropped it in 1918. As in the First World War, German naval strategy was aimed at destroying the sea-borne commerce upon which Britain depended; the submarine attack was therefore especially heavy in the western approaches to the British Isles from the Atlantic Ocean. At the critical time of the German invasion of Norway, British submarine commanders were also authorized to sink vessels on sight but only in a narrow strip of Norwegian coastal water; and similar zones of unrestricted submarine attack were declared later in the year near the coasts of Libya and Italy. But ruthlessness of this kind was not new in submarine warfare. It was merely carried over from the First World War when it had been adopted by the Germans because the submarine lost most of its effectiveness if it adhered to international protocol.

While the influence of Nazi totalitarianism had thus not been responsible for changing the nature of the war at sea, its intensity was very greatly affected by new weapons, and especially by the use of aircraft, which made necessary a revision of many of the old concepts of sea power. This was seen quite early in the Battle of the Atlantic, as the main Nazi submarine attack on the Allied merchant marine in this war came to be called. It is usually regarded as having begun on 6 February, 1941, the date of Hitler's directive on the importance of attacking ships bound for Britain. As submarines and aircraft became more efficient and were used more effectively, naval warfare became more fully three-dimensional, fought under and over the ocean as well as on the surface. Magnetic mines dropped in shallow coastal waters by aircraft, acoustic torpedoes, the operation of wolf-packs of submarines assisted by aerial reconnaisance, greater cruising ranges and speeds, and at the very end of the war the *Schnorkel* tube, which enabled a submarine to remain submerged while charging its batteries, made the *guerre de course* against British maritime commerce in World War II more serious than any experienced before. In 1940, British and Allied merchant-shipping losses in the month of September were heavier than for a similar period of time at the height of the submarine campaign in the previous war. The U-boat menace was gradually brought under control; but sinkings reached a new peak in 1942 when Nazi submarine commanders found rich pickings off the eastern seaboard of the United States and in the Caribbean.

The techniques of anti-submarine warfare rapidly improved. Convoys and escort services had been organized early in the war; aerial search was developed employing land-based aircraft; "jeep carriers" of 10,000 tons were improvised to cover the mid-Atlantic gap out of range of land planes; asdic (sonar) sound detection was improved and supplemented by radar; anti-submarine weapons became much more effective; the wolf-pack was countered by the hunter-killer groups of anti-submarine vessels, including, at times, aircraft carriers. By March,1943,the Battle of the Atlantic reached its crisis; thereafter convoy defense forces slowly gained the upper hand. Already by the end of 1942 the rate of building of merchant ships in Allied yards had topped the rate of losses.In August,1943, more German submarines were sunk than Allied merchant ships. Inflamed by the virus of national socialism, and ably directed from the land by Admiral Doenitz, the German submarine fleet fought to the bitter end; but, when defeat came on land, the submarine crews lost their spirit. The *Schnorkel*, and speedier submarines, came too late to affect the result of the war.

On the surface, German naval power was too weak to bid for mastery of the sea. The Nazis avoided the possibility of being trapped to fight a major sea battle like Jutland by the simple device of never concentrating their small battle fleet. Instead, they used their heavy ships as commerce-raiders and compelled the defenders to use as convoy escorts either ships of equal strength or submarines. At different times between 1939 and 1941 the pocket battleships *Deutschland (Lützow), Graf Spee,* and *Admiral Scheer,* the battlecruisers *Scharnhorst* and *Gneisenau*, the battleship *Bismarck*, the heavy cruisers *Admiral Hipper* and *Prinz Eugen*, and several armed merchant-cruisers were loosed in the sea lanes to work havoc until they were either sunk or driven back to base. When this proved too costly for the Nazis, the new battleship *Tirpitz* was stationed in Norway as a threat to the convoys bound through Arctic waters to Russia. Despite the severe losses inflicted by these ships their efforts only served to prove that surface commerce-raiding, although it imposed a severe strain on British naval resources, was not, in itself, a war-winning weapon.

Through lack of adequate surface sea power, the amphibious operations which the Germans could attempt were severely limited. While Norway was captured by a combined sea and air assault aided by trickery, and futile British attempts to interfere confirmed that surface ships alone could not face strong land-based air power, a Nazi invasion of England was impossible because Hitler lacked sea power. In the Mediterranean, Crete was seized by glider and parachute landings in face of Allied superiority on the sea; but that operation proved that an invasion dependent on aircraft acting alone could not be carried out without suffering prohibitive losses.

In narrow waters air power seriously altered the effectiveness of navies. After Italy had entered the war in 1940, although her fleet showed timidity in seeking action, was crippled in harbor at Taranto by an air strike, and was defeated in the night action called Matapan, the Royal Navy lost control of the Mediterranean because enemy air superiority made it impossible to operate through the narrow channels of that sea. The Royal Navy's shortage of radar until mid-1941 and its lack of the carriers and adequate aircraft to provide air cover for fleet operations until late 1942 severely limited its effectiveness. Supplies for the British Eighth Army had to be carried around the Cape of Good Hope. Malta was beleaguered and, although never invaded, could be relieved only by submarines and by desperate convoys pushed through from each end of the Mediterranean from time to time. On the other hand British submarines, surface vessels, and aircraft took a heavy toll of shipping bound from Italy to Libya. From all these fierce encounters new theories of the relation of air and sea power had to be worked out and new tactics were constantly being evolved.

When the Allies had built up their strength to strike back, the Anglo-American landings in North Africa and in Sicily and Italy, where Canadian and other forces were also employed, were only possible because the United Nations possessed overwhelming naval as well as aerial strength. They were now able to fulfill the requirements of successful amphibious operations—namely, to land strong forces in any one of a number of different places, to prevent enemy interference by sea, to give close support from the guns of the fleet both on the beaches and further inland, and to maintain communications between home bases and the invading forces. Yet the battle for the mountainous terrain of the Italian peninsula, begun by landings at Taranto, Reggio, and Salerno in September, 1943, was fought the hard way. With the exception of the Anzio landing in January, 1944, no attempt was made to turn German positions through the use of sea power because of high-level disputes over the allocation of naval resources. When, in June, 1944, the time came to attack the West Wall, there was no such parsimony. Operation Neptune, the overture to Overlord, the Normandy Campaign, employed 702 warships (excluding the minesweepers) and over 9,000 craft of all kinds.

Technical ingenuity made important contributions to the success of the operation. Frogmen reconnoitered the beaches; specially designed landing craft ferried men and tanks ashore; others gave close rocket artillery support on the beaches; tanks were modified with a device to clear paths through mine-fields; more efficient systems of communications enabled the large naval, military, and air forces involved to be controlled in a single operation; artificial harbors called Mulberries compensated for the lack of a major port at the outset; and oil for the land attack was carried across the Channel by Operation Pluto, pipe lines laid under the ocean. The amphibious landings in Africa, Europe, and the Pacific proved that a dominant sea power had not lost its old advantage of being able to strike virtually where it liked and to exploit surprise to the full.

The Anglo-American drive from the beaches of Normandy to the heart of Germany from June, 1944, to May, 1945, was matched by the even greater effort of the Red Army which had stopped the last great German offensive on the Eastern Front in 1943. For four years of war the Russian front always occupied at least two thirds of the German ground forces and a large part of the *Luftwaffe,* an indication of the power of the Russian military effort. Attacked from east and west, the Nazis were driven back into Fortress Germany and, when that fell, were compelled to surrender unconditionally on all fronts. These great Allied attacks were the product of the industrial resources of Britain, Russia, and the United States, as well as of the rest of the free world, which, when fully mobilized, outweighed Germany's productive capacity even when that was supplemented by the enslaved states of Europe. Victory in Europe was won by the exploitation of superior economic power, superior numbers, superiority in the air and on the sea, and a tactical training on the ground in which the Germans no longer possesed a decided advantage. It was won by the development of close cooperation between the various forces of the Allies, civil and military.

In the course of the Pacific War, begun by a surprise air attack on Pearl Harbor which had caught the defenders off guard, these same factors, the elements of total war, were also clearly revealed. The initial attack, without a declaration of war, was itself in line with the practices of total warfare and was in the Japanese military tradition; for they had begun the Russo-Japanese War in exactly the same way, by a surprise attack on the Russian fleet at Port Arthur. Japan had come to believe that the European War had so weakened the Allies that she could pick up an East Asian empire at will, make herself economically self-sufficient, and form a defensive cordon powerful enough to discourage her enemies from attempting to dislodge her. She planned a line of "unsinkable aircraft carriers" stretching from Rabaul in the Bismarck Archipelago to the Kuriles, north of Japan. Behind this protective screen she intended to swallow and digest the possessions of Great Britain, France, Holland, and the United States while also finishing off her Chinese meal. The Pearl Harbor attack was intended to knock the United States off balance and so prevent the possibility of interference by American fleets while Southeast Asia was overrun. Instead, as Professor S. E. Morison has pointed out, it was a "strategic imbecility," for it ensured that the American people and government would enter the war with their full power without long discussion; and also it made certain that they would be satisfied with nothing less than total victory to atone for that "day of infamy," December 7, 1941.

Meanwhile, the Japanese conquest of Southeast Asia showed once more what could be attempted with superior sea and air strength. The Pearl Harbor attack itself revealed the great offensive power of a carrier task force. In 1939 the Japanese navy was the only one which gave to the carrier a place in its fleet ahead of, or equal to, the battleship. The war was to justify such prescience from the very beginning. In November of 1941 a Japanese fleet stole across the Pacific, refuelling en route and making good use of the cover of weather fronts to hide its movements. Off Hawaii on December 7 it launched 300 aircraft which sank most of the battleships of the United States Pacific fleet in water considered by the Americans to be too shallow for the use of aerial torpedoes. Shortly afterwards, the sinking by Japanese land-based airplanes of the British battleship *Prince of Wales* and the battlecruiser *Repulse* seemed further proof of the vulnerability of surface vessels to aerial attack. In view of these demonstrations of the importance of air power in naval warfare at the outset of the war in the Pacific, the accidental absence at sea of all the United States carriers at the time of the attack on Pearl Harbor must be regarded as an extraordinary stroke of fate.

Within a few months of entering the war Japan had achieved her main territorial objectives in the "southern resources area" of Southeast Asia. Her warships had penetrated to the Indian Ocean and seemed likely to link with Hitler at Suez. The new Japanese Empire stretched from the Home Islands to Sumatra. Elated by these early successes, Admiral Yamamoto, the Commander-in-Chief of the Combined Fleet, succeeded in persuading his superiors to expand the objectives to include Midway, the Aleutians, and the Solomons. This expansion stretched dangerously the sea communications upon which Japan's retention of her conquests obviously depended.

Already in an action in the Coral Sea (May 4-8, 1942), the first action in which surface ships did not exchange a single shot, a Japanese amphibious attack upon Port Moresby had been foiled, compelling the invaders to undertake instead the crossing of the difficult Owen Stanley mountain range in the interior of New

Guinea. Then, a month later, the unsuccessful attack on Midway brought on a naval battle which cost Yamamoto all four assault carriers of his striking force. Thus less than six months after Pearl Harbor, and while Japanese conquests went on, one of the most important battles in history marked the real turning point of the war against Japan. At Midway the Japanese lost 30 per cent of their carrier pilots and two thirds of their big carriers, the vessels which henceforward were to have at least an equal right with battleships to be classed as capital ships. The battle was described by Admiral Nimitz as "essentially a victory of intelligence" (because it resulted from the breaking of the Japanese code). It was also a triumph for the courage of American carrier pilots and for superior technology since the Americans had the advantage in radar.

In the Pacific, carrier-borne planes were used so much that the war is sometimes seen as one fought mainly in the air. In normal weather aircraft and their bombs and torpedoes were the weapons used in fleet actions instead of the big guns of old. In the vast reaches of the Pacific, it was the aircraft of the fleet carriers, and not shore-based planes, that dominated naval warfare. The old belief that carriers were unusually vulnerable ships was proved untrue. Though the United States lost four in the first year of war, thereafter no big ones were lost. Similarly of sixty carriers commissioned by the Royal Navy during the war, only seven were sunk by enemy action and only one after 1942. At Midway the Japanese lost heavily in carriers through lack of adequate air cover.

Big ships, carriers and orthodox surface vessels as well, with their heavy armament, remained a basic ingredient of the fleet largely because of the extra power of defense which radar and the proximity fuse had given. Since radar had added to their offensive power by making possible effective shooting without visible sighting, surface vessels still had an important role. At the Coral Sea it had been surface ships in the background which had barred the way of the Japanese invading force. Off Guadalcanal in late 1942 the United States more than held its own in a series of cruiser battles that were in part responsible for the Japanese decision to withdraw from the island. At Leyte Gulf, when the Americans were recapturing the Philippines, every kind of naval vessel took part and the action included both carrier strikes and gun battles. This battle stands beside Tsushima and Trafalgar among the most crushing naval engagements of all time; only Tsushima was won with as little loss to the victors and in that

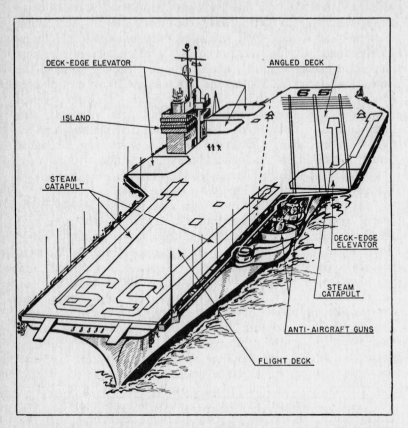

POST–WORLD WAR II DEVELOPMENT OF THE AIRCRAFT
CARRIER.—THE U.S.S. *Forrestal,* a 60,000-ton carrier commissioned in
1955, incorporates the necessary changes for efficient use of jet aircraft
in carrier operations. Planes are launched by the four steam catapults,
expeditiously handled by means of the deck-edge elevators, and safely landed
on the angled deck, which is kept clear of parked aircraft. This ship has a
normal complement of about 100 jet planes, including bombers that can
carry atomic weapons.

engagement the Russian fleet which the Japanese defeated had sailed half round the world and was laden for an ocean voyage. But at Leyte Gulf both fleets were cleared for action. It was a most remarkable victory: Japanese losses were the greatest ever endured in naval warfare in so short a time. They had three battleships (one of them, the *Musashi*, with nine 18-inch guns, was one of the largest warships afloat), four carriers, ten cruisers, and nine destroyers sunk while they accounted for only three small American carriers, two destroyers, and one escort vessel. The most vital part of these statistics was the figures of carriers sunk because, although Japan still had eight or nine built or rebuilding, she had lost at Leyte Gulf all the rest of her experienced carrier pilots and new ones could not be trained in a day. She therefore turned to a desperate expedient to stave off the irresistible advance of her foes, Kamikaze or suicide attacks upon the ships of the United Nations, total warfare in its most absolute form.

In the Pacific War amphibious landings were as essential steps to victory as in the German war, but their relation to the campaign as a whole differed significantly. Whereas the invasions in Europe depended upon the success of a few big landings on hostile shores, and especially upon Operation Neptune, the Pacific campaign was a series of hops from island to island, bypassing strong points which could be safely left because they were isolated by superior sea power. Amphibious operations in this theater were different from those in Europe in two significant ways: they were undertaken at much greater sea distances from base, and they were directed against targets of limited depth where all the shore battles were usually fought within range of the guns of the fleet. Fleets made up of units of all kinds were used. These "task forces" of World War II took the place of the battle fleets of ships-of-the-line which had remained unchallenged from the seventeenth century to World War I. Naval operations over the great distances of the Pacific were made possible by the development of the technique of refuelling at sea. The Americans exploited sea power over greater distances than ever before.

The Japanese garrisons attacked in this way lived up to the traditions of their warrior code by fighting to the last. Thus at Iwo Jima a garrison of 20,000 was attacked by 60,000 Americans and only 200 Japanese lived to be taken prisoner of war. These figures, matched during other assault landings, show that the war was approaching absolute totality. But with all their fanaticism the Japanese troops did not emulate this suicidal conduct when the heat of battle was absent. The Japanese High Command planned that island garrisons left stranded by the leapfrog American advance would resist to the death; instead the Japanese army insisted that isolated garrisons which had been left to starve must be withdrawn by surface vessels, or even by submarines, a diversion which further weakened the shrinking Japanese fleet.

The chief reason for the defeat of Japan's cordon defense was economic. Japan could not maintain the power with which she began the war. Even in the first year of war she had a net loss of warships. Up to the end of 1944 she lost 275 combat ships excluding escort vessels and she replaced only 162 of these. During the same period the United States lost only 128 and added 1005 warships by new construction. Of the latter, more than 200 were submarines; the American underseas fleet made a major contribution to Japan's defeat.

Japan's industrial output was in large part dependent upon supplies from overseas; in fact, the war had been precipitated by the imposition of an American embargo on exports of aircraft, machine tools, chemicals, strategic metals, and gasoline to Japan. The war brought economic collapse. Japan's overseas trade was cut off; as soon as the United States Navy recovered from Pearl Harbor, preparations were made for attacks upon Japan's sea communications which were to prove decisive; 5,000,000 tons of her shipping were sunk; her harbors were mined; many of her industrial cities were bombed; her manpower was drained away in the campaigns in China and Southeast Asia. Japan did not possess the industrial power to defeat the United States, let alone the whole United Nations when the end of the German war allowed them to turn all their resources against her.

The most important aspect of the naval warfare in World War II was the meteoric rise of American sea power. This was based upon the unprecedented ability of both navy and industry to expand enormously without loss of efficiency and upon the United States Navy's rapid appreciation of the revolutionary effect of naval air power. The Americans quickly adopted the strategy, tactics, and techniques in war at sea which air power imposed. With her vast resources, in the course of only four years of war, the United States became by far the strongest naval power in the world.

The most important military and naval development in World War II was the inception of air power as a major factor. It is interesting to examine how far it realized the ideas of the theorists of the twenties. By and large it is possible to say that while air power did not become so dominant as its extreme advocates had prophesied, at least until the development of the atom bomb, it did revolutionize the strategy and tactics of war.

By 1939 the various major powers had developed their air forces on lines dictated by circumstances of geography and politics. Britain, which alone had an independent air force, had been compelled through fear of a German aerial attack and by considerations of economy to concentrate on fighters. As a result she had not been able to build up the strategic bomber force in which many of her airmen believed. Germany, thinking in terms of *Blitzkrieg* and a short war, and Russia, whose greatest asset was her tremendous manpower, had concentrated on the use of air power to support land armies. France, bedevilled by politics, had allowed her air force to decline in quality. The United States, aware that no enemy would be likely to land on her shores, had turned attention to war at a distance and had concentrated on a long-range bombing offensive.

All these characteristics and strategies were to influence the course of the war. Nazi dive bombers, the Stukas, acted like artillery in blasting a path for the columns which overran Poland in 1939 and France in 1940. Because of their slow speed they later proved to be sitting ducks when faced with superior aircraft. The Germans had not grasped the fact that air power cannot be decisive until air superiority has been gained. On the Eastern Front the Russians had produced a superior dive bomber, the Stormovik (IL-2), which played an important part in the Russian winter offensive of 1941-42. Later rocket-equipped versions were famed tank-destroyers. In the West, although there was great pressure from the public for the development of dive bombers (an invention of the United States Marine Corps) to match the Stukas, the air forces eventually used aircraft of a more orthodox type for tactical purposes which quite properly relied on speed.

Having reached the Channel in 1940, the Nazis had failed to win the aerial Battle of Britain because the British had radar, the Hurricane, and the Spitfire. Defeated in the air, and not properly prepared for an amphibious operation, Hitler had had to call off his Operation Sea-Lion to invade Britain. As a result the war settled down to a stalemate just as in the First World War, but without the same bloody conflict in the trenches. At this stage Winston Churchill said that he could see no way to victory except by an "absolutely devastating attack by very heavy bombers from this country upon a Nazi homeland," a comment apparently indicating acceptance of the theories of strategic bombing, but quite unrealistic in terms of the existing strength of the RAF and not in keeping with Churchill's belief in the effects of aerial bombardment. The British Commonwealth Air Training Plan had been set up in December, 1939, to train air crews from the United Kingdom and other British Dominions in Canada for the attack on Germany; but it took time to furnish the large number of crews required, and the four-engined bombers capable of reaching the far parts of the Reich were hardly off the drawing board. Bitter experience had already taught the Royal Air Force that it could operate with reasonable economy only at night, when accurate attacks on industrial targets were unfortunately not possible. Hence in 1941 Churchill informed the Chief of the Air Staff that, while the policy of strategic bombing would continue to receive full support, a decision in the war could be reached only by a simultaneous armored assault on the ground.

The entry of Russia and of the United States into the war made that armored assault possible but, reinforced by the USAAF, strategic aerial attack continued as well. The RAF, because of the difficulty of locating and hitting smaller industrial targets, resorted to heavy night attacks on industrial centers, beginning with thousand-plane raids on Cologne and Essen in May and June of 1942. Only in 1944, when the British had new navigational aids, did they return to attacks on individual factories. Under pressure of war, tremendous improvements had been made by the Royal Air Force in speed, range, bomb load, and armament. The Lancaster and Halifax four-engined bombers were a far cry from the Whitleys and Wellingtons of 1939; the blockbuster, of ten tons, made earlier bombs seem trivial.

The U.S. Army Air Force concentrated on daylight bombing of industrial targets and at first suffered heavy losses. Precision bombing having been found impracticable, it had to develop the technique of pattern bombing. Even so, only 20 per cent of the bombs fell in the target areas—that is within a radius of 1000 feet of the aiming point of attack. The renowned B-17 Flying Fortress, introduced in 1935, was completely overshadowed by the B-29 Superfortress, which appeared at the end of the war.

The prosecution of this policy of strategic bombing, especially by daylight, had been heavily challenged by the *Luftwaffe* and, as has been seen, the Allies had been compelled to vary their tactics. In this regard, whereas the American Air Force had hoped to protect its bombers by building up their fire power, it soon found that it was also necessary to protect them with fighter escorts. Until long-range fighters were available, the daylight bombardment of the remoter parts of enemy territory was not possible. By early 1944, however, fighters, especially the Mustang and the Mosquito night fighter, were able to accompany bombing raids to all parts of enemy territory in Europe, and they were also ordered to seek out Nazi fighters and destroy them. Enemy losses greatly increased, and the air battle of Germany was won.

The defeat of the *Luftwaffe* in the air was the result not merely of errors in production and training policy, but also of Allied bombing. Through overconfidence, the Nazis, failing to appreciate the lessons of the Battle of Britain, had not utilized the full capacity of their aircraft industry until the initiation of the combined Anglo-American bomber offensive in June, 1943, forced them to desperate measures to produce fighters. A year before this time, as a result of a shortage of aviation gasoline (despite more synthetic output), the *Luftwaffe* had cut down the length of flight training by two thirds. The inevitable result was a serious decline in the quality of its personnel. During 1943 and early 1944, continuous Allied attacks on airframe factories contributed significantly to Allied aerial advantage in the ensuing months. By a policy of strategic bombing directed at aircraft and gasoline production, and also by defeating the enemy concentrations sent aloft to ward off the strategic attack, the Allies were able to seize command of the air and so to prepare the way for a combined assault of all arms.

The winning of the air battle had made the landings possible. German air generals have stated in interrogation that on D-Day only eighty fighter planes were operational to oppose the landings in Normandy, and there were certainly no more than 120. But it is important to note that only 28 per cent of all the bombs that were dropped on Germany during the war had fallen before July 1, 1944. Three quarters of the full weight of the air attack came after the ground assault on the heart of the Nazi Empire had been launched in the West. Thus heavier assault was also made possible by the winning of supremacy in the air.

Air power gave invaluable aid to the Anglo-American land forces.

Shortly before the invasion, the weight of the aerial attack had been transferred to transportation; and the communications behind the Atlantic Wall were severely impeded. This was only a part, but perhaps the most important part, of the contribution made by strategic bombing to the success of the landings. As the invasion forces rolled on into Germany they continued to receive invaluable support from the tactical air forces which had been set up. Spitfires, Tempests, Mustangs (P-51), Thunderbolts (P-47), and Typhoons, which were literally flying gun platforms, and medium bombers armed with rockets were used with effect against infantry and armor; and on occasion, the American and British "heavies" were called in to blast a path through strong German defenses, but sometimes with debatable results. Despite serious deficiencies in land-air cooperation throughout the campaign, air power continued to assist the land advance and contributed to the eventual annihilation of the German armies as organized fighting units.

Meanwhile the strategic bombardment continued with ever-increasing ferocity that was sometimes quite unnecessary, as in Coventry, Hamburg, and Dresden. It is not clear how much the bombing contributed to the defeat of Germany. *The United States Strategic Bombing Survey*, which studied the effects of the bombardment immediately after the war, came to the conclusion that "the German experience suggests that even a first-class military power . . . cannot live long under full-scale and free exploitation of air weapons over the heart of its territories. By the beginning of 1945, before the invasion of the homeland itself, Germany was reaching a state of helplessness. . . . Her armies were still in the field. But with the impending collapse of the supporting economy, the indications are convincing that they would have had to cease fighting—any effective fighting—within a few months. Germany was mortally wounded."

At the same time the *Survey* pointed out that the German economy showed tremendous powers of recuperation and that the effects of bombing were far less than the Allied air forces claimed. Despite heavy air attacks, German production actually reached its wartime peak in late 1944. The *Survey's* report showed that even though businessmen and economists had cooperated in working out the strategic bombing plan, there were serious errors in the selection of targets, mainly caused by inadequate intelligence or wrong judgments. It also showed that industries could continue working after raids which had apparently destroyed them, and that the civilian population in a police state showed "surprising" resistance to the terror and hardships of repeated air attacks. One might add that the population of London had also shown that terror bombing did not have the immediate results which its pre-war advocates had claimed. Estimations of the effectiveness of the Allied bombing must not neglect the fact that the Germans had been fighting a major war on their Eastern Front for months before the invasion, and the major Allied bombing effort, began. The Russian campaign had occupied the bulk of the German armies and a considerable part of their air forces.

The appearance of a third armed force, air power, with which the older services must always operate closely but which could also act independently, complicated the problem of inter-service, or "joint," command. For a variety of other reasons also, questions arising out of the exercise of command over the fighting forces became far more important in the Second World War than in any previous conflict. Further, because communications had improved and distances had shrunk, and because the war was world-wide and fought by great coalitions, the problem of "combined," or international, commands had to be settled. Finally, because war had come to involve the whole national life, the age-old problem of the relations of civil and military leadership was greatly aggravated.

It so happened that in this war there was a greater need for amphibious operations. In Europe a landing on the continent had to be forced, and in the Pacific the route to Japan stepped from island to island. The operations which necessitated joint command were therefore far more frequent than ever before. But amphibious operations in the past had often suffered from the inability of co-equal land and sea commanders to work with one another. Yet, when one or the other had been given primacy, he frequently had not sufficiently understood the problems of the other service. The appearance of air power as a third force made co-equal command more difficult and perhaps more dangerous; for two services might conceivably outvote the third and compel it to an action which it knew from its experience to be unfeasible.

The British had had a longer experience than Americans of amphibious operations and had usually, although not always with success, appointed co-equal commanders. In their Chiefs of Staff Committee, they had evolved a form of command which seemed to

be alien to the basic principle of unity but which worked, perhaps
because it was suited to their temperament. Through it they had
achieved a useful degree of successful inter-service cooperation.
However, since Gallipoli, they had been less enthusiastic about
amphibious operations, which seemed to them to be too difficult in
the conditions of modern war. On the other hand, between the wars,
the United States through the Joint Board worked out techniques
for amphibious operations in preparation for the possibility of
having to strike at Japan across the Central Pacific; and in 1935
the principle had been established that when joint operations of
the United States army and navy or marines were undertaken a
single officer would be put in command.

When the war came, the need for an organization to represent
the American services in the Anglo-American Combined Chiefs of
Staff Committee (to be described later) led to formation, for the
first time in United States history, of an American Joint Chiefs of
Staff. Thus the United States conformed at this level to the British
system of coordinating the efforts of the services by a committee.
But at lower levels, where forces of all arms of both countries
acted together in theaters of war, the American practice of appointing a single theater-commander from one of the services was
followed. While these solutions for inter-service command did not
always work without a hitch, they were, on the whole, remarkably
successful. In this war, more than in any previous war, the necessity
for full cooperation between the various arms was apparent; and
by and large it was achieved.

On the German side of the war the problem of international, or
combined, command raised few difficulties. Germany was so much
more powerful than her allies that she invariably took control in
joint operations. Otherwise the three Axis powers merely fought
the war on parallel lines. In the United Nations, however, where
the military strength of the three leading powers was more equal,
no such easy solution could be adopted. Military coalitions in the
past had always found the problem of international command
difficult. In this war also, when there was great disparity of outlook,
as between the western democracies and Communist Russia, it
proved impossible. While the Russians demanded full information
about Allied plans they never revealed their own secrets to the
Allies. The British and Americans found agreement with the Soviet
leaders on general strategy—for instance, on the timing of the Second
Front—difficult to achieve. Even where the political ideals and

systems of government of the Allies were similar, as between Great Britain and the United States, the essential cooperation under a united command was not easy. And it was found that the civil heads of states were often able to come to agreement with their opposite numbers more easily than the leaders of the armed forces, especially those at the operational level.

Nevertheless, Britain and the United States, despite certain difficulties, achieved remarkable degrees of cooperation and of coordinated command. The lessons of the First World War had been learned. For the overall direction of the war an Anglo-American Combined Chiefs of Staff was created with headquarters in Washington. Regional commands in various theaters of war were given to an officer of one nation, usually that which was contributing the larger forces. Harmony between officers of different countries at combined headquarters was a new feature of warfare. Undoubtedly the most outstanding example of it was at General Eisenhower's headquarters in North Africa and Western Europe, where unity by combined command was really achieved. It must be added, however, that the Combined Chiefs of Staff system was never fully extended to include the staffs of the smaller Allied powers.

A noticeable feature of the command at the highest level in the Second World War was that it was exercised by civilians who concerned themselves with many matters that were military in nature. While Churchill, Roosevelt, and Stalin, and Hitler and Mussolini to a lesser degree, might all be said to have had some earlier military office and experience, it was rather limited, and they were, in fact, civilians. The Japanese leaders had a great deal of experience. Yet each of these political heads of state was called upon to make decisions about military strategy; and each one of them paid great attention to matters which in earlier times would have been regarded as being outside the concern of a mere civilian. The top leaders supervised the formulation of grand strategy; and, aided by modern methods of communication, kept a close watch on the conduct of operations. Churchill, as Prime Minister and Minister of Defence, directed Britain's war effort. On military questions, he was advised by the Chiefs of Staff Committee. His volumes on the war showed how much he interested himself in even the minutiae of service matters. Roosevelt, the constitutional commander-in-chief of the United States forces, concerned himself less with military details, but nevertheless he also supervised major strategic policy. Stalin became a Marshal of the Soviet Union and Generalissimo. Hitler went further still and took upon himself the supreme military command. In 1938 he had created a new organization, the *Oberkommando der Wehrmacht* (O.K.W.) through which he could command the armed forces; and in December,1941, he took over personal command of the army as well.

While it was imperative that the supreme civil authority in both democratic and totalitarian states should have ultimate control of military affairs, it was obvious that lack of professional military experience could be a handicap. The successful exercise of this high command by a civilian necessitated great trust in, and dependence on, the professional soldiers who commanded the armed forces. That trust was notably lacking in Germany. In certain spheres, especially those in which military decisions were affected by political affairs, the statesmen were often the best judges of the issues. British actions to support Belgium in 1940 and Greece in 1941 were militarily unsound but politically important. Hitler has been blamed for his insistence on unyielding defense on the Eastern Front and for his repeated orders to his armies to stand and fight. There were times when Hitler was militarily correct, but his policy ultimately led to the destruction of his armies, the strategic retirements contemplated by his generals, which would have prolonged the war, would probably have led to a great loss of prestige that his regime might not have been able to survive.

The relations between statesmen and soldiers in the democracies, where strategy was drawn up by military chiefs under the supervision of the head of the state and on lines indicated by him, and where the operations were, to a great extent, left in the hands of professional military men, were more successful. But the line between military and political decisions is very hard to draw, and it is quite impossible to leave all military decisions to the soldiers and all political decisions to the statesmen. When the United Nations debated whether to invade Southern Europe through France or through the Balkans, Churchill's desire to strike at Central Europe to forestall the Russians had seemed to the Americans to savor of imperialism. It also conflicted with American anxiety to ensure a quick military decision. In fact, however, such decisions, like those which stopped the advancing Anglo-American forces short of Prague and Berlin, should never have been made on purely military grounds. At that level no decision can be non-political.

One reason why problems of command and of politico-military relationships had become so much more important in the Second World War was that war had become total and universal. It had come to permeate thoroughly the national life. As a result of the air attacks the citizen was often as active a participant as the soldier. In the occupied countries he was organized in partisan or underground armies to fight behind the lines for liberation or to commit acts of sabotage. Even where he was not active as a fighter or in civil defense, his life was affected by restrictive regulations, by the rationing of his essential needs, and by the restriction of his luxuries and comforts and pleasures. Government controls instituted for these purposes had to be tied closely into the national military effort and required careful coordination with military policy.

The unleashing of atomic power dramatized another revolutionary development of the Second World War, employment of science and civilian scientists in military effort. Modern science, which had had its birth in the early Renaissance, had been very slow to mature. The scientific renaissance had not fully come until the latter part of the seventeenth century; the technological developments of the Industrial Revolution in the eighteenth had owed little to its inspiration; the marriage of science and technology had been a later development. While soldiers had made use of certain aspects of scientific knowledge in the eighteenth century, especially in the sphere of siegecraft, the full application of science to war had been delayed until chemistry, physics, electronics, and other branches of science had been developed as distinct fields of research.

Thus it was the First World War, in which the technology of the Industrial Revolution had first been fully exploited, which had also seen the beginnings of scientific warfare. Mass-produced electrical and mechanically operated devices of great accuracy and intricacy began to take over various tasks in which the soldier or sailor had formerly made an empiric judgment. As machines are not subject to the emotional stresses and strains of conflict, and as they could perform tasks beyond the capacity of men, the place of the human element in fighting was bound to be affected although, of course, it still remained an essential ingredient. In these circumstances, scientists and laboratories had been absorbed into the war effort, with the result that, by 1918, almost all the principles used in scientific warfare today (with the notable exception of atomic warfare) had made their appearance and had been tried out in practice. It remained only for a greater conflict to put them to their fullest use.

However, after 1918 science and technology had been restricted mainly to developments for peaceful application and their potentialities in war had been little exploited. This was true even in the warlike totalitarian states. On racial grounds, Hitler had ·exiled many of his most brilliant scientists who might otherwise have contributed much to his war effort. Elsewhere, wishful thinking that great wars were things of the past, the one-sided concentration of scientists on the works of peace, and the inability of military men to comprehend the trends of modern science had brought about a serious lag in the further development of the techniques which scientists had produced during the last war. Some few military laboratories existed, but the scientists were relegated to an inferior position by the dominant military direction; and the fundamental principle, which industry had long endorsed, that the scientist must be given freedom to develop his ideas and must be allowed to engage in pure scientific research, was completely alien to the thinking of most senior service officers. Hence, while industry in this period had produced the "most bizarre gadgetry" the world had yet seen, many in the armed forces tended to think of war in terms which were out of date. In a few military fields, notably in the development of radar, scientific advances had been made; but, in the opinion of Dr. Vannevar Bush, the head of the American scientific war effort, "the world slept."

It must be noted that in every nation, and especially in the United States, the extraordinary advance of scientific knowledge and of industrial techniques had produced a reservoir of military power in the form of industrial plants, techniques, skills, and "know-how" which, while developed for purposes of peace, were available for, and were used in, modern war. When the war came a tremendous change took place which can only be regarded as revolutionary. The competition between the scientists on opposing sides in the race to produce new weapons and methods of warfare, and to checkmate those already developed, was as intense as the conflict between the armed forces. In the United States alone, 30,000 scientists and engineers were employed on problems connected with new weapons and new machines. Organizations like the National Research Council, founded during World War I, and the National Defense Research Committee and the Office of Scientific Research and Development, established in the Second, were to some extent paralleled by the British Scientific Advisory Committee to the Cabinet, by Canada's National Research Council, and by her post war Defence Research Board. For the first time, scientists became full and responsible partners in the conduct of war, and as the war progressed the military leaders came to have ever greater confidence in their work. Scientists in or out of uniform were to be found using their peculiar skills and knowledge beside the front-line soldier, in aircraft flying over enemy territory, and in the battle at sea. Through "operational research," the application of scientific techniques to the study of special problems posed by military weapons and operations, science entered into warfare in a new fashion.

No account can be given here of the great number of scientific developments which the war produced, but some mention must be made of a few. Radar, developed at first to give early warning of the approach of enemy aircraft, came to have a multitude of other uses, from directing anti-aircraft fire and night-fighters to aiding navigation and guiding lost aircraft. The proximity fuse, described by Professor J. P. Baxter in *Scientists Against Time* as one of the four or five inventions that helped win the war, was developed by American scientists in response to a British request. It was used against aircraft and also against ground targets. RDX, an explosive nearly twice as powerful as TNT, greatly increased the effectiveness of depth charges, "blockbuster" bombs, and torpedoes. But these are just a very few of the contributions made by the scientists to the war effort.

It is worthy of note that many developments were the result of inter-Allied scientific effort, a new feature in war. While the United States was still neutral, a British Scientific Mission headed by Sir Henry Tizard had taken to Washington and Ottawa information about British secret devices and equipment and a list of urgent requirements. From this visit had come a degree of cooperation between the United States, the United Kingdom, and Canada which had greatly increased productivity. Some groups in both England and America had at first opposed the interchange of information on the ground that their own country would be making the greater contribution. It happened that they were both thinking of the same field, radar, in which they both believed, wrongly, that they had a complete monopoly! It is reasonable to say that inter-Allied cooperation in scientific effort was achieved because the scientists saw with greater clarity than the statesmen and soldiers what its results would be, and because they were successful in their pleas for its introduction. The greatest scientific feat of the war, the releasing of atomic energy, was a product of inter-Allied cooperation, although its full development was left by agreement to the United States. Penicillin, perhaps the greatest medical achievement of the war, was discovered in Britain but made available by a joint effort.

Discoveries of this kind, which could so obviously have a greater value for peace than for war, but which were developed speedily only because war needs were urgent and funds were therefore made available, are evidence that weapon development progresses faster under the stress of war; and they also suggest the theory that war itself has been a stimulant of progress. This theory, which gained a wide public credence at the end of the war, supports those who would attempt to defend war as a creative institution. Against this must be placed the argument that war has always destroyed far more than it has created. War conditions intensify development and investigation but may actually stifle pure research.

Although the United Nations may be said to have won the battle of science it must be emphasized that no single invention was decisive, not even in the war against Japan. The Japanese had already been defeated by conventional weapons before the atomic bomb was dropped at Hiroshima. The Germans were not far behind in the contest in the laboratories. They produced, among other things, the V-1 flying missile, the V-2 rocket, the first operational jet plane, the Messerschmitt 262, the magnetic mine, the snorkel, and the true submarine. This fact is significant because it casts doubt on the old belief that conditions of freedom are necessary for scientific progress. The scientists of the western powers may have had an edge in the contest but, under totalitarian direction, Nazi scientists were foes to be feared.

The use of the atomic bomb was not only a demonstration of the military power of science but also raised important ethical problems which threw light on the declining standards of conduct in modern war. The decision to use the bomb was in line with that trend toward moral nihilism which had marked warfare in the last hundred years. In this it had been preceded in kind by practices like the indiscriminate bombardment of industrial cities and unrestricted submarine warfare. The Hamburg and Dresden fire storms killed in the same order of magnitude as the *Enola Gay*. The Nazis, Japanese, and Russians, partly in retaliation but partly on their own initiative, had perpetrated atrocities on a scale not known before in the history of civilized man. Races marked for extermination were slaughtered wholesale with cold-blooded efficiency (thus creating the new international crime of genocide). Spies, political police, "thought-police," terror, the concentration camp, and forced labor, types of oppression used in the totalitarian states in peacetime, were used in war on a much greater scale to cow subject peoples. These crimes were usually committed, especially in the west of Europe, by political soldiers like the S.S. and the Gestapo rather than by the regulars; but regular troops were not innocent of them.

The United Nations forces were restrained by moral considerations to a greater extent than the totalitarian states but even their decisions were ruled, in the end, by expediency. Moral considerations were important only when they were also expedient; the doctrine of reprisal was used to justify actions which would otherwise have been ruled out; and the ultimate criterion was whether a contemplated policy, operation, or mode of conduct would help to win the war. Any weapon, however frightful, could be justified on these grounds. It is sometimes said that gas was not used because it had aroused the moral conscience of the world in the previous war. Actually gas was not used because of fear of retaliation in kind and even more because it is not a decisive weapon.

Thus the total war brought a decline in moral standards far beyond anything known before. Although offset to some extent by individual deeds of heroism performed through belief in a cause, this decline resulted in a general lowering of traditional standards of behavior. Post war crime waves and increased juvenile delinquency were but minor symptoms of a disease which threatened civilization. Its most serious result would be the failure of moral standards to influence men, parties, and nations. Those lusting for power would then feel free to use any weapon and any practice to gain their ends. With the new weapons which science had developed during the war it was clear that man's control over nature was outrunning his capacity to create a stable social and political system in the world. Total war might lead to total barbarism.

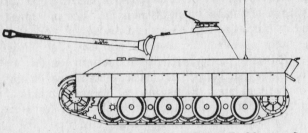

THE GERMAN "PANTHER" TANK.—(From F. M. von Senger und Etterlin, *Die Deutschen Panzer, 1926-1945*, J. F. Lehmanns Verlag, Munich, 1959, p. 61.)

Thus, from being at first a war which was limited in very many ways, World War II had reached a climax in a new degree of totality. It had been fought by great armies of millions, mechanized to an extent beyond the dreams of all but a few peacetime visionaries. Scientists were, for the first time, fully engaged in the war effort; and this war saw technology applied at an astonishing rate to fashion weapons which greatly altered the traditional methods of conflict. The great social and political developments of the twentieth century, the development of democracy on the one hand and of new "popular" autocracies on the other, had also contributed to the revolution in the conduct of war. The harnessing of the whole national life to war had ended, as it must, in the complete destruction of the vanquished state. For the chief enemy, Germany, defeat, like war, was total. The huge losses of manpower that had marked World War I had been surpassed on the battle front, and the wholesale liquidation of civilians had brought the sum total of war deaths to a figure (estimated at 22,000,000) much greater than the number of deaths in World War I. Realization that yet more horrible weapons of mass slaughter were being produced as rapidly as laboratories and factories could turn them out renewed once more the determination which had gripped men everywhere in 1918. Once more the cry was raised that war must be abolished.

19

Cold War

"Cold War" is a term coined to describe the state of tension that developed between the nations of the West and those of the Communist world shortly after the end of the Second World War. International tension is no new thing; in fact, it could be described as a normal condition of relations among states. In the past, when tensions reached a level intolerable to one nation or another, war was frequently resorted to as a means of resolving them. The Cold War was a distinctive phase in the history of international relations not only because of the fundamental cleavage in ideology and objectives between East and West, but even more because the revolution brought about by the development of nuclear weapons and by the perfection of new means to deliver them restricted the use of war as a feasible method of pursuing political ends without diminishing the danger of its occurrence.

If the problem of the Cold War had been simply that of finding a political accommodation between the Soviet and Western blocs in order to lessen tensions and reduce the danger of war, the difficulties would be formidable enough. But relations between the two power blocs were infinitely complicated by contemporary developments that had nothing to do, in origin, with the Cold War, but had become elements in it.

Probably the most significant of these developments was the collapse of the European colonial empires in Asia and Africa, and the emergence of many new sovereign states. European military power had been able to use railways and roads to maintain rigorous control of vast areas formerly subject only to a vague suzerainty. Despite the drastic disruption of ancient societies which European penetration brought about, there had been relatively little partisan resistance, perhaps because the western regimes had made changes that were acceptable either to local ruling classes or to the majority of the people. But imperial authority was spread thin and it collapsed when it was seen to conflict with the principles of Western liberalism and when empires were weakened by World War II. Political and military resistance movements made western imperial rule impossible almost everywhere but proved less effective against Communist totalitarian imperialism. The disturbances that frequently accompanied the passage from colonial status to independence, and the economic and social problems with which the new states were confronted after the achievement of independence, created grave instabilities in the world state system, fostered the spread of the Cold War, and occasioned a series of minor conflicts in which the danger of a major collision between the great power blocs was always present.

Even before the end of the Second World War, the United Nations took measures to erect barriers against the outbreak of a third. At Dumbarton Oaks in 1944 and at San Francisco in 1945, the wartime alliance was converted into a permanent organization to keep the peace. The United Nations Organization, like the League before it, attempted to reconcile the conflicting concepts of national sovereignty and collective security, but, as a result of experience, certain changes in form were introduced to make the new world body more effective. The Charter outlawed private war; and an international military force was planned. The most powerful body in the United Nations was the Security Council, in which the five great powers had permanent seats. Because it was believed that the new plan for collective security would not work unless there was harmony among those great states which would, in the event of a major police action, bear the brunt of the fighting and the responsibility, the veto power (which every state had virtually possessed in the League of Nations as a result of the unanimity rule) was retained only by the five great powers in the Security Council.

The Military Staff Committee of the Security Council, composed of the chiefs of staff of the great powers, was charged with the task of planning the international army and was also expected to discuss the limitation of conventional, or pre-atomic, armament. The atom bomb had not yet been used when the U.N. Charter was drawn up. When it came up for discussion, it was so different in kind from ordinary weapons that it was considered an entirely distinct problem. In order to devote special attention to the abolition of atomic warfare, a U.N. committee on atomic power was created. Plans to create a U.N. army and to control national armaments were moves toward the limitation of national sovereignty.

During the course of the Second World War, the United Nations had prepared plans to bring war criminals and aggressors to justice. The War Crimes Trials, held at Nuremberg and Tokyo between 1945 and 1948, were widely hailed as precedents by virtue of which individuals and groups could be made to answer for crimes against international law. If this were so, then a new chapter in history would have opened in which old concepts of national sovereignty would have radically altered and in which wars between nations would have given place to international police actions.

From the first, however, there was doubt as to whether society had yet reached that stage of development. War crimes are breaches of international agreements, such as the Geneva Conventions, which govern the conduct of military operations and to which most civilized nations have subscribed; and it is arguable that aggression became a crime when private war was outlawed by the nations signing the Kellogg Pact of 1928; accordingly, charges under these headings had some claim to being legal. But some critics pointed out that the third crime brought before the international tribunals, that of genocide, or the wiping out of races, had not formerly been proscribed by international law and that such action thus savored of retroactive justice. Many other people believed that all the proceedings against German and Japanese statesmen and military men represented merely the vengeance of the victors. They noted that no parallel investigation was made of war crimes alleged to have been committed by members of the Allied forces and that the judges were all drawn from the victorious nations. Furthermore, some Allied military leaders objected to the trial and conviction of German generals on charges of committing aggressive war and other offenses. They contended that a soldier must carry out his orders and that the infliction of punishment after a war for offenses committed by a soldier on the orders of his superiors would tend to dissolve all military discipline. There was no general agreement that the War Crimes Trials were inaugurating a new and revolutionary stage in the history of warfare and society.

Many thinkers feared that, just as World War I had led to World War II, the conditions created by the latter might lead to a third war. Drawing on the experience of two world conflicts, one writer has described the aftermath of modern total war as follows:

(a) an increasingly radical domestic orientation of populations in most of the affected areas coupled with a stronger spirit of nationality in foreign relations;

(b) a general economic disturbance growing out of the exigencies of both the war and the peace demands of the victors;

(c) a desire on the part of the defeated powers to upset the peace settlement as soon as possible;

(d) costly disagreement and rivalry among the larger victorious powers;

(e) an apparent need for growing armaments and expanding military commitments despite the existence of international peace machinery.*

While the author of this analysis disclaimed the role of prophet, his examination suggested forcibly that human society, far from having entered a new era in which international conflict will be no more, is still in the midst of a period of chaos of which the end cannot yet be seen and in which the danger of a war more terrible than any yet known is great.

Even without the atom bomb, technological progress in war had made such strides during World War II that the urgency of methods to prevent a third conflagration was augmented by the stark knowledge that another war would lead to even greater devastation and have still greater impact on civilian populations. Recoilless guns, simple to produce and to operate, now gave infantry more protection against the tanks which had brought mobility back into war. Guided missiles, which Hitler's V-1 and V-2 had foreshadowed, were capable of spreading death and destruction far behind the firing line; and no defense against the V-2 had been found. The introduction of supersonic, inter-hemisphere rockets, fitted with atomic warheads, was a probability for the future; "push-button" warfare would enable nations to destroy one another from afar. Deadly nerve gases and bacteriological cultures that could spread disease far and wide were believed to be already available. The atom bomb, in the small crude form used against Japan, was equal to the effect of thousands of tons of TNT. But it also spread a radioactive effect that led to almost as much concern as the immense damage caused by its blast. Men began to ask whether

* W. C. Langsam, "The Political Aftermath of Modern War," *Pennsylvania History*, XXII, January, 1955.

the human race—or, at any rate, civilization as they knew it—
could survive another war.

Western scientists had designed the atom bomb during the war
because they feared that Germany might anticipate the democracies
in atomic warfare. The decision to use the bomb on Japan, made
at the highest political level, had been defended by the argument
that, although Japan was tottering, she still had armies in the field
that would make necessary a bloody and costly invasion of the
Japanese islands. (There were 2,000,000 Japanese troops, 9,000
Kamikaze planes, and ample supplies in the home islands.) The
atom bomb was expected to save hundreds of thousands of Allied
lives.

During the war, however, when consideration was given to the
awful possibilities of the new warfare, many scientists began to
have qualms about prostituting their knowledge and experience in
work that they feared might eventually lead to the destruction of
civilization or of the human race. Man's technological capacity
seemed to have outreached his power of social and political organization. Some scientists declared that, in face of the weapons of the
future, the old law that every new weapon could be countered by
new defenses would fail to operate. Led by Albert Einstein, whose
theoretical work nearly half a century before had prepared the way
for the splitting of the atom, some of the foremost scientists insisted
that man must now abolish war and stop the further development
of thermonuclear weapons; others took it upon themselves to reveal
the secrets of the bombs to foreign powers.

Despite these attitudes on the part of some scientists, weapon
development was extremely rapid after 1945, and the competition between states to create new weapon systems become essentially a contest among scientists. The American monopoly of the
atomic bomb was broken by the Soviet Union in 1949; the first
explosion of a hydrogen bomb by the United States, in 1952, was
followed, the next year, by the Soviet production of an H-bomb.
Great Britain joined the "nuclear club" by exploding its first atomic
bomb in 1952 and its first hydrogen bomb in 1957; then, in 1960,
France tested an atomic device in the Sahara. In both the United
States and Russia, German scientists who had been engaged during
the Second World War in Hitler's V-1 and V-2 programs assisted
in harnessing nuclear weapons to missiles. The rivalry between
the United States and the Soviet Union in the production of missiles, especially the intercontinental ballistic missile (ICBM), was

intense and enormously expensive. Experimentation in rocketry led
to the probing of space. On October 4, 1957, the Soviet Union put
its Sputnik into orbit around the earth, an achievement matched by
the United States on January 31, 1958. Both nations bent their
efforts not only to the launching of satellites but to the perfection
of the technology for manned space flight. Again the Soviet Union
led the way, in the person of Major Yuri Gagarin, whose pioneer
exploit in orbiting the earth was followed by Major Gherman Titov's
flight, in which he circled the earth seventeen times. That the United
States was in the running in the space race was shown by the non-
orbital flights of Commander Alan B. Shepard and Captain Virgil
I. Grissom. Then, on February 20, 1962, Lieutenant Colonel John
H. Glenn successfully rocketed three orbits from Cape Canaveral.
The potential use of space vehicles for military purposes—whether
for reconnaissance, surveillance, communications, or delivery of
nuclear weapons—had doubtless spurred both powers to their remarkable endeavors in this field. The Russian successes in lifting
heavier loads into space, and the spectacular nature of their space
exploits, were of immense propaganda value in the Cold War. Yet
the American launchings, conducted in the full glare of publicity
instead of in secret, were an impressive demonstration of confidence
and technical efficiency that counteracted the effect of the earlier
Soviet successes.

The nature of the new weapons had a revolutionary effect
upon the world state system. In the past, smaller states, if they
possessed superior fighting qualities, more effective military organization, or favorable geographical conditions, always had some
chance of victory in wars against greater powers. Now, the cost of
the newest arms was such that only the largest and wealthiest states
could afford them; and the rate at which arms become obsolescent
meant that smaller states were inevitably equipped with out-of-date
weapons. The ability to feed and equip armies without resort to
foreign aid had become an even greater factor in the reckoning of
military strength. For these reasons, the relative military power of
smaller states greatly declined. There were now only two powers
of the first magnitude, the United States and Soviet Russia. Britain,
shorn of her empire, was not comparable with these. No other
power represented a serious challenge except China. But China's
strength, based on vast manpower and resources, was potential
rather than actual, since she would be occupied for some time to

come with the immense problems arising from the communizing of an economy that was as yet technologically undeveloped.

The reduction of the number of first powers to two made the balancing of power much more difficult than it was in the days when there were more states in the equation. It so happened that the two leading states, the United States and the U.S.S.R., were fundamentally opposed in ideology, in social and economic structure, and in political organization. While both claimed to be "democratic," they had vitally different concepts of the meaning and nature of democracy. The political liberalism that forms the basis of American democracy, and the remnants of her traditional isolationist policy, made it possible for the United States after 1945 to contemplate the continuance of a divided world if a greater unification could not be achieved; but Communist doctrine prevented Russia from accepting a world organization in which her sovereignty would be restricted and her influence outweighed, and from abandoning activities designed to destroy the liberal-capitalist way of life in the other countries. Hence, the reduction of the number of powerful states, the ideological antagonism between the two leading states, and Russian unwillingness to live and let live created great uneasiness and threatened peace. As President Eisenhower put it in a speech to the United Nations Assembly, "Two atomic powers eye each other malevolently across a defenseless world."

In response to this situation, some of the lesser powers, and also groups in some of the major states, talked in terms of "neutralism" or of creating a "third force." But such a policy was practical only for those states which, like India, felt relatively remote from the area of likely conflict or, like Sweden, considered themselves to be too precariously placed between East and West. For some states, as the polarization of the world became clearer, there seemed no alternative to the policy of affiliation with one side or the other. Indeed, by refusing to withdraw her occupation troops from Eastern Europe after the war, Russia quickly forced many of the East European countries into satellite status and imposed Communism upon them. This Soviet policy culminated in 1948 in the *coup d'état* in Czechoslovakia, a little power that had been attempting to make the best of both worlds.

Although Czechoslovakia did not fall to a Russian military assault, the influence of the Red Army encamped along her borders was important. Even before the Czech coup, the Soviet use of the veto in the U.N. and obstruction of attempts to limit arms, to control atomic energy, and to create an international army had suggested that Russia would not accept the establishment of an effective world organization with full power to preserve the peace. The rape of Czechoslovakia brought the rest of the world to the realization that the Soviet Union had not abandoned the Marxist dream of world revolution; and there was reason to believe that that doctrine was now inextricably mingled with Russian imperialistic ambitions for world domination. A Russian note to Turkey in 1945 demanding a share in the control of the Bosporus was in the tradition of the policy bequeathed by Czar Peter the Great to his successors.

Soviet policy immediately after the Second World War would have been better understood if the West had then known more about Russia and especially about Soviet military doctrine; but unfortunately Russia was (and indeed still is) a "mystery wrapped in an enigma." After the Bolshevik Revolution, the Red Army had consciously striven to develop a new "Marxist" military doctrine and military organization. In fact, however, the military theory that evolved was not greatly different in its broad outlines from that of non-revolutionary states. But a few important differences appeared. The difference from western military thought that is, in this post-war world, the most important is the Soviet belief that war and peace are actually indistinguishable in a world in which capitalism continues to exist. This idea is applied in two different dimensions. As was seen during the Second World War, conflict is not limited in Soviet practice to the operations of armies, but is carried on behind the front by partisans and guerrillas, by subversion and sabotage, and by propaganda and indoctrination. In this respect, of course, Soviet military doctrine conforms to the practice of modern total war.

But the Russians carry total war into a second dimension. Although they denounce Clausewitzian thought in certain respects, they in fact develop his doctrine that "war is nothing else than a continuation of political transactions intermingled with different means" to an inverted but quite logical conclusion. They assert that peace is only "a continuance of war by other means." Conflict, though not necessarily armed conflict, between socialist states and capitalism is regarded as inevitable. But it is considered preferable to gain objectives without war if possible. Soviet statecraft turns in peacetime to what are, in effect, lesser forms of war—namely, sub-version, sabotage, colonial rebellion, and satellite aggression. The

Russians have become masters in combining and operating various non-military forms of war—political, economic, and psychological. They support Communist parties if it suits them, they foment disaffection against "imperialist capitalist overlords," they encourage their satellites to fight the Communist battle by aggression, and they can even—as in the Soviet-Japanese fighting on the Manchuria-Mongolia frontier between 1934 and 1939—engage in armed conflict themselves without considering that they are totally involved. All this activity, falling short of total war, formed part of what has come to be called the Cold War.

The most dramatic evidence of the strategy of Cold War was found in the widespread espionage nets that were uncovered in the West, especially the one revealed by the desertion of a Soviet cipher clerk, Igor Gouzenko, in Canada. Communist ideology cuts across national affiliations. Spy rings can easily be built up by the Soviet Union from among the citizens of democratic states. Communist Party members and fellow travelers are potential or active agents of Russia. And the techniques of espionage, not uncommon in the old order of things, are multiplied and intensified.

The upheaval and dislocation caused by the Second World War and its aftermath provided a fertile soil for this new form of warfare. Cities and industries had been destroyed wholesale; populations had been rooted from their homeland and driven, as "displaced persons," to make new homes elsewhere; the Iron Curtain erected by Russia across Central Europe cut off industries from their markets and peoples from their food supplies; a great shortage of consumer goods endangered the stability of national economies; and when industries had to be reconverted to peacetime production in order to restore prosperity, the machinery was not available.

The measures taken to restore shattered economies did not always contribute to a general revival. Every country in Europe strove to maintain full employment by state action, believing that unemployment was a source of unrest. Nations were driven to continue wartime controls and restrictions, the same devices they had criticized when Hitler introduced them in time of peace. Import and export licenses and currency controls, while they protected national economies, hampered the revival of trade among countries that were becoming increasingly interdependent. Most important, the dollar shortage created by an imbalance of trade between the United States and the rest of the world made it impossible for other countries to free their economies. They did not have, and could not earn, the dollars they needed to buy food, manufactured goods, and machinery.

Despite all the emergency measures, Communism made gains in several countries in Western Europe, particularly Italy. Before the time of the Czechoslovak coup in 1948, it had already become amply clear that, in addition to the fear of a renewal of total war with all the terror weapons science could devise, there was a nearer danger that the free civilization of the West might fall from within without a blow being struck.

The defense against such an attack was not weapons, but economic aid—not the long-term economic aid contemplated in the United Nations Charter through the work of the Economic and Social Council and other agencies, but direct and immediate financial assistance. American Lend-Lease, having served its original purpose, had been cut off soon after the end of the war. In 1947, it was, in effect, revived in the form of Marshall Plan aid—that is, dollar grants to countries for the purpose of reviving industries and thus restoring the ability of nations to produce for themselves more of those goods they needed. The Marshall Plan was offered to the whole world, including Russia. The Soviets rejected the offer, however; and when their new satellite Czechoslovakia showed signs of accepting American aid, a word of warning from Moscow soon compelled a change of mind. The Marshall Plan thus became a bridge between the nations of the non-Communist world. It was an important weapon in the Cold War.

At the same time, on the military level, the western nations had given up hope of the creation of a United Nations force and had been compelled to devise a plan to counter Russian moves in Europe and elsewhere. The choice appeared to lie between appeasing the Russians or containing them. When Britain discovered that she could no longer bear the cost of maintaining forces in Greece, which had long been troubled by Communist partisans aided by the neighboring Russian satellites (Albania, Yugoslavia, and Bulgaria), President Truman, in the Truman Doctrine, announced on March 12, 1947, promised American aid to any country threatened by Communist aggression. American military aid to Greece and Turkey was the beginning of a policy of containment which was acceptable to many Americans largely because it contrasted with the appeasement policy that had led to war in 1939. It was a fundamental step away from the isolationism that had traditionally marked American foreign policy.

In furtherance of the policy of containment, the United States worked to achieve the full cooperation of the free states of Western Europe to resist further Soviet aggression. American aid under the European Recovery Program was based on the premise that the countries of Western Europe would increase their trade with one another by reducing the barriers that hindered it; and encouragement was given to plans to create a military union.

A lead was given in this direction in March, 1947, by the Dunkirk Treaty, by which the United Kingdom and France promised to aid one another if attacked by Germany. A year later this alliance was extended by the Brussels Treaty to include the Netherlands, Luxembourg, and Belgium; the new pact was to become operative in the event of attack by any power. Growing sentiment for a wider European union resulted in the creation in 1949 of the Council of Europe, which was believed by its supporters to be the first step towards a United States of Europe. While the reluctance of Britain to commit herself on the Continent chilled the hopes of a general political union within the immediate future, some progress was made towards a "functional" union by the European Coal and Steel Community and by the proposal of a European Defense Community. Exponents of "functionalism" believed that through these agencies European union would eventually be achieved and with it the strength, both military and economic, to resist the further encroachment of Soviet Communism. In the economic sphere, at least, such optimism was rewarded. In 1957 the members of the European Coal and Steel Community agreed to establish the European Economic Community, or European Common Market ("the Six"), and also the European Atomic Energy Community (Euratom). The aims behind the European Common Market were the progressive elimination of tariffs among member states, eventual free movement of labor and capital, wage standardization, and a common investment fund. By 1961, Great Britain, after temporizing with a Free Trade Area of other European states ("the Outer Seven"), had begun negotiations for entry into the Common Market, despite the complications that would result in her relations with the Commonwealth. But these moves for European unity were frustrated by President Charles de Gaulle, who feared Anglo-Saxon dominance in Europe and who sought to revive France's lost *gloire.*

Americans, underestimating the difficulties caused by deep-seated national antagonisms, were inclined to be impatient with the slowness of progress toward European union. Their own attitude toward foreign commitments had undergone a sharp change. In 1948, an attempt by the Russians to blockade Berlin—which, although inside the Russian zone of Germany, had been divided among all four occupying powers—was thwarted by a joint airlift. Then, in 1949, at the suggestion of the Canadian Prime Minister, Louis St. Laurent, nine "like-minded" countries in Western Europe and North America set up the North Atlantic Treaty Organization (NATO) to give each other mutual guarantees against aggression. The United States, Canada, and Britain thereby accepted military obligations on the Continent, and in 1950-52 a NATO army was organized, with an international general staff: Supreme Headquarters, Allied Powers in Europe (SHAPE). Countries like Norway and Belgium abandoned their traditional neutrality, which was no longer an effective shield. Later, in 1954, when France refused to ratify the treaties setting up the European Defense Community because of fear that it would be dominated by West Germany, a wider organization which included Canada, Britain, and the United States was quickly substituted.

Regional alliances of this kind had been provided for in the U.N. Charter; NATO was regarded by its supporters as an attempt to bolster the U.N.; and it differed from military alliances of the old type since it was based on similarity of ideology, had a permanent headquarters and secretariat, and attempted to include other forms of cooperation in addition to the strictly military. The Southeast Asia Treaty Organization (SEATO), formed in 1954 by the United States, Great Britain, France, Australia, New Zealand, Pakistan, Thailand, and the Philippines, was similar to NATO in that it includes non-military modes of cooperation. It was not comparable to NATO in military significance because its members were not obliged to take military action, no supreme headquarters or permanently allocated forces were established, and some of the most important of the non-Communist countries of Asia were not members. The danger of Communist aggression in the Middle East prompted the formation of still another regional defensive alliance in 1955, composed of Great Britain, Turkey, Pakistan, Iran, and Iraq and known as the Middle East Treaty Organization (METO). METO was weakened in 1958 by the withdrawal of Iraq after a nationalist revolt in that country, but in 1959, with the approval of the United States, it was to be reconstructed as the Central Treaty Organization (CENTO).

The necessity for such defensive alliances showed that the plan to build up a system of collective security on a universal scale had once again been checked. On the other hand, under pressure from outside, national states were being forced to enter into new forms of political, military, and economic alliance. The Soviet Union, while criticizing NATO from its inception as a mutual-aggression pact and as a breach of the U.N. Charter, eventually formalized its relationships with its satellites in the Warsaw Pact of 1955, which united the armed forces of the European Communist bloc under a Russian commander, Marshal Ivan Konev, and confirmed the stationing of Russian troops in the satellite countries.

Meanwhile, the Soviet strategic planners, foiled in Europe by NATO, had turned to Asia. Ever since the "liberation" of Southeast Asia by Japan, the colored colonial peoples had been restless. The Japanese conquest had caused the western powers to "lose face" in the East, and their traditional prestige was gone. Indonesia, after a struggle, achieved its independence from the Netherlands. In Malaya, where the population was about equally divided between Malays and Chinese, some of the latter, who had learned guerrilla tactics during the war of liberation, took to the jungle to fight against the re-establishment of British control. Similarly, in Indochina, Vietminh nationalists fought a partisan war against the French-supported Vietnam state. Both the Malayan and the Indochinese rebellions were avowedly Communist in inspiration. A decisive shift in the balance of power in Asia came when the Communist forces of Mao Tse-tung won the long civil war against the Kuomintang government of Generalissimo Chiang Kai-shek. In late 1949 the Nationalist government withdrew with its remaining troops to continue the struggle from the island of Formosa (Taiwan). Mao controlled the whole of mainland China. A Communist victory over all of East Asia seemed imminent.

French colonial rule in Indochina had been made easy in the past by the non-military character and the political apathy of the native peoples. Now, Communist Chinese support for the new nationalist aspirations of the Indochinese peoples, and for widespread Communist agitation in Indochina, turned Vietminh partisan activities into full-scale war against the French. The war was a heavy drain on French military strength, ultimately costing France more than 35,000 lives and more than twice the amount of money she had received under the Marshall Plan. An unwise French decision to fight a major action in 1954 to forestall a compromise settlement by crushing the Vietminh ended in the Dien Bien Phu

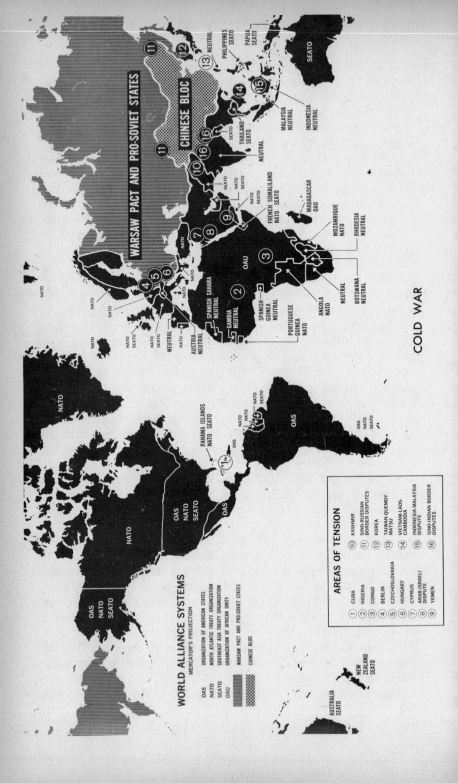

WORLD ALLIANCE SYSTEMS
MERCATOR'S PROJECTION

OAS — ORGANIZATION OF AMERICAN STATES
NATO — NORTH ATLANTIC TREATY ORGANIZATION
SEATO — SOUTHEAST ASIA TREATY ORGANIZATION
OAU — ORGANIZATION OF AFRICAN UNITY
WARSAW PACT AND PRO-SOVIET STATES
CHINESE BLOC

AREAS OF TENSION

1. CUBA
2. NIGERIA
3. CONGO
4. BERLIN
5. CZECHOSLOVAKIA
6. HUNGARY
7. CYPRUS
8. ARAB-ISRAELI DISPUTE
9. YEMEN
10. KASHMIR
11. SINO-RUSSIAN BORDER DISPUTES
12. KOREA
13. TAIWAN-QUEMOY-MATSU
14. VIETNAM-LAOS-CAMBODIA
15. INDONESIA-MALAYSIA DISPUTE
16. SINO-INDIAN BORDER DISPUTES

WARSAW PACT AND PRO-SOVIET STATES

CHINESE BLOC

COLD WAR

disaster, when the Chinese secretly supplied Ho Chi Minh with large numbers of artillery pieces. Although this battle has generally been regarded as a classic example of strategic bungling because faulty intelligence and planning exposed large forces in a weak position without hope of relief, the French chose to view it as a classic example of military valor and gave the baptismal name Dien Bien Phu to a class at St. Cyr.

The fall of Dien Bien Phu was rapidly followed by the withdrawal of the French and the creation of three independent states—Vietnam, Laos, and Cambodia—within the area. However, the continuance of Communist activity supported by Communist China led Secretary of State John Foster Dulles to contemplate the commitment of American military and naval units to the battle for this part of Asia. He was dissuaded by Great Britain, and instead the parties concerned, including Communist China, gathered at Geneva in April, 1954. As a result of their negotiations, a truce supervisory commission was established, with India as chairman and Canada and Poland as members, to arrange for the withdrawal of dissident elements from the territory effectively controlled by the Communist and non-Communist forces in Indochina. Serving officers of all three countries, under the direction of their respective departments of foreign affairs, undertook this arduous and difficult task. But a plebiscite to decide the political future of Vietnam, scheduled for 1956, was not held, and the country remained divided in two parts. Renewed Communist infiltration into South Vietnam and Laos prevented stabilization in this area of Asia.

The Communist technique of utilizing the nationalist aspirations of colonial peoples was particularly effective because those aspirations were very real and won sympathy among many liberal groups in the democracies. Frustrated nationalism is a grievance that can easily be exploited by Russia. It was usually possible to say that, where the colonial rebellions took place in countries close to the Soviet Union, there was certain to be Russian influence at work and perhaps a direct responsibility. But even nationalist upheavals remote from the U.S.S.R., like that in British Guiana in 1953 and the Mau Mau movement in Kenya, showed some signs of Communist inspiration. Others, like the one in Egypt, which threatened the security of the Suez Canal, and that in Iran, which deprived Western Europe for a time of much-needed oil, were not Communist-inspired, but they still helped the Russians because they struck at vital western interests. Communism was able to exploit successfully the strong feeling against domination that had been unleashed by the disturbances of World War II. And the nationalist sentiments of many non-Communist African and Asian states frequently led to the expulsion of western air and naval bases.

In 1950, Communist strategy in Asia passed from the stage of supporting colonial rebellions to that of aggression by satellites. On June 25, the Russian-trained North Korean army crossed the 38th Parallel and invaded South Korea, from which American troops had recently been withdrawn. This challenge to the United Nations was promptly accepted—largely because it happened that a U.N. team of observers on the spot immediately reported the facts of the case, and because the Russians had withdrawn their delegate from the Security Council and thus were not present to veto action taken in the name of collective security. But U.N. action was possible only because of the leadership given by President Truman and because the United States had troops in Japan that could be rushed to Korea. Thus the Cold War between Russian Communism and the free world broke out into large-scale military operations.

The extent of Russian complicity in the aggression by the North Koreans, or that of China, has never been clearly determined. Material aid was undoubtedly given on a large scale; and Russian officers, technicians, and pilots were reportedly seen by prisoners of war. The intervention of the Chinese Peoples' Republic in November, 1950, when United Nations troops neared the Yalu River, was disguised as the action of "volunteers." The pretense that both Russia and China were not legally involved was maintained.

Precedents for indirect war of this kind can be found in the Spanish Civil War, and also in the case of the Spanish "Blue Division," which fought with the Nazis against Soviet Russia during the Second World War. The use of such "volunteers," like the absence of formal declarations, is further evidence of that blurring of the legal boundary between peace and war that has been a feature of warfare in recent times.

On the United Nations side of the conflict, the legal line of demarcation between participants and non-participants in the Korean War was also not clear. Technically, all members of the United Nations were bound to support Security Council action taken under the charter. They could not legally be neutral. But the Charter did not lay down how much aid each member should give. The U.S.S.R. was actually aiding the enemy; and some other member nations limited their support to South Korea to expressions of sympathy, unfulfilled offers of material aid, or non-combatant units. Even among the member states that did send fighting units, the degree of participation varied greatly. Actually, next to the Republic of Korea, the United States provided the greatest proportion of the manpower to the United Nations forces in the Korean War and almost all the materiel. The British Commonwealth was represented by a division which included troops from Britain, Canada, Australia, and New Zealand. For various reasons, other nations provided less, and some none at all. Whatever the legal theory, there was no equality of effort in support of the U.N. cause. But the U.N. army, although commanded by an American, was an international army in which many nations fought. New problems of international military cooperation had to be faced and were overcome. A new international military spirit was evident.

Korea was not really an all-out conflict between the Communist and free worlds. In some ways, it was a limited war. Despite the fact that the principal belligerents came from outside the peninsula of Korea, the war was localized in that country. Although the United Nations had a monopoly of sea power, no general blockade of the Chinese coast was instituted. President Truman directed the U.S. Seventh Fleet to protect Formosa, but also required the Nationalists to stop air and naval operations against the Chinese mainland. Quemoy and Matsu, small islands uncomfortably close to the Chinese coast and still in Chiang Kai-shek's hands, became pawns in jeopardy. While the United Nations had superiority in the air, its airmen were forbidden to strike at the bases beyond the Yalu from which the enemy aircraft came. The military leaders thought that this was fighting with one hand tied behind their backs. When General MacArthur wanted to carry the war to China, he was dismissed by President Truman lest such action might lead to the beginning of a third world war.

The Korean War revealed certain important features in the development of warfare which must be mentioned. To the surprise of many people in the West, United Nations technical superiority in the air and in mechanized forces did not lead to an easy victory. To some extent this was caused by the fact that the war was limited —for instance, by the inviolability of Chinese territory. It was also due to the nature of the country. The tank, which had dominated battlefields in Europe and Africa a few years earlier, was less effective in the mountainous terrain of Korea. The chief Chinese asset was the great reserve of manpower. Hence Communist tactics were based on mass infantry attacks with little reckoning of the cost in lives. Because of the small material needs of the Chinese soldier, the "administrative tail" of the Chinese armies was very small, whereas their opponents, especially the Americans, required great supporting echelons.

Here was evidence of a return to the Napoleonic emphasis on masses of men and a departure from the modern emphasis on masses of materials. The big factories, which had challenged the primacy of the big battalions in the Second World War, were held in check in Korea. It is true that in the course of the war the Communists themselves came to place greater emphasis on matériel, but still in a Napoleonic manner. By secretly regrouping artillery, they could build up a local superiority of fire power greater than that of the United Nations forces. Another interesting development was that defense came to possess a decided advantage. It was a new type of defense-in-depth with complicated bunker systems dug through the tops of hills and mountains. Thus the strategy and the tactics of a localized limited war in a remote mountainous country, fought against an enemy that employed the mass army of the nation-in-arms, were very different from the strategy and tactics that had been used in World War II, a short time before.

The chief lesson of Korea was in the field of grand strategy. It showed that the United Nations—in effect, the United States—could not bear for an indefinite period the burden of a series of such wars of containment around the periphery of the U.S.S.R. In wars like the Korean affair, satellites could be used to wear down the morale and material strength of the nations of the free world, while Russian strength remained unimpaired. Several of the European countries, still struggling to revive their war-shattered economies, found that the task of building up strong military forces was beyond their means. Eventually, in 1967, Britain, perhaps the soundest of all financially, found that she could not meet her planned defense spending and decided to withdraw all her garrisons from east of Suez by 1975, amended a year later to 1971. Unless the United States once again filled the breach it seemed likely that the balance in Asia would swing in favor of the Communists.

Unusual circumstances, unlikely to recur, had enabled the United Nations to wage war against an aggressor in Korea. During the period of Dag Hammarskjöld's Secretary-Generalship (1953–61), a different concept of the United Nations had developed. He saw it as a neutral force, interposing itself between disturbed and chaotic areas of the world and the intense rivalries of the Cold War. Such an area was the oil-rich Middle East, torn by the bitter antagonism between Israel and its Arab neighbors. Here Hammarskjöld, expanding the functions of his office, took the diplomatic initiative and, by stationing observers in the area, did all he could to secure the "United Nations' presence" in order to prevent Middle East discords from pulling the major powers into conflict. His first efforts were nullified by the Israeli invasion of Egypt and the armed intervention by Great Britain and France that followed President Nasser's nationalization of the Suez Company in 1956. The fact that neither the United States nor the U.S.S.R. was directly involved enabled the Secretary-General (at the instance of Lester Pearson of Canada) to create the United Nations Emergency Force and insist upon a withdrawal of invading forces. Thus the United Nations' presence was re-established in a more substantial form, with its troops holding the lines on the Suez Canal temporarily, and in the Gaza Strip up to May, 1967. The strong Soviet reaction to the American and British intervention in Lebanon and Jordan which the General Assembly authorized testified to the wisdom of attempts to isolate the Middle East from the Cold War, but also showed how difficult was the role of the United Nations as peacekeeper if it had to act independently of the great powers. Few states, great or small, were sympathetic to the establishment of a permanent U.N. police force, and the Secretary-General's diplomatic initiative, though substantially increased by Hammarskjöld, was ultimately dependent upon the sufferance of the great powers and the maintenance of a consensus among the member nations in the General Assembly. His policy of strict impartiality tended to antagonize both power blocs in a polarized world, but at the same time was not sufficient in itself to ensure peaceful solutions.

The difficulties attendant upon U.N. action were clearly brought out in 1960 when Belgium suddenly conceded independence to a Congo that was not ready for it. Serious disorders occurred. The central Congolese government of Premier Patrice Lumumba requested United Nations assistance to maintain order because of the breakdown of the police and armed forces, the outbreak of tribal warfare, atrocities against Europeans, and the secession of Katanga and other provinces. An international force, composed chiefly of troops from African and Asian countries (with contingents from Sweden, Ireland, and Canada as well), was dispatched. The U.N. peace-keeping force's orders permitted it at first to use its weapons only in self-defense. Subsequently, its functions were hesitantly extended to the task of maintaining order. Even this was not enough. In effect, civil war raged in the Congo under the general supervision of the United Nations. The whole situation was complicated by the fact that the primitive conflicts of a tribal society were overlaid by the intrusion of the ideological conflicts of the Cold War.

The Secretary-General first called for the dismissal of the white mercenaries who were the mainstay of Katangan secession. When the security of the communications of the United Nations forces was endangered in Katanga, Hammarskjöld was drawn to attempt what the central Congolese government had failed to do—namely, to reduce the province by force and restore the Congo to its territorial extent at the time of the Belgian withdrawal. This military action shattered the consensus upon which the U.N. presence in the Congo rested. The Secretary-General was accused by his opposition of having broken the vital clause of the Charter that bars the United Nations from intervening in the domestic affairs of states. Thus, while the United Nations made strenuous efforts to keep the peace in the Congo, as in the Middle East, such limited success as it achieved was clearly possible only insofar as the two major powers were not directly embroiled. The onset of civil war in Nigeria in 1967 showed that even the most promising of the new African states was unable to overcome the bitter antagonisms inherited from tribalism in order to fashion a modern polity. In this case United Nations intervention proved unacceptable in what some members considered to be a domestic crisis.

In May, 1967, the hope that middle- and small-power forces under U.N. direction might prevent local incidents from precipitating actual war was seriously weakened when President Nasser, after boasting that he was ready to march on Jerusalem, demanded and obtained the immediate withdrawal of the UNEF from Egypt. The Israelis, after a pre-emptive strike against Arab air forces in Egypt and Jordan, drove through to the Suez Canal. They also seized all Arab territory on the west bank of the Jordan, as well as the Golan Heights in Syria. The inert war in the Middle East was reactivated when Israel refused to restore conquered territory without a guarantee that the Arabs would recognize her existence and give other assurances and benefits. Thus, U.N. peacekeeping lost credence: Canada, which had acted out of character in assuming a leading role in this work, began to doubt whether it would be possible again in the future. But attempts to solve Middle East problems by U.S.-Soviet negotiations, and then by four-power talks including France and Britain, were equally unsuccessful. American support for Israel and Russian aid to Nasser prolonged the conflict. The Arab-Israeli confrontation had become a lighted fuse connected to the total-war powder keg.

Meanwhile, there had been a direct confrontation between the two superpowers. In 1962, Khrushchev had tried to extend his military threat to the Americas by putting long-range missiles in Cuba, where Castro's Communist revolution had led to a clash with the United States. President Kennedy, in an eyeball-to-eyeball stance, enforced a quarantine against deliveries. He agreed not to invade Cuba if the missiles were withdrawn. In a separate but perhaps not unrelated move, he withdrew intermediate-range missiles from Turkey. It is possible that the Russians were influenced to back down by the realization that total war would annihilate both sides.

The Cuban confrontation marked a climax in the development of world Cold War bipolarism, which was, however, already disintegrating internally. Few powers except the United States and the Soviet Union had ever fully subscribed to the bipolar concept. In addition to the neutralists, many others had wanted to return to a multilateral system that would permit them greater freedom of action. Moreover, both of the power blocs had, at various times, revealed cracks in their fabric. The withdrawal of France from the NATO military command in 1966 was the most serious breach in the West. On the other side of the Iron Curtain, Tito's break with the Soviet Union in 1951 was followed by a mammoth rift between Russia and China in the 1960's, which was debated in ideological terms but really meant a return to the historic national dispute over boundaries and spheres of interest and influence. The Chinese had attempted to extend their proselytizing to the far parts of the world, including Africa, but only Albania gave them allegiance in East Europe. Although both China and the Soviet Union aided Communist regimes everywhere in conflicts with the West, there were reports of mutual obstruction, and, by the late 1960's, there was fighting on the Soviet-Chinese frontier. Meanwhile, China was racked by internal convulsions, which seemed to presage a return to a new version of the old warlordism.

Before the implications of these cracks in the Communist bloc were understood and appreciated in the West, the United States had

been sucked into direct involvement in the war in Vietnam. John
Foster Dulles, the American Secretary of State, had not liked the
Geneva settlement of 1954, which had partitioned the country, because he feared that it would lead to a Communist takeover of all
Southeast Asia, as small powers fell one after the other like domi-
noes. As a result, he had not encouraged the Saigon government to
hold the elections that, according to Geneva, should have taken
place within two years. The South Vietnamese government was,
therefore, long without a mandate from the people. Meanwhile, the
Communist government in North Vietnam, which had expected to
sweep the polls in the South because of Ho Chi Minh's popularity
as a liberator, resorted to terrorism, acting through local Viet Cong
agents. It soon gave direct military support. United States military
advisers with the Army of the Republic of Vietnam became increasingly involved in operations.

American officers had been critical of French conduct of the war
in Indochina on the grounds that orthodox tactics could not suppress guerrillas. They now found themselves faced with a similar
problem: widespread subversive activity supported by "volunteers"
who were North Vietnamese regulars, often infiltrating by use of
the Ho Chi Minh Trail through neutral Laos and Cambodia. As
American support increased, the North responded by employing
even larger formations, until President Johnson decided, in 1965, to
settle the matter once and for all by bombing the Trail, bombing
North Vietnam, and sending large ground forces to Asia.

The Vietnam conflict was a new kind of war, in which there was
no front line. The Viet Cong dominated most of the countryside
and was able to operate near, and even within, Saigon. Strategic and
tactical deployment had to be prepared to meet attack from any
quarter of the compass. These omnidirectional operations were
made necessary by the fact that the rural population of South Vietnam, normally politically apathetic, was largely disaffected, having
been won over either by coercion or by propaganda. The war had
to be won on a non-military front by gaining the allegiance of the
villages and ensuring them protection against Viet Cong terrorists.
For this purpose, the American trend toward the use of ever greater
force was not proportionately effective, because of the difficulty of
distinguishing between the enemy and innocent civilians. Furthermore, the government of South Vietnam, which was primarily responsible for the pacification of the villages, was an urban clique,

shot through with internal rivalries (especially between Catholics and Buddhists), rotted by corruption, and with little in common with the peasantry. The South Vietnamese army (ARVN) was also very slow to develop its capacity to bear the brunt of the fighting: it seemed to lack the spirit of the Viet Cong and the North Vietnamese. As a result, most of the heavy fighting was undertaken by the better-equipped and better-trained Americans, with the help of a few allies such as Korea, Australia, and New Zealand, countries that, for one reason or another, stood by them in this war. The Americans responded to the omnidirectional tactical problem by, among other things, introducing vast numbers of helicopters over the battlefield.

As in Korea, some of the most serious impediments were limitations on the conduct of the war imposed for what were called "political" reasons. As in Korea, the United States was fighting "with one hand tied behind her back." The chief restriction was that the United States could not use her full strength, especially in nuclear weapons, lest she precipitate total war. Another was that she felt she had to avoid bombing the Russian supply ships in the port of Hanoi. A third, rarely mentioned, was that she could not resort to invasion of the North to finish off the war, lest she provoke overt Chinese intervention, as in Korea. The military intervention and escalation in Vietnam were decided on by the President, with the sanction of the Tonkin Resolution, which gave Congressional approval to retaliation against North Vietnam and the Viet Cong for attacking U.S. forces; there had been no declaration of war. But the President's military advisers had apparently not realized, or at least had not made it clear that they were aware, that the restrictions they must accept were not merely a matter of "politics" but an inevitable result of recent developments in the nature of warfare, and that, with such restrictions, it was no longer possible to guarantee victory by the deployment of bigger and better armed forces.

Overoptimistic reports from the field at the behest of the Pentagon or the White House were often refuted by the news media, sometimes on the basis of statements by on-the-site television reporters, and by the course of events. The nadir of public confidence in the conduct of the war came when the enemy staged his biggest offensive, during the Tet holiday truce in February, 1968, immediately after the Pentagon had given the impression that the enemy's offensive capability had been broken. At home, the government and the military suffered a serious loss of credibility. American youth, subject to the draft but too young to have a say in policy, and concerned more about the morality of the war than about the possibility of an American defeat, had long made Vietnam one of the main planks in a widespread movement of campus protest. Many had defied conscription or fled the country. In addition to demanding a voice in university government and an end to racial discrimination, the students savagely attacked the "military-industrial complex." The United States had thus committed one of the cardinal sins of modern times: fighting a war when the nation had become deeply divided. Although a "silent majority" was said to disapprove of the immediate unilateral withdrawal that many young people demanded, most Americans had come to wish that the United States had never become involved. Furthermore, American intervention in Southeast Asia had alienated large segments of normally friendly opinion throughout the world.

Failure to achieve peace in Vietnam influenced President Lyndon Johnson to withdraw from the Presidential race at the end of his first term, and his successor staked his political career on ending the war without loss of face. Nixon's proposed solution was to "Vietnamese" the war. This policy seemed at first to promise success but ended with the complete collapse of the South Vietnamese Army. Had the original decision to hold back Communism at the border of North Vietnam by committing the United States to a war on the mainland of Asia actually slowed the spread of Communism? This question should be considered in relation to the possibility that the United States and the Soviet Union were, in fact, moving toward a relaxation of the Cold War tension.

20

Nuclear Strategy
and Arms Limitation

In today's shrunken world, war anywhere is likely to involve the whole world and possibly become total. An all-out war, with nuclear weapons, might destroy everything, including the very things it was designed to protect. Therefore, the first aim of the strategic planning of the super-powers should be to prevent war. The defense or advancement of national interests by military means ought to be relegated to an ancillary position. To put this in another way, many people now believe that the prevention of a nuclear war has become the most compelling national interest, greater in importance than the general aim of the preservation of freedom. The development of weapons capable of universal destruction has revolutionized the conduct of war and the ends of diplomacy and has made the discovery of a means of abolishing or controlling war a vital necessity. But a military strategy to prevent war is obviously very different from a military strategy to win a war, and no experience exists to show what such a strategy is like. In previous centuries, defense planning had often aimed at avoiding war. The avoidance of war because it might be an undesirable, ineffective, or uneconomic means of obtaining an end is, however, very different from the prevention of war lest it should prove to be totally destructive.

In these circumstances, proposals for the adoption of non-military, in place of military, measures have become attractive to many people. All such proposals, however, can be shown to depend on a degree of confidence and trust among nations that does not exist. Nothing has happened to suggest that an enemy would refrain from taking advantage of a nation's military weakness, as enemies have always done in the past. Therefore, while efforts must continue to attempt to resolve world problems by non-military means—that is, by measures to forestall subversion and economic dislocation, by plans for distributing capital aid and technical assistance, by negotiations to bring about reduction of armaments under mutually satisfactory guarantees, and by efforts to strengthen international agencies that will build confidence and guarantee peace—military planning must go on. In this respect the technical revolution in weaponry has brought no change. The grand strategist is faced, as he always used to be, with the necessity of maintaining a correct military posture, the right proportion of suitable .weapons, and the armed forces adequate for his purposes to the degree that his country can afford them without destroying its financial and economic stability.

It cannot be emphasized too strongly, however, that, in view of the danger that a conflict might become a suicidal total war, strategic planning continues to be necessary only because no means has been found to provide for national security and arrange disarmament.

In the 1950's and 1960's, a great strategic debate was waged in the West about the form that military planning should take to meet the problems created by these circumstances. The earlier stages of the discussion are well known. The first post-war attempts to plan a strategy to meet the Soviet threat, when that threat was backed only by conventional arms, were described as "long-term, patient but firm and vigilant containment" by an American diplomat and historian, George Kennan, in an oft-quoted anonymous article in *Foreign Affairs* in July, 1947. Military measures based on this concept proved effective in Europe in the NATO build-up. (Kennan later said that he had been misunderstood and that he had not proposed an attempt to encircle the Communist world.)

Containment was, however, found by the American people to be very costly in both life and effort in the case of Korea. Many American civil and military leaders therefore came to believe that another Korea was unthinkable. The most important leader among them, Secretary of State John Foster Dulles, embarked upon a deliberate program of "brink diplomacy"—standing firm to the brink of war—in Indochina and in the offshore islands of China, basing his policy on that American nuclear superiority which, it was argued, had been the really effective force in maintaining the peace in Europe in face of the Soviet advantage in conventional arms ever since the Second World War. Dulles used the phrase "massive retaliation." The theory of massive retaliation was that, though adequate protection against Soviet aggression could not be given around the whole perimeter of Soviet-dominated territory, aggression could be deterred by the threat of a devastating atomic attack from advanced bases surrounding the Soviet Union. It was believed that such an attack would probably never have to be delivered. Like the ancient principle of the "fleet-in-being," the bombardment potential would serve to restrain the enemy.

Obviously, to be effective, this deterrent posture depended upon a Russian appreciation that the U.S. nuclear advantage could and would be employed. Therefore, the deterrent was "credible" only as long as Strategic Air Command gave the United States an overwhelming advantage in the means of delivery. But hardly had this theory of deterrence been evolved than the Russians had the hydrogen bomb. The possibility at once arose that the West might have to accept severe punishment if ever it came to pass that the deterrent had to be used in reprisal.

Long before the U.S.S.R. had astounded the West by Sputnik and Lunik (revelations of a great and unexpected rate of technological development), strategic theorists had shown that there was an intrinsic weakness in Dulles' plan for massive retaliation. Overreliance on the deterrent weakened American capacity to fight anything except a total war and so left wide open the possibility of piecemeal aggression at various points on the perimeter of the free world. From about 1954, Liddell Hart was preaching that defense based on massive retaliation was unsound. In 1956 Henry Kissinger, in his book *Nuclear Weapons and Foreign Policy*, demonstrated the absurdity of relying on deterrence alone and argued that "limited warfare" was still possible. He went on to express a belief in the possibility of the tactical employment of nuclear weapons. Many other writers agreed; and professional soldiers pleaded for the build-up of conventional arms.

The general tenor of all these arguments was that the strategy of massive retaliation provided no military stance between the surrender of appeasement and the devastation of total war and that it therefore provided no room for the application of the art of diplomacy backed by reasonable strength. When the British White Paper on Defence in 1957 followed Dulles in its reliance on the nuclear deterrent, military men and civilian commentators promptly pointed out that Britain possessed colonial interests all over the world for which such a strategy was entirely inadequate. Lester Pearson, in a lecture at Harvard in 1958, also showed that the limitations of diplomacy in the nuclear age made the achievement of political ends much more difficult. All these contentions added up to the need for a more flexible weapons system. Some called this "graduated deterrence."

But there were those who suspected that Kissinger's belief in the possibility of a protracted limited nuclear war was not realistic, especially in Europe, and that any signs of a serious clash in so sensitive an area would bring on an all-out conflict. In fact, they contended, a small war anywhere might lead to total war by an "escalator" effect (rapid and successive moves by each side to resort to more powerful weapons). Some of these theorists feared, however, that an aggressor with nuclear weapons might wish to offset a feeling of inferiority in his armament, or to attempt to reduce the inevitable retaliation to an acceptable minimum, by striking the first blow. They argued, therefore, that pre-emptive war, or a first-strike or forestalling blow, was the only sound strategy. Pre-emptive war is only a shade different from preventive war. While the latter would forestall an attack expected ultimately, the former would forestall an imminent one. Soviet and western writers have each accused the other camp of resorting to this kind of reasoning since as early as 1954 or 1955.

Pre-emptive war was almost as abhorrent in the West as preventive war; but there was always a danger that some determined man might take advantage of the fact that a war once started could hardly be stopped. And the possibility of Russian pre-emptive action was claimed to be even greater, although in all logic it would seem that a power whose relative strength was on the increase would be *less*, not more, likely to take such a desperate step. However, fear and suspicion on either side might easily precipitate a conflict that nobody wanted. And many people were not sure that much-touted "fail-safe" techniques could guarantee against all accidents.

In view of these circumstances, and of the fact that the NATO system had produced close contact with consequent increased danger of friction in Europe, George Kennan, once the advocate of containment, put forward in the BBC's Reith lectures in 1957, "as a proposition for public examination," the idea that disengagement (he never actually used that word, but he meant it) might be both feasible and mutually acceptable in Europe. NATO spokesmen, including Secretary-General Paul Henri Spaak, retorted that the military strength of the alliance depended on depth for military maneuver and that the depth in Western Europe was already uncomfortably shallow. A military withdrawal would increase the difficulty, would abandon areas to infiltration that deterrence could not check, and would shake German morale. Disengagement thus threatened NATO. And the disruption of NATO had long been the Soviet Union's first goal in foreign policy. Nevertheless, many statesmen and writers continued to hope that disengagement might establish controlled disarmament in a small area and so become the first step toward general disarmament and an over all settlement.

With the rise of a Soviet nuclear capability equal or superior to that of the West—as General Pierre Gallois, a French expert on nuclear warfare, has said—what was once a counter-operation was now mutual destruction. Deterrence therefore came to have a new meaning. It was believed by Joseph Alsop and others that, as long as the capacity to retaliate with nuclear weapons could survive a first strike, the initial blow would not be worth delivering. The deterrent could, therefore, still deter. One result of this belief was the rise of a strange new hope—that neither side could contemplate a nuclear war and that a general thermonuclear war, barring accidents, was now unlikely. This so-called mutual deterrence, or balance of terror, might thus abolish total war. Some went even further. As has been shown above, any small war between great powers would, by escalation, be very likely to become a major conflict. It was therefore possible to argue that war might be almost entirely eliminated since no one would dare to take the first step if there was danger of escalation. However, this belief (or rather hope) only served in fact to underline a glaring weakness of deterrence—namely, that it provided no room for diplomatic maneuver short of all-out war. The balance of terror, if it prevented all-out war, might nevertheless shelter a steady nibbling away at local interests and at other values whose defense seemed not worth the risk of suicidal conflict.

In addition, there were also serious doubts about the alleged stability of the balance of terror. The calculation of the balance was complicated by being dependent on intelligence of the enemy's capability. History shows that such intelligence is often likely to be unreliable. The calculation was also clouded by disagreements among scientists about the precise effect of a nuclear strike, including the effects of fallout. Nobody could say with any certainty precisely how much devastation and dislocation would be caused and what would survive. Although there was talk of planning for "broken-backed warfare" so that the fight could be continued even after the spine of the state had been fractured by a nuclear attack, nobody had more than a vague idea what this involved. If, as it seemed, the stage beyond the nuclear strikes could not be planned for, was the prospect of a nuclear war itself an acceptable concept? And how was the power of deterrence affected? It was difficult, therefore, to make the calculations and dispositions that would carry the mutual conviction that all-out war was not worth the candle.

There were even more serious grounds for doubting the stability of the balance of terror. Increased vulnerability for the United States brought fears in Europe that the American deterrent might not be used in Europe's defense. Hence, first Britain and then France strove to develop an expensive nuclear deterrent capability. It was not difficult to imagine where this might lead. Out of forty countries that began nuclear research by 1960, it was said that twenty-seven would be capable of producing the bomb by 1965. This possible multiplication of national deterrents raised the specter of the "nth" nuclear power and of a much greater danger of accidental or irresponsible use. Naturally, there was a great volume of protest in Britain, and there were proposals from the opposition groups that she should reverse her policy and assume leadership of a "non-nuclear club." Some went much further and demanded the renunciation of nuclear arms by Britain, "unilaterally if necessary." Aimed in the first place at British nuclear policy, this movement mingled with the arguments of those who campaigned with Lord Bertrand Russell for the abolition of all western nuclear weapons on the grounds that the U.S.S.R. would have to follow suit. Some even said that, if this example failed, then it would be better to live under Communism than to die by the bomb.

For military men, such reasoning savored only of defeatism, or worse. Their own strategic dilemma was difficult enough. In January, 1959, senior American officers, testifying before a Senate investigating committee, told much about the nuclear weapons problem. Their evidence, excerpts from which can be found in *Survival,* the publication of the British Institute of Strategic Studies, partially drew aside the security veil covering American military thinking and the state of weaponry; but in doing so it revealed the fact that there were as grave disagreements among the experts as among the theorists. Admiral Arleigh Burke, Chief of the Naval Staff, said that America's capacity to fight a limited war had seriously declined in recent years. General Maxwell Taylor, of the Army, said that the U.S. now had more atomic weapons than were needed to deter. On the other hand, General Thomas S. Power, of the Air Force, claimed that it was necessary to have the capability to strike first "because if one does not have that capability an aggressor would be able to take this world away from us piece by piece," knowing that "as long as they do not strike us, we could never do anything about it."

General Thomas D. White and Secretary of Defense Neil McElroy told the Senators that, if one had the initiative, the American target would be enemy missile bases and airfields. But if the enemy delivered a surprise attack, the target for a retaliatory strike would have to be "the Soviet Union as a whole" because, while American capacity to retaliate would possibly be impaired, the enemy's attack would already be delivered or on its way, and therefore no longer worth hitting.

Speaking of the relative state of the development of weapons, General White revealed that the United States had, as yet, no aircraft on the so-called air alert (which theorists had been assuming since 1956) because the Soviets did not, as yet, have a great ICBM capability. The Secretary of Defense, however, stated that the liquid-fueled Atlas would be operational by June, 1959, and that Titan, also liquid-fueled, was not far behind. Furthermore, a "second generation" of rockets with solid propellants, notably the Minuteman, was being developed rapidly. Polaris, which could be fired from the security of submersion, would join the fleet in 1960. All this sounded optimistic. But, as if to counter it, a leak from a confidential session of the Senate Foreign Relations Committee alleged that Secretary McElroy had also told the Senators that, by 1960, the Soviet Union would have 100 more ICBM's than the United States. He described this situation as the "missile gap." It was evident that the strategic theorists had new problems with which to wrestle.

On February 1, 1959, in *The New York Times,* Hanson Baldwin redefined the two kinds of deterrence. Minimum, or finite, deterrence was capable of destroying cities; and infinite deterrence would destroy or substantially blunt the enemy's nuclear delivery capability. The United States was supposed to have a great "overkill" capability for the purposes of minimum deterrence, but probably had insufficient missiles and aircraft for infinite deterrence because that was geared to the size of the enemy's forces, always an inexactly known quantity. Finite deterrence, the *Times* military critic went on, could be just as credible to one's enemies (and, what was equally important, to one's allies) as infinite deterrence; but the deterrent force must be invulnerable. It was realized by this time that Russian advances in rocketry had jeopardized American IRBM (intermediate-range ballistic missile) and air bases in Europe; but it now came to be expected that when both sides had hardened their ICBM bases, then a real system of mutual deterrence would be achieved. This argument was developed at much greater length in Bernard Brodie's book *Strategy in the Missile Age*. Hardening of rocket bases, dispersion and concealment, and the use of mobile launching pads on land and on and under the sea were thus urgent priorities in order to attempt to make the deterrent credible and to stabilize the balance of terror. In this connection, many of America's friends and allies deplored the practice of publicizing in the press the location of bases under construction.

However, cities cannot be hardened or made mobile. Although the United States had long done as much, if not more, than most western countries to prepare the population for civil defense, such measures were not now enough. Finite, or passive, deterrence, which was all that many theorists believed possible, and which many thought would be enough to deter, was aimed at centers of populations. Such an attack could, of course, be aimed both ways. Hardening could not be the answer. Efforts to discover a means of defense against the missiles themselves—for example, by the use of counter-missiles—were therefore pressed. But this quest was hampered in the West by the "no-testing ban" to which the nuclear powers had adhered since 1958 as a result of public fear of the long-term effects of fallout in the form of increased incidence of leukemia and genetic maladjustments.

The search for a protective system precipitated further debate about the weapons most likely to be used, especially about the question as to whether manned bombers or missiles presented the more serious threat. It was understood that, well into the 1960's, even after American ICBM's became operational, the western deterrent would be mainly dependent on the manned bomber. The U.S. Air Force sought to obtain appropriations to maintain a great "air alert." At the same time there was controversy between the army and the air force about the type of defensive missile that should be developed. The army was working on Nike-Zeus and Nike-Hercules, primarily an anti-missile missile that fired up the expected trajectory of an incoming rocket. The air force, to supplement its manned pursuit planes, was developing Bomarc. Opponents claimed that Bomarc was useful only against the manned bomber that presented a dying threat. When an improved model of Bomarc failed in several successive tests, a public outcry against the weapon was strengthened by the prevalent popular belief that the manned bomber was virtually a thing of the past. Against this argument it was strenuously pointed out that an all-out enemy onslaught would obviously include *both* missiles *and* manned aircraft and that, even if no defense against missiles had yet been discovered, the secondary bomber attack against cities could be blunted or prevented. Canada—having chosen Bomarc, and having scrapped its own supersonic fighter, the Arrow, allegedly because the threat of the manned bomber was believed to be fading but probably also because the United States would not buy it—was caught in the eddies of this violent controversy because of her participation in NORAD, a joint American-Canadian air-defense command with tactical regions straddling the international border and radar-warning lines stretched across the north of the continent. Some of those who opposed the building up of North American defense against an air threat on the grounds that it could not be prevented were compelled to place an even greater reliance upon the strengthening of deterrent force protected by hardening and dispersal.

But one school of thought, represented in Oskar Morgenstern's book *The Question of National Defense,* declared that reliance on a retaliatory force alone was too vulnerable. Both the Soviet Union and the United States had for some years been working on the tactical use of atomic weapons. The first American experiments with "atomic cannon" produced artillery of several sizes, but all rather unwieldy for action in the field. Rocket propulsion was found to be more convenient. Weapons like Sergeant and Corporal, with a 200-mile range and a maximum 20-kiloton warhead (that is, the explosive capacity of 20,000 tons of TNT), were followed by close-support weapons, Honest John and Lacrosse, with a 30-mile range, and eventually by "fractional yield" weapons like Davy Crockett, a mortar with less than a one-kiloton warhead. But the development of weapons systems for tactical warfare did not eliminate either reliance upon the deterrent or the necessity emphasized by Morgenstern for more flexibility and diversity as applied to strategic weapons.

A British writer, John Grant, reviewing Klaus Knorr's *NATO and American Security* in *Survival* in November–December, 1959, carried Morgenstern's argument a stage further. He said that, because America had been immune from bombing during the war, Americans had been too slow in coming to grips with the problem of the vulnerability of weapons and the implications that ensued. He went on to say that, as a result, the U.S. posture had hitherto been based upon what the Russians could do, and not upon what they were likely to do. European nations, he said, not being able to match Russian strength, had long been prepared for greater risks. With the vast increase of the number of missiles in the armories of the two powers, it was doubtful whether America could long base defense policy on Russian capabilities exclusively. Here was another argument for the development of much greater flexibility in American policy as well as in weapons systems. These calls for flexibility may have been inspired by the fact that death had removed the great leader of a rigid policy, John Foster Dulles.

Pleas for flexibility were followed by a new look at deterrence. Malcolm Hoag, in *World Politics* in April, 1960, called the two kinds of deterrence "active" and "passive." Active deterrence, also called "counterforce" because it was aimed at the enemy's nuclear bases, was more ambitious and more aggressive than passive, or finite, deterrence. It assumed the possession of the strategic initiative and the capability of striking first. Indeed, one might also add that hardening and dispersal would obviously increase the size of counterforce needed for active deterrence. Hoag declared, however, that counterforce capability does not deter when it exists alone; indeed, because it menaces the Soviet missile capability, it actually invites an all-out enemy attack designed to eliminate it. Hence, the greater the counterforce, or first-strike power, the greater is the need for the simultaneous possession of a passive deterrent to discourage or deter an all-out Russian attack. "A truly active deterrent does not substitute for a passive one; on the contrary it increases the need for one." In other words, if, as many experts had declared was essential, enough missiles existed in sufficient quantities to create a credible first-strike capability against enemy missile bases, even though the size of this counterforce must be proportionately greater according to whether bases were hardened or dispersed, there must also be, at the same time, a proportionately greater need for other missiles poised to strike against non-military targets to act as a deterrent against a surprise blow against the counterforce. Clearly, what was needed, according to this view, was a kind of double deterrent, and the whole effect would be very costly even beyond current expenditures.

These proposals for infinite deterrence were countered by arguments on the other side. In articles in the London *Daily Telegraph* in November, 1960, Sir John Slessor reaffirmed the belief he had often expressed earlier, that deterrence could be effective as a stabilizing factor, but he now admitted that if deterrence aggravated beyond a certain point, it might defeat its own objective. Henry Kissinger interposed another thought along the same lines: "Stability is greatest," he wrote in *Foreign Affairs* in July, 1960, "when numbers [of nuclear missiles] are sufficiently large to complicate the calculations of an aggressor and to provide a minimum incentive for evasion, but not so substantial that they could evade control." A little later he again addressed himself to the possibility of limited warfare. In the Arms Control issue of *Daedalus* in the fall of 1960, he admitted that he now doubted the possibility of tactical nuclear warfare, but maintained that, while flexibility must be maintained by the build-up of conventional forces, nuclear weapons must always be held in reserve in the field because an orthodox war might suddenly become nuclear. Conventional forces, with tactical nuclear weapons held in reserve, and backed by a credible deterrent, would give harmony to the stabilizing process.

In *The Necessity for Choice,* published early in 1961, Kissinger also appeared to have accepted the views of Wohlstetter, Kahn, and others that, for maximum effectiveness, because a President would be unlikely to take so fateful a decision as the delivery of a missile strike, a retaliatory deterrent should be triggered to go off automatically when certain prespecified situations arose. At the same time Kissinger repeated the belief attributed earlier to Brodie —that when neither side can take out the other's hardened or concealed weapons systems, a first-strike will be impracticable. Nevertheless, automatic retaliation, with weapons that cannot be recalled by a "fail-safe" technique, as can the manned bombers of SAC, is a frightening prospect.

Herman Kahn, in *On Thermonuclear War,* pointed out that the last B-52's were to be produced in 1961. Missiles would still be expensive and few in number. A few bombers would be on 15-

minute ground alert, and the Ballistic Missile Early Warning System (BMEWS) would give about 15 minutes' notice of attack. In 1961 the U.S., U.S.S.R., and Britain were entering upon the third year of the moratorium on testing and, while no one could tell whether this had been scrupulously observed by the Soviets, America's weapons development and defensive missile programs had been hampered. Hardened bases, Minutemen on rail cars (an idea later abandoned), and Polaris fired from below the sea had, however, been planned to provide relative invulnerability to the deterrent. A system of invulnerable mutual deterrence thus seemed about to develop that would last until one side or the other made a breakthrough, perhaps by the development of an effective antimissile missile, or perhaps by the use of space vessels for attack as well as reconnaissance. During this period, with or without a missile gap (and there was doubt that one had existed in 1959), the world would live on the edge of the balance of terror. To counter those who, fearing that a thermonuclear war might destroy civilization, would prefer unilateral disarmament and even surrender, Kahn produced a statistical appraisal of the destructiveness of missiles in order to show that a "small" nuclear war, as compared to a major one, could be survived. This argument was developed chiefly to give the necessary morale to civilian populations and to fighting services to stand resolute in the face of the possibility of thermonuclear war: it was reasonable to believe that only by such resolution could war be avoided. Kahn's argument probably had the opposite effect.

But several writers, not merely those infected by the unilateralist virus, also warned against drawing any comfort from the hope of finding stability in a balance of terror. John Strachey, a former British Labour Secretary of War, declared that it is too optimistic to believe that war can abolish itself through the advent of thermonuclear abundance. War cannot abolish itself. All that nuclear weapons have done is to give mankind a choice between abolishing war or being abolished by it. War is only a means of making decisions between completely sovereign states, and it will continue to exist until some alternative means is discovered. Such an alternative presupposes the end of absolute national sovereignty.

Similarly Walter Millis, reviewing Kissinger's *Necessity for Choice,* declared that Kissinger had proved, without so intending, that man is faced with a paradox that cannot be resolved under the existing framework of international relations. "No promising exit exists from the frightful predicament into which giant weapons have plunged our world—not, at any rate, under the concept of international relations which is all that Kissinger, like most of the rest of us, have been able to bring to them."

Kahn also alluded to the immense difficulty of keeping the peace in the nuclear age. He did not deny that a major nuclear war might destroy civilization or humanity. And in a later article he went so far as to say: "It is quite possible that even a 'bad' world government is preferable to an accelerated and uncontrolled arms race. It is to be hoped that this last will not be the only choice available."

Quite apart from the doubts held about the stability of the balance of terror, there were differences of opinion about the ability of the Western world to support the existing financial burden of a series of flexible weapons systems ranging through those for unconventional, conventional, and nuclear forces. C. J. Hitch and R. N. McKean, in *The Economics of Defense in the Nuclear Age,* said that there must be an attempt to maximize the attainment of objectives within the limits imposed by the available resources. But James R. Schlesinger, in *The Political Economy of National Security* (1960), declared that there must be no "artificial" limit to defense spending for national security. Budgets must not be based on premonitions of taxpayer resistance. Comparisons with Russia's defense spending showed that the United States, with its vastly greater GNP, could afford to spend far more freely on defense than it had yet been called upon to do.

It would appear that all that the military strategists had secured was a temporary respite from a devastating holocaust, during which time western economies would be strained by an ever-increasing financial burden and in which the odds of an all-out war in the not-too-distant future were very great. During this same period of armistice, Cold War aggression could continue and would be difficult to counter. The only conceivable strategy for national security in such a period was the maintenance of both deterrent and other forces which, however, made the respite unstable and uncertain.

The development of opinion on grand strategy in the West was paralleled by a similar discussion in the Communist world, though debate there was less public (at least until the disagreement between the U.S.S.R. and Communist China) and was connected intimately with Marxist-Leninist theory. During the period when the United States held a monopoly of atomic weapons, Soviet military thinkers refused to concede that the new weapons had changed warfare in any fundamental way. The five "permanently operating factors" of warfare that Stalin had laid down in 1942 (stability of the rear areas, high military and civilian morale, mass of men and materiel, quality of troops and weapons, and ability of commanders in the field) were still upheld. The underlying assumption was that success in war lay with the superior political and social system, and therefore, because of the inherent superiority of the socialist structure of the Communist states, the U.S.S.R. would always win. War was visualized as a war of attrition, in which the entire resources of states were pitted against each other in a protracted struggle. Surprise attack was therefore of negligible importance, and the failure of Hitler's invasion of Russia seemed to bear out this position; the fact that surprise attack with nuclear weapons might be decisive without social and political factors coming into play was denied.

A major revision in Soviet military thought was one of the elements in the "thaw" that followed the death of Stalin. In November, 1953, Major General Nikolai A. Talensky, the editor of *Military Thought,* was permitted to publish an article specifically rejecting not only the permanently operating factors of Stalin, but also the doctrine that because the Soviet Union was socialist, it would inevitably win in any struggle with capitalism. Instead, Talensky argued that the principles of war were essentially identical for East and West. Though Talensky was removed as editor of *Military Thought* in 1954, his position was ultimately accepted. In the same publication, in early 1955, Marshal Rotmistrov reaffirmed Talensky's arguments, ruled out the war of attrition as unlikely in the nuclear age, and pointed to the dangers of a nuclear surprise attack. By 1957, Premier Khrushchev was arguing that nuclear fire power was the key to victory in any war, and that the large land area of the U.S.S.R. made it less vulnerable in the event of a nuclear war. Thus the Soviet Union committed itself to the doctrine of massive retaliation, while retaining substantial conventional forces of all arms. Warfare between the Communist and capitalist worlds was no longer an eventuality that a Marxist could look forward to with confidence in the outcome. "War would be a calamity for all the peoples of the world," Premier Khrushchev said in February, 1960, and a month later he remarked that "bombs will not distinguish between Communists and non-Communists." As early as 1956, Khrushchev told the Twentieth Congress of the CPSU that despite long-held doctrine, war between Communism and capitalism was not "fatalistically inevitable." While not ruling out the possibility of war, the Soviet leader favored a policy of "peaceful coexistence" between East and West, and repeatedly asserted that Communism would ultimately triumph as the result, not of a final, apocalyptic war, but of the steadily growing economic strength of the Communist bloc.

These striking revisions in Communist doctrine, prompted to a large extent by the implications of the new weapons, did not meet with favor from the Soviet Union's major partner, Communist China. Because, in the Communist world, ideology is closely related to action, the ensuing debate between Moscow and Peking was of fundamental importance. The degree to which advances in Soviet weapons development had changed the power balance in the world was apparently at the root of the division, although Soviet leaders were also cautiously critical of what they regarded as extremism in Chinese domestic policies, such as the commune program. Chinese leaders appeared to believe that the balance of nuclear power had altered decisively in favor of the "socialist camp," and that this development made a forward, or "brinkmanship," policy feasible to advance the Communist cause in those parts of the world emerging from the colonial stage, because the West was now too weak to counter. A spokesman for Mao Tse-tung, writing in *Red Flag* in March, 1960, positively reaffirmed the ultimate inevitability of war with "predatory imperialism" and took a traditional Marxist view of the outcome: "If the imperialists should insist on launching a third world war, it is certain that several hundred million more will turn to socialism."

Prospects of prevention of nuclear war lie in the evolution of a supranational authority or world government to control relations among states, in the achievement of arms control or limitation of arms, in the maintenance of a stable military and political balance in the world, or in some combination of these factors. All have attracted support or enlisted hopes; but the difficulties in the way of each are great, and, in the case of world government, presently insuperable.

Those who hoped in 1945 that the United Nations would provide the framework for world government have been bitterly disappointed, for the United Nations has become the cockpit of conflicting sovereignties, a world forum for the expression of national or bloc policies, and an instrument to be manipulated in the power struggle. Though none of these functions is without its value in informing and shaping world opinion and in affecting materially the course of events, the United Nations has in fact become a battleground of the Cold War rather than the resolver of it. The wartime coalition institutionalized in the Security Council broke up with the emergence of profound disagreements between the Soviet Union and the western powers; and the veto power was then used, chiefly by the U.S.S.R., which was in a minority position on the Security Council, to defend national interests or the interests of associated states against the possibility of collective action through the United Nations. The paralysis of the Security Council as the result of the Russian exercise of the veto was seen in such postwar crises as the Greek border problems of 1946–47 and the Soviet–East German blockade of Berlin in 1948. The response to the Soviet veto by the western powers, led by the United States, was to take remedial action outside the United Nations—as exemplified in the Truman Doctrine and the Berlin airlift. Indeed, actions like these, and the whole structure of regional alliances, merely confirmed that the United Nations was not a workable instrument of collective security.

In 1950, the United States gave the lead in an attempt to bypass the veto through the Uniting for Peace resolution, which, in effect, proposed that a two-thirds majority of the General Assembly could recommend collective action on a voluntary basis, thus supplementing the Security Council as the agency for the operation of the principle of collective security and permitting the United States and its allies to continue using the United Nations to further western policies. The success of this constitutional innovation was relatively short-lived. Since 1950, the number of member nations has been swelled by the addition of many new and highly nationalistic African and Asian states, most of them with neutralist and anti-colonial outlooks, intent upon using the United Nations to further these interests. The Assembly has become, as Lord Avon complained, a place where "nations are anxious to talk but not to bear much of the burden." When there is no assurance of collective action, states fall back on national strategies of national interest. Hence, as in the case of the forcible absorption of Portuguese Goa by India in 1961, the western powers discovered that neither the Security Council nor the General Assembly was available as an instrument to deal with aggression. Even when strong support was secured for Assembly resolutions, as in the condemnation of the Soviet Union for crushing the Hungarian revolt in 1956, in the several indictments of the Union of South Africa for its apartheid policy, in the attempt to discipline Rhodesia for refusing universal suffrage, or in efforts to end civil war in Nigeria and renewed conflict in the Middle East, disapproval by the United Nations was ineffective. Far from realizing the aspirations of some of its founders, the United Nations has increasingly become an accurate mirror of a divided world.

Negotiations on the subject of disarmament, limitation of arms, and arms control have been going on intermittently since the end of World War II, although it has often appeared that negotiations have had less to do with arms control than with the political objectives of the participants. As early as 1946, at the time of the establishment of the United Nations Atomic Energy Commission, Bernard Baruch, the American representative, proposed an international atomic-energy authority for the benefit of all peoples, an end to the manufacture of atomic weapons, international inspection, and the destruction of existing stocks of atomic weapons as soon as an acceptable inspection system had been instituted. The Soviet Union objected that the Baruch proposal meant conceding to the United States a perpetual monopoly of the knowledge required for assembling atomic weapons, thus posing a perpetual danger to Soviet security. The Soviet Union, from that time, consistently maintained that inspection is an intolerable invasion of national sovereignty and that, moreover, no satisfactory inspection system has yet been devised. After the U.S.S.R. acquired its own nuclear weapons, both atomic powers became concerned with the danger of surprise attack and, while continuing to affirm their interest in nuclear disarmament, put forward plans to limit the possibility of surprise. To the Russians, American bases on the perimeter of their territory constituted the greatest menace, and they called for American withdrawal. The United States countered with President Eisenhower's "open skies" proposal of 1955, which would have permitted mutual aerial inspection. The Soviet Union rejected this proposal. The United States, however, secretly inspected the U.S.S.R. from the air. This violation of Soviet air space provided Premier Khrushchev with the pretext for scuttling the summit meeting of May, 1960, after an American U-2 reconnaissance aircraft was shot down over Russian territory.

Negotiations toward a ban on the testing of nuclear weapons moved very slowly. At Geneva in 1959 some progress was made when the Soviet Union accepted as satisfactory the technical procedures for the identification of atomic explosions put forward by the United States. Subsequently, however, American experts began to fear that their procedures were inadequate for the detection of underground nuclear explosions, which could not be distinguished from natural disturbances. Between 1958 and 1961, the Soviet Union, the United States, and Great Britain observed a *de facto* suspension of tests; but because of fear that Russia was testing secretly, President Eisenhower withdrew the American moratorium on testing in 1959. Beginning on September, 1961, the Soviets exploded a series of massive nuclear devices in the atmosphere. The United States immediately resumed testing underground.

Soviet propaganda has attributed the repeated failure of arms-control talks to the aggressive designs of western imperialists and militarists; the western response has been that arms control is incompatible with Soviet plans for world conquest and Soviet suspicion of any inspection of its territory. But behind the propaganda, and behind the mutual accusations of insincerity and the political fencing that have constituted so large a part of these negotiations and contributed to the air of unreality that surrounds them, there are genuine and serious obstacles to agreement. It will be remembered that one of the chief obstacles to the achievement of disarmament between the two world wars was inability to overcome the technical problems involved. The additional problem of nuclear weapons, and the question whether their control should be negotiated apart from or together with control of conventional weapons, prevented the post-1945 discussion from reaching an exchange of views on the technicalities of control of conventional weapons. If trust existed between the power blocs, technical impediments to agreement could be overcome; but it is precisely because mutual trust does not exist that agreement has become vitally necessary to a world menaced by nuclear war.

Were nuclear disarmament actually to be achieved without the resolution of the political and ideological differences that divide the world, the likelihood of war, even though only "conventional" war, would be increased. But nuclear disarmament appears unlikely, or at least extremely difficult; Pandora's box, once having been opened, can hardly be closed. The destruction of all nuclear weapons would not destroy the knowledge of how to make them, and the temptation to resort to their manufacture and use in any limited or conventional war would also remain. Nuclear technology for peaceful purposes, now becoming a part of the economy of many nations, is the basis of a military nuclear potential as well. No inspection system yet devised is foolproof enough to satisfy responsible planners that evasion is impossible. In a non-nuclear world, the possession of even a small number of nuclear weapons would give mastery, or at least great power, to the evader. On these points, the United States and the Soviet Union are in agreement. There is at present no inspection system secure enough to override their mutual distrust, though the use by both superpowers of reconnaissance satellites which cannot be intercepted seems to promise some amelioration of suspicion.

Arms control must, however, rest ultimately upon the power to impose sanctions for evasion. In the past, the breaking of an arms-control agreement by one state could be punished by the resumption of the arms race by other parties to the original agreement. But this would scarcely be an adequate sanction against a country that had secretly stockpiled nuclear weapons. In such a situation, it is the evader who would be in control, having used arms limitation to alter decisively the military balance. The only possible check on such evasion, a central world body equipped with a nuclear deterrent, does not exist at present. Nor does there appear to be development toward such an authority.

However, the arms race involves weapons other than hydrogen bombs and states other than nuclear powers. Thus it has been argued, for example by Philip Noel-Baker in *The Arms Race* (1958), that only general and comprehensive disarmament, proceeding in stages and commencing with an arms freeze at existing levels, can meet the problems of the present state of international society. Such a scheme would rest upon initial, and universal, acceptance of the level at which armaments are to be frozen—or, in other words, upon universal agreement that the present distribution of power in the world is satisfactory. It is the unlikelihood of such agreement that has permitted the Soviet Union, from time to time, to issue grandiose proposals for total disarmament within a limited period, such as that made by Premier Khrushchev at the United Nations in 1959. Such proposals, made in the full glare of publicity, have had propaganda value for the Soviet Union. They have not furthered the cause of disarmament.

Pending agreement upon some measure of arms control, prevention of nuclear war must continue to depend upon the maintenance of a balance of political and military forces between East and West. This balance is precarious because there are many conceivable ways in which it could be upset. A new weapon, a new defense system, a new method of delivering an attack, or any similar radical innovation might disrupt the balance by giving a decisive edge to one side. Such an edge, being of necessity temporary, might tempt the power possessing it to exploit its advantage. Fear caused by the revelation in 1967 of Soviet deployment of antiballistic missiles to defend vital areas of the Soviet Union led Secretary of Defense Robert McNamara to announce the installation of a "thin" antiballistic-missile defense system, allegedly designed to protect vital areas against Chinese attack. Both sides were also developing new forms of weapons, which would make interception infinitely more difficult and costly, if not impossible: the Soviets, their Fractional Orbital Bombardment System, using satellites; the Americans, their Multiple Independent Re-entry Vehicle, carrying several warheads.

The relative simplicity of the present nuclear balance would be infinitely complicated were the nuclear club expanded to include the other states that are now capable of manufacturing nuclear weapons. It has been argued that the balance of mutual deterrence will be stable because a rational government would never resort to nuclear warfare. Such an assumption is invalid. Nuclear war could occur by accident—through a technical breakdown, by the escalation of a limited war, or by some other mischance or miscalculation. It is remotely conceivable that in certain circumstances—for example, a radical shift in the political alignment of states—a rational government could consider a nuclear war the lesser of two evils. "Rational" governments must be assumed to be composed of "strategic" men—men deeply knowledgeable in the attitudes and probable reactions of their opposite numbers in the other camp, deeply versed in diplomacy and in the interpretation of the complex currents of international events, not prone to sudden excesses of hope, fear, or despair, and acutely conscious of the probable consequences of their actions or of their failure to act. To rely solely upon the rationality of governments is to trust that such "strategic" men will be thrown up by the palace politics of the Kremlin and by the capricious democratic processes of the West—surely a vain hope.

But the first essential step toward eliminating the possibility of world destruction must, obviously, be achieved by cooperation between the Soviet Union and the United States. In 1963, it had been found impossible to obtain agreement to a complete test-ban agreement, because Britain and the United States were unwilling to accept the Soviet claim that underground tests could be adequately monitored by national, rather than international, inspection systems. It was, therefore, necessary to proceed toward the ultimate objective in a piecemeal fashion. In December, 1966, the United States and the Soviet Union reached agreement on eliminating war and testing from outer space, which was to be kept open to all nations for peaceful purposes. This was followed in 1968 by an agreement about the rescue and return of astronauts and objects launched into outer space. There was also the widespread feeling that the seabed should not be used for military purposes. Finally, on July 1, 1968, a Treaty on the Non-proliferation of Arms was presented for the signatures of all nations. On the same day, President Johnson announced an agreement with the Soviet Union to discuss the limitation and reduction of offensive strategic nuclear weapons and antiballistic missiles.

This decision to reopen negotiations leading toward general disarmament had been furthered by the earlier limited-arms-control agreements and by virtual abandonment of the Soviet propaganda stand for immediate "general and complete disarmament." But the most important factor forcing the super-powers to return to the conference table was the acceleration of the arms race. Not merely did the Soviet FOBS and the American MIRV once again raise the specter of a preventive total war, but the cost of these weapons— and, even more, of the defensive systems they would soon make obsolescent—had reached unacceptable proportions. In the world as a whole, military expenditures had risen steadily from 1951. The U.S. Arms Control and Disarmament Agency revealed in 1969 that, in the four years from 1964 through 1967, making allowances for inflationary costs, the total world outlay had grown by 24 per cent, more rapidly than world population. In the first half of the twentieth century, the world had spent $4 trillion in wars and preparation for wars. Although military expenditure thus so far remained at a fairly constant 7 per cent of world GNP, this represents 50 per cent more than was spent on public education and three times as much as was spent on public health.

Military expenditures in the United States run at about 9 to 10 per cent of GNP and are rising. Military expenditures in the underdeveloped countries are a little lower, in proportion to GNP, than those of the super-powers. But they constitute about twice as much as those countries received in international aid, and they are a serious drag on development. Meanwhile, pressing economic and social problems are being allowed to rot civilization: urban decay and environmental pollution increase steadily, while transportation, education, housing, medical care, hospitals, and social welfare suffer because of the diversion of wealth for military preparations. The U.S. contribution to international aid (which already included a large proportion of military aid instead of the economic aid underdeveloped nations need to obtain a better life) has been cut by more than half. The United States put man on the moon in 1969 but neglected more immediate problems on earth. Undoubtedly, the Soviet Union is experiencing the same frustration at the possibility that military expenditures might increase further and destroy all hope of maintaining the economic and financial health of the Soviet state. This was a contributory factor in making possible the Strategic Arms Limitation Talks (SALT), which opened in November, 1969. Nevertheless, the road to international control will be long and arduous.

The likelihood is that both West and East will continue to prepare themselves for a war they do not wish to fight, while carrying on the power struggle by other means and with the now-familiar accompaniment of nuclear threats and counterthreats. War now appears capable of destroying society, yet the means adopted to avert it consist in building up the means to wage it. In such a world, for the western powers to keep the middle way between catastrophe and capitulation, while meeting the challenge of the Communist powers, will put to the ultimate test their social discipline, strength of will, political aptitude, and all the values implicit in the western tradition.

21
Détente and Derangement

Beginning in the late 1950's, signs had multiplied that the two super-powers were seeking means for the achievement of a less rigid and less aggressive posture toward each other than had obtained during the height of the Cold War. Détente, an easing of the tensions of the Cold War, came about a decade later primarily because, in the shadow of nuclear balance, it was mutually desirable for the United States and the Soviet Union to lower the risk of nuclear war. This was not the result of any basic alteration in the fundamental clash of ideology and objective; indeed, neither power abandoned the prosecution of its interests and ambitions in many parts of the world. Nevertheless, signalized by a series of agreements placing restrictions of various kinds upon nuclear arms, there was a distinct slackening of intensity in their competitive relationship. In 1959 nuclear arms were barred in the Antarctic region; in 1963 the major nuclear powers agreed to a partial test ban; and in 1967 treaties were negotiated to prohibit the use of nuclear weapons in outer space. Other factors contributing to the climate of détente were the 1967 decision of twenty-one Latin American countries (out of a possible twenty-three, Cuba and Guyana abstaining) to establish a non-nuclear area, the signing of a nuclear non-proliferation treaty in 1968 by eighty-three countries (more than fifty other nations chose not to adhere to the treaty), a U.N. General Assembly Resolution in 1969 to declare ocean seabeds to be outside national sovereign jurisdiction, and the 1972 adoption of a treaty by thirty-one states to outlaw biological warfare.

The super-powers had come to realize that they had a mutual interest in limiting the expansion of the nuclear club, in reducing the possibility of nuclear accidents, and in preventing the onset of war with each other through misunderstanding or miscalculation. Neither the Soviet Union nor the United States stood to gain by the poisoning of the earth's surface, atmosphere, or oceans, and both wished to avoid repetition of dangerous confrontations like the Cuban missile crisis of 1962. The "hot line" between the White House and the Kremlin, first established in 1963 and improved in 1971, was a recognition of this understanding. So was the 1972 agreement on procedures to minimize the effects of nuclear accidents on the high seas. These efforts reached a climax in the Strategic Arms Limitation Talks (SALT). In 1972 the two powers agreed to restrict antiballistic (ABM) sites in each country to two, and the number of possible launchings from them to one hundred. In 1973 they agreed to continuing consultation on the development of strategic weapons, looking ahead to the need to renegotiate SALT I upon its expiration in late 1977. In 1974 ABM sites were reduced to one in each country. The SALT agreement had brought a temporary limitation upon the number and types of offensive strategic weapons deployed by the U.S.S.R. and the United States and a start toward limitation of defensive weapons.

These developments might seem to suggest a rapport between the two super-powers that promised hope of a more stable relationship resting on the maintenance of a nuclear balance and on the avoidance of clashes in peripheral areas or over less important matters. This hope was carried further by President Nixon's visit to China in 1972, a dramatic move that signalled a diplomatic about-face for the United States. Arrangements were made in Peking for the exchange of representation, but not for full diplomatic recognition; and both Japan and the U.S.S.R. were kept advised of developments and assured that there would be no deterioration of old alliances or new harmonies. As the Chinese and the Russians were at odds, however, the United States had to take especial care not to revive the Cold War in a new form. But continued recognition of the Nationalist Chinese regime in Formosa made it unlikely there would be an alignment with Red China against Russia.

Détente was clearly an advance from the Cold War, yet something quite different from entente. Considerable mutual suspicion remained. Progress toward the second round of SALT talks was therefore slow. The U.S.S.R. had been permitted to catch up in the number of nuclear weapons, but it had always had an advantage in the delivery weight of individual missiles, and therefore a seeming edge. On the other hand American weapons were more accurate. Multiple Independent Re-entry Vehicles (MIRV), developed first by the United States, helped to strengthen the U.S. side of the balance but greatly complicated the problems both of defense and of arms control. On each side military leaders suspected that arms-control negotiations were being used by the opposing side to secure an advantage; the U.S. Congress resolved that further steps in SALT must ensure real parity. SALT I had in fact been followed by an increased effort in both Russia and the United States to develop weapons not restricted by the agreement; for example, the Soviet Union, possibly spurred by its loss of face in the Cuban confrontation, developed multi-headed weapons (that were not independently targeted) much faster than had previously been expected. In some respects SALT I had increased, rather than diminished, the competitive nuclear arms race.

Cultural exchanges and the negotiation for a trade treaty to give the U.S.S.R. most-favored-nation status in the United States tariff system broadened the basis of détente somewhat further. Then in 1974 President Ford, meeting Soviet leader Brezhnev in Vladivostok, obtained what he claimed was a breakthrough in progress toward a SALT II agreement, a proposed permanent ceiling on the stockpiles of nuclear weapons. But when Congress qualified the trade treaty by tacking on it an amendment to require Soviet relaxation of restrictions on the emigration of Jews, the Soviet Union withdrew. Yet Soviet leaders emphasized that rejection of the trade treaty did not mean the end of détente. Clearly, progress toward the establishment of better relations as a basis for reducing the possibility of nuclear war was still possible, though difficult. Faced with a close presidential election in 1976, Gerald Ford was hampered in his negotiations with the Soviets. Domestic political opposition in the United States, and the tendency in both countries to be suspicious of the other's military-industrial complex, portended long negotiations which some observers thought might take years to complete. For instance, President Carter's first attempt to cope with the problem failed when the American position was stated in advance of negotiations.

In two areas in particular the consequence of the continuance of suspicion between the two super-powers showed the limitations of the détente. Military budgets had not been reduced as a result of the SALT I agreement: there were stepped-up research and development programs. Budgets in fact continued to grow. In the United States concentration of the American military effort for the war in Vietnam had been at the expense of the strategic arms sector. The end of the war, therefore, did not lead to the reduction in military spending that the public expected. Appropriations were increased to make up for deficiencies and to replace lost, worn-out, and outmoded equipment. Signs of an increase of the Russian military and naval presence in various parts of the world were offered as evidence of the continuance of the Cold War spirit. In particular the growth of Soviet naval power in the Indian Ocean by use of the Berbera naval base in Somalia, and in the eastern Mediterranean based at Egyptian and Syrian ports, was countered by American plans to establish a naval base on a British island in the Indian Ocean, Diego Garcia, and at Bahrein in the Persian Gulf. At the same time American hard-liners produced figures of the number of individual Russian ships opposing the Sixth Fleet to suggest that it was being outmatched. The growth of the Soviet underwater fleet also seemed sinister. Some defense specialists therefore argued that détente was a snare. They stressed the need for continued vigilance.

The Vladivostok agreement had brought renewed attention to manned bombers. It also limited missile capability on both sides to equal numbers of delivery vehicles (2,400) and MIRV missiles (1,320). But the Soviet Union was said to possess 308 vehicles that had a much greater "throw weight" than any American weapon. Mated with MIRV missiles, these could provide a very great advantage in the number of deliverable warheads. Hence, as the United States could not under the agreement develop a new delivery vehicle, the proposed equivalence required by Congress in future SALT talks could in fact be reached only if the United States were to produce a greater throw-weight by developing up to the approved numerical limits one or all of the MX missile (an improvement on Minuteman), the projected B–1 bomber, and the Trident submarine. The sticking point in SALT II negotiations came when the Soviets insisted that the United States' new air-launched Cruise missile, which the Americans claimed was only an intermediate-range weapon, should be included in the reckoning. At the same time they objected to counting their Backfire bomber, which, when refueled, was comparable in range, if not in performance, with the American intercontinental bomber, FB-111. Two Canadian observers, Albert Legaut and George Lindsey, in *The Dynamics of the Nuclear Balance* agreed that Backfire seemed designed for use in Europe and over the seas, but said that it might be later redesigned for other purposes.

Détente had a bearing on strategic doctrine and especially upon the debate among strategic experts over the most effective forms of targeting. In 1974 American Secretary of Defense James R. Schlesinger revealed that in the future Russian missile sites, rather than cities, would be prime objectives, on the grounds that this was made possible by new small weapons and by precision delivery. This was seen as a contribution to, and a consequence of, the spirit of détente; but the change in target was not very significant. Furthermore, a previous shift in targeting in the early 1960's had been based on the assumption that cities, not missile sites, were preferred targets because in the event of a hostile pre-emptive attack, it would be futile to retaliate against empty silos. At that time targeting against cities had been introduced as the most effective form of deterrent. If a return to targeting on missile sites was a result of détente, it could also be regarded as a weakening of the deterrent. These shifts merely show, however, that since completely safe deterrence was unattainable, neither forms of targeting could be accepted with confidence. The planners had grounds for warning against concessions.

On the other hand, many people argued that to increase, or even maintain, the number of nuclear weapons in existence was futile, since the amount of destruction that would occur in the event of war was such that overkill in mutually assured destruction was an unnecessary burden on already overtaxed economies. The debate revolved between proposals for reducing the overkill and efforts to anticipate and plug loopholes in the deterrent balance that derived from the SALT I agreement. But the latter attempts were claimed by opponents to be a reopening of the arms race and so a move against the stabilizing trend. As the arms agreement talks had been bogged down by technicalities to the point of stalling, and as they had been thrust into the background for a long time by the public debate about involvement in Vietnam and its domestic consequences, strategic discussion received less public attention than a decade earlier.

But politicians and the military were divided much on the same lines as the split between doves and hawks in the Vietnam controversy. Discussion of the intricacies of strategic arms and their limitation now made less impression on the public despite attempted explanations in the publications of such institutions as the Georgetown University Center for Strategic and International Studies, which often voiced the Pentagon's views.

Meanwhile, doubts about the reality of this balance between the super-powers had led to a suggestion that unless European nations could come together to establish agreement on the use of nuclear weapons for their own defense—and perhaps even on the establishment of a tactical nuclear deterrent in Europe—there was a serious possibility that Western nations might fall piecemeal into a Russian orbit during the next ten years or so. On the other hand, deployment of tactical weapons would reverse the trend toward reducing nuclear potential in Europe that was initiated when NATO removed nuclear mines from the German approaches and intermediate-range missiles from Turkey after the Cuban crisis.

One obstacle to the achievement of an agreement between the opposing super-powers, and also among allies, arose from the impossibility of anticipating technical developments in the next ten years. Nuclear powers and powers with nuclear potential were unwilling to make firm agreements that might limit their freedom to react to unforeseeable technical development in the more remote future; and non-nuclear powers with serious international problems were reluctant to commit themselves to perpetual repudiation of nuclear weapons as a means of solution.

The United States and the U.S.S.R. had stockpiled enough nuclear weapons to destroy every person on earth. Security was still assumed by most political leaders and the general public to rest on the capacity for mutually assured destruction, a position that hard-line strategists feared and disliked. A contrary argument is that a minimum nuclear deterrent may be all that is needed to prevent war. The Carter Administration appeared to accept this when it proposed a mutual reduction of present holdings. Nevertheless, as it was still theoretically possible to achieve a breakthrough in technology by discovering the perfect weapon or the perfect defense against a nuclear attack, one side might someday gain a supreme advantage. The balance of terror was therefore still intrinsically unstable. For this reason reduction of offensive weapons, even more than of defensive weapons, was more difficult to achieve than had been the ceiling imposed by SALT I.

Ominously, on another level, other powers had already developed a nuclear potential or were believed to have done so. France, a nuclear power, had refused to participate in the non-proliferation treaty or in other proposals to limit the weapons already possessed. Some fifteen to twenty other nations were capable of producing an atomic weapon. A first step in that direction had come when China exploded an atomic bomb in 1964 and a thermonuclear weapon in 1968 and announced that it was working on means of delivery. Other Asian powers were inevitably forced to review their position. The most disturbing move came when India, having evaded restrictions required by the powers that had helped her with nuclear development, announced in 1974 that she had the capacity to utilize nuclear power for explosive purposes. The statement that the atom bomb would be used only for peaceful purposes did not calm the fear spread by this step taken by what had traditionally been a great pacifist state. During the 1980's several other countries can undoubtedly follow suit. The United States therefore strives to restrict the further spread of nuclear knowledge and capacity. In 1977, as an example, the United States decided it would not use plutonium as a fuel because the residue could be used to make bombs.

A most serious possibility for the future is therefore the proliferation of nuclear weapons in the possession of perhaps twenty, thirty, or even forty nuclear powers. Localized nuclear war that had seemed unthinkable, and even unlikely or impossible, in the European area (though Henry Kissinger once thought it might take place there) began to appear rather less unlikely in areas like the Middle East or parts of Asia or Africa where the possibility of containment seems greater. No one can predict what effect such a war would have on international relations. An agreement on non-intervention by the super-powers might develop to restrict the possibility of spreading nuclear conflict. But such a policy would open the door to exploitation by potential empire-builders. As a result, the super-powers would then be compelled to show their willingness to intervene, and this would bring the danger of total global devastation. Hence what the effects of outbreaks of a local nuclear war would be are difficult to envisage. They might bring a radical change in the structure of the international nation-state system. Without some such change, the future elimination of war seems impossible. A new world order might be theoretically possible if the threats of localized nuclear war to the existence of mankind were to become so critical that a more effective system of international security became the inescapable alternative to the destruction of all life or of civilization. Such a turn of events might, however, impede those peoples who feel that they have legitimate grievances.

SALT negotiations to reduce the danger of nuclear war have not brought a diminution of other kinds of warfare. Nor has that desirable result been brought about by the nuclear confrontation known as the balance of terror, even though the possibility of escalation has made any war more dangerous. Indeed, in the shadow of mutually assured destruction, limited local wars continue to be sheltered and therefore possibly are more likely. Great powers that in earlier times would have exercised restraint on allies and satellites lest they become involved themselves were now tempted to tolerate or even encourage war by satellite. So, while unwilling to accept restrictions on the use of military pressure at the highest level, the U.S.S.R. also encouraged and armed North Vietnam in order to maintain a military leverage against South Vietnam and therefore against its American sponsors. Despite Russian differences with China, that latter power was also an aider and abettor of communist militancy in Vietnam.

Even though the United States had little economic interest and had no obvious strategic involvement in the area, as we have seen it had become committed militarily in Vietnam because a succession of presidents from Truman to Johnson had been prisoners of the ideology of the Cold War. In 1968 Richard M. Nixon, emulating the 1952 campaign of Eisenhower, had won election in part because of his promise that within twelve months of his inauguration significant progress would have been made toward ending the war. His determination to achieve "peace with honor," yet his acceptance of the same restrictions upon the full exertion of American military power that had shackled his predecessors, meant that United States involvement in the war lasted much longer than he had hoped or apparently expected. The Johnson Administration had attempted to lure Hanoi to the peace table by a technique of gradual escalation of the war. Nixon rejected that, because he believed that such a policy gave the enemy time to adjust, militarily and psychologically, to higher levels of conflict. Since the Johnson approach had also been tied to assurances, both to Hanoi and to its chief backers, that the United States had no desire to overthrow North Vietnam but wished merely to stop the North Vietnamese from "doing what they were doing" in the South, Nixon believed that Hanoi had therefore had no real inducement to seek terms. His solution was to escalate the war in a fashion calculated to place an intolerable strain upon North Vietnam's capacity to wage it. At the same time he sought to ensure presidential freedom of action by reliance upon the silent and patriotic majority at home.

Hence in 1969 American forces made a dramatic and successful sweep into Laos to cut the Ho Chi Minh trail; and heavy bombing raids were begun against North Vietnamese sanctuary areas in Cambodia. The President also announced the beginning of staged troop withdrawals from Vietnam, looking to a "Vietnamization" of the struggle whereby the ground war would be carried on exclusively by South Vietnam. This policy served to blunt somewhat the intensity of agitation against the war at home, but it weakened the psychological effect his military strategy had upon Hanoi and its supporters. Failing a positive response from North Vietnam, American forces invaded Cambodia in 1970. Though this operation undoubtedly severely damaged North Vietnam's capacity to mount a campaign in the South, it also rekindled and embittered domestic opposition to the war at home, a development (such was the unhappy logic of the war) that stiffened the resolve of Hanoi. An attempt in 1971 to duplicate the success of the Laotian sweep of 1969, this time employing South Vietnamese forces with U.S. air support (Operation Dewey Canyon II), served only to demonstrate that the army of the Thieu government was not yet strong enough to operate effectively in this manner.

The Nixon Administration was accordingly induced to place its chief reliance upon a bombing offensive, especially against North Vietnam. Use of air power did not produce the high level of casualties that had been suffered in the ground war, and it was not so brutally visible on television to the American public. Therefore it was much less damaging politically. Its aim was to destroy the North Vietnamese logistical system and to convince Hanoi that it was in the interest of North Vietnam to end the war. The air offensive did not have the hoped-for result. With its capacity to fight seemingly little diminished, Hanoi launched a ground offensive in South Vietnam in 1972. At the risk of Russian military intervention, the United States responded by blockading Haiphong, Hanoi's port and the main entry for Soviet arms, and by heavily bombing Hanoi itself.

These measures were combined with the diplomatic offensive in which Nixon established direct contact with China. The issue of Vietnam was also linked with the arms and other negotiations then proceeding with the Soviet Union. Nixon's diplomacy finally brought a truce settlement in 1973; and, promising a resumption of American operations should the truce be broken, the United States secured the reluctant adherence of South Vietnam to the agreement. For its part, the United States agreed to withdraw American troops on the conditions that North Vietnam would bring no new supplies into South Vietnam except for the replacement of arms and ammunition, and also that American POW's would be released. But the truce proved impossible to police. Canada, which had somewhat unwillingly agreed to participate in a peacekeeping role along with Indonesia, Poland and Hungary, called attention to gross infractions by North Vietnam and then withdrew after the minimum contracted period had elapsed.

The Vietnam war, the longest war in American history, had been most costly in money and lives. It had been an almost unrelieved disaster. The United States had been defeated politically with military consequences. The war had raised questions about the capacity of the American political system and of the American people to sustain the hard demands of limited war. At most, the enormous American effort had managed to stave off the collapse of South Vietnam and its neighbors for only a few years; in the process, that country and its neighbors had been scourged, many hundred of thousands had been killed, and millions of South Vietnamese peasants had been dislodged from their ancestral lands and reduced to the status of refugees living in the squalor of *bidonvilles* in the cities. The assumption underlying American policy, that it was necessary to stop the spread of communism in order to prevent a falling domino effect, was by no means incorrect, as subsequent events in Southeast Asia were to show. American policy, however, was based in part on the belief that with proper bolstering the government of South Vietnam would be able to sustain itself. However, the links between the Saigon regime and the peasant population of the South had never been strong. Despite large-scale American military and civil aid, successive South Vietnamese governments were never able to command the unflinching loyalty of their people. It became more and more difficult for many Americans at home to accept the government of South Vietnam as a genuinely democratic one. When the press disclosed cases of the misuse of United States aid by corrupt Vietnamese officials, American revulsion against the war increased.

Neither the South Vietnamese government nor its American allies were able effectually to combat the grip which the Viet Cong and North Vietnamese military elements established over many villages. From the Mekong Delta to the outskirts of Saigon the lives of the peasants were controlled, at least at night, by VC covert operations and directives; in turn, the villagers supplied cover and subsistence to these troops. Much of this was involuntary, since the ascendancy won by the Viet Cong and North Vietnamese owed much to their chief weapon: terror. The ruthlessness with which they were prepared to commit atrocities in order to maintain and extend their hold upon the population was most shockingly laid bare when the old capital of Hué was retaken after the Tet offensive. There they had carried out mass murders, including the slaughter of the intellectual leaders of the community.

The war not only had impact upon South Vietnam and the surrounding states; it also affected virtually every American institution and virtually every aspect of American life. For the armed forces, Vietnam was a nightmare. It provided combat experience for career officers and a laboratory for the testing of weapons systems. But its professional military advantages were outweighed by the damage done to the morale of the military establishment and by the loss of confidence in the military engendered among broad sections of the American public. The spectacle of a super-power thwarted by the regular troops of a small and underdeveloped country supported by peasant guerrillas was humiliating. The resilience of a revolutionary country in the face of a powerful adversary was scarcely new—history affords many examples of such phenomena—but it was nevertheless unexpected. By 1968 there were about 550,000 American servicemen in South Vietnam, together with large supplies of the most advanced equipment. But this force could never be fully exerted against the enemy, partly because of the political and social circumstances in the countryside, which gave the war its omni-directional character, and even more by the rules of engagement, which forbade penetration into the territory of North Vietnam. The American military felt itself shackled in Vietnam, but to outsiders it appeared that the war could be ended only by the uprooting of the population and by severe damage to the natural environment. Though in the end the bombing offensive had contributed to the achievement of a truce, the use of a strategic bombing force against the trails, wooden bridges, and pedestrian and cycle-mounted porters that made up the enemy's logistical system, at heavy cost in air crew and material, had not achieved notable success. Neither search-and-destroy operations nor bombing strikes had brought light at the end of the tunnel. Neither had critically impaired the enemy's chief resource, manpower. Neither had materially affected the enemy's will to fight on.

The internal problems that had sapped the morale of the American forces had damaged the American public's esteem for the military. Some of these were doubtless inflated by the ubiquitous press, but scandals in post and supply administration, clashes between white and black troops, mutinous behavior by some units, "fraggings" of officers, and the use of heroin and other drugs by American personnel in Vietnam were dispiriting evidence that all was not well within the forces. The disclosure of the My Lai massacre, and then of other outrages committed by American troops, further widened the gap between the military and large sections of the American public. As anti-military feeling spread in the United States, draft resistance and desertion increased, and thousands of young Americans chose to go into voluntary exile in Canada, Sweden, and elsewhere. Recruiting officers for the military and for companies that had military contracts were excluded from many universities. ROTC enrollments dropped from 212,400 in 1968 to about 75,000 in 1973.

These difficulties within the American forces had arisen in part because of the nature of the struggle in Vietnam. But drug problems, black-white tensions, racist attitudes that lay behind atrocities, and disrespect for constituted authority were all projections from American society itself. The war coincided with an unprecedented explosion of a youth culture that rejected parental and other established authority and traditional norms of attitude and behavior. Not only did the war intensify and radicalize the youth culture, it also deepened hostility toward government policy in Vietnam among those seeking to alleviate urban poverty and to guarantee civil rights, especially in the black community. Opposition to the war became the central and rallying issue of many groups dedicated to domestic change. Their cause was furthered by uncensored war reporting and by television selected for its shock effect. (Hanoi, on the other hand, permitted only the most favorable reporting of its operations.) To a degree without parallel in history, war in all its horror and violence was brought into the American living room. The agonies of Vietnam, the urban riots in the United States, and the disturbances on American campuses such as the shooting of anti-war protestors at Kent State University in 1970, were all depicted on the TV screen, and impressed many Americans with a deep fear that their institutions and their society were disintegrating. For those less susceptible to such images, the war-born inflation and the devaluation of the dollar, with prolonged economic consequences, provided concrete evidence of a crisis in American life.

These events, for which the war was the focus, weakened governmental authority, called into question the quality of American leadership, polarized society, and cast doubts upon hitherto powerful American national myths. Yet the war had greatly strengthened existing tendencies toward the proliferation of the federal civil service, toward greater governmental secrecy and a penchant for covert security operations, and, most of all, toward a concentration of power in the executive branch. The Tet offensive, surely one of the most successful surprises in recent military history, drew all these conflicting tendencies into focus. The fact that it was a tactical failure because of crippling losses suffered by the North Vietnamese was less important than its dramatic political success. The shock was so great that it brought down a president. Partly because of it, more and more Americans came to distrust their government, doubt the motives of their political leaders, and fear the activities of agencies like the CIA. Many therefore condoned the abandonment of traditional ideals of loyalty and patriotism, which was, in effect, symbolized by Daniel Ellsberg's breach of his oath of secrecy when he released the Pentagon Papers.

Although the ultimate military and political consequences of the Vietnam war for the United States were to take a long time to emerge, several suggestive developments appeared promptly. The decision to abandon the draft, and to rely instead upon all-volunteer forces, was intended to heal the wounds opened in the body politic by the war. The heavy costs of long-service volunteer forces, reinforcing the wartime diversion of funding from strategic weapons, meant that a lesser share of the budget could be devoted to the production of high-technology weapons such as the Cruise missile and the new precision-guided missiles (PGM), including the neutron bomb. Constitutionally, opposition to the war had caused a reversal of a trend, dating from 1939–1945, when Congress had begun to accept a minor role in the determination of foreign policy. So, in 1973 Congress denied to the executive the monies needed for the bombing of Cambodia. Then, in November, it overrode the presidential veto of the War Powers Act. By so doing Congress reversed the *carte blanche* that had been granted to the President by the Tonkin Gulf resolution and so restricted the war-making power of the executive.

President Nixon, weakened by the Watergate scandal as well as by the rising hostility to the war, warned that the consequences of Congressional action, and particularly the denial of additional military aid, were a betrayal of the guarantees given to the Government of South Vietnam. But he was in no position to coerce Congress. By the spring of 1975 his Vietnamese policy—and hence that of his predecessors—had ended in debacle. Laos had already succumbed to the communists. A surprise North Vietnamese offensive crumbled the Army of South Vietnam. The last American forces were hurriedly evacuated. The Cambodian regime, which had been kept alive by American arms and subsidies, went under at the same time. Shortly thereafter the government of Thailand demanded the withdrawal of all American forces from its soil.

In the wake of the Vietnam experience, it seemed clear that the United States would not intervene again in a colonial war for a long time. All sections of American opinion were resolved that there should be "no more Vietnams." Thus in 1976 the Ford Administration would refrain from any involvement in the conflict in Angola which followed upon the withdrawal of Portugal, the colonial power, despite the fact that Cuban troops with Soviet backing aided the anti-Western insurgents. The long-range effects that Vietnam will have upon American ability to check future limited wars cannot be foreseen. It may be assumed that many such wars will occur, for even while the Vietnam war dragged on, stimulated rather than prevented by the nuclear stalemate and by the precarious balance of the super-powers, small wars continued. War flared up when East Pakistan (now Bangladesh) revolted, precipitating conflict between India and West Pakistan. On this occasion the great powers were in little danger of being sucked in; but an American fleet moved into the Bay of Bengal and the Peoples' Republic of China watched warily. When Greek officers in the Cypriot Civil Guard threatened the regime of Archbishop Makarios and an uprising expelled him, Turkish forces seized one-third of the island; and Greece and Turkey, both members of NATO, nearly went to war. Greece withdrew from NATO. Limited wars like these, which perpetuated old antagonisms and hatreds and kept the international situation unstable by weakening associations and alliances, were a continuing reminder that total nuclear war was a possible consequence if the super-powers became involved.

Of all the crisis areas, the Middle East was the most dangerous and its problems were the most intractable. A chronic tendency to resort to war there seemed most likely to bring the super-powers in eventually. The Arab-Israeli conflicts of 1948, 1956, and 1967 were repeated in the Yom Kippur war in 1973, but with some differences. The Israelis were taken by surprise by Egyptian attacks and suffered severe early reverses. Ultimately they recovered ground lost in the Sinai and crossed the Suez Canal; they also seized the Golan Heights and advanced within artillery range of Damascus. They were halted by the great drain on their manpower and resources and by the intercession of the United States and the Soviet Union. This was the first, perhaps the only, occasion on which the super-powers moved quickly together to suppress a local conflict. It showed what they might do if they were not bedevilled by mutual antagonism.

The Yom Kippur war brought Arab cooperation, never very strong, to a pitch not known before. Iraq sent troops to aid Syria; Lebanon, usually inactive, mobilized; and Saudi Arabia, Libya, and the Persian Gulf states provided arms. Token forces came from other parts of the Moslem world. Against this appearance of unity, Israel continued to hold some of the territory gained during the war as a security because of Arab unwillingness to recognize its right to exist. On the other hand, as a result of Israel's successful recovery, the Arab states, led by Saudi Arabia, took up a new weapon—the oil embargo. In view of the West's dependence on Middle East oil, this move threatened to alter the world strategic balance by tipping the scales against the industrialized West. At the same time it placed a new burden on oil-poor Third World states striving to develop their economies.

One contribution made by the Arab-Israeli Wars to the development of military knowledge was of more immediate consequence. The powers that supplied arms to one side or the other—especially the United States, which aided Israel, and the Soviet Union, which aided the Arabs—saw those weapons tested under combat conditions. In the Yom Kippur War the dominance of great tank formations, which in 1967 had been deployed in the Sinai on a greater scale than in Libya during World War II, was broken when Egyptian infantry used Soviet-made hand-held rockets as tank destroyers. The Israelis hurriedly worked out new tactics that became effective before the fighting was halted. This was some indication that in the development of the electronic battlefield concept for major wars in Europe or elsewhere, the infantryman could still be a decisive factor.

A complex of technological innovations, taken together, had created the "electronic battlefield." Vietnam had been a significant laboratory for such innovations. In the air war the effect of heavy bomber attacks was greatly increased when the first precision-guided missiles (PGM's) were developed—"smart" bombs capable of hitting pinpoint targets such as bridge piers and powerhouses. Such missiles were at first controlled by operators aboard the aircraft, through TV cameras mounted in the nose. Later versions were fully automated; once the camera was "locked on" to a target, the missile guided itself to its destination. Similarly, ground-to-air "homing" missiles using radar, infrared, and anti-radiation devices found fast-moving airborne targets with a high degree of accuracy. On the ground, electronic surveillance and warning equipment monitored the covert movements of men and materials though vital areas of mountain and jungle by day and by night, using radio waves, light amplification, or infrared techniques. The development of each new electronic system initiated a search for an electronic counter-measure (ECM), thus setting in train an escalatory process that continued apace in the 1970's.

Both the Vietnam and the Middle Eastern conflicts brought out the importance of tactical air power in the land battle. In Korea helicopters had been used for reconnaissance and medical evacuation, and occasionally for battlefield command and control. But in Vietnam this employment was much more extensive. Infantrymen were transported to the forward edge of the battle area (FEBA) and sometimes inserted directly into the firefight, while helicopter "gunships," armed with two or more 50-calibre machine guns, delivered suppressive fire. Rocket-armed helicopters were also successfully used in the anti-tank role. At An Loc in 1972 they destroyed three T54 tanks. Nevertheless, helicopter losses were heavy, even in the comparatively permissive air environment of Vietnam. However, "nap of the earth" tactics, with the helicopters flying below treetop height, cut losses. The renewed importance of tactical air power, and doubts about the potential of the helicopter as a part of the combat team, led the United States to develop a fixed-wing aircraft, the Fairchild A-10, which was designed especially for close air support in a more hostile air environment than that of Vietnam, and it possessed advanced navigation and target acquisition systems. Vietnam also saw the first use of improved conventional munitions (ICM's). Compression bombs, utilizing an explosive gas-air mixture that created intense pressure over a given area when ignited, were originally employed to clear helicopter landing zones of pressure-sensitive mines. They were subsequently applied against armored fighting vehicles. Their pressure waves killed crewmen and disabled vehicles by rupturing fuel and hydraulic lines.

The post-Vietnam era saw a continuance of the rapid development of new battlefield technology. Among the most significant innovations were laser-ranging, energy-absorbing Chobham armor, and fin-stabilized, discarding sabot (FSDS) ammunition. The battlefield communications web was vastly improved. Calls for artillery fire, for example, were now transmitted directly to fire-direction center computers, and engagement data were fed immediately to battery positions and individual guns. Solid-state electronics and component engineering for quick testing and replacement greatly simplified front-line maintenance and improved reliability in all the combat arms. Most dramatic of all was the appearance of new high-technology weapons systems and the building of electronic network links that enabled full advantage to be taken of the surveillance and sighting techniques that had been pioneered in Vietnam.

Traditional weaponry had been severely limited, whether directed against targets covering a substantial area of ground, such as an armored division, or against small targets such as a single tank or gun. Newly developed ICM's went far to overcome these limitations. Thus "cluster" bombs or artillery projectiles, sometimes rocket-assisted, could saturate ground with anti-armor or anti-personnel "bomblets" or "minelets" capable of canalizing an enemy's advance, slowing it down, or destroying it altogether. Small targets were now subject to the "first round hit" capability of PGM's, using laser marking or electro-optical homing techniques. Such sophisticated guidance systems and new rocket propellants which increased velocity, accuracy, and range gave the individual soldier a vastly greater hitting power. Moreover, all direct fire weapons could now be fitted with "passive" devices, such as light amplification for night firing and thermal imagery, permitting accurate sighting through haze or battle smoke. But they were not susceptible to ECM's. When combined with "active" radar and infrared, and vibration- and sound-detection systems, they enabled a small unit to maintain close surveillance over its area of interest at all times.

Many of these surveillance devices could now be linked directly to higher headquarters. Along with other data links, such as the fire-control systems already mentioned, they brought computer technology onto the conventional battlefield. When combined with additional electronic innovations like the high-gain directional tactical antennas, spread-spectrum transmission techniques, laser telephones, fiber-optical cable, digital message devices, and frequency-hopping radars, they enabled unit commanders to survey and dominate a larger area.

Aside from demonstrating the continuing impact upon warfare of science and technology, these devices were significant in a number of other ways. For one thing, the new battlefield technology seemed to give a radical advantage to the defense. Successful attack against such systems, failing a technological revolution that reversed prevailing trends, could require immense numerical preponderance and a willingness to absorb heavy casualties. Secondly, and perhaps even more important, the sophistication and power of the new technology led, at least among the NATO forces, to a de-emphasis of tactical nuclear weapons. It therefore conceivably reduced the danger of escalation toward an all-out nuclear war.

Another trend in macro-strategy also emphasized mini-tactics. This was the remarkable increase of terrorist activity in many parts of the world. The period of the 1960's and 1970's, an uneasy calm in the nuclear strategic balance when weapon development produced new electronic marvels, may nevertheless come to be known as "the age of the guerrilla." It has already been noted that during World War II partisan operations played a much bigger role than in World War I; but they were normally associated with, or supplemental to, conventional operations. When that war ended, the rapid process of decolonization was frequently hastened by nationalist or social revolutionary movements. Resort to systematic violence replaced the non-violent resistance punctuated by sporadic rioting that had marked pre-war anti-colonial movements. The long struggle of Mao Tse-tung's communist forces against Chiang Kai-shek's nationalists, both before the war against Japan and afterward, when wartime cooperation ceased, was a most important source of example and inspiration for insurgents. Mao's writings on guerrilla tactics became the bible of communists and other militants.

It has been seen that in Indochina guerrilla action against French colonial rule led up to conventional operations and that this pattern was repeated by North Vietnam against the American-backed regime in the south. In Africa in the 1970's long, drawn-out guerrilla campaigns against the Portuguese in Angola and Mozambique similarly escalated until they took the form of continuous campaigns and operations. An ominous epilogue was that when the three groups which had fought the colonial government were victorious, Cuban troops with Soviet connivance intervened on behalf of the Popular Movement for the Liberation of Angola (MPLA). The National Front for the Liberation of Angola (FNLA) and the Union for the Total Independence of Angola (UNITA) were defeated, and fled to the bush. The United States did not intervene on their behalf because, as was noted above, the Vietnam War had made Americans wary lest they be sucked into another interminable and bloody struggle against communism on a far-off continent with divisive effects at home.

At the other end of Africa a prolonged guerrilla campaign by Eritreans against the Lion of Judah was continued against the leftist military regime which overthrew him and was parallelled by what was claimed to be a rising of Somalis seeking to liberate another part of Ethiopia, the southeastern desert, to attach it to Somalia. A Somali invasion aided the insurgents. A striking feature of this war was that when it broke out the two super-powers had recently exchanged sides. Formerly, the United States had supplied the Emperor with arms, and the Somalis had given the Soviet navy use of a naval base. But the Western powers were now sympathetic to the Somali cause and the Russians supported Ethiopia. In all these cases guerrilla war had merged into conventional operations as popular support increased or as terrorist methods enforced acquiescence.

In the three decades after the end of World War II a new pattern for the conduct of war had emerged. Based on Mao's teachings and example, with or without some contact with Peking or Moscow, movements for social revolution or national liberation set up underground general staffs, publicly sought by every possible psychological means to advertise their political aims, and secretly organized operational cells and rudimentary communications systems of couriers or messengers. They robbed banks to obtain funds, exploited terror to control populations, suborned local officials, established safe areas in remote mountains or safe houses in cities, conducted campaigns of civil disobedience, "liberated" rural regions by establishing control away from highways or during the hours of darkness, and worked toward a general offensive to eliminate the last vestige of a governmental presence and to secure the transfer of power. This overall strategic plan had proved eminently successful in Indochina, but had failed in some other parts of Southeast Asia—for instance, in Malaysia. A similar game plan was adopted for subversion in southern Africa, by the Palestine Liberation Organization in the Middle East, and by the Irish Republican Army in Ulster.

A parallel development came from the growing expectation of the American black population, nursing resentment for past ill-treatment and struggling to free itself from the historical restrictions of segregation, to cope with economic dislocation caused by migration to the cities to share American prosperity. Riots occurred in the ghettos, and acts of terrorism became widespread. In the late 1960's student movements in many parts of the world, feeding on, among other things, objections to American imperialism, resorted to violence. Student activism in the United States was reinforced by opposition to conscription for service in Southeast Asia. Disorder and incendiarism in Los Angeles, Washington, and Detroit, and widespread bombings, were in fact forms of urban guerrilla warfare.

These political and social upheavals were accompanied by a breakdown of law and order that had a history among juveniles going back to the end of World War II. In some ways criminal activity was as serious a challenge to social stability as organized violent political activism. Furthermore, the decline of public order, the rise of terrorism, and the greater frequency of violence in the streets in formerly law-abiding societies created a situation that could no longer be considered remote from the relationship between military forces and society. In some countries, for instance Argentina, Italy, and West Germany, kidnappings and other terrorist acts by obscure political extremists that were hard to distinguish from criminality had become a way of life by the late 1970's.

A growing concern for human rights has accompanied the in-

creasing tendency on the part of minorities to assert their views and
on the part of small groups to attempt to enforce their ideas by
violence. Defense needs compete with social welfare for funds, and
the protection of civil liberties conflicts with the need to maintain
authority. But internal subversion and terrorist campaigns, the hi-
jacking of aircraft, the taking of hostages, and indiscriminate
bombings—often claimed by their perpetrators to be "legitimate"
war—can present a severe threat to the state. In addition to the
possibility of escalation, they are themselves disruptive of stability.
They constitute a new dimension in warfare and must be taken into
consideration in a study of the relations of warfare and society. Although soldiers traditionally dislike participation in internal security
duties, aid to the civil power is a normal part of their duties even in
democracies, and of course more so in autocracies and military
dictatorships. Wise use of the military to back civil authority, to
prevent disruption, and to restore order has always been a factor in
the stability of states and in their capacity to cope with major
problems.

Another source of friction must also be mentioned. Competition
for scarce natural resources such as oil, natural gas, and even water
is causing increasing tension among industrialized states. In addition
it promises to heighten the hostility between rich and poor nations.
Hitherto it had always been considered that in the struggle between
the North and the South (as the rich and poor nations are sometimes
called) the wealthy countries had an advantage, especially if they
were disposed and able to use their military strength. But industrialized nations may be more vulnerable to modern terrorist tactics
than less advanced states. Furthermore, modern nation states are
often weakened by internal ethnic or regional activists. Finally, Arab
use of the oil embargo suggests that economic weapons may be
employed by weaker military powers with considerable effect.
Competition for scarce resources is therefore a potential source of
friction and war. The international state system thus promises to become even more anarchic than it has been. It is clear that the role of
the soldier in society has not been reduced despite the possibility
that an effective nuclear agreement between the super-powers might
come one day.

Questions arising from the uncertainties of the future have begun
to attract the attention of serious scholars formerly interested in
strategic studies. Herman Kahn's Hudson Institute is but one of the
groups (though perhaps the most committed) concerned with such
matters. Talking about what he called "surprise-free projections,"

Kahn avoided predictions of the vague, general kind that had often marked earlier studies of the future. Kahn's projections in *Things to Come* (1972) related mainly to the development of the military relations among the powers in the light of the technical changes that he had noted in earlier studies and that could be confidently expected within the next ten years. Kahn believed that the Cold War was over, at least in Europe; that the United States had abandoned its one-time belief that superiority in weaponry over the Soviet Union was the key to stability; and that the arms race was being brought under control and was therefore less dangerous. He expected no revolutionary technological innovation in weapons before the mid-1980's, and he stated that the allegation that the United States was dropping behind the U.S.S.R. in research and development depended on how one did the calculation. He suggested that the alleged research-and-development gap of the 1970's might turn out to be as spurious as the missile gap of the late 1950's. Finally, Kahn believed that there might be a long-term trend toward an increase of military capability despite efforts to limit armament. "The total weight of the power of military hardware in 1985 is certain to be much more deadly than today." Kahn assumed, however, that multipolarity might provide a degree of stability. So, just as he once said in *On Thermonuclear War* that a total war could be survived (a forecast that fortunately has not been tested), he now said the same kind of thing about a continued arms race and the further development and proliferation of nuclear weapons.

On the other hand, Alastair Buchan, a British scholar, wrote in *International Interactions* that current discussion in the United States about the research-and-development gap suggested that there might be limits to American willingness to accept loss of military superiority over the Soviet Union. But the transference of wealth to the Arab states as a result of the oil squeeze might mean that the United States would be faced with the possibility of having to take second place behind the communist world plus the Arabs. Buchan also thought it possible that the Arabs might seek to get all they can from oil now because they know that they have a transitory monopoly. Like Kahn he postulated the breakdown of bipolarity and its replacement by a "multiple balance" of five or more major power centers—for instance, the United States, U.S.S.R., China, Japan, and possibly Western Europe—but he said that this could bring greater stability only if the United States refrained from attempting to keep its superiority by maintaining a community of interest with either Japan or Western Europe. Clearly, however, continued great-power rivalry in any kind of power system, whether bipolar or multipolar, would serve to obstruct the development of the international cooperation that is needed to solve the macro-problems that face the world—unequal distribution of resources and prosperity, and overpopulation in poor states. Continued efforts to balance power among the great powers might increase the leverage that underprivileged states could assert, especially those with a monopoly of essential raw materials.

A third possibility is what Richard Brody has called in another article in *International Interactions* "polyarchical multi-polarity," which would take in more than a small group of advanced states. He argued that there are signs of this in the economic sphere as well as in the political and the military. Such a state of affairs would please the middle states and perhaps also the smaller ones. But the great powers might find it hard to accept, and it might therefore not bring stability. Their efforts to solve world problems according to their own views could be frustrated if an underprivileged majority continues to use the United Nations as a sounding board for polit-ical and ideological propaganda and for the passage of resolutions challenging great-power interests or concerns. An end to the Cold War confrontation might thus prolong the present anarchy.

Kahn showed in *Things to Come* that the world economic system is now so complex that it has become much more sensitive to dis-ruption from any direction. He was very critical of lawyers and judges who, he said, have a "learned incapacity" to see the nature of the problem arising within the state from the growth of violence. An anarchical international system, or a polyarchical multi-polarity which hamstrings the great powers, could compound the issues arising in many states from the increase of assassinations, kidnap-pings, bombings, and hijackings. When it is also considered that the proliferation of nuclear weapons is among lesser states, which might not exercise the same self-restraint as the super-powers thus far have shown, the future becomes darker. States like India, one of the most successful practitioners of democracy in the Third World but now possibly weakening in that respect, may be tempted to solve their problems of poverty by extreme measures. International rivalries like that between Arab and Zionist, and international friction like that in Northern Ireland, which now appear insoluble by any kind of compromise, may precipitate either nuclear black-mail or nuclear war. Nuclear weapons in the hands of terrorist groups could present a menace that an anarchical international system could not meet. And behind all these problems is the scarcity of essential resources for an increasing world population.

Problems like these require some kind of global authority or some degree of international cooperation of a kind not now in sight. The way in which national military forces would fit into the exercise of such an authority or such cooperation is unclear and is as yet unconsidered. What is certain is that military force will continue to play a role in the world of the future and that the structure of society will be affected by it even though that role may change. Meanwhile it is clear that the soldier of the immediate future must be capable not merely of handling the technical problems of electronic warfare but also the quasi-diplomatic problems of a changing international system and some of the internal law-enforcing problems in domestic disruption.

PROBLEMS OF TODAY AND TOMORROW

Brody, Richard, "The Emergency International System: Policy Implications," *International Interactions,* Vol. I, No. 4 (1974), pp. 217–227.

Buchan, Alastair, "The Emerging International System: A European Perspective," *International Interactions,* Vol. I, No. 4 (1974), pp. 195–196.

Fitzgerald, Frances, *Fire in the Lake: the Vietnamese and the Americans in Vietnam.* Boston: Little Brown, 1972.

Hoopes, Townsend, *The Limits of Intervention: An Inside Story of How the Johnson Policy of Escalation in Viet Nam Was Reversed.* New York: McKay, 1970.

Kahn, Herman, and B. Bruce Briggs, *Things to Come: Thinking About the Seventies and Eighties.* New York: Macmillan, 1972.

Lake, Anthony (ed.), *The Vietnam Legacy: The War, American Society, and the Future of American Foreign Policy.* New York: New York University Press, 1976.

Legault, Albert, and George Lindsey, *The Dynamics of the Nuclear Balance.* Rev. ed., Ithaca: Cornell University Press, 1976.

Luttwak, Edward, *The U.S.-U.S.S.R. Nuclear Weapons Balance.* The Washington Papers, Vol. II, No. 13, Beverly Hills/London: Sage Publications, 1974.

Mesarovic, Mihajlo, and Eduard Pestel, *Mankind at the.Turning Point: The Second Report to the Club of Rome.* New York: Dutton, 1974.

Moss, Robert, *Urban Guerrillas: The New Face of Political Violence.* London: Maurice Temple Smith, 1972.

Paret, Peter, and John W. Shy, *Guerrillas in the 1960's.* New York: Center of International Studies, Praeger, 1966.

Preston, Richard A. "War Peace and Society in the 1980's: An Historian's View," *Naval War College Review* (Winter 1976), pp. 34–44.

Sully, Francois, *The Age of the Guerrilla.* New York: Avon Books, 1968.

Willrich, Mason, and John G. Rhinelander, *SALT: The Moscow Agreements and Beyond.* New York: Free Press, 1977.

Bibliography

(References are to the latest American editions. Entries are not repeated even when they are appropriate in more than one section.)

GENERAL

(Including Introduction and Chapter One)

MILITARY DICTIONARIES

Beadnell, C. M., *An Encyclopaedic Dictionary of Science and War*. London: C. A. Watts, 1943.

Eggenberger, David, *A Dictionary of Battles*. New York: Crowell, 1967.

Farrow, E. S., *Farrow's Military Encyclopaedia*, 2d ed. 3 vols. New York: Military-Naval Publishing Co., 1895.

Garber, Max, *A Modern Military Dictionary*, 2d ed. Washington: Bond, 1942.

Gaynor, Frank, *The New Military and Naval Dictionary*. New York: Philosophical Library, 1951.

HISTORIES OF WAR

Albion, R. G., *Introduction to Military History*. New York: Century, 1929.

Birnie, Arthur, *The Art of War*. London: Nelson, 1942.

Burne, A. H., *The Art of War on Land*. Harrisburg, Pa.: Stackpole, 1966.

Coblentz, S. A., *From Arrow to Atom Bomb: The Psychological History of War*. Cranbury, N.J.: A. S. Barnes, 1966.

Craven, F., "Why Military History?" *Harmon Memorial Lectures in Military History*, no. 1. Colorado Springs: USAF Academy, 1959.

Earle, E. M. (ed.), *Makers of Modern Strategy: Military Thought from Machiavelli to Hitler*. New York: Atheneum, 1966 (paperback).

Falls, Cyril, *The Art of War: From the Age of Napoleon to the Present Day*. London: Oxford University Press, 1961.

Fuller, J. F. C., *Armament and History: A Survey of the Influence of Armament on History from the Dawn of Classical Warfare to the Second World War*. New York: Scribners, 1945.

Fuller, J. F. C., *The Decisive Battles of the Western World and Their Influence upon History*. 3 vols. London: Eyre & Spottiswoode, 1954–1956.

Fuller, J. F. C., *The Foundations of the Science of War*. London: Hutchinson, 1926.

Hamley, E. B., *The Operations of War Explained and Illustrated.* London: Blackwood, 1907.

Henderson, G. F. R., *The Science of War.* London: Longmans Green, 1912.

Liddell Hart, B. H., *Strategy: The Indirect Approach.* New York: Praeger, 1954.

Mathews, Joseph J., *Reporting the Wars.* Minneapolis: Minnesota University Press, 1957.

Mitchell, W. A., *Outlines of the World's Military History.* Harrisburg, Pa.: Military Service, 1940.

Montgomery, Bernard L., *A History of Warfare.* London: Collins, 1968.

Montross, Lynn, *War through the Ages,* 3d ed. New York: Harper, 1960.

Oman, Charles, "A Plea for Military History," *On the Writing of History.* London: Methuen, 1939.

Paret, Peter. "Innovation and reform in warfare . . . ," *Harmon Memorial Lectures in Military History,* no. 8. Colorado Springs: USAF Academy, 1966.

Phillips, T. R. (ed.), *Roots of Strategy.* Harrisburg, Pa.: Military Service, 1940.

Ropp, Theodore, *War in the Modern World,* rev. ed. New York: Crowell Collier & Macmillan, 1965 (paperback).

Schneider, Fernand, *Histoire des Doctrines Militaires.* Paris: Presses Universitaires, 1957.

Spaulding, O. L., Hoffman Nickerson, and J. W. Wright, *Warfare: A Study of Military Methods from the Earliest Times.* Washington: Infantry Journal Press, 1939.

Turner, G. B. (ed.), *A History of Military Affairs in Western Society since the Eighteenth Century.* New York: Harcourt Brace, 1953.

Vagts, Alfred, *A History of Militarism,* rev. ed. Glencoe, Ill.: The Free Press, 1967 (paperback).

Willoughby, C. A., *Maneuver in War.* Harrisburg, Pa.: Stackpole, 1939.

Zook, D. H., and Robin Higham, *A Short History of Warfare.* New York: Twayne, 1965.

Histories of Weapons

Brodie, Bernard, and Fawn Brodie. *From Cross-Bow to H Bomb.* New York: Dell, 1962 (paperback).

Carman, W. Y., *A History of Firearms from Earliest Times to 1914.* New York: St. Martin's, 1956.

Held, Robert, *The Age of Firearms.* Chicago: Gun Digest, 1969 (paperback).

Newman, J. R., *The Tools of War.* New York: Doubleday, Doran, 1943.

Wintringham, T. H., *Weapons and Tactics.* London: Faber & Faber, 1940.

Histories of Branches of Armed Forces, etc.

Denison, G. T., *History of Cavalry,* 2d ed. London: Macmillan, 1913.

Lloyd, E. M., *A Review of the History of Infantry.* London: Longmans Green, 1908.

Turner, E. S., *Gallant Gentlemen: A Portrait of the British Officer, 1600–1956.* London: Michael Joseph, 1956.

MILITARY HISTORIES OF VARIOUS COUNTRIES

Dupuy, R. E., and T. N. Dupuy, *The Military Heritage of America*. New York: McGraw Hill, 1956.

Sheppard, E. W., *A Short History of the British Army*. London: Constable, 1950.

Stacey, C. P. (ed.), *Introduction to the Study of Military History for Canadian Students,* rev. ed. Ottawa: Queen's Printer, 1955.

Stacey, C. P., *The Military Problems of Canada*. Toronto: Ryerson, 1940.

Stanley, G. F. G., *Canada's Soldiers*, rev. ed. Toronto: Macmillan, 1960.

Weighley, R. F., *History of the United States Army*. New York: Crowell Collier & Macmillan, 1967.

MARITIME WARFARE

Brodie, Bernard, *A Guide to Naval Strategy*, 5th ed. New York: Praeger, 1968.

Callender, Geoffrey, and F. H. Hinsley, *The Naval Side of British History, 1485–1945,* rev. ed. London: Chatto, 1960.

Corbett, Julian, *Some Principles of Naval Strategy*. New York: Longmans Green, 1911.

Knox, D. W., *A History of the United States Navy*. New York: Putnam, 1948.

Lewis, Michael, *History of the British Navy*. New York: Oxford University Press, 1959.

Lewis, Michael, *The Navy of Britain*. London: Allen & Unwin, 1948.

Mahan, A. T., *The Influence of Sea Power upon History, 1660–1783*. New York: Hill & Wang 1957, (paperback).

Mathew, David, *The Naval Heritage*. London: Collins, 1945.

Potter, E. B., *et al., Sea Power: A Naval History*. Englewood Cliffs, N.J.: Prentice-Hall, 1969.

Richmond, Herbert, *Sea Power in the Modern World*. London: G. Bell, 1934.

Tunstall, Brian, *Realities of Naval History*. London, 1936.

GEOGRAPHIC AND ECONOMIC FACTORS IN WARFARE

Cole, D. H., *Imperial Military Geography*, 11th ed. London: Sifton Praed, 1953.

Emeny, Brooks, *The Strategy of Raw Materials*. New York: Macmillan, 1934.

STRATEGY AND PRINCIPLES OF WAR

Brodie, Bernard, "Strategy as a Science," *World Politics,* I. 1948–1949.

Brown, C. R., "The Principles of War," *United States Naval Institute Proceedings,* LXXV. June 1949.

Maurice, Sir F. B., *British Strategy: A Study of the Application of the Principles of War*. London: Constable, 1938.

Voysey, R. A. E., *An Outline of the Principles of War*. London: Riss, 1934.

WARFARE AND SOCIETY

Andrzejewski, Stanislaw, *Military Organization and Society*. London: Routledge and Kegan Paul, 1954.

Aron, Raymond, *On War*. Garden City, N.Y.: Norton, 1968 (paperback).

Aron, Raymond, *War and Industrial Society*. New York: Oxford University Press, 1958.

Buchan, Alastair, *War in Modern Society*. London: Watts, 1966.

Clarkson, J. D., and T. C. Cochrane, *War as a Social Institution: The Historians' Perspective*. New York: Columbia University Press, 1941.

Davie, M. R. *The Evolution of War: A Study of its Role in Early Societies*. New Haven, Conn.: Yale University Press, 1929.

Fuller, J. F. C., *The Conduct of War, 1789–1961: A Study of the Impact of the French, Industrial, and Russian Revolutions on War and its Conduct*. London: Eyre & Spottiswoode, 1961.

Howard, Michael (ed.), *Soldiers and Governments: Nine Studies in Civil-Military Relations*. Bloomington, Ind.: Indiana University Press, 1957.

Huntington, S. P., *The Soldier and the State: The Theory and Politics of Civil-Military Relations*. Cambridge, Mass.: Harvard University Press, 1957.

Kranzberg, Melvin, and C. W. Pursell (eds.), *Technology in Western Civilization*. 2 vols. New York: Oxford University Press, 1967.

Lauterbach, A. T., "Militarism in the Western World: A Comparative Study," *Journal of the History of Ideas,* V. 1944.

Masland, J. W., and Lawrence I. Radway, *Soldiers and Scholars: Military Education and National Policy*. Princeton, N.J.: Princeton University Press, 1957.

Millis, Walter, *Arms and the State: Civil-Military Elements in National Policy*. New York: Twentieth Century Fund, 1958.

Mumford, Lewis, *Technics and Civilization*. New York: Harcourt Brace, 1934 (paperback).

Nef, J. U., *War and Human Progress: An Essay on the Rise of Industrial Civilization*. New York: Russell, 1968 (paperback).

Nickerson, Hoffman, *Can We Limit War?* Bristol: Arrowsmith, 1933.

Redlich, Fritz, *The German Military Enterpriser and His Work Force*. 2 vols. Wiesbaden, W. Germ.: Steiner, 1965.

Shotwell, J. T., *War as an Instrument of National Policy*. New York: Harcourt Brace, 1929.

Sombart, Werner, *The Quintessence of Capitalism*, new ed. New York: Fertig, 1967.

Strachey, Alix, *The Unconscious Motives of War: A Psychoanalytical Contribution*. New York: Hillary, 1957.

Toynbee, A. J., *War and Civilization*. New York: Oxford University Press, 1950.

Turney-High, H. H., *Primitive War*. Columbia, S.C.: University of South Carolina Press, 1949.

Wright, Quincy, *A Study of War,* 2d. ed. 2 vols. Chicago: University of Chicago Press, 1965; abridged ed., 1964 (paperback).

THE CLASSICAL PERIOD AND BYZANTIUM

Adcock, F. E., *Greek and Macedonian Art of War*. Berkeley, Calif.: University of California Press, 1957 (paperback).

Adcock, F. E., *The Roman Art of War under the Republic*, rev. ed. New York: Barnes & Noble, 1963.

Amit, M., *Athens and the Sea: A Study in Athenian Sea Power*. Brussels: Collection Latomus, no. 75, 1965.

Baynes, N. H., "The Emperor Heraclius and the Military Theme System," *English Historical Review*, LXVII. 1952.

Bell, M. J. V., "Tactical Reform in the Roman Republican Army," *Historia*, XIV. 1965.

Brunt, P. A., "The Army and the Land in the Roman Revolution," *Journal of Roman Studies*, 52. 1962.

Burn, A. R., *Persia and the Greeks: The Defense of the West, 546–478 B.C.* New York: St. Martin's. 1962.

Bury, J. B., *A History of Greece*, 3d ed. London: Macmillan, 1959.

Caesar, *War Commentaries: De Bello Gallico and De Bello Civili*. New York: Dutton, 1953 (paperback).

Cambridge Medieval History, IV, Parts I and II, *The Byzantine Empire*, new ed. 2 vols. Cambridge: Cambridge University Press, 1966–1967.

Casson, L., *The Ancient Mariners: Sea Farers and Sea Fighters of the Mediterranean in Ancient Times*. New York: Funk & Wagnalls, 1967 (paperback).

Clark, F. W., *The Influence of Sea Power in the History of the Roman Republic*. Menasha, Wis.: Banta, 1915.

Delbrück, H., *Geschichte der Kriegskunst, I, Das Altertum*, 3d ed. Berlin, 1920.

Dodge, T. A., *Caesar: A Hisory of the Art of War Among the Romans down to the End of the Roman Empire*. 2 vols. New York: Houghton Mifflin, 1892.

Dodge, T. A., *Hannibal: A History of the Art of War Among the Carthaginians and Romans down to the Battle of Pydna, 168 B.C.* 2 vols. New York: Houghton Mifflin, 1891.

Domaszewski, A. von, *Die Rangordnung des römischen Heeres*. Bonn, 1907.

Eadie, J. W., "The Development of Roman Mailed Cavalry," *Journal of Roman Studies*, 57. 1967.

Fuller, J. F. C., *The Generalship of Alexander the Great*. New York: Funk & Wagnalls, 1968 (paperback).

Fuller, J. F. C., *Julius Caesar: Man, Soldier, and Tyrant*. New York: Funk & Wagnalls, 1969 (paperback).

Glover, R. G., "The Elephant in Ancient War," *Classical Journal*, XXXIX. Feb. 1944.

Graves, Robert, *Count Belisarius*. London: Cassell, 1938.

Griffith, G. T., *Mercenaries of the Hellenistic World*. Chicago: Argonaut, 1935.

Grundy, G. B., *The Great Persian War*. New York: AMS Press, 1969.

Grundy, G. B., *Thucydides and the History of his Age*. 2 vols. Oxford: Blackwell, 1948.

Harmand, J., *L'Armée et le Soldat à Rome*. Paris: Picard, 1967.

Henderson, B. W., *The Great War between Athens and Sparta*. London: Macmillan, 1927.

Herodotus, *The History*. 2 vols. New York: Dutton (Everyman's Library), 1936–1937.

Hignett, C., *Xerxes' Invasion of Greece*. Oxford: Oxford University Press, 1963.

How, W. W., "Arms, Strategy and Tactics in the Persian Wars," *Journal of Hellenic Studies*. 1923.

Jouguet, Pierre, *Macedonian Imperialism*. New York: Knopf, 1928.

Kromayer, J., *Antike Schlachtfelder*. Berlin, 1907–1931.

Launey, Marcel, *Recherches sur les Armées Hellénistiques*. 2 vols. Paris: Boccard, 1949.

Liddell Hart, B. H., *A Greater than Napoleon, Scipio Africanus*. London: Blackwood, 1930.

MacMullen, R., *Enemies of the Roman Order: Treason, Unrest and Alienation in the Empire*. Cambridge, Mass.: Harvard University Press, 1966.

MacMullen, R., *Soldier and Civilian in the Later Roman Empire*. Cambridge, Mass.: Harvard University Press, 1963.

Marsden, E. W., *The Campaign of Gaugamela: Alexander's Most Decisive Battle*. Chicago: Argonaut, 1964.

Marsden, E. W., *Greek and Roman Artillery*. Oxford: Clarendon, 1969.

Mellersh, H. E. L., *Roman Soldier*, New York: Taplinger, 1964.

Ormerod, H. A., *Piracy in the Ancient World*. Chicago: Argonaut, 1924.

Ostrogorsky, G., *History of the Byzantine State*, rev. ed. New Brunswick, N.J.: Rutgers University Press, 1969.

Parker, H. M. D., *The Roman Legions*, 2d ed. New York: Barnes and Noble, 1958.

Partington, J. R., *A History of Greek Fire and Gunpowder*. Cambridge: Heffner, 1960.

Rodgers, W. L., *Greek and Roman Naval Warfare*. Annapolis, Md.: United States Naval Institute, 1937.

Scullard, H. H., *Scipio Africanus in the Second Punic War*. Cambridge: Cambridge University Press, 1930.

Smith, Richard Edwin, *Service in the Post-Marian Army*. Manchester: Manchester University Press, 1958.

Snodgrass, A. M., *Arms and Armour of the Greeks*. Ithaca, N.Y.: Cornell University Press, 1967.

Starr, C. G., *The Roman Imperial Navy*, 2d ed. New York: Barnes & Noble, 1960.

Tarn, W. W., *Alexander the Great*. 2 vols. Boston: Beacon Press, 1956 (paperback).

Tarn, W. W., *Hellenistic Military and Naval Developments*. Cambridge: Cambridge University Press, 1930.

Thucydides, *Complete Writings*. New York: Random House (Modern Library), 1934 (paperback).

Toynbee, A. J., *Hannibal's Legacy: The Hannibalic War's Effect on Roman Life*. 2 vols. London: Oxford University Press, 1965.

Ure, P. N., *Justinian and His Age*. Harmondsworth, Eng.: Penguin, 1951.

Vegetius Renatus, Flavius, *The Military Institutions of the Romans*. Harrisburg, Pa.: Military Service, 1944.

Watson, G. R., *The Roman Soldier*. Ithaca, N.Y.: Cornell University Press, 1969.

Webster, Graham, *The Roman Imperial Army*. London: Black, 1969.

Xenophon, *The Persian Expedition*. Harmondsworth, Eng.: Penguin, 1949.

THE MIDDLE AGES

Beeler, John, *Warfare in England, 1066–1189*. Ithaca, N.Y.: Cornell University Press, 1966.

Blair, Claude, *European Armour circa 1066 to circa 1700*. London: Batsford, 1958.

Burne, A. H., *The Agincourt War: A Military History of the Latter Part of the Hundred Years' War from 1369 to 1453*. New York: Oxford University Press, 1956.

Burne, A. H., *Battlefields of England*. London: Methuen, 1950.

Burne, A. H., *The Crecy War: A Military History of the Hundred Years' War from 1337 to the Peace of Bretigny, 1360*. New York: Oxford University Press, 1955.

Cheyney, E. P., *The Dawn of a New Era, 1250–1453*. New York: Harper, 1936.

Foulkes, Charles, *Arms and Armament*. London: Harrap, 1945.

Glover, R. G., "English Warfare in 1066," *English Historical Review*, LXVII. Jan. 1952.

Hewitt, H. J., *The Black Prince's Expedition of 1355–1357*. Manchester: Manchester University Press, 1958.

Hewitt, H. J., *The Organization of War under Edward III, 1338–62*. New York: Barnes & Noble, 1966.

Heymann, F. G., *John Ziska and the Hussite Revolution*. New York: Russell, 1969.

Hollister, C. W., *Anglo-Saxon Military Institutions*. New York: Oxford University Press, 1962.

Hollister, C. W., *The Military Organization of Norman England*. Oxford: Clarendon, 1965.

Lewis, A. R., *Naval Power and Trade in the Mediterranean, A.D. 500–1100*. Princeton, N.J.: Princeton University Press, 1951.

Lot, Ferdinand, *L'Art Militaire et les Armées au Moyen Age en Europe et dans le Proche Orient*. Paris: Payot, 1946.

Oman, Sir Charles, "The Art of War in the Fifteenth Century," *Cambridge Medieval History*, VIII. New York: Macmillan, 1936.

Oman, Sir Charles, *The Art of War in the Middle Ages, 378–1515*, rev. ed. Ithaca, N.Y.: Cornell University Press, 1960 (paperback).

Oman, Sir Charles, *A History of the Art of War in the Middle Ages*. 2 vols. New York: Burt Franklin, 1969.

Painter, Sidney, *A History of the Middle Ages, 284–1500*. New York: Knopf, 1961.

Perroy, Edouard, *The Hundred Years' War*. London: Eyre & Spottiswoode, 1951 (paperback).

Powicke, Michael, *Military Obligation in Medieval England*. Oxford: Clarendon, 1962.

Rodgers, W. L., *Naval Warfare under Oars from the Fourth to the Sixteenth Centuries*. Annapolis, Md.: United States Naval Institute, 1939.

Runciman, Steven, *History of the Crusades*. 3 vols. Cambridge: Cambridge University Press, 1951–1955 (paperback).

Sanders, I. J., *Feudal Military Service in England*. London: Oxford University Press, 1956.

Sellman, R. R., *Medieval English Warfare*. London: Roy, 1964.

Smail, R. C., *Crusading Warfare, 1097–1193*. London: Cambridge University Press, 1967.

Thompson, A. Hamilton, "The Art of War to 1400," *Cambridge Medieval History*, VI. New York: Macmillan, 1911–1936.

Thompson, A. Hamilton, *Military Architecture in England during the Middle Ages*. London: Oxford University Press, 1912.

Toy, Sidney, *A History of Fortification from 3000 B.C. to 1700*. New York: Dufour, 1954.

THE RENAISSANCE TO NAPOLEON

GENERAL AND MILITARY

Alden, John R., *The American Revolution*. New York: Harper, 1954 (paperback).

Alden, John R., "The Military Side of the Revolution," *Manuscripta*, IX. 1957.

Ashley, M. P., *Cromwell's Generals*. New York: St. Martin's, 1954.

Ashley, M. P., *The Greatness of Oliver Cromwell*. New York: Crowell Collier & Macmillan, 1966 (paperback).

Atkinson, C. T., *Marlborough and the Rise of the British Army*. New York: Putnam, 1941.

Baurmeister, Karl, *Revolution in America: Confidential Letters and Journals, 1776–1784*. New Brunswick, N.J.: Rutgers University Press, 1957.

Bayley, C. C., *War and Society in Renaissance Florence: The De Militia of Leonardo Bruni*. Toronto: University of Toronto Press, 1961.

Belloc, Hilaire, *The Tactics and Strategy of the Great Duke of Marlborough*. London: Arrowsmith, 1933.

Blomfield, Reginald, *Vauban*. London: Methuen, 1938.

Bryant, Arthur, *The Age of Elegance, 1812–1822*. London: Collins, 1950.

Bryant, Arthur, *Years of Endurance, 1793–1802*. New York: Harper, 1947.

Bryant, Arthur, *Years of Victory, 1802–1812*. London: Collins, 1944.

Buchan, John, *Oliver Cromwell*. Mystic, Conn.: Verry, 1957.

Burne, A. H., *The Great Civil War: A Military History of the First Civil War, 1642–1646*. London: Eyre & Spottiswoode, 1959.

Burton, I. F., *The Captain-General* (Marlborough). London: Constable, 1969.

Chandler, David, *The Campaigns of Napoleon*. New York: Crowell Collier & Macmillan, 1966.

Chandler, David (ed.), *Robert Parker and Comte de Merode-Westerloo: The Marlborough Wars*. London: Longmans, 1968.

Churchill, Winston, *Marlborough*. 4 vols. London: Harrap, 1933–1938.

Colby, Eibridge, *Masters of Mobile Warfare* (chapters on Marlborough, Frederick the Great, and Napoleon). Princeton, N.J.: Princeton University Press, 1943.

Colin, J. L. A., *L'Education Militaire de Napoléon*. Paris: Chapelot, 1900.

Colin, J. L. A. (ed.), *La Tactique et la Discipline dans les Armées de la Révolution.* Paris: Chapelot, 1902.

Craig, G. A., *The Politics of the Prussian Army, 1640–1945.* New York: Oxford University Press, 1964.

Craig, G. A., "Problems of Coalition Warfare: The Military Alliance Against Napoleon, 1813–1814," *Harmon Memorial Lectures in Military History,* no. 7. Colorado Springs: USAF Academy, 1965.

Cruickshank, C. G., *Elizabeth's Army,* rev. ed. London: Oxford University Press, 1950.

Davidson, Philip, *Propaganda and the American Revolution.* Chapel Hill, N.C.: University of North Carolina Press, 1967 (paperback).

Davies, Godfrey, *Wellington and His Army.* Oxford: Oxford University Press, 1954.

Deiss, J. J., *Captains of Fortune: Profiles of Six Italian Condottieri.* New York: T. Y. Crowell, 1966.

Dodge, T. A., *Gustavus Adolphus: A History of the Art of War from the Middle Ages to the War of the Spanish Succession.* Boston: Houghton Mifflin, 1895.

Ergang, R. R., *The Myth of the All-Destructive Fury of the Thirty Years' War.* Pocono Pines, Pa.: Craftsmen, 1956.

Ergang, R. R., *The Potsdam Führer.* New York: Cambridge University Press, 1941.

Firth, C. H., *Cromwell's Army,* 2d ed. London: Methuen, 1962.

Fisher, H. A. L., *Napoleon,* 2d ed. New York: Oxford University Press, 1967.

Fortescue, J. W., *Six British Soldiers* (Cromwell and Marlborough). London: Williams & Norgate, 1928.

Fortescue, J. W., *Wellington.* London: Williams & Norgate, 1928.

Frederick II of Prussia, *Instructions for His Generals.* Harrisburg, Pa.: Stackpole, 1951.

Fuller, J. F. C., *British Light Infantry in the Eighteenth Century.* London: Hutchinson, 1925.

Fuller, J. F. C., *Sir John Moore's System of Training.* London: Hutchinson, 1925.

Gershoy, Leo, *From Despotism to Revolution, 1763–1789.* New York: Harper, 1944 (paperback).

Gilbert, Felix, "Machiavelli," E. M. Earle (ed.), *Makers of Modern Strategy.* Princeton, N.J.: Princeton University Press, 1948.

Glover, R. G., *Peninsular Preparation: The Reform of the British Army, 1759–1809.* Cambridge: Cambridge University Press, 1963.

Guerlac, H., "Vauban: The Impact of Science on War," E. M. Earle (ed.), *Makers of Modern Strategy.* Princeton, N.J.: Princeton University Press, 1948.

Hall, A. R., *Ballistics in the Seventeenth Century: A Study in the Relations of Science and War with Reference Principally to England.* New York: Cambridge University Press, 1952.

Hegemann, Werner, *Frederick the Great.* London: Constable, 1929.

Hibbert, Christopher, *Wolfe at Quebec.* Cleveland: World, 1959.

Jacobs, J. R., *The Beginnings of the U.S. Army, 1783–1812.* Princeton, N.J.: Princeton University Press, 1947.

Jameson, J. F., *The American Revolution Considered as a Social Movement.* Princeton, N.J.: Princeton University Press, 1926.

Kamen, Henry, *The War of Succession in Spain, 1700–1715.* Bloomington, Ind.: Indiana University Press, 1969.

Kennett, Lee, *The French Armies in the Seven Years' War: A Study of Military Organization and Administration.* Durham, N.C.: Duke University Press, 1967.

Leach, D. E., *Flintlock and Tomahawk: New England in King Philip's War.* New York: Norton, 1966 (paperback).

Lewis, Michael, *Armada Guns: A Comparative Study of English and Spanish Armaments.* New York: Fernhill, 1961.

Liddell Hart, B. H., *The Ghost of Napoleon.* New Haven, Conn.: Yale University Press, 1933.

Luvaas, Jay (ed.), *Frederick the Great on the Art of War.* New York: The Free Press, 1966.

McCardell, Lee, *Ill-Starred General: Braddock of the Coldstream Guards.* Pittsburgh: University of Pittsburgh Press, 1958 (paperback).

Macdonell, A. G., *Napoleon and His Marshals.* London: Macmillan, 1934.

Machiavelli, Nicolo, *The Art of War.* Indianapolis, Ind.: Bobbs-Merrill, 1965.

Machiavelli, Nicolo, *The Prince.* Harmondsworth, Eng.: Penguin, 1961.

Mackesy, Piers, *The War for America, 1775–1783.* Cambridge, Mass.: Harvard University Press, 1964.

Macleod, W. C., *The American Indian Frontier.* New York: Knopf, 1928.

MacMunn, George, *Gustavus Adolphus.* London: Hodder & Stoughton, 1930.

Miller, J. C., *Triumph of Freedom.* Boston: Little Brown, 1948 (paperback).

Montross, Lynn, *Rag, Tag, and Bobtail: The Story of the Continental Army, 1775–1783.* New York: Harper, 1952.

Napoleon, "Maxims," T. R. Phillips (ed.), *Roots of Strategy.* Harrisburg, Pa.: Military Service, 1940.

Nicholson, G. W. L., *Marlborough and the War of the Spanish Succession.* Ottawa: Queen's Printer, 1955.

Nickerson, Hoffman, *The Armed Horde, 1793–1939: A Study of the Rise, Survival, and Decline of the Mass Army.* New York: Putnam's, 1940.

Oman, Carola, *Sir John Moore.* Mystic, Conn.: Verry, 1953.

Oman, Charles, *History of the Art of War in the Sixteenth Century.* London: Methuen, 1937.

Oman, Charles, *A History of the Peninsular War.* 5 vols. Oxford: Clarendon, 1902.

Oman, Charles, *Studies in the Napoleonic Wars.* London: Methuen, 1929.

Oman, Charles, *Wellington's Army, 1809–1814.* New York: Longmans Green, 1912.

Omond, J. S., *Parliament and the Army.* Cambridge: Cambridge University Press, 1933.

O'Neil, B. H., *Castles and Cannon: A Study of Early Artillery Fortifications in England.* Oxford: Clarendon, 1960.

Palmer, R. R., "Frederick the Great, Guibert, Bülow," E. M. Earle (ed.), *Makers of Modern Strategy.* Princeton, N.J.: Princeton University Press, 1948.

Pargellis, S. M., "The Four Independent Companies of New York," *Essays in Colonial History Presented to Charles McLean Andrews by his Students.* New Haven, Conn.: Yale University Press, 1933.

Pargellis, S. M., *Lord Loudoun in North America.* Hamden, Conn.: Shoe String Press, 1968.

Parkman, Francis, *Montcalm and Wolfe.* 2 vols. Boston: Little Brown, 1905–1907; New York: Crowell Collier & Macmillan (paperback).

Peckham, H. H., *The War for Independence: A Military History.* Chicago: Chicago University Press, 1958 (paperback).

Phipps, R. W., *The Armies of the First French Republic and the Rise of the Marshals of Napoleon.* 5 vols. London: Oxford University Press, 1926–39.

Prebble, John, *Culloden.* Harmondsworth, Eng.: Penguin, 1967 (paperback).

Quimby, R. S., *The Background of Napoleonic Warfare: The Theory of Military Tactics in Eighteenth Century France.* New York: AMS Press, 1957.

Roberts, Michael, *The Military Revolution, 1560–1660.* Belfast: Belfast University Press, 1956.

Roberts, Penfield, *The Quest for Security, 1715–1740.* New York: Harper, 1947.

Rose, J. Holland, *The Personality of Napoleon.* London: G. Bell, 1912.

Russell, C. P., *Guns on the Early Frontiers: A History of Firearms from Colonial Times through the Years of the Western Fur Trade.* Berkeley, Calif.: University of California Press, 1957 (paperback).

Savory, Reginald, *His Britannic Majesty's Army in Germany during the Seven Years' War.* New York: Oxford University Press, 1966.

Saxe, Maurice de, *Reveries on the Art of War.* Harrisburg, Pa.: Military Service, 1944.

Scheer, G. F., and H. F. Rankin, *Rebels and Redcoats.* Cleveland: World, 1957; New York: Mentor, 1959 (paperback).

Scouller, R. E., *The Armies of Queen Anne.* New York: Oxford University Press, 1966.

Snyderman, G. S., *Behind the Tree of Peace: A Sociological Analysis of Iroquois Warfare.* Philadelphia: University of Pennsylvania Press, 1948.

Spaulding, O. L., H. Nickerson, and J. W. Wright, *Warfare.* Washington: Infantry Journal Press, 1937.

Stacey, C. P., *Quebec, 1759: The Siege and the Battle.* New York: St. Martin's, 1959.

Stoye, John, *The Siege of Vienna.* London: Collins, 1964.

Taylor, Frank, *The Wars of Marlborough, 1702–1709.* 2 vols. Oxford: Blackwell, 1921.

Thompson, J. W., *The Wars of Religion in France, 1559–1576.* New York: Ungar, 1964.

Trevelyan, G. M., *England under Queen Anne.* 3 vols. New York: Longmans Green, 1932–1934.

Vaillant, G. C., *The Aztecs of Mexico,* 2d ed. Harmondsworth, Eng.: Penguin, 1962.

Ward, Christopher, *The War of the Revolution.* 2 vols. New York: Macmillan, 1952.

Wedgwood, C. V., *The Common Man in the Great Civil War.* Leicester: Leicester University Press, 1957.

Wedgwood, C. V., *The King's War, 1641–1647.* New York: Macmillan, 1959.

Wedgwood, C. V., *The Thirty Years' War.* Harmondsworth, Eng.: Penguin, 1961 (paperback).

Weller, Jac, *Wellington in the Peninsula, 1808–1814.* London: N. Vane, 1962.

White, J. M., *Marshal of France: The Life and Times of Maurice, Comte de Saxe.* New York: Rand McNally, 1962.

Wise, S. F., "The American Revolution and Indian History," *Character and*

Circumstance: Essays in Honour of D. G. Creighton. Toronto: Macmillan, 1970.

Woodhouse, A. S. P. (ed.), *Puritanism and Liberty: The Army Debates, 1647–49.* Chicago: University of Chicago Press, 1951.

Yorck von Wartenburg, Maximilian, *Napoleon as a General.* 2 vols. London: Paul Trench, Trübner, 1902.

NAVAL

Albion, R. G., *Forests and Sea Power: The Timber Problem of the Royal Navy, 1652–1862.* Hamden, Conn.: Archon, 1965.

Anderson, Romola & R. C., *The Sailing Ship.* New York: Norton, 1963.

Bamford, P. W., *Forests and French Sea Power, 1660–1789.* Toronto: University of Toronto Press, 1956.

Bryant, Arthur, *Samuel Pepys.* 3 vols. Cambridge: Cambridge University Press, 1933–1936.

Cipolla, Carlo, *Guns and Sails in the Early Phase of European Expansion, 1400–1700.* London: Collins, 1965.

Clark, G. N., *The Dutch Alliance and the War against French Trade, 1688–1697.* New York: Longmans Green, 1923.

Corbett, Julian, *The Campaign of Trafalgar.* London: Longmans Green, 1910.

Corbett, Julian, *Drake and the Tudor Navy.* 2 vols. New York: Burt Franklin, 1965.

Corbett, Julian, *England in the Seven Years' War.* 2 vols. London: Longmans Green, 1907.

Corbett, Julian (ed.), *Fighting Instructions, 1530–1816.* London: Navy Records Society, 1905.

Corbett, Julian, *The Successors of Drake.* New York: Burt Franklin, 1969.

Ehrman, John, *The Navy in the War of William III, 1689–1697.* Cambridge: Cambridge University Press, 1953.

Graham, G. S. *Empire of the North Atlantic: The Maritime Struggle for North America,* 2d ed. Toronto: University of Toronto Press, 1958.

Great Britain, Admiralty, *Evidence Relating to the Tactics . . . at Trafalgar.* London: HMSO, 1913.

Grenfell, Russell, *Nelson, the Sailor.* London: Faber & Faber, 1949.

James, William, *The British Navy in Adversity.* New York: Longmans Green, 1926.

Laughton, J. K. (ed.), *State Papers Relating to the Defeat of the Spanish Armada.* London: Navy Records Society, 1894.

Lewis, Michael, *A Social History of the Navy, 1793–1815.* London: Allen & Unwin, 1960.

Mackesy, Piers, *The War in the Mediterranean, 1803–1810.* Cambridge, Mass.: Harvard University Press, 1957.

Mahan, A. T., *The Life of Nelson.* 2 vols. New York: Haskell, 1968.

Mahan, A. T., *The Major Operations of the Navies in the War of American Independence.* New York: Greenwood, 1968.

Mahan, A. T., *Sea Power in its Relations to the War of 1812.* 2 vols. New York: Greenwood, 1969.

Malone, J. J., *Pine Trees and Politics: Naval Stores and Forest Policy in Colonial New England.* Seattle: University of Washington Press, 1964.

Mattingly, Garrett, *The Defeat of the Spanish Armada.* New York: Houghton Mifflin, 1962; Harmondsworth, Eng.: Penguin (paperback).

Morison, S. E., *Admiral of the Ocean Sea.* Boston: Little Brown, 1942.

Oakeshott, W. F., *Founded upon the Seas.* Cambridge: Cambridge University Press, 1942.

Oman, Carola, *Nelson.* Mystic, Conn.: Verry, 1967.

Owen, J. H., *War at Sea under Queen Anne.* Cambridge: Cambridge University Press, 1938.

Parry, J. H., *The Age of Reconnaissance.* New York: Praeger, 1969.

Perrin, W. G., *Nelson's Signals: The Evolution of the Signal Flags.* London: HMSO, 1908.

Pool, Bernard, *Navy Board Contracts, 1660–1832.* London: Longmans, 1966.

Powley, E. B., *The English Navy in the Revolution of 1688.* Cambridge: Cambridge University Press, 1928.

Richmond, Herbert, *The Navy as an Instrument of Policy, 1558–1727.* Cambridge: Cambridge University Press, 1953.

Rose, J. Holland, "Napoleon and Sea Power," *The Indecisiveness of Modern War.* Port Washington, N.Y.: Kennikat, 1968.

Rowse, A. L., *Sir Richard Grenville.* London: Cape, 1937.

Taylor, A. H., "The Battle of Trafalgar," *Mariners' Mirror,* XXXVI. 1950.

Tunstall, Brian, *Admiral Byng and the Loss of Minorca.* London: P. Allan, 1928.

Tunstall, Brian, *Nelson.* New York: Dufour, 1950.

Williamson, J. A., *The Age of Drake.* New York: Barnes & Noble, 1960.

Williamson, J. A., *Hawkins of Plymouth,* 2d ed. New York: Barnes & Noble, 1969.

Woodrooffe, Thomas, *The Enterprise of England: An Account of her Emergence as an Oceanic Power.* London: Faber & Faber, 1958.

THE NINETEENTH CENTURY

GENERAL AND MILITARY

Andreano, Ralph, *The Economic Impact of the American Civil War.* Cambridge, Mass.: Schenkman, 1962 (paperback).

Angell, Norman, *The Great Illusion: A Study of the Relation of Military Power in Nations to their Economic and Social Advantage.* New York: Putnam's, 1911.

Black, R. C., *The Railroads of the Confederacy.* Chapel Hill, N.C.: University of North Carolina Press, 1952.

Bourne, Kenneth, *Britain and the Balance of Power in North America, 1815–1908.* Berkeley, Calif.: University of California Press, 1967.

Brinton, Crane, G. A. Craig, and F. Gilbert, "Jomini," in E. M. Earle (ed.), *Makers of Modern Strategy.* Princeton, N.J.: Princeton University Press, 1948.

Bruce, R. V., *Lincoln and the Tools of War.* Indianapolis, Ind.: Bobbs-Merrill, 1956.

Caemmerer, Rudolf von, *The Development of Strategical Science during the Nineteenth Century.* London: Rees, 1905.

Catton, Bruce, *The Centennial History of the Civil War.* 3 vols. Garden City, N.Y.: Doubleday, 1961–1965 (paperback).

Challener, Richard D., *The French Theory of the Nation in Arms, 1866–1939.* New York: Russell, 1955.

Clausewitz, Karl von, *On War.* New York: Random House (Modern Library), 1943; abridged ed., Harmondsworth, Eng.: Penguin, 1968.

Coggins, Jack, *Arms and Equipment of the Civil War.* Garden City, N.Y.: Doubleday, 1962.

Curtiss, John S., *The Russian Army under Nicholas I, 1825–1855.* Durham, N.C.: Duke University Press, 1965.

De Weerd, H. A., "Churchill, Lloyd George, Clemenceau: The Emergence of the Civilian," E. M. Earle (ed.) *Makers of Modern Strategy.* Princeton, N.J.: Princeton University Press, 1948.

Dowdey, Clifford, *Death of a Nation: The Story of Lee and his Men at Gettysburg.* New York: Knopf, 1958.

Downey, F. D., *The Guns at Gettysburg.* New York: Crowell Collier & Macmillan, 1962 (paperback).

Du Picq, A., *Battle Studies.* Harrisburg, Pa.: Military Service, 1947.

Earle, E. M., "Smith, Hamilton, and List," *Makers of Modern Strategy.* Princeton, N.J.: Princeton University Press, 1948.

Falls, C. B., *A Hundred Years of War, 1850–1950.* New York: Crowell Collier & Macmillan, 1962 (paperback).

Fite, E. D., *Social and Industrial Conditions in the North during the Civil War.* New York: Ungar, 1963.

Fortescue, J. W., *History of the British Army,* XI–XIII. New York: Macmillan, 1902–1930.

Freeman, D. S., *R. E. Lee.* 4 vols. New York: Scribner's, 1951.

Fuller, J. F. C., *War and Western Civilization, 1832–1932: A Study of War as a Political Instrument and as an Expression of Mass Democracy.* London: Duckworth, 1932.

Goerlitz, Walter, *History of the German General Staff, 1657–1945.* New York: Praeger, 1953 (paperback).

Greene, Francis Vinton, *The Russian Army and its Campaigns in Turkey in 1877–78.* New York: Appleton, 1879.

Greene, J. I., *The Living Thoughts of Clausewitz.* Philadelphia: McKay, 1943.

Henderson, G. F. R., *Stonewall Jackson and the American Civil War.* New York: Longmans Green, 1963.

Hilton, Richard, *The Indian Mutiny: A Centenary History.* London: Hollis & Carter, 1957.

Hittle, J. D., *The Military Staff, its History and Development,* rev. ed. Harrisburg, Pa.: Stackpole, 1961.

Howard, Michael, *The Franco-Prussian War: The German Invasion of France, 1870–1871.* New York: Crowell Collier & Macmillan, 1969 (paperback).

Irvine, D. D., "The French and Prussian Staff Systems before 1870," *Journal of the American Military History Foundations,* II. 1938.

Irvine, D. D., "The French Discovery of Clausewitz and Napoleon," *Journal of the American Military Institute,* IV. 1940.

Irvine, D. D., "Origins of Capital Staffs," *Journal of Modern History,* X. 1938.

Jessup, P. C., *et al.*, *Neutrality: Its History, Economics and Law*. 4 vols. New York: Columbia University Press, 1935–36.

Jomini, Henri, *Summary of the Art of War*. Harrisburg, Pa.: Stackpole, 1952.

Kitchen, Martin, *The German Officer Corps, 1890–1914*. Oxford: Clarendon, 1968.

Livermore, T. L., *Numbers and Losses in the Civil War in America, 1861–65*. New York: Kraus, 1968.

Luvaas, Jay, *The Civil War: A Soldier's View: A Collection of Civil War Writings*. Chicago: University of Chicago Press, 1958.

Luvaas, Jay, *The Education of an Army: British Military Thought, 1815–1940*. Chicago: University of Chicago Press, 1964.

Luvaas, Jay, *The Military Legacy of the Civil War: The European Inheritance*. Chicago: University of Chicago Press, 1959.

Luard, C. E., "Field Railways and their General Application in War," *R.U.S.I. Journal*, XVII. 1873.

Maurice, J. F., *The System of Field Manoeuvres Best Adapted for Enabling our Troops to Meet a Continental Army*. Edinburgh: Blackwood, 1872.

Milton, G. F., *Conflict: The American Civil War*. New York: Coward-McCann, 1941.

Moltke, H. K. B. von, *The Franco-German War of 1870–71*. London: Harper, 1907.

Nelson, O. L., *National Security and the General Staff*. Washington: Infantry Journal Press, 1946.

Nickerson, Hoffman, *The Armed Horde, 1793–1939: A Study of the Rise, Survival, and Decline of the Mass Army*. New York: Putnam's, 1940.

Oppenheim, L. F. L., *International Law, II. Disputes: War and Neutrality*, 7th ed. New York: Longmans Green, 1963.

Possony, S. T., and E. Mantoux, "Du Picq and Foch," E. M. Earle (ed.), *Makers of Modern Strategy*. Princeton, N.J.: Princeton University Press, 1948.

Pratt, E. A., *The Rise of Rail Power in War and Conquest, 1833–1914*. London: King, 1916.

Preston, R. A., *Canada and "Imperial Defense": A Study of the Origins of the British Commonwealth's Defense Organization, 1867–1919*. Durham, N.C.: Duke University Press, 1967.

Randall, J. G., and David Donald, *The Civil War and Reconstruction*, 2d ed. Boston: Heath, 1961.

Ritter, E. A., *Shaka Zulu: The Rise of the Zulu Empire*. New York: Longmans Green, 1964.

Rothfels, Hans, "Clausewitz," E. M. Earle (ed.), *Makers of Modern Strategy*. Princeton, N.J.: Princeton University Press, 1948.

Schellendorff, Paul von, *The Duties of the General Staff*. London: HMSO, 1907.

Sen, Surendra Nath, *Eighteen Fifty-Seven*. Delhi: Government of India, 1957.

Stacey, C. P., *Canada and the British Army: A Study in the Practice of Responsible Government*, rev. ed. Toronto: University of Toronto Press, 1963.

Stacey, C. P., "The Myth of the Unguarded Frontier, 1815–1871," *American Historical Review*, LVI. 1950.

Stackpole, E. J., *Chancellorsville: Lee's Greatest Battle*. Harrisburg, Pa.: Stackpole, 1958.

Stackpole, E. J., *Drama on the Rappahannock: The Fredericksburg Campaign.* Harrisburg, Pa.: Military Service, 1957.

Steele, M. F., *American Campaigns.* 2 vols. Washington: U.S. Infantry Association, 1939–43.

U.S. Military Academy, Department of Military Art and Engineering, *Jomini, Clausewitz, and Schlieffen.* West Point: Government Printing Office, 1951.

Upton, Emory, *The Military Policy of the United States.* New York: Greenwood, 1968.

Vandiver, Frank, *Mighty Stonewall.* New York: Mc-Graw-Hill, 1957.

Webster, Charles, *The Congress of Vienna.* New York: Barnes & Noble, 1963.

Whitton, Frederick E., *Moltke.* London: Constable, 1921.

William, K. P., *Lincoln Finds a General.* 5 vols. New York: Macmillan, 1949–1959.

Williams, T. H., *Lincoln and His Generals.* New York: Random House, 1952 (paperback).

Woodham-Smith, Cecil, *The Reason Why.* New York: Dutton, 1952 (paperback).

NAVAL

Albion, R. G., and J. B. Pope, *Sea Lanes in Wartime: The American Experience: 1775–1942.* Hamden, Conn.: Shoe String Press, 1968.

Anderson, Bern, *By Sea and by River: The Naval History of the Civil War.* New York: Knopf, 1963.

Bartlett, C. J., *Great Britain and Sea Power, 1815–1853.* Oxford: Clarendon, 1963.

Baxter, J. P., "The British Government and Neutral Rights," *American Historical Review,* XXXIV. Oct. 1928.

Baxter, J. P., *The Introduction of the Ironclad Warship.* Hamden, Conn.: Shoe String Press, 1968.

Brodie, Bernard. *Sea Power in the Machine Age,* 2d ed. Princeton, N.J.: Princeton University Press, 1944.

Callendar, G. A. R., and F. H. Hinsley, *The Naval Side of British History, 1485–1945.* London: Chatto, 1960.

Chapelle, Howard I. *The Search for Speed under Sail, 1700–1855.* New York: Norton, 1967.

Cotter, C. H., *A History of Nautical Astronomy.* New York: American Elsevier, 1968.

Daly, Robert W., *How the 'Merrimac' Won: The Strategic Story of the C.S.S. Virginia.* New York: Crowell, 1957.

Gardiner, C. Harvey, *Naval Power in the Conquest of Mexico.* Austin, Tex.: University of Texas Press, 1956.

Hearnshaw, F. J. C., *Sea Power and Empire.* London: Harrap, 1940.

James, W. M., *The Influence of Sea Power on the History of the British People.* Cambridge: Cambridge University Press, 1948.

Lewis, Michael, *The Navy in Transition: 1814–1864.* Mystic, Conn.: Verry, 1965.

Lloyd, Christopher, *The Navy and the Slave Trade: The Suppression of the African Slave Trade in the Nineteenth Century.* New York: Barnes & Noble, 1968.

Marder, A. J., *The Anatomy of British Sea Power: A History of British*

Naval Power in the Pre-dreadnought Era, 1880–1905. London: F. Cass, 1964.

Marder, A. J., "From Jimmu Tenno to Perry," *American Historical Review.* Oct. 1945.

Penn, Geoffrey, *"Up Funnel, Down Screw!": The Story of the Naval Engineer.* London: Hollis & Carter, 1955.

Preston, Antony, and John Major, *Send a Gunboat: A Study of the Gunboat and its Role in British Policy, 1854–1904.* London: Longmans Green, 1967.

Puleston, W. D., *The Life and Work of Captain Alfred Mahan.* New York: Yale University Press, 1939.

Richmond, Herbert, *Statesmen and Sea Power.* Oxford: Clarendon, 1946.

Robertson, F. L., *The Evolution of Naval Armament.* London: Constable, 1921.

Savage, Carlton, *The Policy of the United States toward Maritime Commerce in War, 1776–1918.* 2 vols. New York: Kraus, 1969.

Schurman, D. M., *The Education of a Navy: The Development of British Naval Strategic Thought, 1867–1914.* Chicago: University of Chicago Press, 1965.

Smith, D. B., and A. C. Dewar (eds.), *The Russian War, 1854–55.* 3 vols. London: Navy Records Society, 1943–1945.

Sprout, H., and M. T. Sprout, *The Rise of American Naval Power.* Princeton, N.J.: Princeton University Press, 1943 (paperback).

Sprout, M. T., "Mahan," E. M. Earle (ed.), *Makers of Modern Strategy.* Princeton, N.J.: Princeton University Press, 1948.

Wescott, A. F. (ed.), *American Sea Power Since 1775.* Philadelphia: Lippincott, 1947.

Westcott, A. F. (ed.), *Mahan on Naval Warfare: Selections from the Writings of Rear Admiral Alfred T. Mahan.* Boston: Little Brown, 1918.

Wilson, H. W., *Ironclads in Action.* 2 vols. London: S. Low & Marston, 1896.

THE TWENTIETH CENTURY TO 1939

Albertini, Luigi, *The Origins of the War of 1914.* 3 vols. New York: Oxford University Press, 1952–1957.

Aron, Raymond, *The Century of Total War.* Boston: Beacon, 1955 (paperback).

Aston, George, *The Study of War for Statesmen and Citizens.* New York: Longmans Green, 1927.

Baldwin, Hanson W., *World War I: An Outline History.* New York: Harper & Row, 1962.

Banse, Ewald, *Germany Prepares for War.* New York: Harcourt Brace, 1934.

Barnett, Correlli, *The Swordbearers: Supreme Command in the First World War.* New York: Morrow, 1964.

Bliss, Tasker, "The Evolution of the Unified Command," *Foreign Affairs,* I. Dec. 1922.

Bloch, I. S., *The Future of War in its Technical, Economic and Political Relations.* Boston: Ginn, 1902.

Boyle, Andrew, *Trenchard.* London: Collins, 1962.

Bruntz, G. F., *Allied Propaganda and the Collapse of the German Empire in*

1918. Stanford, Calif.: Stanford University, Hoover War Library Publications, 1938.

Buell, R. L., *The Washington Conference.* New York: Putnam's, 1922.

Chambers, F. P., *The War Behind the War, 1914–1918.* London: Faber & Faber, 1939.

Chatterton, E. K., *The Big Blockade.* London: Hurst & Blackett, 1932.

Churchill, W. L. S., *The Unknown War: The Eastern Front.* London: Butterworth, 1931.

Churchill, W. L. S., *The World Crisis, 1911–1918.* 6 vols. New York: Scribner's, 1923–1931.

Coffman, Edward M., *The War to End all Wars: the American Military Experience in World War I.* New York: Oxford University Press, 1969.

Cruttwell, C.R.M.T. *A History of the Great War, 1914–1918.* Oxford: Oxford University Press, 1940.

Dawson, R. M., "The Cabinet Minister and Administration: Asquith, Lloyd George, Curzon," *Political Science Quarterly,* LV. Sept. 1940.

Dawson, R. M., "The Cabinet Minister and Administration: Winston Churchill at the Admiralty," *Canadian Journal of Economics and Political Science,* VI. Aug. 1940.

De Gaulle, Charles, *The Army of the Future.* Philadelphia: Lippincott, 1941.

Douhet, Giulio, *The Command of the Air.* London: Faber & Faber, 1943.

Dunlop, J. K., *The Development of the British Army, 1899–1914.* London: Methuen, 1938.

Edmonds, J. E., *A Short History of World War One.* London: Oxford University Press, 1951.

Ehrman, John, *Cabinet Government and War, 1890–1940.* Hamden, Conn.: Shoe String Press, 1969.

Erickson, John, *The Soviet High Command: A Military-Political History, 1918–1941.* New York: St. Martin's, 1962.

Falkenhayn, Erich von, *General Headquarters, 1914–1916, and its Critical Decisions.* New York: Dodd Mead, 1919.

Falls, C. B., *The First World War.* London: Longmans, 1964.

Fay, S. B , *The Origins of the World War,* 2d ed. New York: The Free Press, 1966.

Fedotoff-White, Dimitri, *The Growth of the Red Army.* Princeton, N.J.: Princeton University Press, 1944.

Foerster, Wolfgang, *La Stratégie Allemande . . . 1914–1918.* Paris: Payot, 1929.

Fredette, R. H., *The Sky on Fire: The First Battle of Britain, 1917–18 and the Birth of the Royal Air Force.* New York: Holt, Rinehart & Winston, 1966.

Frost, H. H., *The Battle of Jutland.* London: Stevens & Brown, 1936.

Fuller, J. F. C., *Armoured Warfare.* Harrisburg, Pa.: Military Service, 1943.

Fuller, J. F. C., *Lectures on Field Service Regulations II.* London: Sifton Praed, 1931.

Fuller, J. F. C., *Memoirs of an Unconventional Soldier.* London: Nicholson & Watson, 1936.

Fuller, J. F. C., *The Reformation of War.* London: Hutchinson, 1923.

Fuller, J. F. C., *War and Western Civilization, 1832–1932.* London: Duckworth, 1932.

Garthoff, R. L., *Soviet Military Doctrine.* Glencoe, Ill.: The Free Press, 1953.

Gibson, Irving, "Maginot and Liddell Hart: The Doctrine of Defense," E. M. Earle (ed.), *Makers of Modern Strategy*. Princeton, N.J.: Princeton University Press, 1948.

Gibson, Langhorne, and J. E. T. Harper, *The Riddle of Jutland*. New York: Coward-McCann, 1934.

Golovine, N. N., *The Russian Campaign of 1914: The Beginning of the War and Operations in East Prussia*. London: Rees, 1933.

Goodspeed, D. J., *Ludendorff: Genius of World War I*. Toronto: Macmillan, 1966.

Gordon, H. J., *The Reichswehr and the German Republic, 1919–1926*. Princeton, N.J.: Princeton University Press, 1957.

Gottman, Jean, "The Background of Geopolitics," *Military Affairs*, VI. 1942.

Hammond, P. Y., *Organizing for Defense: The American Military Establishment in the Twentieth Century*. Princeton, N.J.: Princeton University Press, 1961.

Hankey, M. P., *The Supreme Command, 1914–1918*. 2 vols. New York: Fernhill, 1961.

Harper, J. E. T., *The Truth about Jutland*. London: Murray, 1927.

Higham, R., *Armed Forces in Peacetime: Britain, 1918–1940*. London: Foulis, 1963.

Higham, R., *The British Rigid Airship, 1908–1931*. London: Foulis, 1961.

Higham, R., *The Military Intellectuals in Britain, 1918–1939*. New Brunswick, N.J.: Rutgers University Press, 1966.

Hoffman, Max., *War Diaries and Other Papers*. 2 vols. London: M. Secker, 1929.

Holley, I. B., *Ideas and Weapons: Exploitation of the Aerial Weapon by the United States during World War I: A Study in the Relationship of Technological Advance, Military Doctrine and the Development of Weapons*. New Haven, Conn.: Yale University Press, 1953.

Holt, Edgar, *The Boer War*. London: Putnam, 1958.

Howard, Michael, "Strategy and Policy in Twentieth Century Warfare," *Harmon Memorial Lectures in Military History*, no. 9. Colorado Springs: USAF Academy, 1967.

Hunter, T. M., *Marshal Foch: A Study in Leadership*. Ottawa: Queen's Printer, 1961.

Johnson, R. M., *First Reflections on the Campaign of 1918*. New York: Holt, 1920.

Levine, I. D., *Flying Crusader: The Story of General William Mitchell*. London: Davies, 1943.

Liddell Hart, B. H., *The Defence of Britain*. London: Faber & Faber, 1939.

Liddell Hart, B. H., *Europe in Arms*. London: Faber & Faber, 1937.

Liddell Hart, B. H., *The Future of Infantry*. London: Faber & Faber, 1933.

Liddell Hart, B. H., *The Real War, 1914–1918*, rev. ed. Boston: Little Brown, 1964.

Liddell Hart, B. H., *The Remaking of Modern Armies*. London: Murray, 1927.

Liddell Hart, B. H., *The Revolution in Warfare*. New Haven, Conn.: Yale University Press, 1927.

Liddell Hart, B. H., *The Tanks*. London: Cassell, 1959.

Lloyd George, David, *War Memoirs*. 6 vols. London: Nicholson & Watson, 1933–1936.

Ludendorff, Erich, *My War Memories, 1914–1918.* 2 vols. New York: Harper, 1919.

Mackinder, Halford, *The Scope and Methods of Geography and The Geographical Pivot of History.* London: Murray, 1951.

Madariaga, Salvador de, *Disarmament.* New York: Coward-McCann, 1929.

Marder, A. J., *Fear God and Dreadnought: The Correspondence of Admiral of the Fleet Lord Fisher of Kelverstone.* 3 vols. London: Cape, 1952–1959.

Marder, A. J., *From the Dreadought to Scapa Flow,* 3 vols. to date. London: Oxford University Press, 1961–.

Maurice, F. B., *Governments and War.* London: Heinemann, 1926.

Maurice, F. B., *Lessons of Allied Cooperations, Naval, Military and Air, 1914–1918.* London: Oxford University Press, 1942.

Miksche, F. O., *Blitzkrieg.* London: Faber & Faber, 1942.

Millis, Walter, *The Road to War: America, 1914–1917.* New York: Fertig, 1935.

Moorehead, Alan, *Gallipoli.* New York: Harper, 1956.

Morgan, J. H., *Assize of Arms: The Disarmament of Germany and Her Rearmament, 1919–1939.* New York: Oxford University Press, 1946.

Morton, Louis, "The Origins of American Military Policy," *Military Affairs,* XXII. 1958.

Moyse-Bartlett, Hubert, *The King's African Rifles: A Study in the Military History of East and Central Africa, 1890–1945.* Aldershot, Eng.: Gale & Polden, 1956.

Obermann, Emil, *Soldaten, Bürger, Militaristen: Militär und Demokratie in Deutschland.* Stuttgart, W. Germ.: Cotta, 1958.

O'Callaghan, Sean, *The Easter Lily: The Story of the I.R.A.* New York: Roy, 1956.

Parkes, Oscar, *British Battleships: Warrior 1860 to Vanguard 1950: A History of Design, Construction and Armament.* London: Seeley, 1958.

Pollard, A. F., *A Short History of the Great War.* London: Methuen, 1950.

Puleston, W. D., *High Command in the World War.* London: Scribner's, 1934.

Raleigh, Walter, and H. A. Jones, *The War in the Air.* 6 vols. Oxford: Clarendon, 1922–1937.

Read, J. M., *Atrocity Propaganda, 1914–1919.* New Haven, Conn.: Yale University Press, 1941.

Renouvin, Pierre, *The Forms of War Government in France.* New Haven, Conn.: Yale University Press, 1927.

Ritter, Gerhard, *The Schlieffen Plan: Critique of a Myth.* New York: Dufour, 1968.

Robertson, William, *Soldiers and Statesmen.* London: Cassell, 1926.

Robinson, D. H., *The Zeppelin in Combat,* rev. ed. London: Foulis, 1966.

Root, Elihu, *The Military and Colonial Policy of the United States.* Cambridge, Mass.: Harvard University Press, 1916.

Rosinski, Herbert, "The Role of Sea Power in Global Warfare of the Future," *Brassey's Naval Annual.* 1947.

Royal Institute of International Affairs, *International Sanctions.* London: Oxford University Press, 1938.

Scammel, J. M., "Spenser Wilkinson and the Defense of Britain," *Journal of the American Military Institute,* IV. 1940.

Sikorski, Wladyslaw, *Modern Warfare.* New York: Roy, 1943.

Siney, M. C., *The Allied Blockade of Germany, 1914–1916.* Ann Arbor, Mich.: University of Michigan Press, 1957.

Slessor, J. C., *Air Power and Armies.* London: Oxford University Press, 1936.

Spaight, J. M., *Air Power and War Rights.* New York: Longmans Green, 1924.

Spaight, J. M., *Air Power Can Disarm.* London: Pitman, 1948.

Spaight, J. M., *The Beginnings of Organized Air Power.* London: Longmans Green, 1927.

Spears, E. L., *Prelude to Victory.* London: Cape, 1939.

Sprout, H. M., *Toward a New Order of Sea Power: American Naval Policy and the World Scene, 1918–1922.* Princeton, N.J.: Princeton University Press, 1946.

Strausz-Hupé, Robert, *Geopolitics.* New York: Putnam's, 1942.

Sueter, M. F., *Airmen or Noahs.* London: Pitman, 1928.

Sueter, M. F., *The Evolution of the Tank.* London: Hutchinson, 1937.

Sykes, F. H., *Aviation in Peace and War.* London: Arnold, 1922.

Taylor, Edmond, *The Strategy of Terror.* Boston: Houghton Mifflin, 1940.

Thomas, Hugh, *The Spanish Civil War.* New York: Harper, 1961 (paperback).

Tschuppik, Karl, *Ludendorff: The Tragedy of a Military Mind.* Boston: Houghton Mifflin, 1932.

Tuchman, Barbara, *The Guns of August.* New York: Macmillan, 1962 (paperback).

Vagts, Alfred, "Geography in War and Geopolitics," *Military Affairs,* VII. 1943.

Vagts, Alfred, *The Military Attaché.* Princeton, N.J.: Princeton University Press, 1967.

Wavell, Archibald, *Allenby.* 2 vols. London: Harrap, 1940–1943.

Wheeler-Bennett, J.W., *The Nemesis of Power: The German Army in Politics, 1918–1945.* New York: Viking Press (Compass), 1964 (paperback).

White, Howard, *Executive Influence in Determining Military Policy in the United States.* Urbana, Ill.: University of Illinois Press, 1925.

Whittlesey, D. S., *German Strategy of World Conquest.* New York: Farrar & Rinehart, 1942.

Wilkinson, Spenser, *The Brain of an Army: The German General Staff.* London: Constable, 1895.

Woodward, E. L., *Great Britain and the German Navy.* London: E. L. Cass, 1964.

Wynne, G. C., *If Germany Attacks: The Battle in Depth in the West.* London: Faber & Faber, 1940.

WORLD WAR II

Allport, G. W., and Leo Postman, *The Psychology of Rumor.* New York: Russell, 1965.

Amrine, Michael, *The Great Decision: The Secret History of the Atomic Bomb.* New York: Putnam, 1959.

Andrews, Marshall, *Disaster through Air Power.* New York: Rinehart, 1950.

Bacon, Reginald, *Modern Naval Strategy.* London: Muller, 1950.

Badoglio, Pietro, *Italy in the Second World War*. New York: Oxford University Press, 1948.

Baxter, J. P., *Scientists against Time*. Cambridge, Mass.: MIT Press, 1965 (paperback).

Benoist-Mechin, J., *Sixty Days that Shook the West: The Fall of France, 1940*. New York: Putnam, 1963.

Bloc, Marc, *Strange Defeat: A Statement of Evidence Written in 1940*. New York: Norton, 1968 (paperback).

Bradley, Omar, *A Soldier's Story*. New York: Holt, 1951.

Brodie, Bernard, *Strategic Air Power in World War II*. Santa Monica, Calif.: Rand Corporation, 1957.

Bryant, Arthur, *Triumph in the West, 1943–1946: Based on the Diaries and Autobiographical Notes of Field Marshal the Viscount Alanbrooke*. Garden City, N.Y.: Doubleday, 1959.

Bryant, Arthur, *The Turn of the Tide: A History of the War Years Based on the Diaries of Field Marshal Lord Alanbrooke, Chief of the Imperial General Staff*. Garden City, N.Y.: Doubleday, 1957.

Buckmaster, M. J., *They Fought Alone: The Story of British Agents in France*. London: Odhams, 1958.

Burne, A. H., *Strategy as Exemplified in World War II*. Cambridge: Cambridge University Press, 1946.

Canada, Department of National Defence, *Official History of the Canadian Army in the Second World War*. 4 vols. Ottawa: Queen's Printer, 1955–1970.

Carroll, Wallace, *Persuade or Perish*. Boston: Houghton Mifflin, 1948.

Chuikov, Vasilii, *The Battle for Stalingrad*. New York: Ballantine, 1968 (paperback).

Churchill, W. L. S., *The Second World War*. 6 vols. Boston: Houghton Mifflin, 1948–1953.

Ciano, Galeazzo, *The Ciano Diaries, 1939–1943*. New York: Fertig, 1946.

Clark, Alan, *Barbarossa: The Russian-German Conflict, 1941–1945*. New York: Morrow, 1965.

Clark, Mark, *From the Danube to the Yalu*. New York: Harper, 1950.

Cookridge, E. H., *Inside SOE: The Story of Special Operations in Western Europe, 1940–45*. London: Arthur Barker, 1966.

Craven, W. F., and J. L. Cate (eds), *The Army Air Forces in World War II*. 6 vols. Chicago: University of Chicago Press 1948–1955.

Creswell, John, *Sea Warfare, 1939–1945*, rev. ed. Berkeley, Calif.: University of California Press, 1967.

Dallin, Alexander, *German Rule in Russia, 1941–1945: A Study of Occupation Policies*. New York: St. Martin's, 1957.

De Guingand, Francis, *Operation Victory*. London: Hodder & Stoughton, 1947.

De Seversky, A. P., *Air Power: Key to Survival*. New York: Simon & Schuster, 1950.

De Seversky, A. P., *Victory through Air Power*. New York: Simon & Schuster, 1942.

De Weerd, H. A., *Great Soldiers of the Two World Wars*. New York: Norton, 1941.

Dickens, G. C., *Bombing and Strategy*. London: S. Low, Marston, 1947.

Draper, Theodore, *The Six Weeks' War*. London: Methuen, 1946.

Eisenhower, D. D., *Crusade in Europe.* New York: Doubleday, 1948 (paperback).

Erickson, John, *Stalin's War Against Germany.* London: 1966.

Falls, C. B., *The Second World War: A Short History,* 3d ed. London: Methuen, 1950.

Feis, Herbert, *Churchill, Roosevelt, Stalin: The War They Waged and the Peace They Sought.* Princeton, N.J.: Princeton University Press, 1957 (paperback).

Fleming, Peter, *Invasion, 1940: An Account of the German Preparations and the British Counter-measures.* London: Hart-Davies, 1957.

Fuller, J. F. C., *The Second World War.* London: Eyre & Spottiswoode, 1954.

Galland, Adolf, *The First and the Last: The Rise and Fall of the German Fighter Forces, 1938–1945.* New York: Ballantine, 1969 (paperback).

Garthoff, R. L., *Soviet Military Policy.* New York: Praeger, 1966.

Gilbert, Felix (ed.), *Hitler Directs His War.* New York: Oxford University Press, 1950.

Goebbels, Joseph, *The Goebbels Diaries, 1942–43,* New York: Doubleday, 1948.

Goerlitz, W., *Paulus and Stalingrad.* London: Methuen, 1963.

Great Britain, Privy Council, *History of the Second World War.* 55 vols. to date. London: HMSO, 1952–.

Guderian, Heinz, *Panzer Leader.* London: Michael Joseph, 1952; abridged ed., New York: Ballantine, 1967.

Harris, Arthur, *Bomber Offensive.* London: Collins, 1947.

Higgins, Trumbull, *Winston Churchill and the Second Front, 1940–1943.* New York: Oxford University Press, 1957.

Hinsley, F. H., *Hitler's Strategy: The Naval Evidence.* Cambridge: Cambridge University Press, 1951.

Irving, T. A., "Psychological Analysis of Wartime Rumour Patterns in Canada," *Bulletin of the Canadian Psychological Association,* III. 1943.

Jacobsen, H. A., and J. Rohwer (eds.), *Decisive Battles of World War II: The German View.* New York: Putnam's, 1965.

James, William, *The British Navies in the Second World War.* London: Longmans Green, 1947.

Kilmarx, R. A., *A History of Soviet Air Power.* New York: Praeger, 1962.

Kris, Ernst, and Hans Speier, *German Radio Propaganda.* New York: Oxford University Press, 1944.

Liddell Hart, B. H., *Defence of the West.* London: Cassell, 1950.

Liddell Hart, B. H., *The Other Side of the Hill,* 3d ed. London: Cassell, 1956.

Liddell Hart, B. H. (ed.), *The Rommel Papers.* London: Collins, 1953.

Liddell Hart, B. H., *Strategy,* 2d rev. ed. New York: Praeger, 1967.

Lundin, C. L., *Finland in the Second World War.* Bloomington, Ind.: Indiana University Press, 1957.

Manstein, Erich von, *Lost Victories.* Chicago: Regnery, 1958.

Marshall, G. C., *The Winning of the War in Europe and the Pacific.* Washington: Simon & Schuster, 1945.

Marshall, S. L. A., *Men Against Fire: The Problem of Battle Command in Future Wars.* New York: Apollo (paperback).

Martienssen, A. K., *Hitler and His Admirals.* London: Secker & Warburg, 1948.

Matloff, Maurice, "Mr. Roosevelt's Three Wars: FDR as War Leader,"

Harmon Memorial Lectures in Military History, no. 6. Colorado Springs: USAF Academy, 1964.

Maund, L. E. H., *Assault from the Sea.* London: Methuen, 1949.

Mellenthin, F. W. von., *Panzer Battles, 1939–1945.* London: Cassell, 1955; Norman, Okla.: University of Oklahoma Press, 1964.

Montgomery, Bernard, *El Alamein to the River Sangro.* British Army of the Rhine, 1946.

Montgomery, Bernard, *Memoirs.* Cleveland, Ohio: World, 1958.

Montgomery, Bernard, *Normandy to the Baltic.* London: Hutchinson, 1946.

Morison, S. E., *History of United States Naval Operations in World War II.* 15 vols. Boston: Little Brown, 1947–1962.

Morton, Louis, "The Decision to Use the Atomic Bomb," *Foreign Affairs,* XXXV. 1957.

Morton, Louis, "Pacific Command: A Study in Interservice Relations," *Harmon Memorial Lectures in Military History,* no. 3. Colorado Springs: USAF Academy, 1961.

Nickerson, Hoffman, *Arms and Policy, 1939–1944.* New York: Putnam's, 1945.

Puleston, W. D., *The Influence of Sea Power in World War II.* New Haven, Conn.: Yale University Press, 1947.

Rohwer, Jürgen, *Die U-boot-Erfolge der Achsenmächte, 1939–1945.* Munich: Lehmann, 1968.

Rohwer, Jürgen, and G. Hümmelchen, *Chronik des Seekrieges, 1939–1945.* Oldenburg, Germ.: Stalling, 1968.

Ruge, Friedrich, *Sea Warfare, 1939–1945: A German Viewpoint.* London: Cassell, 1957.

Schull, J. J., *The Far Distant Ships: An Official Account of Canadian Naval Operations in the Second World War.* Ottawa: King's Printer, 1950.

Sherwood, R. E., *Roosevelt and Hopkins.* New York: Harper, 1950.

Shulman, Milton, *Defeat in the West.* London: Secker and Warburg, 1947; rev. ed., New York: Ballantine, 1968 (paperback).

Slessor, J. C., *The Central Blue: Recollections and Reflections.* New York: Praeger, 1956.

Slim, William, *Defeat into Victory.* New York: McKay, 1956.

Speidel, Hans, *Invasion 1944.* Chicago: Regnery, 1950.

Stacey, C. P., *The Canadian Army, 1939–1945.* Ottawa: King's Printer, 1948.

Sykes, Christopher, *Orde Wingate.* London: Collins, 1961.

Taylor, Edmond, *The Strategy of Terror.* Boston: Houghton Mifflin, 1940.

Tedder, A. W., *Air Power in War.* London: Hodder & Stoughton, 1948.

Terrell, Edward, *Admiralty Brief: The Story of the Inventions That Contributed to Victory in the Battle of the Atlantic.* London: Harrap, 1958.

Tuker, Francis, *The Pattern of War.* London: Cassell, 1948.

U.S. Army, Chief of Military History, *The United States Army in World War II.* 65 vols. to date. Washington: Government Printing Office, 1947–.

U.S. Marine Corps Historical Branch, *History of U.S. Marine Corps Operations in World War II.* 5 vols. Washington: USMC Headquarters, 1958–1968.

U.S. Military Academy, *The War in Eastern Europe (June 1941 to May 1945).* West Point, 1949.

United States Strategic Bombing Survey, *Summary Report (European War).* Washington: Government Printing Office, 1945.

Webster, Charles, and Noble Frankland, *The Strategic Air Offensive against Germany, 1939–1945*. 4 vols. London: HMSO, 1961.

Werth, Alexander, *Russia at War, 1941–1945*. New York: Dutton, 1964.

Westphal, Siegfried, *The German Army in the West*. London: Cassell, 1951.

Wheatley, Ronald, *Operation Sea Lion: German Plans for the Invasion of England, 1939–1942*. Oxford: Clarendon, 1958.

Wheeler-Bennett, J. W., *The Nemesis of Power: The German Army in Politics, 1918–1945*. New York: St. Martin's, 1956.

Wilmot, Chester, *The Struggle for Europe*. London: Collins, 1952.

Wright, Gordon, "The Ordeal of Total War, 1939–1945," *The Rise of Modern Europe*. New York: Harper and Row, 1968.

Wright, Quincy, "The Present Status of Neutrality," *American Journal of International Law*, XXXIV. July 1940.

Young, Desmond, *Rommel*. London: Collins, 1951.

THE WORLD SINCE 1945

Alsop, Joseph, "The New Balance of Power," *Encounter*. May 1958.

Ambler, John S., *The French Army in Politics, 1945–62*. Columbus, Ohio: Ohio State University Press, 1966. (Reissued by Doubleday in paperback as *Soldiers Against the State*.)

Aron, Raymond, *Peace and War: A Theory of International Relations*. London: Weidenfeld & Nicolson, 1967.

Barclay, C. N., *The First Commonwealth Division . . . in Korea 1950–53*. Aldershot, Eng.: Gale & Polden, 1951.

Bator, Victor, *Viet Nam, a Diplomatic Tragedy: The Origins of the United States Involvement*. Dobbs Ferry, N.Y.: Oceana, 1965.

Beaton, Leonard, *The Struggle for Peace*. New York: Praeger, 1967 (paperback).

Berger, Carl, *The Korean Knot: A Military-Political History*, rev. ed. Philadelphia: University of Pennsylvania Press, 1964.

Blackett, P. M. S., *Fear, War, and the Bomb: Military and Political Consequences of Atomic Energy*. New York: McGraw-Hill, 1948.

Bowett, D. W., *United Nations Forces: A Legal Study*. New York: Praeger, 1965.

Brodie, Bernard, *Strategy in the Missile Age*. Princeton, N.J.: Princeton University Press, 1959 (paperback).

Bull, Hedley, *The Control of the Arms Race: Disarmament and Arms Control in the Missile Age*. New York: Praeger, 1961 (paperback).

Burgess, Eric, *Guided Weapons*. New York: Macmillan, 1961.

Caidin, Martin, *Spaceport U.S.A.: The Story of Cape Canaveral and the Air Force Missile Center*. New York: Dutton, 1959.

Devillers, Philippe, and Jean LaCouture, *End of a War: Indochina, 1954*. New York: Praeger, 1969.

Dinerstein, H. S., *War and the Soviet Union: Nuclear Weapons and the Revolution in Soviet Military and Political Thinking*. New York: Praeger, 1959.

Fall, Bernard, *The Two Viet Nams: A Political and Military Analysis*, 2d ed. New York: Praeger, 1967.

Fehrenbach, T. R., *This Kind of War: a Study in Unpreparedness*. New York: Macmillan, 1963.

Foot, M. R. D., *Men in Uniform: Military Manpower in Modern Industrial Societies.* New York: Praeger, 1961.

Gallois, Pierre, *The Balance of Terror: Strategy for the Nuclear Age.* Boston: Houghton Mifflin, 1961.

Garthoff, R. L., *The Soviet Image of Future War.* Washington: Public Affairs Press, 1959.

Gavin, J. M., *War and Peace in the Space Age.* New York: Harper, 1958.

Goodspeed, D. J., *A History of the Defence Research Board of Canada.* Ottawa: Queen's Printer, 1958.

Gordenker, Leon, *The United Nations Secretary General and the Maintenance of Peace.* New York: Columbia University Press, 1967.

Hahn, W. F., and J. C. Neff, *American Strategy for the Nuclear Age.* Garden City, N.Y.: Peter Smith, 1961.

Halperin, M. H., *Limited War: An Essay on the Development of the Theory and an Annotated Bibliography.* Cambridge, Mass.: Harvard University Center for International Affairs, Occasional Papers in International Affairs, No. 3, May, 1962.

Higgins, Rosalyn, *United Nations Peacekeeping Operations: Documents and Commentary.* London: Royal Institute of International Affairs, 1969.

Hitch, C. J., and R. N. McKean, *Economics of Defense in the Nuclear Age.* Cambridge, Mass.: Harvard University Press, 1960; New York: Atheneum, 1965 (paperback).

Howard, Michael, and Robert Hunter, *Israel and the Arab World: The Crisis of 1967.* London: Institute for Strategic Studies, 1967.

Horowitz, Irvine L., *The War Game: Studies in the New Civilian Militarism.* New York: Ballantine, 1963.

Irmscher, W. F. (ed.), *Man and Warfare: Thematic Readings for Composition.* Boston: Little Brown, 1964 (paperback).

Jessup, P. C., and H. J. Taubenfeld, *Control for Outer Space and the Arctic Analogy.* New York: Columbia University Press, 1959.

Kahn, Herman, *On Escalation: Metaphors and Scenarios.* New York: Praeger, 1965.

Kahn, Herman, *On Thermonuclear War.* Princeton, N.J.: Princeton University Press, 1960; New York: The Free Press, 1969 (paperback).

Kahn, Herman, *Thinking about the Unthinkable.* New York: Horizon Press, 1962; Avon, 1969 (paperback).

Karig, Walter, M. W. Cagle, and F. A. Manson, *Battle Report: The War in Korea.* New York: Rinehart, 1952.

Kingston-McCloughry, E. J., *The Direction of War: A Critique of the Political Direction and High Command in War.* New York: Praeger, 1955.

Kissinger, Henry A., *The Necessity for Choice: Prospects of American Foreign Policy.* New York: Harper, 1961; Norton, 1969 (paperback).

Kissinger, Henry A., *Nuclear Weapons and Foreign Policy.* New York, Harper, 1957; Norton, 1969 (paperback).

Knorr, Klaus (ed.), *NATO and American Security.* Princeton, N.J.: Princeton University Press, 1959.

Knorr, Klaus, and Thornton Read (eds.), *Limited Strategic War.* New York: Praeger, 1962.

Liddell Hart, B. H., *Deterrent or Defense.* New York: Praeger, 1960.

McClelland, C. A., *Nuclear Weapons and Future War: Problem for the Sixties.* San Francisco: Chandler, 1960.

Mao Tse-tung, *On Protracted War*. Peking: Foreign Language Press, 1954.

Mao Tse-tung, *Strategic Problems of China's Revolutionary War*. Peking: Foreign Language Press, 1954.

Martin, Andrew, *Collective Security: A Progress Report*. Paris: UNESCO, 1952.

Middleton, Drew, *The Defense of Western Europe*. New York: Appleton, 1952.

Miksche, F. O., *The Failure of Atomic Strategy—And a New Proposal for the Defense of the West*. New York: Praeger, 1959.

Miksche, F. O., and E. Combaux, *War between Continents*. London: Faber & Faber, 1948.

Miller, Linda B., *World Order and Local Disorder: the United Nations and Internal Conflicts*. Princeton, N.J.: Princeton University Press, 1967.

Morison, Samuel E., *Strategy and Compromise*. Boston: Little Brown, 1958.

Noel-Baker, Philip, *The Arms Race*. New York: Oceana, 1960 (paperback).

O'Ballance, Edgar, *The Arab-Israeli War, 1948*. London: Faber & Faber, 1956.

Pearson, L. B., *Diplomacy in the Nuclear Age*. Cambridge, Mass.: Harvard University Press, 1959.

Possony, S. T., *Strategic Air Power: A Pattern of Dynamic Security*. Washington: Infantry Journal Press, 1949.

Preston, Richard A., "The Great Debate on Strategy: A Survey of the Literature," *R.C.A.F. Staff College Journal*. 1961.

Pruitt, D. G., and R. C. Snyder, *Theory and Research on the Causes of War*. Englewood Cliffs, N.J.: Prentice-Hall, 1969 (paperback).

Pustay, J. S., *Counter-insurgency Warfare*. New York: Free Press of Glencoe, 1965.

Rapoport, Anatol, *Strategy and Conscience*. New York: Harper & Row, 1964; Schocken, 1969 (paperback).

Rees, David, *Korea: The Limited War*. New York: St. Martin's, 1964.

Rovere, Richard, and Arthur Schlesinger, *The General and the President*. New York: Farrar, Straus, & Young, 1951.

Royal Institute of International Affairs, *Defence in the Cold War*. London: R.I.I.A., 1950.

Saunders, M. C. (ed.), *The Soviet Navy*. New York: Praeger, 1958.

Schelling, Thomas C., *Arms and Influence*. New Haven, Conn.: Yale University Press, 1966 (paperback).

Schelling, Thomas C., *Strategy and Arms Control*. New York: Twentieth Century Fund, 1961 (paperback).

Schelling, Thomas C., *The Strategy of Conflict*. Cambridge, Mass.: Harvard University Press, 1960; New York: Oxford University Press, 1963.

Schlesinger, James R., *The Political Economy of National Security*. New York: Praeger, 1960.

Singer, J. D., *Deterrence, Arms Control, and Disarmament*. Columbus, Ohio: Ohio State University Press, 1962.

Slessor, J. C., *The Great Deterrent: A Collection of Lectures, Articles, and Broadcasts on the Development of Strategic Policy in the Nuclear Age*. New York: Praeger, 1957.

Slessor, J. C., *Strategy for the West*. London: Cassell, 1954.

Smyth, J. G., *The Western Defences*. London: Wingate, 1951.

Sokolovsky, Vasilii D. (ed.), *Military Strategy: Soviet Doctrine and Concepts*. New York: Praeger, 1963.

Spanier, J. W., *The Truman-MacArthur Controversy and the Korean War.* Cambridge, Mass.: Harvard University Press, 1959.

Stern, F. M., *The Citizen Army: Key to Defense in the Atomic Age.* New York: St. Martin's, 1957.

Taylor, Maxwell D., *The Uncertain Trumpet.* New York: Harper, 1960.

Thomas, R. C. W., *The War in Korea, 1950–1953: A Military Study.* Aldershot, Eng.: Gale & Polden, 1954.

Tucker, Robert W., *The Just War: Exposition of the American Concept.* Baltimore: Johns Hopkins, 1960.

Turner, Gordon B., and R. D. Challener, *National Security in the Nuclear Age: Basic Facts and Theories.* New York: Praeger, 1960.

United States, Department of the Army, *Korea—1950.* Washington: Office of the Chief of Military History, 1952.

Waltz, Kenneth N., *Man, the State, and War: A Theoretical Analysis.* New York: Columbia University Press, 1964 (paperback).

Ward, Barbara, *Policy for the West.* London: Allen & Unwin, 1951.

Welles, Sumner, *Where Are We Heading?* New York: Harper, 1946.

Wise, S. F., "The Balance of Nuclear Terror," *Queen's Quarterly,* LXVII. 1960.

Wolfers, Arnold, *et al., Developments in Military Technology and their Impact on United States Strategy and Foreign Policy.* Washington: Washington Center of Foreign Policy Research, 1959.

Wood, Herbert F., *Strange Battleground: The Operations in Korea and their Effects on the Defence Policy of Canada.* Ottawa: Queen's Printer, 1966.

Young, Oran R., *The Intermediaries: Third Parties in International Crises.* Princeton, N.J.: Princeton University Press, 1969.

Index